Computation and Cognition

⌐┕ Bradford Books

Edward C. T. Walker, Editor. EXPLORATIONS IN THE BIOLOGY OF LANGUAGE. 1979.
Daniel C. Dennett. BRAINSTORMS. 1979.
Charles E. Marks. COMMISSUROTOMY, CONSCIOUSNESS AND UNITY OF MIND. 1980.
John Haugeland, Editor. MIND DESIGN. 1981.
Fred I. Dretske. KNOWLEDGE AND THE FLOW OF INFORMATION. 1981.
Jerry A. Fodor. REPRESENTATIONS. 1981.
Ned Block, Editor. IMAGERY. 1981.
Roger N. Shepard and Lynn A. Cooper. MENTAL IMAGES AND THEIR TRANS-FORMATIONS. 1982.
Hubert L. Dreyfus, Editor, in collaboration with Harrison Hall. HUSSERL, INTENTIONALITY AND COGNITIVE SCIENCE. 1982.
John Macnamara. NAMES FOR THINGS. 1982.
Natalie Abrams and Michael D. Buckner, Editors. MEDICAL ETHICS. 1982.
Morris Halle and G. N. Clements. PROBLEM BOOK IN PHONOLOGY. 1983.
Jerry A. Fodor. MODULARITY OF MIND. 1983.
George D. Romanos. QUINE AND ANALYTIC PHILOSOPHY. 1983.
Robert Cummins. THE NATURE OF PSYCHOLOGICAL EXPLANATION. 1983.
Irwin Rock. THE LOGIC OF PERCEPTION. 1983.
Stephen P. Stich. FROM FOLK PSYCHOLOGY TO COGNITIVE SCIENCE. 1983.
Jon Barwise and John Perry. SITUATIONS AND ATTITUDES. 1983.
Izchak Miller. HUSSERL, PERCEPTION, AND TEMPORAL AWARENESS. 1984.
Elliot Sober, Editor. CONCEPTUAL ISSUES IN EVOLUTIONARY BIOLOGY. 1984.
Norbert Hornstein. LOGIC AS GRAMMAR. 1984.
Paul M. Churchland. MATTER AND CONSCIOUSNESS. 1984.
Ruth Garrett Millikan. LANGUAGE, THOUGHT AND OTHER BIOLOGICAL CONSIDERATIONS. 1984.
Myles Brand. INTENDING AND ACTING. 1984.
Herbert A. Simon and K. Anders Ericsson. PROTOCOL ANALYSIS. 1984.
Robert N. Brandon and Richard M. Burian. GENES, ORGANISMS, POPULATIONS. 1984.
Owen J. Flanagan. THE SCIENCE OF THE MIND. 1984.
Zenon W. Pylyshyn. COMPUTATION AND COGNITION. 1984.

Computation and Cognition

Toward a Foundation for Cognitive Science

Zenon W. Pylyshyn

A Bradford Book
The MIT Press
Cambridge, Massachusetts
London, England

First MIT Press Paperback Edition, 1986
Fifth Printing, 1989
Copyright © 1984 by
The Massachusetts Institute of Technology

This book was set in Palatino
by The MIT Press Computergraphics Department
and printed and bound by Halliday Lithograph
in the United States of America.

Library of Congress Cataloging in Publication Data

Pylyshyn, Zenon W., 1937–
    Computation and cognition.

    "A Bradford book."

    Bibliography: p.
    Includes index.
    1. Cognition. 2. Artificial intelligence.
I. Title.
BF311.P93   1984   153'   84–2913
ISBN 0-262-16098-6 hardcover
ISBN 0-262-66058-X paperback

For Sonia and Joel

Contents

Preface

What Is Cognitive Science?

This book concerns the foundational assumptions of a certain approach to the study of the mind, which has lately become known as *cognitive science*. A more realistic way to put it might be to say that the material contained here is to the foundations of cognitive science what a hole in the ground is to the foundation of a house. It may not seem like what you eventually hope to have, but you do have to start some place.

It is possible that despite considerable recent interest in the field, and despite the appearance of much commonality, cognitive science may have no single foundation; it may be just an umbrella title for a number of different sciences, all of which are, like the proverbial blind men trying to understand the elephant, attempting to understand the workings of the mind. If that is the case, cognitive science might be simply a political union based on an interest in a broad set of questions, and perhaps on a shared need for certain techniques, say, experimental methods or the techniques of computer simulation. Academic departments, such as schools of engineering or departments of psychology, are probably based on just such ties.

But there is another, much more exciting possibility: the prospect that cognitive science is a genuine scientific domain like the domains of chemistry, biology, economics, or geology. In scientific domains it is possible to develop theories based on a special vocabulary or reasonably uniform set of principles independent of the principles of other sciences—that is, principles with considerable autonomy. Many feel, as I do, that there may well exist a natural domain corresponding roughly to what has been called "cognition," which may admit of such a uniform set of principles. Just as the domain of biology includes something like all living things (for which a strict definition is probably impossible outside of biological theory), so the domain of cognitive science may be something like "knowing things," or, as George Miller (1984) colorfully dubbed it, the "informavores."

Humans are living things, and consequently advances in biological science will contribute to a fuller understanding of human nature. Similarly, because we are informavores, or cognizers, understanding human nature can also gain from the study of principles governing members of that domain. At the moment it appears that included in this category are the higher vertebrates and certain computer systems. In any case, in view of the kinds of considerations we will explore in this book, and the impressive successes in recent work on artificial intelligence, one ought to take such a possibility seriously.

Lest the prospect of being a sibling of the computer appear as disturbing as the prospect of being the nephew or niece of the great ape once was, we should keep in mind that these are merely ways of classifying individuals for the purpose of discovering some of their operating principles. After all, we are classified along with rocks, atoms, and galaxies for the purpose of revealing how we move in response to physical forces. No classification—including "parent," "sentient being," or "fallen angel"—can capture *all* that is uniquely human. Indeed, even considering all the natural kinds to which we belong will not render a vision of humans as "merely" something or other; but each gives us special insight into some aspect of our nature.

What, then, is the common nature of members of the class of cognizers? I will suggest that one of the main things cognizers have in common is, they act on the basis of *representations.* Put another way, to explain important features of their behavior, we must take into account their (typically tacit) knowledge and goals. Knowing the representations they possess, together with the assumption that much of their behavior is connected with their representations by certain general principles, we can explain an important segment of the regularities in behavior exhibited by these cognizers. This view (sometimes called the "representational theory of mind") is what brings the study of cognition into contact with both classic philosophical problems (the sort of problem that concerned Franz Brentano when he talked about the "intentionality of the mental") and ideas from computer science. In chapters 1 and 2 I introduce this set of issues in the context of the demands placed on the task of providing psychological explanations.

Even assuming that this general picture is correct, it raises important and deep puzzles. How is it possible for a physical system (and I assume that cognizers are physical systems) to act on the basis of "knowledge of" objects and relations to which the system is not causally connected in the correct way? Clearly, the objects of our fears and desires do not cause behavior in the same way that forces and energy cause behavior in the physical realm. When my desire for the pot of gold at the end of the rainbow causes me to go on a search, the (nonexistent) pot of gold is not a causal property of the sort that is involved in natural laws. It appears that what is responsible is something we call a belief or "representation" whose semantic content is the hoped-for goal. If that is the case, however, it gives the explanation of my behavior a highly different character from the explanation of why, say, my automobile moves forward.

There is much we would like to know about this sort of explanation, and about the kinds of processes that demand such an explanation— including how these explanations are related to those that appeal to natural laws. We would also like to know just what sort of regularities are explainable precisely in this way. Surely not everything about an organism's behavior need be explained in this way, for the organism also behaves in ways that can be explained quite well in terms of the laws of optics, acoustics, dynamics, chemistry, endocrinology, association, and so on. The natural category "cognizer" not only encompasses a population of objects such as people and computers but a subset of phenomena as well. Do we know what is included in this subset?

These are some of the issues for which we would like, if not final answers, at least a hint of the direction from which answers might come.

What I try to do in this book is address such questions in a way that places a premium on suggestive and provocative possibilities rather than on rigorous analyses. One of the central proposals that I examine is the thesis that what makes it possible for humans (and other members of the natural kind *informavore*) to act on the basis of representations is that they instantiate such representations physically as cognitive codes and that their behavior is a causal consequence of operations carried out on these codes. Since this is precisely what computers do, my proposal amounts to a claim that cognition *is* a type of computation.

Important and far-reaching consequences follow if we adopt the view that cognition and computation are species of the same genus. Although "computer simulation" has been a source of much interest to psychologists for several decades now, it has frequently been viewed as either a useful metaphor or as a calculation device, a way to exhibit the consistency and completeness of independently framed theories in some domain of cognition.[1] The very term *computer simulation* suggests

1. For example, Juan Pascual-Leone characterizes computational models as follows: "Simulation models . . . of modern psychology play an epistemic role not unlike the illustrative analogies, case examples, and language-games which Wittgenstein made popular in modern analytical philosophy . . . which the investigator uses as figurative supports (arguments) on which to apply his analytical mental operations." Pascual-Leone, 1976, p. 111.

Even the practicing computationalist John Anderson does not take computational models as making literal claims: "Our aspiration must be the correct characterization of the data. If a computer simulation model provides it, fine. On the other hand,

verisimilitude—imitation—rather than a serious proposal as to how things really are. This way of viewing the relevance of computation has unfortunate consequences. Thinking of a model as a metaphor or a mnemonic removes the need to be rigorous in the way we appeal to the model to explain behavior; what does not fit can be treated as the irrelevant aspect of the metaphor. (See the section "What Theoretical Claim about Imagery Is Being Made?" in chapter 8, for an example of the consequences of appealing to a metaphor.) If the model is empirically adequate, however, there is no need to qualify one's interpretation by taking refuge in a metaphor. After all, no one believes that physical theories are a metaphor, or that they specify a way of imitating nature. Nor does anyone believe that physical theories represent a counterfeit, a device for calculation. Physics does not claim that the world behaves "as if" it were following the laws of physics, whereas it might actually be behaving that way for an entirely different reason or reasons. Physics purports to present a *true* account of how things really are.

The difference between taking a system as depicting truth, literally, and taking it to merely behave "as if" it were running through the lines of a cleverly constructed copy of nature's script, may be only a difference in attitude, but it has a profound effect on the way science is practiced. An important aspect of the acceptance of a system as a true account of reality is that the scientist thus can see that certain further observations are possible, while others are not. In other words, taken realistically true scientific theories tell us what possibilities exist in nature, what *might be* observed under different conditions from those that obtain at present. According to this view, theories do much more than assert that when we make observations we find that certain things happen in certain ways, as is commonly believed by psychologists concerned with "accounting for variance." Building theories thus becomes a way of perceiving, a way of thinking about the world, of seeing things in a new way.

Plane geometry is an outstanding example of how the acceptance, as a view of reality, of what was once a tool for calculation made a fundamental difference in science. The Egyptians were familiar with geometry and used it widely in surveying and building. The Greeks later developed geometry into an exquisite formal instrument. For the Egyptians, geometry was a method of calculation—like a system of ciphers—whereas for the Greeks it was a way of demonstrating the

---

there are those (for example, Newell and Simon, 1972) who seemed committed to arguing that at an abstract level, the human and the computer are the same sort of device. This may be true, but the problem is that a unique characterization of man's cognitive functioning does not exist. So it's . . . pointless to try to decide what kind of device he is." Anderson, 1976, p. 15.

perfect order in that platonic world of which the observable one is but a shadow. It would be two millennia before Galileo began the transformation that resulted in the view so commonplace (and mundane) today that virtually no vestige remains of the Aristotelian ideas about natural places and motions. We conceive of space as a completely empty, infinite, three-dimensional, isotropic, disembodied receptacle distinct from the earth or any object that might be located on the earth, one that is capable of housing not only things but also such incorporeal mathematical entities as points and infinite straight lines. Such a strange idea—especially if it were taken to describe something that exists in *this* world—was unthinkable before the seventeenth century; yet not even Galileo fully accepted the idea of such a world as real. For him, a "straight line" was still bound to the earth's surface. Not until Newton was the task of "geometrization of the world" (to use Butterfield's 1957 phrase) completed. The transformation that led to reification of geometry, though basically one of attitude and perception rather than of empirical observation, profoundly affected the course of science.

What would it take to treat computation the same way we treat geometry today—as a literal description of some aspect of nature (in this case, mental activity)? Clearly we are not justified in viewing any computer simulation of a behavioral regularity as a literal model of what happens in the mind. Most current, computational models of cognition are vastly underconstrained and ad hoc; they are contrivances assembled to mimic arbitrary pieces of behavior, with insufficient concern for explicating the principles in virtue of which such behavior is exhibited and with little regard for a precise understanding of the class of behaviors for which the model is supposed to provide an explanation. Although I believe that the computational view is the correct one, I have little doubt that we need to better understand the assumptions underlying this approach, while at the same time grasping what it would be like to use such models in a principled way to provide rigorous *explanations*—as opposed to merely mimicking certain observed behaviors. This much is clear: In order that a computer program be viewed as a literal model of cognition, the program must correspond to the process people actually perform at a sufficiently fine and theoretically motivated level of resolution. In fact, in providing such a model what we would be claiming is that the performances of the model and the organism were produced "in the same way" or that they were carrying out the *same* process. To conclude that the model and the organism are carrying out the same process, we must impose independent constraints on what counts as the same process. This requires a principled notion of "strong equivalence" of processes. Obviously, such a notion is more refined than behavioral equivalence or mimicry; at the very least it corresponds to equivalence with respect to a theoretically motivated set of basic operations. Further, what may count as a basic operation must be constrained independently. We cannot accept an operation as basic just because it is generally available on conventional computers. The operations built into production-model computers were chosen for reasons of economics, whereas the operations available to the mind are to be discovered empirically. Choosing a set of basic operations is tantamount to choosing an appropriate level of comparison, one that defines strong equivalence. Such a choice must be independently and empirically motivated.

The requirements of strong equivalence and independent constraints lead us to recognize a fundamental distinction between rule-governed or representation-governed processes and what I call *functional architecture*. By "functional architecture" I mean those basic information-processing mechanisms of the system for which a nonrepresentational or nonsemantic account is sufficient. The operation of the functional architecture might be explained in physical or biological terms, or it might simply be characterized in functional terms when the relevant biological mechanisms are not known. This particular distinction is crucial to the enterprise of taking the computational view of mind seriously; thus considerable attention is devoted to it in chapter 4 and thereafter. For example, in chapter 5 several methodological criteria are discussed for determining whether a particular function should be viewed as falling on one or the other side of the cognitive-noncognitive or architecture-process boundary. As a rule, practical methodologies for making theoretically relevant distinctions such as this one develop with the growth of the science, and thus cannot be anticipated in advance. Nonetheless, I single out two possible methodological criteria as being especially interesting; they follow directly from the basic assumptions of the metatheory, and some version of them is fairly widely used in information-processing psychology. Although these criteria are analyzed at length, I will outline them as a way of providing a preview of some issues to be discussed.

The first criterion (or class of criteria) derives from ideas in computer science. It appeals to the notion of strong equivalence identified with what I call the "complexity-equivalence of computational processes." From this perspective two processes are equivalent only if they are indistinguishable in respect to the way their use of computational resources (such as time and memory) varies with properties of their input, or, more accurately, they are equivalent only if the relation between properties of their input and some index of resource use takes the same mathematical form for both processes. In order for this to be true, it must be the case that primitive operations have constant computational complexity or fixed resource-use. These notions are implicit in the use of such measures as reaction time for investigating cognitive processes.

The second criterion attempts to draw the architecture-process boundary by distinguishing between systematic patterns of behavior that can be explained directly in terms of properties of the functional architecture and patterns that can be explained only if we appeal to the *content* of the information encoded. Much is made of this distinction throughout, but especially in the discussions in chapters 5 and 7. For the purpose of using this distinction as a methodological criterion, what is important is the *way* in which the pattern of regularities can be systematically altered. In the case of patterns attributable to representations, often the regularities can be systematically altered by the information conveyed by stimulus events. In such cases the change from one regular pattern of behavior to another, induced by such information-bearing "modulating" events, usually can be explained if we assume (1) that the organism interprets the "modulating" events in a particular way, so as to change its beliefs or goals, and (2) that the content of new beliefs and goals enter into the rational determination of actions. In practice this type of modulation is usually easily discerned, at least in humans, since it typically consists of the person "finding out" something about a situation that normally produces a regular pattern of behavior. Thus, for example, the systematic pattern of behavior I normally exhibit in response to being offered money can be radically altered if I am given certain information (for example, that the money is counterfeit, that it was stolen, that I will have to give it back). This observation translates into the following methodological principle (discussed at length in chapter 5): If we can set up situations demonstrating that certain stimulus-response regularities can be altered in ways that follow these rational principles, we say that the input-output function in question is *cognitively penetrable*, concluding that at least some part of this function cannot be explained directly in terms of properties of the functional architecture; that is, it is not "wired in" but requires a cognitive, or computational, or representation-governed, explanation.

These two criteria are discussed in various parts of the book in connection with a number of alternative theories of aspects of cognition. In particular, they (among others) figure in constraining theories of perception to prevent the trivialization of the problem that one encounters in "direct realism," and they are appealed to in analyzing the notion of analogue process and in examining the proposal that imaginal reasoning involves a special kind of functional architecture or "medium" of representation.

The picture of cognitive (or "mental") processing we end up with is one in which the mind is viewed as operating upon *symbolic represen-*

tations or *codes*. The semantic content of these codes corresponds to the content of our thoughts (our beliefs, goals, and so on). Explaining cognitive behavior requires that we advert to three distinct levels of this system: the nature of the mechanism or functional architecture; the nature of the codes (that is, the symbol structures); and their semantic content (see chapter 9). This trilevel nature of explanation in cognitive science is a basic feature of the computational view of mind. It is also the feature that various people have objected to, on quite varied grounds. For example, some think all of it can be done solely at the level of mechanism, that is, in terms of biology; others (for example, Stich, 1984) believe it can be done without the semantic level. Others (for instance, Searle, 1980) claim that cognitive behavior can be explained without the symbol or the syntactic level. I discuss some of my reasons for believing we need all three levels—one of which is that different principles appear to govern each level, and that the levels appear to have considerable autonomy. One can describe regularities at each level, to a first approximation, without concern for the way the regularities are realized at the "lower" levels. Elaborating on this view (one which, I believe, is implicit in cognitive-science practice), and providing some justification for it, occupies much of this book. Readers will have to judge for themselves whether the justification is successful.

Why Bother with Foundations?

I have said that this book is intended merely to be a modest start in the task of developing an inventory and an understanding of some assumptions underlying cognitive science. Not everyone believes that this is a task worth starting at all. One frequently held view is that we should plunge ahead boldly, doing science as best we can, and leave questions of a more foundational nature for the historians and philosophers who follow—cleaning up behind us, as it were. I must confess that I have considerable sympathy for this point of view. Historically, good work is often (perhaps typically) done by people with inadequate understanding of the larger picture into which their work fits. Even when scientists indulge in painting the larger picture, they are frequently wrong in their analysis. The more frequent pattern is for scientists to "sleepwalk" their way to progress, as Koestler (1959) put it. So, why do I bother worrying about foundational questions?

The answer, I hope, will become evident as the story unfolds. The reason I personally bother (putting aside psychopathological reasons) is that I have been driven to it over the years, first, in trying to understand what I did not like about certain theories of imagery (for example, in Pylyshyn, 1973, 1978b, 1981), or certain claims about the value of computational models (Pascual-Leone, 1976; Dreyfus, 1972, to which I replied in Pylyshyn, 1974), or the nondeterminacy of computational models (for example, Anderson, 1978, to whom I replied in Pylyshyn, 1979c). That, of course, may be a personal itch I have to scratch; yet, in my view, there is a more pressing need for the sort of inquiry I have undertaken in this book, quite apart from my personal proclivity. Contrary to some interpretations (for instance those expressed in the responses to Pylyshyn, 1980a, published in the same issue of the journal), this need has nothing to do with a desire to prescribe the field of cognitive science. Rather, it has to do with the need to expose what by now have become some stable intuitions which cognitive science researchers share and which to a great extent guide their work, but which have been articulated only in the most fragmentary ways.

Thus I see my role in writing this book as that of investigative reporter attempting to tease out the assumptions underlying the directions cognitive science research is taking and attempting to expose the foundations of this approach. The reason I am convinced that the project is worth undertaking is that cognitive science *practice* is far from neutral on these questions. I try to show (especially in chapters 6 to 8) that the kind of theories cognitive scientists entertain are intimately related to the set of tacit assumptions they make about the very foundations of the field of cognitive science. In cognitive science the gap between metatheory and practice is extremely narrow. There is a real sense in which the everyday research work done by scientists is conditioned by their foundational assumptions, often both implicit and unexamined. What convergence there is is due in large part to the existence of some commonality among these scientists' assumptions.

Many of the issues raised in this book have a long and venerable history within the philosophy of mind; many are hotly debated among philosophers today. Although I realize that I am adding to this debate, this book is not intended as primarily a philosophical analysis. For one thing, it is not written in the style of philosophical scholarship. I have tried to say what is implicit in the best cognitive science work being done, as well as defend the assumptions I think worth defending. As a result, I suspect that many psychologists and artificial-intelligence people will find the discussions somewhat on the philosophical or abstract side, missing the usual copious descriptions of experimental studies and models, while philosophers will miss the detailed argumentation, exegesis, and historical allusions. In addition, I have chosen not to provide a review of work in information-processing psychology (except for some of the results that bear directly on the points I am making) because of the many readable reviews available, for example, Massaro, 1975, and Posner, 1978.

As for the philosophical tradition, I have tried to present several different points of view which bear directly on the issues discussed. Many of the philosophical discussions of cognitivism are concerned with certain issues, however, such as the proper understanding of "meaning" or the role of consciousness, about which I simply have little to say. I am, in fact, treating these topics as among the "mysteries" (rather than the technical "puzzles") of cognitive science (to use Chomsky's [1976] useful distinction). While these questions may be fascinating, and while our understanding of the mind may benefit from a careful conceptual analysis of these issues, they may well be precisely the kind of questions that are irrelevant to making scientific progress. Indeed, they may be like the question, How is it possible to have action at a distance? Although physicists—or, as they were called until the nineteenth century, "natural philosophers"—debated such questions with much acrimony in the eighteenth century, the question remains unresolved today; people merely have decided that the question is not worth pursuing or that it is a question with no answer that falls within physical theory.

Similarly, some questions that appear to be philosophical in nature are largely empirical, in that they can be illuminated (or refined) only as the empirical and theoretical work takes shape. In such cases it may be that only limited analysis is worth doing in the absence of scientific understanding of the details of the phenomena. For example, while I devote some space to discussing "folk psychology," the question of whether it is misleading to view the mind in such terms cannot be entirely divorced from the development of detailed theories, for the reason that folk psychology is a mixture of generalizations held together by considerable mythical storytelling. Some generalizations are almost certain to be valid, whereas many explanations of their truth are likely to be false or at least not general enough. If it is true that folk psychology is a mixture of generalizations, then a developed cognitive theory is likely to contain some folk psychology terminology, but it will also leave much out, while adding its own constructs. I don't see how the development of the picture can be anticipated in detail except perhaps in the few areas where considerable progress is already evident (perhaps in such areas as psycholinguistics and vision). Thus I see no point in undertaking a defense (or a denial, as in Stich, 1984) of folk psychology in general.

These considerations, together with my personal predilections, have led to a style of presentation that is both eclectic and, at times, presumptive. I hope the benefits outweigh the discomfort the specialist may feel at having certain problems central to his or her discipline given less care here than they typically receive in the scholarly work of that field.

Some Personal Background and Intellectual Debts

Works such as this frequently are more a chronicle of personal search than they are the text of a message. This book has haunted me for more years than I ever imagined I could sustain an interest. I owe its completion to several pieces of good fortune. The first good fortune consisted of a number of fellowships and grants. My original ideas on the topics discussed here germinated long ago during 1969–70 spent at the Institute for Mathematical Studies in the Social Sciences at Stanford University, a year made possible by Patrick Suppes, the Foundations' Fund for Research in Psychiatry, and the Ontario Mental Health Foundation. Some of the ideas presented here appeared in a widely circulated but unpublished report (Pylyshyn, 1972), parts of which were later incorporated in my critique of models of mental imagery (Pylyshyn, 1973). Also, I considerably rethought these issues while a visiting professor at the MIT Artificial Intelligence Laboratory in 1975, thanks to Marvin Minsky, Seymour Papert, and Pat Winston. The first draft of what is questionably the same book as this was outlined while I was a fellow at the Center for Cognitive Science at the Massachusetts Institute of Technology in 1978–79. The bulk of the writing, however, was done in 1979–80, in idyllic circumstances provided by my fellowship at the Center for Advanced Study in the Behavioral Sciences, a special place that can make possible many things. I thank these institutions for their generosity, as well as the Social Science and Humanities Research Council of Canada for its support by granting a leave fellowship in 1978–79.

The second piece of good fortune was the generous provision of help by friends and colleagues. Two people, in particular, contributed so extensively to the ideas presented in this book that it would be difficult, not to mention embarrassing, to acknowledge it at every appropriate point in the text. The idea of functional architecture grew out of discussions with Allen Newell, discussions that began in the summers of 1972 and 1973 while I was a participant in a series of workshops in information-processing psychology at Carnegie Mellon University. Newell's production-system architecture (Newell, 1973b) was the catalyst for most of our discussions of what I initially referred to as "theory-laden language" and later called "functional architecture." Our continuing dialogues, by telephone, computer networks, and face to face, helped me shape my ideas on this topic. If there is anything to the idea, Newell deserves much of the credit for introducing it. The second person who contributed basic ideas on the representational view of mind, and who patiently explained to me what philosophy was for, is Jerry Fodor. Fodor's influence is evident throughout this book. Were it not for his interest, I would probably have made fewer but less defensible claims than I do. In addition to contributing to the content of this book, Fodor and Newell, from nearly opposite poles of intellectual style, have the following important trait in common, one which undoubtedly has affected the writing of this book: they are among the few people in cognitive science who appear to be guided by the premise that if you believe P, and if you believe that P entails Q, then even if Q seems more than a little odd, you have some intellectual obligation to take seriously the possibility that Q may be true, nonetheless. That is what it means to take ideas seriously, and that is what I have been arguing we should do with the idea of cognition as computation.

Because various pieces of paper bearing the same title as this book have been around for so long, I have received much advice from numerous people on what to do with them. Among those whose advice I did not ignore entirely are Sue Carey, Ned Block, and Steve Kosslyn, colleagues at MIT who argued with me about mental imagery; Noam Chomsky and Hilary Putnam, who argued about the philosophy of mind; Dan Dennett, John Haugeland, Pat Hayes, John McCarthy, and Bob Moore, my colleagues at the Center for Advanced Study in the Behavioral Science, in Palo Alto; and John Biro, Bill Demopoulos, Ted Elcock, Ausonio Marras, Bob Matthews, and Ed Stabler, colleagues or visitors at the University of Western Ontario's Centre for Cognitive Science. In addition, the following people read parts of the manuscript and offered useful suggestions: Patricia Churchland, Bill Demopoulos, Dan Dennett, Jerry Fodor, Allen Newell, John Macnamara, Massimo Piatelli-Palmarini, Steve Pinker, and Ed Stabler. You might wonder (as does the publisher) why, with all this support and advice, the book was not ready years ago.[2]

2. For those interested in such intimate details, the book was primarily composed using the EMACS editor at the MIT-AI Laboratory and at the Xerox Palo Alto Research Center (for the use of which I am very grateful), with final (massive) revisions using the Final Word editor on an IBM-PC. A handful of TECO macros prepared it for the Penta Systems International phototypesetting system at The MIT Press. Were it not for all this electronic wizardry, the book probably would have been shorter; but very likely it would still be in process.

Finally, a personal note. Any piece of work as involving and protracted as this inevitably takes its toll. I am thankful to those close to me for putting up with the somewhat higher level of neglect, not to mention abuse, that my attention to this book engendered.

Computation and Cognition

Chapter 1

The Explanatory Vocabulary of Cognition

The truth is that science started its modern career by taking over ideas derived from the weakest side of the philosophies of Aristotle's successors. In some respects it was a happy choice. It enabled the knowledge of the seventeenth century to be formularised so far as physics and chemistry were concerned, with a completeness which has lasted to the present time. But the progress of biology and psychology has probably been checked by the uncritical assumption of half-truths. If science is not to degenerate into a medley of *ad hoc* hypothesis, it must become philosophical and must enter upon a thorough criticism of its own foundations.

A. N. Whitehead, *Science and the Modern World*, New York: The New American Library of World Literature, Inc., p. 18

Cognitive Phenomena and Folk Psychology

In science, the process of seeking to understand is called *explanation*. What distinguishes different sciences is that they seek to answer different questions and explain different phenomena. Frequently, however, different sciences address the *same* events, though in highly different ways. This would be the case, for example, if a physicist, a psychologist, and a biologist addressed the event in which a baseball pitcher throws a curve ball and attempts to say why and how the event occurred. Often, the most distinct characteristic of explanations provided by two disciplines is the vocabulary used to express both their phenomena and their explanations. This is more than a superficial question of terminology. Scientists cannot choose a vocabulary entirely for its interest and convenience, though they can (and frequently do) augment and refine the vocabulary to suit their needs. This situation exists because at least part of the vocabulary specifies the *explananda*, which carries the initial puzzle and which occurs in the substantive portion of such questions as:

Why does such and such happen?

What (hidden) things are responsible for such and such phenomenon? and
How do these things bring about that phenomenon?

Cognitive psychology is fundamentally tied to a certain class of terms which in part define the phenomena it seeks to explain (but only in part, for a consequence of explanation is that it frequently redefines its explananda) and in part dictate the sort of accounts that qualify as putative explanations. Questions of *why, what,* and *how* are bound so intimately to certain terms that an account based on a completely different vocabulary is simply, and correctly, dismissed as a misunderstanding of the question.

My purpose in this chapter is to introduce the reader to the idea that explanations are relative to particular vocabularies. The chapter is not intended as a contribution to the philosophy of science. I will be discussing what, at least in certain quarters, is fairly standard material but with the purpose of setting the stage for ideas to be developed in the remainder of the book. Although my goal here is not primarily to show the inadequacy or incompleteness of explanations based strictly on behaviorist ideas or neurophysiology, some discussion early in this chapter is devoted to confronting what I have discovered to be some major recurring objections to cognitive science (or "cognitivism") from members of the psychology community. The reason I bother is that contrasting the cognitivist approach with behavioral and biological approaches is a good way to introduce cognitive science and discuss its nature. I do this chiefly by using informal, mundane examples and by playing on the reader's intuitions. Thus, anyone familiar with the standard arguments (for example, Chomsky, 1957, Fodor, 1963b) may do well to skip to the next chapter.

The major message of this chapter is that although many of us are committed materialists, believing in physical causality and similar reasonable propositions (such as the importance of the brain in causing behavior), the problem of explanation in psychology forces us to adopt a certain kind of taxonomy of behavior. Specifically, it is because explanations attempt to capture generalizations, and different vocabularies reveal different generalizations, that we find ourselves forced to resort to what I call a *cognitive vocabulary* in revealing certain fundamental patterns of intelligent, largely rational behavior in certain creatures, and, I might add, artifacts. We will also find, perhaps not surprisingly, that the cognitive vocabulary is roughly similar to the one used by what is undoubtedly the most successful predictive scheme available for human behavior—folk psychology.

I will return to the question of choosing an appropriate descriptive vocabulary later in this chapter; for now, an informal example will serve to illustrate this point. Suppose you are standing on a street corner and observe a sequence of events that might be described as follows. A pedestrian is walking along a sidewalk. Suddenly the pedestrian turns and starts to cross the street. At the same time, a car is traveling rapidly down the street toward the pedestrian. The driver of the car applies the brakes. The car skids and swerves over to the side of the road, hitting a pole. The pedestrian hesitates, then goes over and looks inside the car on the driver's side. He runs to a telephone booth at the corner and dials the numbers 9 and 1.

What has happened? Why did the pedestrian run to the phone booth? What will he do next, and why? If you are a determinist and a materialist, you believe that every movement that occurred in that event, no matter how small, and every change in the physical state of people and objects in that scene instantiates some natural physical law, as well as any applicable law of chemistry, biology, or neurophysiology.[1] Neglecting quantum-mechanical effects, nothing is left either to chance or to non-physical vital principles. Since, according to this view, everything that happened follows from some natural law, you might think it possible, at least in principle, to explain the entire sequence of events in this incident by recourse to the terms and laws of natural science (that is, physics, chemistry, biology, and so on).

Explaining, however, is a special activity whose success in a given case depends to great extent on how the explanation relates to the way we describe the phenomenon to be explained. A typical way to explain phenomena in natural science is to cite nomological, or universal, laws and relate them to descriptions of phenomena couched in the same vocabulary as that of the laws (or to descriptions of the phenomena defined in terms of this vocabulary). Thus physics might explain the trajectory of the car and of various objects, including people and people's limbs, in terms of their earlier states, the forces and energy transfers taking place, and the structural properties (or initial conditions) of the situation, together with the relevant physical laws.

---

1. Outside of quantum mechanical effects, science does seem to subscribe to the general belief in determinism, as well as to materialism, this in spite of the fact that scientists often offer opinions to the contrary. For example, in a survey of physics professors, John Macnamara (personal communication) found that 75 percent of the respondents claimed they do not believe the world is truly deterministic. Fortunately, such libertarianism appears to surface only when scientists are asked specifically to give a philosophical opinion. As far as I can determine, no one actually practices science according to that view. Invariably, theories are built to account for deterministic causes (again, outside quantum mechanics, where the situation is unclear either way). This merely demonstrates the futility of asking practicing scientists for philosophical opinions concerning the foundations of their work.

Obviously, such an explanation would provide an inadequate answer to the question, "Why did the pedestrian run to the telephone booth?" Many answers to this question are possible that would be more satisfactory:

> Giving *reasons* (for example, in order to phone).
> Giving *conditions* (because of the accident witnessed).

Or more systematic explanations could be given:

> A rule is that, in the event of an accident, one should get help. A prerequisite for obtaining help is to communicate the request. One way to do that is by phone. A prerequisite for using a phone is to be located beside one. One way to accomplish that, if a phone is in view, is to run to it. And so on.

However, neither an answer in physical terms or in biological terms (for example, by innervating a cycle of opposing tenser muscles, which causes the position of one foot to be placed ahead of the other) would be an adequate answer to any of the *why, what,* or *how* questions, though they *might* form part of the overall story of how it was possible for the organism to carry out the actions mentioned in the psychological account; that is, they might form part of the explanation of the organism's *capacity* (a topic that will be treated at greater length in chapter 7).

There are general reasons why one account of a sequence of events might qualify as an explanation while another *true* account of the same sequence does not. These reasons have to do with the fact that such claims as "The occurrence of X (together with . . .) *explains* the occurrence of Y" are not, in general, equivalent (that is, they need not preserve truth values) when we replace the X or the Y by phrases that refer to exactly the same event or to the same objects (in general, "explains" provides what philosophers refer to as an "opaque context").[2] I will return to this point briefly, because the entire issue of the nonequivalence of neurophysiological, behavioral, cognitive, and perhaps other modes of description rests on the fact that this discussion is conducted in the context of *explanation*, where we are concerned not just with the veracity (or even the general usefulness of certain kinds of descriptions) but with the ability of different descriptions to *capture generalizations*, and hence with the adequacy of *explanations* couched in these different vocabularies.

2. I owe this point to an unpublished paper by Block and Fodor (1972). I don't know how standard the view is, but it seems correct to me. I should also point out that I am making a small point here; the more general question of *when* something counts as an explanation—particularly, to a *why* question—is enormously difficult (see, for example, Bromberger [1966]).

To return to the example of the pedestrian and the automobile, it appears—at least, intuitively—that an adequate explanation of the events in the incident must mention, among other things, that the pedestrian *perceived* the collision, *recognized* it as an event that is classified as an accident, *inferred* that there might be an injury, went over to *determine* whether anyone had in fact been injured, *deduced* from what he saw that that might be the case, *decided* to seek help based on the *knowledge* he possessed of the proper treatment of injured persons, *noticed* a telephone booth nearby, *recalled* the number for emergencies, and dialed the number with the *intention* of seeking help. While a more technical explanation might not use these particular terms, or might use more or fewer of them, it is clear that this class of vocabulary—as opposed to a physical or biological class—is precisely what appears to be needed actually to explain the *why*, *what*, and *how* of the event. These are cognitive terms, what many philosophers, following Franz Brentano's analysis of the special aspects of mental activity (see, for example, McAlister, 1976), call *intentional terms*. Although Brentano's thesis is not discussed in this book, the idea of an "intentional vocabulary" plays an important role in the discussion of psychological explanation.

It should be noted that I imply no contradiction here in suggesting that a cognitive description refers to the person following rules or doing things for a reason or reasons. It is no contradiction, as Ryle (1949) once put it, to speak of baseball players simultaneously following the laws of physics and the rules of baseball. All I am suggesting in this informal example is that some phenomena seem to demand explanations couched in a certain vocabulary.

However one views the merits of a particular explanation in the example, it at least suggests that prima facie constraints exist on what counts as an explanation of some phenomena. Of course we cannot let the case rest on intuitive examples alone; perhaps the intuitive criteria for the "cognitive satisfaction" of explanations are too naive; perhaps when we ask for an explanation, we do not actually want a scientific explanation, just some informal common-sense *reasons*. Perhaps all we are looking for is a story that *makes sense*. Whereas many psychologists (especially those with a biological or a behavioral orientation) seem to take this view for granted, there is reason to believe that biological or behavioral accounts are grossly inadequate for addressing certain questions because they are incapable of expressing the relevant generalizations.

What I argue in this book (primarily by example and by trying to make a plausible case, rather than by philosophical rigor, which I leave to those better equipped for the latter) is that, no matter how scientific and technical an explanation one might wish to give, whether from a physical, a biological, or a behavioral perspective, it is still true in a most fundamental sense that if the pedestrian in our example does not *perceive* the event as an emergency, does not *know* what to do, or does not *remember* the phone number, the entire sequence could be quite different. Here, I claim that this is both true *and* relevant to our making sense of the situation. For example, it is crucial in distinguishing this sequence from one that starts off the same way in every respect (that is, with the same environmental conditions) but in which the pedestrian has, say, interpreted some feature of the situation so as to warrant the *inference* that the accident was not serious, or does not *know* what to do, or has *forgotten* the phone number. Further, I claim that any explanation which denies, say, that *being told* X (for instance, being told that the emergency phone number is 911 instead of 91) is, under specifiable conditions of motivation, a sufficient condition for *knowing* X and consequently behaving in certain predictable ways, will encounter considerable difficulty in explaining even the simplest psychological regularities—to take a random example, those of human conditioning. As Brewer (1974) shows persuasively, an account of human conditioning experiments that makes use of the notion that a subject is being *informed* of what will happen, or what he or she is expected to do, provides a better explanation of the observed phenomena than does an account based on reinforcement contingencies.

Also, I argue that a reason why this language (that is, talk of "knowing," "perceiving as," "being informed of," and so on) is needed is that other sequences of behavior that are equally regular and systematic *could* be induced merely by varying the information available to the person, that is, by changing the person's beliefs. This concern with counterfactual cases, with *what might have been*, is a hallmark of explanatory—as opposed to merely descriptive—accounts. Furthermore, it is the way the counterfactual states of affairs could be brought about that constitutes one of the features of "cognitive" systems. These points will be raised again at length in connection with the notions of cognitive penetrability and cognitive capacity that occupy much of the later chapters. All I want to do in this chapter is provide some familiar, informal examples of the phenomena by way of illustrating the point that behavior which you and I naively know to be both systematic and rational may nonetheless appear plastic in the extreme, even to the extent of seeming nondeterministic, when described using a vocabulary or taxonomy drawn from biology or behaviorism.

Capturing Generalizations

There are many reasons for maintaining that explanations of behavior must involve cognitive terms in a way that does not serve merely as a heuristic or as something we do while waiting for the neurophysiological theories to progress. One of the principal reasons involves showing that there are regularities and generalizations which can be captured using cognitive terms that could not be captured in descriptions using behavioral or physical (neurophysiological) terms.

This sort of argument has frequently been made in the philosophical literature, and so will not be repeated here in detail. (See, however, Fodor, 1980a, 1980c, 1978a, 1968b; Putnam, 1960, 1967, 1973; Davidson, 1970; Dennett, 1978a.) I do, however, want to sketch the argument briefly and informally, because some of the principles are directly relevant to various points that arise in this book—bearing, for example, on such issues as the nature of mental processing, transduction, and mental representation. Also, I claim later on that the reasons which lead us to believe that cognitive theories must be stated in terms such as those used in the examples above—rather than in physical, neurological, or behavioral terms—are precisely those that lead us to believe that the cognitive system is correctly described as performing computations—for the reason that computation is the only detailed hypothesis available for explaining how it is possible for a physical system to exhibit regularities that must be explained as "rule following" or even as being governed by goals and beliefs.

Notice, first, that giving an account in cognitive terms is not simply to give an explanation that is more intellectually satisfying. Also, because it captures relevant generalizations, such an account is more predictive. Recall that in the example cited, we left our pedestrian in the phone booth, having dialed the digits 9 and 1. You might now ask: What will he do next? The answer is obvious when the situation is described using the particular terms I used. Because the pedestrian knows that the emergency number is 911, and because he perceives the situation to be an emergency, his next behavioral act is overwhelmingly likely to be: dial 1. The way I describe the situation, no account stated solely in behavioral terms (that is, in terms that do not incorporate the person's knowledge or goals) can make such a prediction. The reason is, if a systematic account is to connect the prediction that the person's next act will be to dial 1 with the "stimulus" conditions, such an account must at the very least mention: that the pedestrian *interpreted the scene as an accident*; that the pedestrian *knows* or *remembers* the phone number; and that the pedestrian's behavior is an instance of the category "phone for help." That this is true can be seen by considering the other possibilities, that is, by considering certain counterfactual possibilities. There are physically identical situations in which the prediction *does not hold* (for example, telling the person in advance that there is to be a rehearsal of a television show on this street). And there are situations in which the prediction *does hold*—for exactly the same reason (that is, the explanation is the same) but the physical situation is vastly different (for example, instead of the person seeing the injured driver, he hears the driver's cries for help or is told by a passerby that someone has been injured). Or the physical conditions may be the same but the detailed behavior different (the person's arm is in a cast, so he asks *someone else* to dial 911, thereby realizing the prediction with highly different behavior). The point is, there are innumerably many physically distinct ways in which the same generalization can be realized; yet they remain cases of the same generalization. If that generalization were not recognized, *each instance would count as a different sequence*, and we would miss an important regularity.

It is true that such things as "beliefs" are derived from past experiences (perhaps even from experiences that were "reinforced"). Thus one might think this story could be retold using behavioral terms. The behavioral story, however, is not equivalent to the cognitive one—for an important reason. In the behavioral story past experiences must be classified in terms of a particular, *objective* taxonomy, a taxonomy that partitions classes of histories according to the physical properties of stimuli and behaviors. The way histories must be partitioned in order for them to correspond to states of knowledge, however, requires that we be capable of speaking of such things as the meaning of a sentence, or the interpretation the person placed on a certain stimulus, or the action intended by a certain behavior that formed part of the history. Unless the history leading to a particular functional state is categorized this way, we cannot use it to explain why someone does what he does.

For example, we have to classify certain events in a person's past as instances of the event type "finding out that the telephone number for emergencies is 911." If we did not classify past events in this way, we could not express a certain generalization that relates an indefinite range of antecedent histories (namely, all the different ways of finding out the telephone number for emergencies) to their common tendency to cause people to behave in certain ways, namely, to dial the digits 9-1-1. Further, without a category such as "emergency" or something similar, we could not say what was common between conditions in which people might dial 911 and those in which they are disposed to utter such exclamations as Help! or answer questions in characteristic ways.

In practice—though not in theory—the way behaviorists get around the need for such a mentalistic vocabulary is to load the description of conditions or behavior with cognitive content. Instead of a physical vocabulary, they use a "behavioral" vocabulary in which things are described as *stimuli, responses, reinforcers,* and so on. The reason this works is that, in practice, such categories are cognitive: What serves as the functional stimulus depends on how a person interprets the situation (for example, the stimulus in the pedestrian-automobile example is *accident;* but, of course, if that person is told it is a rehearsal for a television show, the stimulus is no longer *accident* but *rehearsal* and engages the habits appropriate for that category). Similarly, what constitutes the response is also implicitly cognitive. Some particular bit of movement (accidentally bumping into a telephone while in a booth keeping out of the rain) does not count as a "response," only movements intended a certain way are counted.

The critical aspect of the connection between stimulus conditions and subsequent behavior—the aspect that must be incorporated in the theoretical account if the latter is to capture the systematicity of the person's behavior—is that it is (a) the environment or the antecedent event *as seen or interpreted by the subject,* rather than as described by physics, that is the systematic determiner of actions; and (b) actions performed with certain *intentions,* rather than behaviors as described by an objective natural science such as physics, that enter into behavioral regularities. For example, it is only under the description that the person's action is an intended telephone-dialing—rather than, say, the mere rotation of a black dial in a certain way—that the connection between the perceived stimulus situation and the action becomes systematic.

The reason for this is revealing. Even though the dial-rotating description may correspond exactly to what actually happens on a particular occasion, it does not correspond to the equivalence class of all behaviors that can be systematically related to certain previous experiences. For example, viewed thus, the description cannot be systematically related to such events as those in which the subject was told (or otherwise found out) the phone number for emergencies or those that can be systematically related to the perception of the preceding events as an accident requiring urgent assistance. The reason is, presumably, there are no valid generalizations of the form that when people know the emergency number, and when they recognize an emergency, they tend to rotate a small dial with holes in it. Such behavior as rotating a dial in a certain way is neither necessary for the generalization to hold (for example, they might use touch buttons or ask an operator), nor—even more important—sufficient. The occurrence of a certain kind of dial rotation, in which the digits 9-1-1 are rotated, is not a sufficient condition for behavior to fall under the generalization, for there are cases in which a dial might be rotated in this way without the action having anything to do with the generalization in question.

For example, a person would dial 911 as part of the general action of dialing 679-1124, or while acting in a play. That person might even dial the sequence for some thoroughly rational reason, all the while knowing the phone is out of order. These, however, are not behaviors covered by the generalization we are considering. To come under that generalization, the behavior must fall in the category of a certain intended action.

If there is any validity to the view that at least some human behavior is rational, then the systematicity of people's behavior in those cases will be stateable only when their actions are described in what I refer to as *cognitive* or *intentional* terms. On such an account the relation between conditions and actions is seen as mediated by beliefs as well as, perhaps, considerable reasoning or cognitive processing, rather than merely being linked by nomological laws. It is this remarkable degree of *stimulus-independent control* of behavior that has been the Achilles' heel of behaviorism.

The same argument can be brought to bear against attempts to predict the next behavior in the sequence from a neurophysiological or biological account. Here, I do not deny that the minute muscular movements that unfold in the instants following the point at which our story leaves off are governed precisely by physical and biological laws, and therefore are, in principle, predictable from the current physical and neurophysiological state of the person making the movement. Such a prediction, however, is both too strong and too weak a requirement to demand of our theoretical apparatus. It is too strong in the sense that it will, in principle, predict every microscopic movement that occurs, rather than predict the behavior in terms of the most systematic or regular feature that such behaviors exhibit under relevantly similar circumstances. Furthermore, to make such a strong prediction, one would need a complete description not only of the organism's current neurophysiological state but of the state of the environment as well, since that, in part, also determines the particular movements that occur.

An even more serious problem is that such a prediction is also too weak, for it does not—indeed, *cannot*—tell us that the minute sequence of movements *corresponds to the act of dialing a "one"*, which is what we really need to know in this situation. The reason this is what we need to know is not merely that it is useful or that it corresponds to our everyday way of speaking; it is that there are many situations in which we can predict correctly that a person will perform an action such as "dialing 1" although the precise way he or she does it may lie outside a uniform set of regularities covered by the theory. The sequence of movements may be *psychologically indeterminate*, inasmuch as the choice of alternative realization or alternative element of the equivalence class is under the control of such noncognitive factors as the actual physical circumstances. In spite of this situation there may yet be an important generalization that *can* be stated in psychological terms. This is just another way of saying that, taken under a cognitive description certain kinds of behavior enter into a system of generalizations.

Another, perhaps more revealing way to cast the discussion concerning the limitations of physiological explanation is to note that the difficulty with such explanations is that they provide a distinctly different causal account linking each of a potentially unlimited number of ways of learning the emergency phone number, each of a potentially unlimited number of ways of coming to know that a state of emergency exists, to each of a potentially unlimited number of sequences of muscular movements that correspond to dialing 911. In so doing, the neurophysiological story misses the most important psychological generalization involved: regardless of how a person learns the emergency number, regardless of how he or she comes to perceive a situation as an emergency, and regardless of how the person's limbs are moved in dialing the number, a single, general principle is implicit in the entire set of these sequence. That principle can be exhibited only if we describe the events, using the kinds of terms invoked above, for example, recognizing an emergency and remembering a way to get help. Moreover, a theory's failure to exhibit such a principle is a serious shortcoming. Not only would such a theory fail to tie together various related phenomena, it would also fail to support certain relevant counterfactuals, that is, make predictions about what *would* have happened had the circumstances differed in various ways from the way they actually were. For instance, in our example such a theory would be silent on such counterfactual conditionals as what would have happened had the phone not been visible from where the pedestrian was standing; what would have happened had it been out of order; had the line been busy; or even had the phone been a Touch-Tone, as opposed to a dial phone, thus requiring different finger movements.

My point here is that phenomena can be described using a variety of terms that carve up, or taxonomize, the world in various ways. A hierarchy of type-token relationships exists among such terms. For example, there is an infinite variety of acoustical descriptions of events corresponding to the utterance of a word, an infinite variety of ways to communicate a word (spoken, typed, printed, handwritten, morse code, and so on), an infinite number of ways to tell someone something, an infinite variety of ways someone comes to know something. At each level of such a hierarchy important and interesting generalizations exist. It seems to be the case that in cognitive psychology (that is, the psychology of perception, thought, problem-solving, and so forth—the psychology of intellectual processes), the interesting and important generalizations are best captured by what I call "cognitive terms".

Cognitive science rests on the foundational assumption that there exist a natural set of generalizations that can be captured by using such cognitive terms, therefore that there is a natural scientific domain that is the subject matter of cognitive science. (Later, I will have more to say concerning the question of what characterizes this domain.) So long as such a domain exists, capturing generalizations within it is an important scientific goal. To succeed, however, we must adopt the right taxonomy or descriptive vocabulary. Another, equally important goal is to capture the generalizations in a manner that does more than merely tap our informal knowledge of the way people behave. We also want to be able to relate these generalizations to possible, physically realizable mechanisms, and that's where computation can serve the important bridging role.

The Stimulus-Independence of Cognitive Behavior

I have claimed that an important reason for requiring a cognitive vocabulary for explaining behavior is that behavior, at least human behavior, is highly plastic in certain well-defined ways. This characteristic emerges most clearly in the degree to which behavior is stimulus-independent. Most nonbehaviorists believe that the reason behavior is stimulus-free is that what people do depends to a great extent on what they believe at the moment, how they perceive a situation at the moment, on what they think will be the consequences of various behaviors, and so on. This stimulus-independence thus is not capricious or stochastic; it is merely governed by different principles. This is an empirical, not a logical, point. As far as we know, it is not true of much of the behavior of a frog, many of whose responses appear to be the under control of the environment, as the environment is objectively described in physical terms. If we attempt to describe human behavior in terms of physical properties of the environment, we soon come to the conclusion that, except for tripping, falling, sinking, bouncing off walls, and certain autonomic reflexes, human behavior is essentially random. Yet we know that human behavior, if described in cognitive terms, is highly regular and systematic. And that, of course, is not very good news for behaviorism.

There have been attempts to capture the antecedents of cognitive regularities in physical terms, notably in the study of perception. We shall see in chapter 6 that it is important to build a bridge between physical and cognitive terms; at that point I make some proposals about how the bridge might be built. Traditional attempts to relate perceptual regularities to physical properties, however, have encountered much the same difficulties that I alluded to. That is, the regularities that exist are to be found among perceived (cognitively described) properties or what Pike (1967) calls *emic* properties, not among objective (physically described) or *etic* properties. For example, the well-known perceptual psychologist Julian Hochberg has spent a lot of time trying to translate some of the Gestalt laws of perception into physical terms as part of what was to be a psychophysics of form perception. Despite some success in specifying "perceived complexity" in physical terms, the enterprise was abandoned. Hochberg (1968) reported that his earlier optimism had been premature; he could not specify, in physical terms, the relevant stimulus attributes that determine the way a pattern is perceived. He goes on to provide persuasive demonstrations that virtually no candidate physical properties (for example, particular physical features) are either necessary or sufficient for a person perceiving some situation in a certain way—for perceiving a stimulus *as* a something or other in the distal scene.[3] Following are some examples of the sort of radical variations in the physical properties of proximal stimulation that give rise to the same perception.

A line drawing of a cube in perspective, which includes the back (potentially hidden) lines, is called a Necker cube. Except for apparent motion, which I will ignore in these illustrations, it displays the marks of a perceptual reaction referred to in note 3. Clearly the cube need not be presented as drawn lines; dashes, points, and even end points of other lines can produce the same percept. If a field is uniformly filled with random points, the same percept can be produced by arranging for the points that would lie along the lines of a superimposed Necker cube to be perceptually distinct in almost *any* way—including being a different color, size, and shape (within interesting limits—cf. Julesz, 1975) or undergoing a small synchronous movement relative

3. It should be noted that in these demonstrations Hochberg is careful to distinguish between a true perceptual product (percept) and the results of deliberate reasoning. It would be less surprising (though the same principle is involved) if it proved impossible to physically specify environmental conditions that lead eventually to the same beliefs, since clearly the same conclusions can be inferred from very different methods of presenting the information. In all cases where a claim is made that the same percept occurs, a subject not only reports the same perceived form but also reports properties that are taken as distinguishing marks of an involuntary perceptual reaction, namely, spontaneous interpretation of the two-dimensional form as a three-dimensional object, spontaneous reversals of ambiguous patterns, and spontaneous apparent motion (when a sequence is presented).

to the other points.[4] The percept can also be produced sequentially over time by moving a screen containing a slit over any of the static forms described above (at a suitably high speed). Although one might view the latter procedure as painting the form on the retina, it turns out not to be necessary even to produce the actual spatial distribution of the pattern on the retina. The perceptual pattern can also be produced by moving the figure behind a stationary slit, thus ensuring that all stimulation is superimposed on a single line on the retina (Parks, 1965; Howard, personal communication). Various other sequential methods are possible as well. The most intriguing (and exotic) presentation, however, employs the random-dot stereogram method developed by Julesz (1971). Here, two random-dot patterns are presented, one to each eye. The patterns are identical except along the lines or regions that would be covered by a Necker-cube drawing (there, the dots of one random figure are systematically displaced relative to the other figure). Both figures are completely random patterns, but a systematic cross-correlation between the two figures carries information about the location of lines. Such a display also produces the perception of a Necker cube when—and only when—viewed stereoscopically. This exotic display can be combined with other forms of variation mentioned above.

It is not obvious what, if any, limits exist on ways to present stimulation compatible with the same perceptual interpretation. Furthermore, in each case the same regularities among perceived aspects have been found. For example, when a particular line is perceived as the top edge, the surface it bounds and the other contiguous lines are perceived as part of the top face; and when a particular face is perceived as the near face, it is perceived simultaneously as being somewhat larger than the far face. This holds true even when the figure undergoes a spontaneous reversal.

No wonder Hochberg despairs at the prospect of giving an account of perception in physical terms:

> (1) because we don't have a single physical dimension of stimulation by which to define the stimulus configuration to which a subject is responding, or by which we can decide what it is that two different patterns, which both produce the same form percept, have in common . . . [and] (2) because the subject can perceive very

---

4. There are a few restrictions here, and a fair amount is known about the optical properties that can serve to generate the perception of lines and edges (see, for example, Julesz [1975], Marr [1982]). Nonetheless, the range of alternative physical causes of a perceived line remains unbounded.

different forms in response to the same physical stimulus, . . . which form he perceives critically determines the other answers he gives to questions about shape, motion, size, depth, and so on.

This is not to deny that *some* causal chain connects stimulation and perception. The point is simply that there exist regularities stateable over perceptual (or cognitive) categories that are not stateable over properties of the stimulation itself. This, in turn, is true because it appears that virtually no physical properties (including arbitrarily complex combinations and abstractions over such properties) are necessary and sufficient for the occurrence of certain perceptions; yet it is these perceptions that determine psychological regularities in behavior. In fact, there could not be such properties in general since, as perceptionists are well aware, the way something is perceived can vary radically with physically identical stimuli and can be the same with physically very different stimuli.

Another way to put the matter is to say that organisms can respond selectively to properties of the environment that are not specifiable physically, such properties as being beautiful, being a sentence of English, or being a chair or a shoe. These properties are not properties involved in physical laws; they are not *projectable properties*. Fodor (1984) views a system's capacity to respond selectively to nonprojectable properties as precisely what differentiates inferencing systems from systems that merely react causally to environmental stimulation. I return to this view in chapter 5 and again in chapter 7, where I take a slightly different position; for now, it suffices to remark that it is not surprising that an organism reacts to nonphysical or nonprojectable properties of the environment inasmuch as "reacting to an environment" (at least for humans, and probably for many animals) typically involves such processes as drawing inferences to the best available hypothesis about what, in fact, is out there in the distal world.

This is not to say that everything in perception involves inference (the output of transducers, discussed at length in chapter 6, does not), only that some things do. In particular, recognizing or identifying a stimulus as an instance of some category does involve inference; that's what we mean when we speak of seeing a stimulus *as* something. This recognition, in turn, is why what we see a stimulus *as* depends on what we know. And, of course, it is what we see things as that determines their effect on our behavior. When we see a certain red light *as a traffic light*, we stop—and our seeing the light as a traffic light depends on knowledge of our culture's conventions. That, in a nutshell, is why the physical properties of stimuli do not determine our behavior.

Phenomena as "Events under Descriptions"

The question, which vocabulary is the appropriate one for a particular domain, can be viewed in a slightly different way, one that helps introduce the discussion in chapter 2, in which I claim there is a need for different levels of explanation.

If an event is to be explained by some theory, it must be viewed as being nonunique. It must be seen as a sample from a large equivalence class of events among which no distinction is made by the theory. Within the domain of a theory there is an unlimited number of distinct events (in principle, distinguishable in *some* respect) that nonetheless are counted as equivalent; that is, they are, to use the linguistic term, considered to be in "free variation." Thus if what we are interested in is providing a theoretical explanation, there is no such thing as a phenomenon in some fixed or absolute sense. One cannot *point* to a phenomenon except as a rough way of distinguishing a problem domain. Any time we seek to explain a phenomenon we always do so in relation to some way of conceptualizing, or dividing, the space of possible alternatives—indeed, some way of characterizing what constitutes potential alternatives.

The particular way in which one chooses to divide a set of alternatives is revealed by the vocabulary used to describe the phenomena. Take the case of human or animal behavior. If one describes the behavior in terms of the trajectories of limbs in space and time, then two behaviors are automatically considered equivalent if they have identical trajectory descriptions, regardless of the particular muscles or neural mechanisms responsible, the goals served by the movement, the intentions realized, or its final consequences on the immediate environment. If the behavior is described physiologically, in terms of the muscles that are innervated, a wide range of trajectories and purposive actions will be treated as equivalent. On the other hand, if the behavior is described in terms of certain end results (for example, a button being depressed), as it is to some extent in operant conditioning, the description collapses over an even larger range of trajectories, muscle contractions, and goals; it does not, for instance, distinguish between the deliberate act of pressing a lever and merely bumping into it accidentally. Similarly, if behavior is described in terms of such meaningful units or actions as reaching, grasping, walking, writing, or speaking, then a far different equivalence relation is imposed, that defines what will be counted as the "same behavior."

To summarize: Different descriptive vocabularies entail different structures in the space of possible events from which some particular, observed instance is assumed to be a sample. A theory never explains an entirely unique event, only an event viewed against a background of distinctions and equivalences defined by the vocabulary with which the events are described. That is what I mean when I say that theories address phenomena as "events under descriptions."

Two factors are relevant to the specification of this structure of phenomena, and hence to choosing a descriptive vocabulary. One is our pretheoretical notion of the domain of inquiry, or of the set of questions we take as requiring a systematic answer. The other factor is the empirical structure of the phenomena in that general domain. The informal example discussed above is intended to show the relevance of both factors. For instance, in the accident example an account can, in principle, be given solely in biological or physical terms. There are two problems with this sort of account, however. The first is that the account does not address the questions in the original domain of inquiry; it simply fails to deal with the *psychological* puzzles or with the phenomena under the intended interpretation. The second, closely related problem is that such an account does not capture the relevant regularities in the behavior.

It is an empirical fact about some behavior of humans and other animals that the regularities we are primarily interested in cannot be expressed listing certain biological and physical descriptions. This is true not only because we have various "culture-specific" notions of what regularities are "interesting" (though that in itself is enough to warrant the study of such regularities), but also because many regularities in our own behavior are clearly a result of our acting in certain ways *in order* to achieve certain results—that is, we act intentionally. Further, there must be a fairly reliable, systematic relation between the intentions we have when we act and the consequences of these acts, since such a reliable relation is precisely what is required for getting along in both social and natural environments. (For example, we need to know such things as that it is dangerous to walk off the edge of a cliff, a generalization that requires such nonphysical categories as *danger* and *walk*.) Physical and neurophysiological terms taxonomize the world in ways that do not permit us to express such generalizations. They often distinguish aspects of the world and of behavior that are equivalent with respect to their psychological import, and sometimes fail to make distinctions that are psychologically relevant. For this reason, descriptions cast in such terms typically fail to capture important psychological generalizations concerning human behavior.

Perhaps it is not surprising that strikingly different regularities emerge under different descriptions of events, and consequently that the descriptions suitable for stating the regularities of physics, chemistry, and biology are unsuitable for stating the regularities of cognitive psychology. As Fodor (1975) puts it,

> Any pair of entities, however different their physical structure, must nevertheless converge in indefinitely many of their properties. Why should there not be, among those convergent properties, some whose lawful interrelations support the generalizations of the special sciences? Why, in short, should not the kind predicates of the special sciences *cross-classify* the physical natural kinds?
>
> Physics develops the taxonomy of its subject matter which best suits its purposes . . . . But this is not the only taxonomy which may be required if the purposes of science in general are to be served—e.g., if we are to state such true, counterfactual supporting generalizations as there are to state. So there are special sciences, with their specialized taxonomies, in the business of stating some of these generalizations. If science is to be unified, then all such taxonomies must apply *to the same things*. If physics is to be basic science, then each of these things had better be a physical thing. But it is not further required that the taxonomies which the special sciences employ must themselves reduce to the taxonomy of physics. It is not required, and it is probably not true. (p. 25)

One could, in fact, turn the entire question around and ask why the referents of such physical terms as energy are so abstract, removed from experience, and psychologically complex. The taxonomy of physics, the set of basic terms in its vocabulary, was chosen to make the statement of physical laws simple, elegant, and revealing. In a remarkable study of the relationship of geometry and sense perception, conducted in 1924, Jean Nicod (1970) makes the same point:

> . . . the formation and growth of physics are dominated completely by the pursuit of simple laws or, better, of the simple expression of laws. This expression can in fact only be obtained by marking complex things by simple names. For nature is constituted in such a way that it is not the simple things that enjoy simple laws, and so, in order to simplify the laws, we must complicate the meanings of the terms. Energy, matter, object, place and time themselves, taken in the physical sense, and, more generally all the terms which are employed by physics and which do not express elementary observations, derive all their utility, their whole *raison d'etre*, from this compelling need for simple and striking statements of the laws of the sensible world. (p. xviii)

The statement of cognitive regularities as symbolic processes is another matter, however, and may require that we give "simple names" to very different "complex things."

Whatever the reason for the radical cross-classification provided by biological, physical, and cognitive taxonomies, the observation that different descriptive vocabularies are appropriate in these different domains should be clear from the example discussed above. My point here is that our pretheoretical notions of what constitutes the domain of cognitive psychology have been shaped by our experience with certain kinds of empirical regularities, so that the notions bear some prima facie validity, at least, as a first approximation (we see some examples in chapter 9 where these intuitions go astray as the science progresses and a more refined perspective on its boundary develops). Thus we intuitively count as psychological, regularities which, for example, relate "perceived" properties (such as the identity of objects we see in a scene) to meaningful or intentional actions (for example, "reaching for the salt"), whereas we count as at least partly nonpsychological the relation between tripping over a stone and hitting one's knee. With no such pretheoretical distinction pressed upon us by various extrinsic considerations, the need for a separate science of psychology might not have arisen; the study of our behavior might simply have proceeded by treating humans as merely another physical, biological object. Among the considerations that suggest at least the first-order view of an autonomous psychological domain of inquiry, and thus argue for the importance of considering events "under a psychological description," are some of our strongest intuitions concerning the reasons for our own actions. These considerations provide plausible empirical—hence, falsifiable—hypotheses concerning the nature of regularities in human behavior. Some of them are:

(a) The intuitive presuppositions of our naive questions (for example, How do we solve problems? What happens when we read, speak, or think?), presuppositions that determine to some extent the sort of an account that will be viewed as addressing the questions on their terms. Of course, we might discover that such naive questions are poorly formulated because they have false presuppositions, but this discovery would then be a substantive discovery of some intrinsic interest. Further, it can hardly be true that all the *why* and *how* questions concerned with the aspects of behavior important to us have false presuppositions. If it were true, we would have to conclude that no science dealing with such puzzles was possible. In view of even the modest success of both artificial intelligence (which addresses some of these questions) and folk psychology, this seems unlikely.

(b) The compelling view each one of us possesses regarding why or how we do certain things (because we are paid to, because we were taught a way to do it). While many such accounts undoubtedly turn out to be incorrect, or at least inadequate in some respect, there can be no question that *some* such accounts are correct yet they can be expressed only using certain kinds of cognitive terms to describe the environment and the behavior. In other words, there exist what appear to be clear-cut cases in which we know our behavior must be characterized over a certain nonphysical vocabulary that mentions such things as our intentions and goals. Even explaining something as mundane as why a subject in an experiment pressed the left rather than the right button must mention the subject's intent in pressing the button (for example, to indicate which of two stimuli were perceived, or to indicate agreement versus disagreement), which, in turn, depends on the subject's interpretation of the task, and so on. Thus we have to view the behavior in terms of how the subject intended it or in terms of an intentional description of the behavior.

(c) The fact that a certain rough taxonomy of the world and of other people's actions results in a reasonably successful and predictive folk psychology. While it is likely that many, perhaps most, hypothetical mechanisms that folk psychology appeals to are impotent to provide adequate explanations of behavior (since, for example, homuncular explanations abound in folk psychology), the fact that the predictions made concerning the everyday social behavior of people are so often correct strongly suggests that we have made some of the correct cuts through phenomena (that is, that the taxonomy or descriptive vocabulary over which our beliefs are expressed is more or less the right one).

(d) The rationality of much (though not all) of our behavior, which can be exhibited only if we have a taxonomy that allows us to relate beliefs and goals to intended actions. Rationality itself cannot be applied to descriptions cast in terms of biology or physical trajectories, yet it is one of the properties of at least some of our activity that must somehow enter into an explanation of our behavior; at least some explanations of our behavior take the form: Person S had goal G and beliefs $B1$, $B2$, $B3$, . . . , Bn, one or more of which had the content that action A could help achieve goal G, and hence, on the assumption that S acts rationally, *that is why S* carried out a certain behavior as an instance of A. Obviously, much remains to be said about rationality, especially since there are large areas in which people do not appear to behave in accordance with normative principles of rationality (cf. Nisbett and Ross, 1980; Tversky and Kahneman, 1974; but see Kyburg, 1983). Nonetheless, the principle of rationality—suitably embedded within a system of limited, imperfect mechanisms—is indispensable in giving an account of human behavior, for reasons explored in chapter 2.

These considerations provide us with a first-draft specification of a domain of inquiry, or to put it as I did above, they specify what it is to view phenomena *under a cognitive description*. I have suggested that lawlike generalizations or regularities in behavior of special concern to cognitive psychology are likely to be captured only if the behavior and its antecedent conditions are described in terms of such a taxonomy. I have also claimed that such a taxonomy is distinct from that provided by other disciplines, especially physics and biology, and that the taxonomy typically is not only more abstract than that of these sciences but that it classifies events in equivalence classes whose boundaries typically do not coincide with the boundaries of classifications based on the other sciences. So far, though, I have said nothing that is not also true of all the "special sciences," that is, of every science other than basic physics. In each case, generalizations from each science are stateable only over their own special vocabulary; consequently, the lawlike generalizations of these sciences are not reduceable to some finite combination of physical laws. Each category over which regularities are stated in a special science stands in a type-token relation to categories of physics, which means a category in, say, economics cannot be reduced to a finite disjunction of categories of physics. I will have more to say about type-token hierarchies in chapter 2, inasmuch as I argue that there is more than one principled level of this hierarchy within cognitive science itself.

What I suggest is that there is an important difference between the generalizations that belong to the "cognitive sciences" and those that occur in physical or other "natural" sciences, because, in cognition, there is another type-token level that does not apply in natural-science accounts that is relevant to the notion of rationality, as well as to what Brentano first described using the term *intentionality*, a property he took to be the mark of the mental. I do not discuss the issue of intentionality in its full philosophical complexity (there is an enormous technical, philosophical literature on the subject); I do examine one aspect of intentionality because it is closely related to the notion of *representation*, a notion which plays a fundamental role in cognitive explanation. Chapter 2 is devoted to a discussion of this topic. I might just note in anticipation of later discussion, however, that the need to appeal to representations in providing explanations of cognitive phenomena constitutes one of the main reasons why cognition is fundamentally a *computational* process.

Chapter 2

The Explanatory Role of Representations

... To unfold the secret laws and relations of those high faculties of thought by which all beyond merely perceptive knowledge of the world and of ourselves is attained or matured is an object which does not stand in need of commendation to a rational mind.

George Boole, *Laws of Thought*

Introduction

In this chapter I attempt to elaborate on the idea of levels of explanatory principles. Because one of the levels is the semantic level, I will be right in the middle of what is probably the second hardest puzzle in philosophy of mind: the puzzle of meaning. (The hardest puzzle, in my view, is consciousness, which probably is not even well enough defined to qualify as a puzzle.) I want to reassure the reader that I do not propose to solve the puzzle of what meaning is or how it gets into the head; my aims are somewhat more modest: to describe how the idea of the semantic content of representations is implicitly viewed within the field of cognitive science, and discuss why this view is justifiable. Although it is appropriate to raise this issue early, to provide a background for the more detailed analysis of cognitivist theorizing presented throughout the book, this strategy prevents me from using certain ideas and distinctions that will be developed later (notably, the notions of functional architecture and cognitive capacity). So bear with me; I will anticipate just enough of this material to lay out the story.

The first thing to do is introduce the idea that in order to express certain cognitive generalizations, we must refer to *representations*. This necessity is related to the point made in chapter 1, concerning certain generalizations being "under a cognitive description." Here, though, I try to be more precise about what is entailed. In particular, I make the point that generalizations stated over the contents of representations are not mere *functional* generalizations in the usual sense. What is traditionally viewed as a functional description or a functional theory (roughly, a theory that does not refer to physical properties of the particular system in question, only the way it operates; see, for example, Cummins, 1975; Fodor, 1968b; Haugeland, 1978; Putnam, 1973; Dennett, 1971), where it concerns cognition, needs to be refined. It is this refinement that forces us to raise, somewhat prematurely, the notion of computation, or symbol manipulation. In the refinement we will see that there are actually two distinct levels above the physical (or neurophysiological) level—a representational or semantical level and a symbol-processing level. Allen Newell (1982) refers to the first level as the "knowledge level" and to the second as the "symbol level."

Having thus forewarned you of my intentions, I can now back up to where the discussion of explanation by appeal to generalizations left off.

The Appeal to Representations

Lawlike generalizations or explanatory principles that use different vocabularies can differ in several ways. Consider the following examples, each of which represents a fragment of a longer explanation. Account (1) says that a certain object accelerated at a meters per second per second because a steady force was applied to it that was equal to ma, where m is the mass of the object. Account (2) says that a certain neuron fired because a potential of v millivolts was applied along two of its dendrites and that it had been inactive during the previous t milliseconds. Account (3) says that the bit pattern in a certain computer register came to have a particular configuration because of the particular contents present in the instruction register and the program counter, and because the system is wired according to a certain register transfer protocol. Compare accounts (1) to (3) to account (4), which states that the computer printed the sequence of numbers 2,4,6, . . . because it started with the number 2 and added 2 repeatedly or because it applied the successor function repeatedly and doubled the value before printing it out; or with account (5), which says (as in our example in chapter 1) that the pedestrian dialed the phone number 911 because he believed it to be the emergency number and had recognized the urgent need for assistance.

In the first three accounts all terms refer to properties of objects within a closed system.[1] For example, the mass and force on an object,

1. In using the term *closed system* I do not mean to imply that the system has a well-defined physical boundary, or "skin". The term is used in the systems-theory sense, where a system is defined in terms of a set of properties or parameters, together with some characterization of how they interact. The point here is that a closed system is one with no causal connections other than the set of variables that define the system. Although

the electrical potential across a dendritic membrane, the bit pattern in a computer register are all properties of a system that causally determine the sequence of states the system goes through. These accounts make no reference to entities or properties other than those that determine what is sometimes referred to as the *location* of the system in its state or phase space. Because these are deterministic systems (what Ashby [1956] calls "absolute" or "state determined" systems), closed to the outside except for effects explicitly recognized as inputs or outputs, such an explanatory account is also closed and complete.

Accounts (4) and (5) differ in an important respect: Both make substantive reference to entities or properties that are not an intrinsic part of their state description, for example, *numbers* or *need for assistance*. It is important to recognize that such terms do not refer to properties of the system whose behavior we are explaining (that is, the computer or the person doing the phoning) nor necessarily to properties causally connected to such states or to the system's behavior, that is, the behavior of the system cannot be explained in terms of a chain of causal laws connecting such extrinsic entities as those mentioned in accounts (4) and (5) to the current state of the system. The reason for this has already been discussed in chapter 1, that is, the causal chain would have to contain an arbitrarily large disjunction of possible physical causes, since the relevant connections between the extrinsic events and the current state includes such relations as: being told about them by someone, reading about them, inferring from what one has seen or heard, and so on. Neither numbers nor the anticipation of help can in any sense be viewed as *causal inputs* to the system. Numbers are abstract mathematical objects; and the successor function is defined only over these abstract objects. Similarly, the content of anticipations or goals are possible future states of affairs; none can enter directly as causes in the usual sense. The case is even clearer when we find people's behavior being a function of such nonexistent things as Santa Claus, the pot of gold at the end of the rainbow, a hoped-for raise, or beliefs that are false (for instance, in the example in chapter 1, the perceived *need for assistance* could be an illusion: the pedestrian could have happened upon a rehearsal of a movie scene).

As materialists we must ask how behavioral regularities such as those captured by statements that mention extrinsic but causally unconnected entities (or perhaps nonexistent objects) are possible in a world governed

---

no segment of the universe is truly closed, it is often possible to define a set of properties and a configuration such that the behavior of the configuration is determined almost entirely from its initial state. We can then extend the notion to any configuration that has well-defined interactions with extrinsic properties by viewing the interactions as occurring through inputs and outputs to the system, which then become part of the system description.

by physical laws. How is it possible for properties of the world to determine behavior when the properties are not causally related in the required sense to the functional states of the system, which is what we seem to be claiming when we say, for example, that what determines the person's behavior in rushing to the phone is something like his anticipation of, or desire to obtain help? This conundrum is sometimes called "Brentano's problem," after the psychologist who first appreciated its force. Brentano saw no way out of the puzzle except by accepting that mental events are not governed by physical laws but by their own mental principles. The answer I ultimately give to this puzzle is that the causes of the behavior are not literally numbers, anticipated future events, or other "intentional objects" but rather some physically instantiated *internal representation* of such things, that is, a physical code or a symbol.

To introduce this discussion it should again be emphasized that the notion of representation is necessary only in the context of explanation; it is needed to state generalizations concerning the behavior of systems under certain descriptions. (Recall that explanation is relative to particular descriptions of the behavior of a system.) Thus, if under a particular description of a system's behavior, a physical, neural, or purely functional account captures all the relevant generalizations hence serves the explanatory function, then appealing to representations is not essential. Included in examples of such heuristic uses of representation-talk are, for example, explaining the operation of a television set, watch, or thermostat by referring to certain properties of the device as representing, say, time or color or temperature. In such cases the representational character of certain properties enters in only in order to connect the operation of the device to the intentions of its designer. What is crucial here is that we do not need the notion of representation to explain how a device works, only to explain how it performs the function intended by its designer. In other words, the content of the representations—or, what the properties in question actually represent—is not part of the explanation itself. We need not say that the system does such and such *because* it has a certain representation, though frequently we use such language to express the reason why the system was designed in a particular way. Here, the test is that, by viewing the device as transforming physical patterns of inputs into physical patterns of outputs, we lose no explanatory power, inasmuch as everything that must be accounted for—all relevant generalizations— can be captured in an account that makes no mention of what various properties and states represent. This is in marked contrast with the case of explaining genuine representational or intentional processes.

To see what makes the crucial difference between mere design descriptions (what Dennett [1978] refers to as descriptions from the "design stance") and genuine cases of epistemic states, consider the following example, in which the important generalization cannot be captured unless we refer to the semantic content of the representation.[2] Suppose I wish to explain what I am doing at this moment as I sit here in front of my computer terminal, alternately typing these sentences and thinking about other things. I look out over the Stanford campus below, and my mind wanders. I think about the Santa Cruz mountains behind me and wonder why I didn't go for a walk after lunch instead of confining myself to my study. Clearly, my current behavior (including writing this paragraph) is caused by my current thoughts and goals. They include the goal of having a completed chapter and the thought that there are walking trails in the hills behind me. If there is any sense in which this behavior is *caused* by the nonexistent, completed chapter or by the hills, it is an entirely obscure sense of causation. Plainly, what is going on is, my behavior is being caused by certain states of my brain. Yet—and this is the crux of the problem—the only way to explain why those states caused me to type the specific sentences *about* walking, writing, the mountains, and so on is to say that these states themselves are in some way related to the things referred to (writing, walking, mountains).

This is not simply a case of the explanations having to be more complicated or less comprehensible if the content of the representation is not mentioned; the relevant generalization or connection to my behavior, viewed under the appropriate description, cannot even be expressed. My brain states are not, as we have noted, causally connected in appropriate ways to walking and to mountains. The relationship must be one of content: a semantic, not a causal, relation. Brain states cause certain movements. If these movements are viewed as members of the equivalence class of behaviors described as "writing a sentence about walking in the Santa Cruz mountains" the brain states must be treated as embodying representations or codes *for* such things as walking and hills. In this way the behavior can be seen as rationally connected to the representational content of these codes by certain rules (logical, heuristic, associative, etc.). That must be the case in part because the meaning of my words derives from the semantics of my mental states, from my intention to mean something or other by expressing them. If the mental states that caused *those* sentences to be produced were about

---

2. Here, the notion of content is roughly that of what the states are about or what they represent. It is in itself not entirely unproblematic, though the general idea is clear enough. In End Note 2, I discuss some of the distinctions that have to be kept in mind when talking about content.

nothing (or were about something quite different), then my producing the sentences would be just like a tape recorder's or photocopier's producing sentences, it would not constitute the making of an utterance; therefore, an explanation cast in these terms would not explain the event under the description that something was being asserted. Presumably, it is under *that* description that we will find my keyboard pressings to be explainable in terms of certain of my experiences (that is, related in terms of some system of regularities or generalizations).

On the other hand, in the case of such artifacts as watches, the semantic interpretation is gratuitous, since the set of movements corresponding to the "interpreted" behavior is coextensive with, or type-equivalent to, the set of movements corresponding to the physical description of the behavior. Whether you call something the position of a lever or the time of day is determined merely by whether you are interested in conveying to someone the intended use of the device; it has no bearing on capturing generalizations about the possible behaviors of the device, since the device *exhibits no other behavior* that falls under generalizations involving time of day as an open-ended category (a category realizable in arbitrarily many distinct physical forms). The same is true of a description of more complex devices, for example, a television set. In terms of the discussion above of explanations being relativized to phenomena "under descriptions," the two forms of explanation (say, of the behavior of a clock or a television set, or any other artifacts designed for a specific function), the physical account and the representational account end up explaining their behavior under a coextensive taxonomy; hence, one captures no generalizations missed by the other. On the other hand, the two ways of explaining certain human behavior capture extremely different generalizations.[3]

Representational and Functional Levels

The burden of these examples (as well as the example in chapter 1) is to suggest that it is not enough to give a *functional* description of mental processes; we must also discuss the content of certain representational states. If, however, the content makes a difference to behavior, is it not, by definition, also a functional difference? There is a sense in which functional and representational states might be viewed as identical except for the way we choose to describe them (and some, notably Stich [1984] take precisely this view). If that were the case, one might

---

3. In End Note 1, I discuss some indicators of when the attribution of representational content or semantics to functional states of a system plays an ineliminable part in the explanation.

think nothing could be gained by adding the semantic vocabulary to the account; that is, nothing is gained by mentioning what states represent. While it is true that differences in content always result in functional differences, the converse may very well not be true. Thus the question we need to ask is whether we can have differences in functional states *without* there being differences in content, or without there being differences in what is being represented. To answer this question we need to be somewhat more specific about how representational states and functional states are related. What I shall try to do at this point is anticipate some of the discussion to come in the next several chapters, in order to deal with the content-attribution issue here.

The view I take in chapters 3 and 4—with a few exceptions to be mentioned when the topic comes up for discussion, and which is fairly widespread in cognitive science—is that, to be in a certain representational state is to have a certain symbolic expression in some part of memory.[4] That expression *encodes* the semantic interpretation and the combinatorial structure of the expression encodes the relation among the contents of the subexpressions, much as in the combinatorial system of predicate calculus. The details are very much in dispute and, I might add, subject to empirical investigation; but the general picture seems to be widely accepted. This picture is discussed in the following chapters, where some of its aspects are defended.

The reason there must be symbolic codes, of course, is that, because they are instantiated as physical patterns, they can enter into causal relations. Unlike semantic contents, tokens of symbols can actually cause the system to behave in certain ways. Now, if there is a unique symbolic expression corresponding to each content, one might expect

---

4. Within philosophy, this corresponds to the view championed by Fodor (1980c), that to have a certain propositional attitude that is, to "believe" or "want" or "fear" P is to be in a certain computational relation to a representation of P. Others, such as Davidson (1970) and Geach (1957,1980), insist that it is unnecessary to assume that something (an internal property or a symbol) corresponds to P to explain how people can be in the state of "believing P." All we need, according to this view, are certain states of an organism which function in a particular way—namely, in a way correctly described (from the outside) as "P-believing." This is a kind of adverbial theory of intentional states which simply pairs functional states with belief (or other propositional attitude) descriptions without the step of positing any articulated substates or symbols that are the representations of P. This idea is discussed briefly in chapter 3, where I argue that within the context of explanation it is necessary that a functional theory take a certain articulated form, that it have a symbolic level or a level of syntactic structure. The regularities of a system with arbitrarily many functional states cannot be captured in a finite manner without some language-like combinatorial mechanism that ties together the systematic features of the set of state transitions. Indeed, this is a primary reason for a computational model appearing to be the appropriate one for cognitive processes.

functional states and representational states to once again be in a one-to-one relation; hence, the ascription of content still does not gain us any explanatory leverage—it remains merely heuristic.[5] That need not be the case, for two reasons:

(a) There may be synonymous expressions—sets of codes with the same semantic content. Such codes might be functionally, but not semantically, distinguishable. For example, one might be structurally more complex than another and, consequently, might take more time to process or lead to certain systematic errors—predictable according to certain functional principles at what is referred to below as the "symbol level." (The problem of distinguishing differences in content from differences in structure remains to be solved. According to Putnam (1975,1981), it may be one of those puzzles better left alone.)

(b) Merely possessing a certain symbolic expression that encodes semantic content is, by itself, insufficient to produce behavior. Another part of the story remains to be told; it is a part that has been of much greater concern to computer scientists than to philosophers or psychologists (see, however, Newell, 1972,1973b). What is needed is a set of mechanisms to make the system run or, as is sometimes said, "interpret" the symbols. It is because of these mechanisms that the symbolic expressions do not exhaust what we have informally been referring to as the "functional state" of the system.

The set of mechanisms needed is approximately what I refer to below as the "functional architecture" of the system (though I place severe constraints on what qualifies as functional architecture). It includes the basic operations provided by the biological substrate, say, for storing and retrieving symbols, comparing them, treating them differently as a function of how they are stored, (hence, as a function of whether they represent beliefs or goals), and so on, as well as such basic resources and constraints of the system, as a limited memory. It also includes what computer scientists refer to as the "control structure," which selects which rules to apply at various times. (See the brief discussion of the problem of control structure at the end of chapter 3.)

Some of these mechanisms may be quite rigid, whereas others may be alterable in various ways by the environment. For example, retrieval

---

5. Even in this case, the word *merely* overstates the case. Content ascription may still be crucial insofar as there may be no way to discover the functional states—no independent motivation for positing equivalence classes of physical states—than by treating the system as an "intentional system" and in this way inferring its beliefs, goals, and other semantic contents. After all, there are infinitely many ways to map physical states onto functional ones. Presumably, the correct way is the one that captures generalizations stated over the appropriate vocabulary, which, in the case of cognition, is extremely likely to be the intentional one.

and control processes may be sensitive to anything from intoxication and sleep to the association strength among codes, which reflects, say, the repetition or the temporal proximity of token occurrences of their referents. Of course, the mechanisms themselves are not sensitive to the *content* of incoming information, since, by hypothesis, semantic content is precisely what is encoded in terms of the symbolic codes (this point is quite central in later discussions, where I talk about the "cognitive impenetrability" of the basic mechanisms).

The importance of the distinction between semantically interpreted symbolic codes and functional architecture arises when we relate the functional description to the representational one. When we claim that functional states are semantically interpreted (that is, they have representational content), we are referring only to the symbolic code part of the states, not the functional architecture. Differences in functional architecture, though they affect behavior, are not considered related to differences in content; the representation can remain the same despite changes in functional architecture. What that means is: If we individuate states according to their content, then two systems in exactly the same representational state (all the same goals, beliefs, fears, desires, and so on) can nonetheless still be functionally distinguished. That's because behavior is determined by more than the mere content of all one's beliefs, goals, and so forth. Behavior is also determined by the functional architecture, including the control structure and all available mechanisms.

Take a simple case. Two people whose beliefs and goals are all the same may nevertheless be functionally distinguishable if they have, say, slightly different memory-retrieval mechanisms, short-term memory capacities, degrees of alertness, or, possibly, different reinforcement histories, insofar as these cause differences in some aspect of the functional architecture rather than the content of certain beliefs (assuming reinforcement indeed has such an effect, as is claimed by behaviorists though denied by others, for example, Brewer, 1974). Two people who differ in this way might take different amounts of time on different classes of problems; they might make predictably different errors, find various tasks easy or hard, and so on. That is why psychologists devote so much time to studying failures; failures provide evidence of humans' functional architecture. On the other hand, people in artificial intelligence spend considerably more time studying expert performance and determining what knowledge these experts bring to bear on problems with which they are fluent—because in artificial intelligence one is more or less stuck with a relatively limited class of functional architectures, namely, those of available computers equipped with available high-level languages.

It thus appears that when we provide the kind of functional explanation provided in cognitive science—in terms of both semantically interpreted symbol structures and properties of the functional architecture—we find that many functionally distinct systems have the same representations. In other words, precisely the same representational state may lead to behaviors that differ in predictable ways. Thus generalizations can be captured by referring to the content of representational states that differ from those captured by referring to functional mechanisms. Generalizations expressible in terms of the semantic content of representations are referred to in this book as "semantic-level generalizations," whereas generalizations expressible in terms of functional properties of the functional architecture are referred to as "symbol-level generalizations." The latter term is taken from Newell (1980,1982), who uses the term "knowledge level" where I use "semantic level." Although "knowledge level" conveys the correct idea to people in artificial intelligence, it has the unfortunate property of failing to distinguish between knowledge and belief; further, it gives the appearance (perhaps incorrectly) of leaving out such other representations as goals. That is why I will continue to use the term "semantic-level generalization."

Representational Content as Defining a Level of Description

Although the need to use a special class of terms (especially terms that refer to semantic content) may surprise some, the situation here is no different from one we have already encountered. The principle that leads us to postulate representational states (individuated by their content) that are distinct from functional states is exactly the same as the principle that leads us to postulate functional states that are distinct from physical states. In both cases we want to capture certain generalizations. We discover that in order to do this, we must adopt a new vocabulary or taxonomy; hence we find ourselves positing a new, autonomous level of description.

Recall that our reason for abandoning a biological vocabulary in describing cognitive processes is that we found there are many generalizations (at least in such central processes as thinking and problem-solving) we have reason to believe correspond to arbitrarily large disjunctions of sequences of brain states, that is, there is multiple realization of functional states as neurophysiological states.[6] We therefore concluded

6. Even if some functional states or properties did correspond to particular neurological properties on *every* occasion, it would be a *discovery* of some importance. It would be a "discovery" precisely because there would have been two independent sets of considerations or methodologies that happened to converge on one of their categories, a con-

that biologically distinguishable brain states are not identical to functionally distinguishable states, consequently, functional generalizations cannot, in general, be captured in a finite neurophysiological description.

It is the fact that certain arbitrary sets of physical properties have something in common at the functional level, which cannot be captured in terms of a finite description at the physical level, that leads us to postulate the existence of a new level with a distinct taxonomy or vocabulary. In this case it is a purely functional vocabulary in which theoretical constructs are identified by their role in explaining or generating the behavioral regularities in question (for example, the symbolic terms that appear in any computational or information-processing model of a psychological process). When we have principles of operation that cannot be stated within a certain vocabulary—but that *can* be captured in another, more abstract (here, *functional*) vocabulary to which the terms of the first vocabulary stand in a multiple-realization relation— we have a prima facie case for the existence of an independent level of description. This is exactly the situation we find ourselves in with regard to regularities expressible in semantic terms. That was the idea behind the analysis above of such examples as the one in which a pedestrian who witnesses an accident dials the emergency telephone number, or in which we consider how my writing the particular sentences I wrote might be explained. On the basis of these considerations we can conclude that the representational, or semantic, level represents a distinct, autonomous level of description of certain kinds of systems. The notion that there is something special about certain systems, that requires their description in terms of representations or representation-governed processes is only beginning to be appreciated by those concerned with the foundations of cognitive science (Fodor, 1980c; Dennett, 1978,1982; Newell, 1982), though it is implicit in nearly all the work done by cognitive psychologists and researchers in artificial intelligence.

One way such an implicit view manifests itself is in the general acceptance of the assumption that there are certain *principles* constraining transitions among states individuated in terms of content and that these principles do not apply to states individuated by function

---

vergence that is a contingent empirical fact, not a logical necessity (indeed, it might not even be true in another species or for other categories). Further, even if, as seems unlikely at present, there were an abstract physical description that in some sense always preserves the functional types, this would still not provide a basis for arguing against the existence of an autonomous, functional level, since one would not be able to read off the functional generalizations from the physical description alone, inasmuch as the *same* physical system has many functional descriptions, depending on what we call its inputs and what its outputs, that is, depending on the description under which we view its behavior. Here, the abstract, physical description would still have to be after the fact and would have to be relativized to at least some prior functional considerations.

alone. Despite the acceptance of this assumption by virtually everyone who uses what philosophers call intentional terms (who talks about beliefs, goals, fears, and other "propositional attitudes"), such principles are understood only roughly. Chief among them is the principle of *rationality*. To the extent we are justified in appealing to such a principle that is, to the extent that, by using this principle, we can give a general account of certain classes of regularities and thereby render coherent a range of behaviors that would otherwise just be an unprincipled collection of empirical generalizations—to that extent we are justified in claiming to have discovered a distinct level of analysis beyond the functional level. What I am claiming is that the principle of rationality (and perhaps other principles that are stated over the content of rep-resentations) is a major reason for our belief that a purely functional account will fail to capture certain generalizations, hence, that a distinct new level is required. It is because of this belief that the principle of rationality figures so prominently in the writings of people intent on understanding intentionality. It is also due to this belief that practitioners of cognitive science who speak of goals and beliefs take rationality for granted. For example, we take it for granted that when we say someone does A because they have goal G, and because they believe that doing A will help them achieve G, we are, in fact, giving a *principled* expla-nation (rather than merely an ad hoc description) of what happened.

For example, in explaining how a subject was able to assign the correct anaphoric reference to a certain pronoun (say, the italicized pronoun in the sentence "The doctor did not try to help the nurse because *he* needed the practice"), we do not hesitate to refer to what the subject believes (or "knows") about the world, including beliefs about stereotypical sex roles, which, for example, would explain the difficulty many people have in interpreting the sentence. Not only do we unhesitatingly give such explanations, we tacitly assume that they are principled. That is, we do not feel compelled to add something like, "and if the person *was acting rationally at the time*"; it is assumed to be part of the "normal background conditions."

It is not simply that rational action occurs frequently; rather, it is that there is something special and nonarbitrary about concluding Q from P and "P entails Q" that makes it the unmarked case. If people have the beliefs we attribute to them—but consistently arrive at con-sequent beliefs whose content bears no such privileged relation to these beliefs (say, if a man asserts that he is Napoleon whenever he learns it is raining)—then, that *would* require a further analysis and explication, precisely because it lies outside such a principled relation. I will return to this issue by a somewhat different route.

Levels and Constraints on Realizability

Throughout our discussion of levels up to this point I have referred to the need to capture generalizations. Indeed, this is the main argument for the existence of levels, that is, that there be valid generalizations at one level that are not expressible at a lower level. There is another, closely related way of looking at this notion, however, that can help illustrate the role played by the principle of rationality while simultaneously relating the idea of a level to constraints rather than actual performance. This approach is related to the notion of *capacity*, one of the main points of focus in chapter 7. What I suggest is that the existence of a new level can often be recognized by the presence of constraints on the behavior of a system over and above the constraints that can be expressed in terms of principles currently available. I make the point that the purely functional constraints imposed by the functional architecture are compatible with the existence of systems whose behavior clearly falls outside what is natural for a "cognizing" system like us, hence that the explanation of such constraints, if they are principled ones, must be provided at another level. There is an interesting analogy here with biology, which I will take a page or so to examine first, to show how the existence of genuine explanatory levels provides for a kind of emergence of constraining principles.

One way in which this emergence is exhibited is that at one level of description, the principles of operation of a system may be compatible with a much wider range of behaviors than actually occurs. For example, the laws of physics are compatible with the existence of all the observed types of creatures as well as an indefinite number that do not exist. Why does only this subset exist? One answer might be that it's just a fluke; the initial state of the universe had to take some form, and the form it took led to the evolution of precisely this subset of creatures, and no others. Another answer might be that members of the existing subset had a survival advantage; but that is no explanation unless one can identify particular properties of the existing creatures and can explain how those properties increase the chances of survival of the group, by what mechanisms the property is realized and propagated, especially if it is a functional property, such as a high rate of reproduction. A more interesting answer to the question of why only certain patterns exist would be possible if there were a set of principles that characterized the existing patterns as a class. For example, if biology picks out a natural domain of inquiry—that is, if *living thing* is a natural kind— then there will be principles that apply to all entities in that domain and only entities in that domain. In other words, if some phenomenon falls within that domain, it must obey the laws of biology. On the assumption that this or something like it is true of biology, there may be principles living organisms cannot fail to follow and still qualify as living organisms. If some configuration of atoms failed to obey such principles, the configuration would automatically fall outside the domain, hence would be subject to *no* biological principles. For example, universal biological laws may exist that constrain the possibilities for tissue structures, say, laws of genetics or embryology. Systems that do not obey such laws simply would not be living organisms, not by definition but by an empirical theory, because biology claims that living organisms as a class must follow such principles. Consequently, whereas physics provides a set of constraints on what is physically possible, there may be cases for which one can give a principled *explanation* of why a certain class of these possibilities do not occur, by appealing to principles at another level, say, to principles of biology, genetics, embryology, or evolution. Thus, in cases where there are such principles (and there may not always be such principles; as I state above, the exclusion might merely be an accident of the initial state), the existence of another level (and, typically, a different nonreducible science) is usually indicated.

Now, if we take the *symbol level* to be more or less as described above, and if we identify the principles that govern this level with some very general properties of what I have been calling "functional architecture," we will find that the existing (empirically observed) functional architecture of humans, and perhaps of other creatures, is compatible with a wide range of processes and regularities that do not occur in human cognition. Some of these processes and regularities may not occur simply because the right conditions do not happen to be present, that is, they *could* occur within some class of variation of such conditions—for example, if the cultural or social context were substantially different (here, the relevant class of variations is an important consideration, one we will take up in detail in chapter 5). On the other hand, there are other types of processes that would not occur under this class of variation of antecedent conditions, though conceivably they could be caused by brain damage or similar noncognitive intervention. What are some of these processes? I suggest below that they are processes that are characterizable as *semantically deviant*.

Even with no detailed theory of human functional architecture, we already see that principles of the architecture can only constrain transitions among representational states in certain ways, specifically in certain structural ways that are *independent of the content* of these representational states. For example, limitations in the size of working memory may constrain the number of items that can be interrelated at one time, or they may necessitate certain recodings that lead to certain memory-time tradeoffs (see, for instance, the proposal in Newell,

1973b). It is clear that whatever constraints there may be in detail, the functional architecture permits application of arbitrary rules governing transitions among functional states so long as the rules conform to certain very general structural or functional principles. There is reason, though, to think there are other sorts of principled constraints not specifiable in terms of properties of information-processing mechanisms that constrain rules in certain cases, including some of the clearest cases of what might be called "high-level cognitive processes."

As far as the constraints of the functional architecture are concerned, rules are permitted that would be viewed as nonsensical or bizarre or incoherent by someone who interpreted the functional states as having representational content. For example, there could be a regularity among functional states that would be interpreted as the rule that if one believes all ravens are black, and that there is a raven in the tree, then that person goes into a state corresponding to the belief that the sky is falling; or there might be a regularity that, under the representational interpretation, would come out as the rule that if someone tells you a building is on fire, you come to believe that $2 + 3 = 12$.

Clearly, nobody would choose to interpret the functional states that way, and no empirically adequate model would contain such rules, since the rules would not generate the right behaviors. Whether anyone would ever hypothesize such rules is not the point. The question still arises in a cognitive system—What principle prevents them from occurring?—as it does in the case of the biological examples discussed. Why don't certain rules permitted by the constraints of the functional architecture, in fact, occur? More to the point, since the absolute nonoccurrence of such cases is not what is crucial, what distinguishes one kind of rule (the incoherent or nonsensical ones) from the other kind (the coherent or sensible ones), when both kinds are permitted within the constraints of the functional architecture? As in the example from biology, there are two possible answers. One is that the nonoccurrence of one kind of rule may be due to the initial state of the world from which organisms evolved; hence, the distinction between the two kinds of rules could be considered an accident, since the distinction between the kinds of rules that occur and those that do not occur could, in principle, have been quite different. The other answer is that there may be additional principles, perhaps universal in human cognitive systems, not stateable in terms of constraints on the functional mechanisms. (I will have more to say about the importance of distinguishing different sources of constraints in chapter 7, since that is one of the main issues raised by the proposal that certain kinds of cognitive processes are *analogue*.)

To say that the distinction between the two kinds of rules is due to the survival advantage of having truth-preserving transformations (that is, valid inferences) may be correct—though it is easy to overestimate the explanatory value of such appeals to evolution—but it does not diminish the present point: that principles must be imported from outside the symbol level, or the level of functional architecture, to explain these particular constraints, and that these principles must be stated in terms of what the functional states represent, here, in terms of "truth preservation."[7] Although many doubt the possibility of couching the principle of rationality in terms of survival value, the present point is neutral on this question.

We thus come once again to the view that, in a cognitive theory, the reason we need to postulate representational content for functional states is to explain the existence of certain distinctions, constraints, and regularities in the behavior of at least human cognitive systems, which, in turn, appear to be expressible only in terms of the semantic content of the functional states of these systems. Chief among the constraints is some principle of rationality. It is also a consequence of this view that deviations from rationality can arise because of interactions of intentional-level (or knowledge-level) regularities with functional-level constraints (that is, constraints of the functional architecture), just as certain functional regularities may not be realized because of intrusions of physical-level properties (such as when computer program failures are due to faulty electronic components). Effects can penetrate upward through levels, since each level is supervenient on levels below; that is, there can be no differences at level n unless there is some difference at level $n-1$, even though the converse is not true (because of the multiple-instantiation property of ascending levels; supervenience of psychological states on biological states entails that there cannot be two different thoughts unless there are *some* biological differences between the two underlying brain events).

Where Does the Semantic Interpretation Come From?

It appears that we need to appeal to the content of representations in

---

7. It is one of the tasks of modern logic to show that to some extent—at least, within deductive logic—it *is* possible to specify such principles as validity (surely a constitutive property of rational thought) purely in formal or syntactic terms, that is, without reference to the content of nonlogical terms. Even if all rational rules could be specified in this way, the point at issue here would be unaffected. Every rational rule might be specified in a formal notation, and the set of such rules that characterize an ideally rational individual might be listed; but one could still not express syntactically what it was that all such rules have in common which distinguishes them from other syntactically well-formed rules—because *that* is a semantic property (a property that cannot be stated without reference to what is represented by the expressions in the rules).

order both to account for certain kinds of generalizations and to give a principled account of certain constraints and capacities, such as those embodied in the principle of rationality. It also appears that, in a certain sense, it may be possible to accommodate this need within a functional framework by providing an interpretation of inputs and outputs and of at least some states of the model. Doing so, however, does not solve the entire problem, for it might still be argued that such interpretations are not the model's interpretations, that they are merely attributions made by the theorist. It does matter to us whether the states are representational for the model or merely for us. This is a question of whether the semantics of the states are original—as the semantics of our thoughts presumably are—or whether they are derived, as is the case with books. The meanings books have are in a derived sense; they mean something *only for us* because their authors intend them to have certain meanings when they write them. In cognitive science, however, we want something stronger than derived semantics, inasmuch as we want to explain the system's behavior by appealing to the content of its representations.

A dilemma is presented here. As we have already noted, the semantics of representations cannot literally cause a system to behave the way it does; only the material form of the representation is causally efficacious. When we say that we do something because we desire goal G or because we believe P, we are attributing causality to a representation, though it is not the content that does the causing. As we have noted, what is being represented need not exist, and even when it does, its only relevant aspect is the way it is conceptualized. What actually do the causing are certain physical properties of the representational state—but in a way that reflects the representational state's content. There is, if you like, a parallel between the behavioral patterns caused by the physical instantiation of the representational states and the patterns captured by referring to the semantic content of these states. How can this be? How can such a parallel be maintained coherently over time?

Only one nonquestion-begging answer to this dilemma has ever been proposed: that what the brain is doing is exactly what computers do when they compute numerical functions; namely, their behavior is caused by the physically instantiated properties of classes of substates that correspond to *symbolic codes*. These codes reflect all the semantic distinctions necessary to make the behavior correspond to the regularities that are stateable in semantic terms. In other words, the codes or symbols are equivalence classes of physical properties which, on one hand, cause the behavior to unfold as it does, and on the other, are the bearers of semantic interpretations that provide the needed higher-level principle for their individuation and for stating the gen-eralizations. As dyed-in-the-wool realists, we propose as the next step exactly what solid-state physicists do when they find that postulating certain unobservables provides a coherent account of a set of phenom-ena: we conclude that the codes are "psychologically real," that the brain is the kind of system that processes such codes and that the codes do in fact have a semantic content.

Many people are quite familiar with this idea, though it remains fairly controversial outside cognitive science. The uneasiness this causes in some people is absent among those who work with computer models, because this story is precisely, and literally, what happens in com-puters—with one difference. The states of a computer can be given many different semantic interpretations; indeed, the same symbolic states are sometimes interpreted as words, sometimes as numbers, chess positions, or weather conditions. In the case of a psychological model we want to claim that the symbols represent one content and no other, since their particular content is part of the explanation of its regularities. Thus, even if we accept the "syntax parallels semantics" view, there remains the question, What determines what a given (syntactically articulated) state represents? I shall examine several proposals for dealing with this problem that have surfaced over the years and then offer some extremely modest proposals for thinking about this problem in its relation to computational theories. My proposals are incomplete as answers to the puzzle because the entire problem of semantics is, in general, poorly understood. The proposals are intended only to suggest that the lack of a definitive answer need not be taken as an indictment of the cognitive-science enterprise, since no proposal concerning mental content is free of all problems.

Early versions of mentalism, all of which place conscious experience in a central methodological position, had an answer to the question, What causes certain mental events to have certain contents? In these versions, at least some mental contents represent certain things because they *resemble* them. An image of X represents X precisely because the conscious mental representations, or images, *look like* X. Such a view probably is not far from the common notion of visual imagery. If you were to ask a group of people how they know their image of a duck actually represents a duck, rather than, say, a rabbit, they might reply that the image looks like a duck. For several reasons, however, this answer does not explain why the image is a representation of a duck. For example, even in the introspectionist approach, the image need not closely resemble a duck for people to take it as a duck since it is *their* image, they can take it as virtually anything they wish; after all, the word *duck* refers to a duck without in any way resembling a duck. As Wittgenstein points out, the image of a man walking up a hill may look exactly like the image of a man walking backward down a hill; yet, if they were my images, there would no question of their being indeterminate—I would know what they represented.

The relation of resemblances is not well defined. Whether one thing resembles another is not a physically (or geometrically) definable property; resemblance depends on what the viewer knows or believes. To me, most birds closely resemble one another, but to a birdwatcher friend they are as different as ducks and rabbits. Resemblance cannot be specified except in relation to a viewer, which, in the case of mental contents, amounts to positing an intelligent, knowledgeable, problem-solving homunculus. Resemblance provides no basis for specifying the semantic content of mental representations. In any case, this kind of mentalism has little to say about the second part of the issue of representation: how behavior can be caused by the property that gives them their content—which, in this case, is resemblance. One can have something called "association of ideas," and one can apply consciously memorized rules; but there is no room in this mentalism for appeal to consciously unavailable, content-dependent processes. Even with memorized rules there is the problem of who (what sort of mechanism or homunculus) applies them. This problem, in fact, formed part of the criticism frequently leveled at early mentalistic cognitivism: that these theories "left the organism lost in thought," with no way to generate behavior from their stock of images without the intervention of a homunculus.

In addition, certain schools of behaviorism have a proposal for the first part of the task of explicating representational content. Mediational behaviorists (especially Osgood, 1963) and certain speculative neurophysiologists (for example, Hebb, 1949) take the position that a brain event can be said to represent something if that event is sufficiently like (possesses a subset of the properties of) the event that takes place when that something actually is perceived. Another, more radically behaviorist version requires that the mediational event evoke an internal "preparatory response" (as in Hull's "anticipatory goal response") that is sufficiently like the response that would have been evoked by the corresponding stimulus. Neither position is satisfactory, because of the properties of representations we have already noted (for example, we can think about objects we have neither perceived nor have any disposition to behave toward, such as, perhaps, quarks). In any case, the only mechanism behaviorism provides for explicating the representing relation is that of association. Association, in turn, must be established by such principles as contiguity and evoked by the activation of other associated items (otherwise we would not have provided the naturalistic account of the semantics of the functional states sought by behaviorism). A chain of contiguous events mediating between a brain state and an object, however, cannot form the basis of representation, for reasons discussed above, namely, that it is neither necessary nor sufficient that the state of an organism be linked by a series of contiguous events to the object that the state represents. Not only can I think of things to which I obviously am not in this sort of relation (for example, nonexistent things), but when I do think of X, I do not thereby think of associates of X; indeed, I need not think of properties that are necessarily coextensive with X, such as shape, size, weight, color, and so on.

The basic problem is that *representing* is a semantic relation, that semantic relations, like logical relations, appear not to be causally *definable*, at least not in any direct way (see Fodor, 1980a) even though they may on various token occasions be established by or realized in various, different, causally explainable ways. It may be that representation requires that certain causal relations with the world were established at some point in the organism's history. For example, in order to represent the sensory feature *red* as a particular sensory quality, some aspect of the representational state must be causally related to an occasion on which the organism was in sensory contact with a color in the category red. However, the general attempt to define or reconstruct semantic relations in terms of associatively established links—or any other straightforward series of causal events—is bound to encounter difficulty. It is like all the other cases of multiple-instantiation relations we encountered in our discussions—though each case of a semantic relation may be accompanied by *some* causal relation, the two are not type equivalent.

In contrast with naturalistic approaches to representation, at least one version of the functionalist approach (the "coherence view," popular with computationalists) does not attempt to specify the semantics of functional states in terms of a purely causal link between the functional state and the object represented. Rather, the relation of representing is taken as arising from the role of the functional state within the complete theory, including the way the organism interacts with its environment through mechanisms called transducers, the way it relates to those of its inputs and outputs that are considered to be interpreted (which, for humans, is clearest in the case of the linguistic signals they receive and emit) and the relation of the organism's behavior and its own history of such interactions.

Although, in the computational model, the symbolic codes themselves do not specify their intended interpretation (and the model's behavior is not influenced by such an interpretation), the cognitive theory that makes claims about what it is a model of, which aspects of it are supposed to model something and which are not, *does* have to state what the states represent, for reasons already noted, having to do with explanation and with capturing generalizations. The cognitive theory would be gratuitous, or, at best, weakly equivalent or "mere mimicry," if the ascription of some particular representational content to states of the model were not *warranted*. The particular interpretation placed on the states, however, appears to be extrinsic to the model, inasmuch as the model would behave in exactly the same way if some other interpretation had been placed on them. This observation is what has led some (for example, Searle, 1980) to claim that functional models (at least of the computational type) do not actually contain representations, that it is we, the *theorists*, who, for reasons of convenience, hold that functional states in computer models have representational content—and that adds up to what Searle (1980) calls *weak artificial intelligence*, that is, a functionalist account in which formal analogues "stand in" for but neither have nor explain the representational (or intentional) contents of mental states.

Notice that if this view were correct, it would undermine my claim that functional models, at least of the computational variety, address the issue of representation-governed behavior. That is because I want to maintain (see chapter 4) that computation is a literal model of mental activity, not a *simulation* of behavior, as was sometimes claimed in the early years of cognitive modeling. Unlike the case of simulating, say, a chemical process or a traffic flow, I do not claim merely that the model generates a sequence of predictions of behavior, but rather that it does so in essentially the same way or by virtue of the same functional mechanisms (not, of course, the same biological mechanisms) and *in virtue of* having something that corresponds to the same thoughts or cognitive states as those which govern the behavior of the organism being modeled. Being the same thought entails having the same semantic content (that is, identical thoughts have identical semantic contents).

Now, Searle is surely right in saying that it does not follow merely from the fact that computational models produce the same behavior, and that their states are given a certain semantic interpretation, that such systems work in the same way as humans do. By the same token, it does not follow from the fact that it was the theorist who provided the interpretation of the symbols that such an interpretation is simply a matter of convenience or that there is a sense in which the interpretation is the theorist's rather than the system's. Much depends on the theorist's reasons for giving that particular interpretation. In my view, the question of whether the semantic interpretation resides in the head of the theorist or in the model itself is the wrong question to ask. A better question is: What fixes the semantic interpretation of functional states? or, What latitude does the theorist have in assigning a semantic interpretation to the states of the system?

Admittedly, in many models that take the form of computer programs, there is much latitude in assigning semantic interpretations to the symbols, hence, to the model's states. Indeed, we routinely change our interpretation of the functional states of a typical computer, sometimes viewing the states as numbers, sometimes as alphabetic characters, sometimes as words or descriptions of a scene. Even when it is difficult to think of a coherent interpretation different from the one the programmer had in mind, such alternatives are, in principle, always possible. (There is an exotic result in model theory, the Lowenheim-Skolem theorem, which guarantees that such programs can always be coherently interpreted as referring to integers and to arithmetic relations over them.) If, however, we equip the programmed computer with transducers so it can interact freely with a natural environment and a linguistic one, as well as the power to make inferences, it is far from obvious what if any latitude the theorist (who knows how the transducers operate and therefore what they respond to) would still have in assigning a coherent interpretation to the functional states so as to capture psychologically relevant regularities in behavior. If the answer is that the theorist is left with no latitude beyond the usual inductive indeterminism all theories have in the face of finite data, it would be perverse to deny that these states had the semantic content assigned to them by the theory.

Suppose such constraints (and, possibly, others not yet considered) fixed the possible interpretations that could be placed on representational states. Would that resolve the argument concerning whether we are warranted in ascribing a particular semantic content to these states? Here, I suspect that one would run into differences of opinion that could prove unresolvable. There arises immediately the question whether such functional models are fundamentally different from us, inasmuch as we alone possess special, privileged access to the content of our thoughts, presumably something our model would lack unless it, too, was conscious. Even if we have strong intuitions concerning such questions, many of us believe that such intuitions should be considered no more than secondary sources of empirical constraint, whose validity should be judged on the basis of how successful the resulting theoretical systems are in accounting for all aspects of the phenomena in question. Information-processing theories have achieved some success in accounting for such as aspects as problem-solving, language-processing, and perception, by deliberately glossing over the conscious-unconscious distinction—by grouping under common principles processes necessary to account for functional capacities and for patterns of behavior, independent of whether people are aware of the underlying processes and representations. At the same time the theories have set aside questions about what constitutes qualia, or "raw feels"—dealing only with some of their reliable functional and semantic correlates (for example, the *belief* that one is in pain, as opposed to the *experience* of the pain)—and have to a large extent deliberately avoided the question of what gives functional states their semantics, opting instead to assign such semantic interpretations according to a principle of global coherence and waiting to see whether the resulting theory lives up to the usual canons of scientific performance.

This is about as much as I need say about semantic level and representations. After completing the tour of the cognitive-science program in the next six chapters, we will return to reconsider the fundamental proposal that human cognition and certain computer systems share the remarkable feature that they are what Dennett (1978) calls "semantic engines" or what George Miller (1984) has referred to as "informavores." At this point I have introduced computers, as it were, through the back door; I have been using the idea of symbol system without properly introducing computers and computation. Because computing plays a major role in the cognitive science project, in the next chapter I take a step backward and examine the symbol-system phenomenon in some detail.

End Note 1: When Are Functional States Representations?

It is not straightforward to give either necessary or sufficient conditions for when a system can be said actually to be governed by internal representations. These conditions, it should be appreciated, are rarely available even for the clearest distinctions; no unproblematic defining conditions are available for such basic notions as cause, explanation, and cognition or for most other fundamental concepts in science. Yet, in all such cases there are usually good indications (at least, for most clear cases) of when the concepts are applicable. So, too, are there indicators of when the explanation of certain phenomena cannot avoid appeal to representations without losing important principles and generalizations. As is shown by many of the examples we have discussed, there are clear cases where the relation between stimulus and response (again, under the appropriate cognitive description) is itself unsystematic in general, yet where the relation between a certain interpretation (hence, representation) of the stimulus and a certain interpretation of the response is not only systematic but may even be seen as rational. In general, we find that when we have a situation in which appealing to the semantic content of functional states enables us to explain regularities that would otherwise go unexplained, it is because the relation between the ascribed content and the functional states is not a simple one-to-one correspondence. Typically, we get only an explanatory advantage by appealing to representational content, when the semantic interpretation S we give to certain states I happens to have such characteristics as the following:

(a) According to our method of assigning content there will more than one distinct I in our model that corresponds to some actual or possible S; that is, there will, in general, be more than one distinguishable way of representing something in our scheme).

(b) According to our method of assigning content, I's will also occur in our model for which no corresponding S exists—or is even possible; that is, according to our theory, the system can, in general, represent states of affairs that are contrary to fact.

(c) Given our content-assigning scheme and the functional model that accompanies it, there may also be an unlimited number of ways for the system to come to be in state I other than as a direct causal consequence of the occurrence of the corresponding state of the environment identified as S. Here, a representational account might be able to show how these different ways of achieving state I are related under the appropriate semantic interpretation. In particular, we may be able to explain the transition from I' to I by showing that under the particular interpretation we have selected, the transition instantiates some logical, heuristic, or associative rule.

(d) Closely related to point (c), we may also find that the state-to-state transition regularities that do occur in certain circumstances can be distinguished from other possible transitions that do not occur, by viewing the individual states I as representing some S and by appealing to regularities that exist in the domain of S, including purely conceptual ones. We encounter excellent examples of this case in discussing models of mental imagery in chapter 8.

Again, it must be emphasized that these are neither necessary nor sufficient conditions for a system to be genuinely representational. The criterion for their being genuinely representational remains whether generalizations are missed when one is denied a representational vocabulary that refers to objects and properties represented by the system and whether there are principled constraints on the system's behavior that can be captured only using such semantic principles as rationality. Nonetheless, various conditions such as those sketched above are among the conditions that provide prima facie indications that certain functional states should be viewed as semantically interpreted, since such conditions are symptomatic of an independence of the state's role from its causal antecedents and of a dependence of its role on its semantic content, that is, on what it represents. For example, these conditions entail that the way cognitive, or representational, processes unfold has a high degree of independence from the organism's causal interactions with the world. They separate the content of the representation from the stimulus conditions by an act of interpretation or encoding, which itself may involve an act of inference, as opposed to instantiating a natural, causal law. As Dretske (1981, p. 188) puts it, an important property of a representation is "its muteness about the particular manner in which the information (constituting its semantic content) arrived." What regularities follow from the presence of a certain stimulus depend not only on what the stimulus was but on what it was taken to be (on what it was "seen *as*"). The latter, in turn, depend on the system's other semantically interpreted structures (beliefs, goals, fears, imagination).

Conditions (c) and (d) arise because a representation that serves an ineliminable role in the explanation of a system's behavior is generally one that enters into logical (or, at least, quasi-logical) relations, as well as other relations governed by rules and arbitrary conventions, stated in terms of the domain represented. This helps to explain how organisms appear capable of anticipating novel situations, and of explaining what appears to be suboptimal behavior—behavior that occurs when the organism has false beliefs. Because precisely the same event or object can be represented in different ways, the system, or organism, can behave differently with respect to the object on different occasions or in different "states of knowledge." All are characteristics of intentional (or epistemic) or representational states (states individuated by their content or by their semantic properties, which causes them to differ substantially from functional states in general, that is, states individuated in terms of their role in generating different behaviors).

Note that the characteristics of representations discussed above are not present in any examples of purely functional explanations mentioned earlier, including cases in which the explanation adverts to a design vocabulary. Clearly, these are not characteristics of the functional states of television sets or watches. Nor are they true of neural states, that is, states individuated in terms of their neurophysiological properties Although certain neural states could be described as representing the state of the retina, the motor system, or some other part of the nervous system (as P. S. Churchland, 1980, does), the relation between the neural state in question and what it is taken to represent fails to meet numerous conditions on representation suggested above; for example, transitions among them cannot be described in terms of such content-dependent rules as inference. These relations are purely causal and must be sharply distinguished from *semantic* relations. Describing a certain neural pattern as "representing" the position of a limb is exactly the same as describing the pattern of gears in a clock as representing the position of the hands on the face of the clock or of the time of day: both are a derivative senses of *representing* which gains us no explanatory advantage over a neurophysiological or mechanical description.

End Note 2: On the Notion of Representational Content

I have been speaking of representational content as though it were a simple, straightforward notion. Although the points made in this chapter do not depend crucially on precisely how content is understood, the idea of content does raise some thorny philosophical problems. First, it should be kept in mind that content refers to the *conceptual* content of representations (thoughts, images, goals) and not to the reference of these representations. The contents of representations are not actual objects in the world. For one thing, most of our mental contents have no referents in the world. This is patently true of goals, since goals describe nonactual states of affairs, and it is also true of many of the fears and beliefs that motivate us. Moreover, even when mental representations succeed in referring, what they in fact refer to is not what is relevant. The grain of mental contents is not the same as the grain of distinct, objective states of the world; precisely the same state of the world can correspond to numerous, different conceptual contents. A thought about the person who just drove up in a car has a different content from a thought about my daughter, even though, as it happens, the person who just drove up in my car is my daughter. A desire to marry the girl who lives on Piccadilly Street has a quite different content from the desire to marry Mary Jones, whether or not Mary Jones is the girl on Piccadilly Street toward whom both desires are directed. Oedipus had no desire to marry his mother, even though the person he wished to marry was, in fact, his mother, as he later tragically discovered. In all cases the two contents have different meanings, or what Frege calls different senses, though they refer to the same actual states of affairs or to the same individuals. They are said to be intensionally distinct though extensionally equivalent. Thus we see that we want to count two token mental states (thoughts and goals) as having the same content only if they are intentionally the same.

Chapter 3

The Relevance of Computation

A bird is an instrument working according to mathematical law, which instrument it is within the capacity of man to reproduce with all its movements.

Leonardo da Vinci (1452–1519)

Some Background: Formalism, Symbols, and Mechanisms

The possibility of imitating life by artifact has intrigued people throughout history (Cohen, 1966); but it is only in the second half of this century that the possibility of using the special type of artifact called a computer has been considered seriously as a means of understanding mental phenomena. What is different about this latest interest is that the focus is not primarily on the imitation of movements (as was the case with early clockwork mechanisms) but on the *imitation* (to the extent that this word is even appropriate) of certain unobservable internal processes. This notion became conceivable only with the gradual emergence, in several disparate areas of intellectual development, of a certain abstract way of understanding *mechanism*.

It is difficult to say where the relevant ideas originated, since the structure-function or form-substance distinction implicit in notions of symbol and mechanism dates from the ancient Greeks. In modern times, one of the earliest concerns with mechanism is closely related to attempts to develop a completely formal, content-free foundation for mathematics. The "Hilbert program" is one of the most ambitious attempts to build up mathematics by purely formal means, without regard to questions of what the formalism was about. In the work of Frege, as well as Russell and Whitehead, some of this enterprise was successful. On the other hand, a great intellectual achievement of the modern age has been the demonstration by purely formal means that the ultimate goal of complete formalization is, in principle, not achievable. (The original work was done by Godel and subsequently by Turing, Church, Post, and others; see the collection of papers in Davis, 1965.)

The same work that provided demonstrations of some in-principle limitations of formalization provided demonstrations of formalization's universality as well. Thus Alan Turing, Emil Post, and Alonzo Church independently developed distinct formalisms that were shown to be complete in the sense that they are powerful enough to formally (that is, "mechanistically") generate all sequences of expressions capable of interpretation as proofs, and hence, can generate all provable theorems of logic. In Turing's work this took the form of showing that there exists a universal mechanism (called the Universal Turing Machine [UM]) that can simulate any mechanism describable in its formalism. The machine does this by accepting a description of the mechanism to be simulated; it then carries out a procedure which, in a special sense, is formally equivalent to the procedure that would have been followed by the machine whose description it was given. Here, the sense of formal equivalence is that the inputs and outputs of the UM can be decoded uniformly as the inputs and outputs of the machine being simulated. We say that the UM "computes the same function" as the target machine, where, by *same function*, we mean the same input-output pairs or the same *extension* of the function. That is, there is no implication that the UM performs the same steps as the target machine. That would be a stronger sense of equivalence, one to which we return presently.

What is interesting about Turing's work from our point of view is that, to derive these results concerning the limits and universality of formalization, it was necessary to understand the notions of proof and deduction in a formal system in terms of the manipulation of symbol tokens or marks on a piece of paper, where the manipulation is specified "mechanistically" in a manner entirely independent of the way the symbols might be interpreted. This understanding took a long time to develop, for, in a sense, it meant crystallization of the platonic ideal of "pure form" divorced from all content. Logic became a game played with meaningless symbol tokens according to certain rules of form (that is, syntactic rules).

The only property symbol tokens have in these systems is a nominal one: *type identity*. A particular symbol token has to be recognizable as belonging to a certain type regardless of the context in which it occurs. Another way of stating this is to say that symbol tokens were themselves assumed to be unstructured; one could not say two symbol tokens are *more* or *less* similar, or that they are similar in certain *ways*, any more than one can say two electrons are more or less similar. Further, it was assumed that one could make indistinguishable copies of symbols (in order to identify two marks as distinct occurrences or tokens of the same symbol).

The notion of a discrete atomic symbol is the basis of all formal understanding. Indeed, it is the basis of all systems of thought, expression, or calculation for which a *notation* is available. It is important to stress that such an idea not only has deep roots in what is sometimes called the intellectualist tradition but that no one has succeeded in defining any other type of atom from which formal understanding can be derived. Small wonder, then, that many of us are reluctant to dispense with this foundation in cognitive psychology under frequent exhortations to accept symbols with such varied intrinsic properties as continuous or analogue properties. Unless these notions can be reduced to either atomic symbol foundations or to physical foundations, they remain intellectual orphans, hence, are a poor basis for explanation. The problem is, such notions lack systematic foundations; we do not know what can be done with them. To state the matter more precisely, when we refer to such symbolic (or mental) entities, there is an important sense in which we do not understand what we are talking about! (See chapter 7.)

It was the development of the notion of the universality of formal mechanism, first introduced in the work on foundations of mathematics in the 1930s, that provided the initial impetus for viewing the mind as a symbol-processing system. Allen Newell (1980) provides an insightful way of viewing both the universality and the limitations of formal symbol-manipulation systems. I borrow Newell's points in the next several paragraphs.

Universality implies that a formal symbol-processing mechanism can produce *any* arbitrary input-output function. Now, even within the confines of symbolic functions, where we abstract from the physical properties of inputs and outputs, such arbitrary flexibility seems paradoxical. After all, if the mechanism is deterministic, it obviously can realize only one function—the one that pairs its inputs with its determinate outputs. To view the mechanism as universal, its inputs must be partitioned into distinct components. One component is assigned a privileged interpretation as instructions or as a specification of a particular input-output function, the other is treated as the proper input to that function. Such a partition is essential for defining a universal mechanism. This way of looking at the phenomenon of universality is important also because it shows that there can only be arbitrary plasticity of behavior if there is some *interpretation* of its inputs and outputs (though, of course, the converse does not hold: interpretation is a necessary but not sufficient condition for universality).

Once we take the step of viewing some of the input symbols as designating or identifying a certain function, we encounter a remarkable difficulty: there are simply too many potential input-output functions to allow specification by a finite set of instructions—or by any other finite means. The set of functions is not only infinite, it is uncountable. That is, it cannot be mapped onto the integers in a one-to-one fashion; therefore, the functions cannot be listed even on an infinitely long list. One of this century's great intellectual achievements has been to show that there exist functions that cannot be specified by finitary means. Thus it seems that, contrary to the claim made above, the input-output behavior of a mechanistic system is not really arbitrarily plastic; if such behavior is to be described finitely, the behavior cannot be arbitrarily varied. On the other hand, it is natural to ask just how flexible such behavior can be. What sort of behaviors *can* be described finitely?

It might understandably be objected that what behaviors can be described finitely surely must depend on how one describes the behaviors. I can describe behavior as, say, "adaptive," thereby describing an infinite set of behaviors in a simple, flexible way. Clearly, we want to exclude such highly general, partial descriptions. For the purpose of providing a theory of the behavior, we need a description that somehow captures the entire class of behaviors without requiring additional knowledge or additional intelligent interpretation. If we could achieve that description we would have a theory that provides a noncircular analysis of the behavior into simpler behaviors, in which case we might even possess a way of capturing the extension of the set of behaviors or of providing a way to decide, for a given input-output pair, whether the pair is an instance of that set of behaviors. But how can we constrain our theoretical apparatus to provide only this kind of exhaustive characterization of behavior? The question has no general answer. What there is, however, is another remarkable empirical result. In the last fifty years a rather large variety of formalisms have been developed, all with the idea of their being maximally expressive yet mechanistic in spirit. Intuitively, all these formalisms can specify functions in a way that does not presuppose an intelligent agent to apply the specification. In every case, however, it turned out that as each new scheme was proposed, it was found to be intertranslatable with all the other schemes. It appears that every scheme picks out exactly the same set of finitely specifiable functions—the "recursive" or "effectively computable functions." Many different schemes can be used to finitely specify functions in this class; thus many different ways are available for capturing the notion of a universal mechanism. It appears, though, that they are all variations on the same underlying idea—that of a completely specifiable set of behaviors or behavioral propensities—consequently, it is generally accepted that they provide a definition of the intuitive notion of a "mechanistic process."

We thus have a notion of maximally plastic behavior that circumscribes *interpreted* behavior, just as the notion "nomological," or lawlike, circumscribes *physically possible* behavior. This extreme plasticity in behavior is one reason why computers have been viewed all along as artifacts possibly capable of exhibiting intelligence. Those not familiar with this view frequently have misunderstood the capacity of computers. For example, the Gestalt psychologist Wolfgang Kohler (1947) viewed machines as too rigid to serve as models of mental activity, claiming that mental activity is governed by "dynamic factors"—an example of which are self-distributing field effects such as those that cause magnetic fields to be redistributed when new pieces of metal are introduced—as opposed to structurally rigid "topographical factors." "To the degree to which topographical conditions are rigidly given," Kohler (1947, p. 65) says, "and not to be changed by dynamic factors, their existence means the exclusion of certain forms of function, and the restriction of the processes to the possibilities compatible with those conditions. . . . This extreme relation between dynamic factors and imposed topographical conditions is almost entirely realized in typical machines . . . we do not construct machines in which dynamic factors are the main determinants of the form of operation." That computers violate this claim is one of their unique and most important characteristics. The topographic structure of computers is completely rigid, yet they are capable of maximal plasticity of function. It is this property that led Turing (1950) to speculate that computers are, in principle, capable of exhibiting intelligent behavior. For example, he devoted an important early philosophical paper (Turing [1950]) to an exposition of this idea, arguing that a computer can, in principle, be made to exhibit intelligent activity to an arbitrary degree. Turing argued that a machine would qualify as intelligent if it could play the "imitation game" successfully, that is, fool a human observer with whom it could communicate only through a teletype so that the observer could not discriminate between it and another person. The possibility of a computer successfully passing what has become known as the Turing test is based entirely on recognition of the plasticity of behavior entailed by symbolic systems, which can be programmed to behave according to any finitely specifiable function.

It should be recognized that plasticity is only part of the story. Even if it were true that a Turing machine can behave in a manner indistinguishable from that of a human, given certain constraints on what is allowed to count as appropriate observations of behavior, producing such behavioral mimicry is a far different matter from providing an *explanation* of that behavior. Explaining behavior is a much more stringent task than generating behavior. Specifically, explanation entails capturing the underlying generalizations as perspicuously as possible and relating them to certain universal principles. To do that, I have argued, it is necessary to appeal to, among other things, semantically interpreted representations. Thus I provided some indications that explanatory adequacy requires a much finer-grain correspondence between a computational model and an organism than is implied by input-output, or "Turing" equivalence. Most of the remainder of this book is devoted to examining the constraints a computational system must satisfy in order for it to serve as an explanation. For the time being, however, I am concerned with showing that the notion of computational mechanism and formal symbol system implicit in the preceding discussion is in fact closer in spirit to the requirements of cognitive explanation than is apparent from the arguments based on plasticity alone.

We already have one indication that this is the case, from the fact that maximal plasticity is achievable only by introducing interpretation of some of the inputs. It must be the case that some part of the input is viewed as consisting of symbols that designate instructions or that otherwise specify the function in a finite manner. This much semantics is indispensable. If, however, we are, in fact, to view the mechanism as carrying out a certain function on semantically interpreted inputs and outputs—say, on numbers—then the rest of the symbols in the system must also be interpreted, as must the rules for transforming expressions. Further, in this case, the explanation of why the system produces certain interpreted outputs (for example, why it prints out certain *numbers*) must appeal to numerical algorithms, to rules of arithmetic applied to representations of numbers. As we saw in chapter 2, these processes must appeal to semantically interpreted representations. When we take into account the requirements of explanation, we find that a much finer-grained analysis of the symbol-processing functions carried out by the computational mechanisms becomes relevant. In the next section I introduce the notion of computation as the rule-governed transformation of formal expressions viewed as interpreted symbolic codes.

Computation as a Symbolic Process

The early developments mentioned provided the key ideas of symbol and mechanism. From the earliest writings about these ideas—by such people as Turing, Von Neumann, Shannon, Wiener, McCulloch, McCarthy, Minsky, Newell, and Simon—it was apparent that what was incubating was not just another industrial technology but an intellectual tool that was directly relevant to unraveling the mystery of intelligence (two of the earliest papers on this issue, published in the same year, are still worth reading: Turing, 1950, and Shannon, 1950).

As I have suggested, the formal universality of computation made it most attractive. Such universality implied that any process specifiable formally (in the sense, for example, required by a Turing machine) can be performed by a computer. More precisely, a computer can compute a formally equivalent function, which means that, in principle, it can be made to exhibit the same input-output behavior as that of a specified function. This "black box" equivalence is now considered a weak equivalence criterion. As we see below, in the case of cognitive psychology, explanatory adequacy depends on a stronger sense of equivalence, particularly on knowing the details of the process at a suitable level of abstraction. What, then, recommends computation as the appropriate vehicle for *that* task? To provide a framework for discussing this question, let us first look at computation from a more abstract point of view. That will help bring out further similarities in the relationship of computational devices and computational processes, on the one hand, and brains and cognitive processes, on the other. It is the failure to distinguish computation as a type of process from the particular physical form it takes in current computing machines that has prevented many people from taking computation as a literal account of mental process. If we understand computation at a fairly general level (as, in fact, it is understood in theoretical computer science), we can see that the idea that mental processing is computation is indeed a serious empirical hypothesis rather than a metaphor.

A computer is a physical object whose properties vary over time in accordance with the laws of physics. In principle, one might characterize a computer's dynamic behavior as a causally connected sequence of physical-state descriptions, with transitions subsumed under various physical laws. Because an unlimited number of physical properties and their combinations can be specified in the physical description, there is, in fact, an unlimited number of such sequences. By itself, however, the record of a particular sequence of physical states tells us nothing about the computational process going on in the machine, for two basic reasons.

(1) Very few of the physically discriminable properties of the machine are relevant to its computational function—for example, its color, temperature, and mass, as well as its very slow or very fast electrical fluctuations, variations in electrical properties above or below relevant ranges, variations in electrical properties that are within tolerance limits, and so on. In fact, *any* variations in physical properties of distinct components, other than those few properties to which other designated components are meant to react in *particular* specified ways, can be said

to be irrelevant to the machine's operation as a computer. Thus, in a given computer, only a minuscule subset of physically discriminable states are computationally discriminable. Of course, each of the infinitely many sequences of physical descriptions could correspond to some computational sequence. At least in principle, there is nothing to prevent such an interpretation. In other words, computational states are relativized to some convenient mapping, which I shall call the *instantiation function* (IF). By mapping from physical to computational states, such a function provides a way of interpreting a sequence of nomologically governed physical state changes as a *computation*, and therefore of viewing a physical object as a *computer*.

(2) A computational state of the machine corresponds to an equivalence class of physical states indistinguishable from the point of view of their function in the machine's abstract computational description. In typical computers, physical descriptions of these equivalence classes are extremely complex. To give a physical description of some arbitrary computational state of a computer involves an extremely long story covering myriad topographic and electrical properties and giving the ranges of parameters and combinations of parameter values that leave the state invariant.

Even for a particular computer the situation is much more complex than can be indicated here. Under the ordinary interpretation of "computational state," a computer executing a program written in, say, LISP is in a unique computational state whenever it begins with some given input and arrives at a certain point in the program. Of course, the class of physical states corresponding to *this* sense of computational state depends, among other things, on which LISP interpreter was used. Even a slight change in interpreter results in a radically different class of physical descriptions, corresponding to a particular LISP computational state. In fact, simply storing a program in a different sequence of memory registers of a stored-program computer radically alters the physical description corresponding to what would be considered the same computational state. This example shows that what I call the instantiation function is not fixed in a particular machine but can itself be altered, in this case under control of the interpreter, which translates from LISP statements to machine operations, or a loader program, which stores a program in specified storage locations. The point here is that there need be no uniform way of giving a physical description of the equivalence class of physical states of a machine that correspond to each of its computational states.

For a particular, finite computer, such a mapping from physical to computational states can, in principle, be found if we know the relevant physical parameters, since we can enumerate all relevantly discriminable physical states; in general, however, because of the independence of structural and functional descriptions of states, this is not possible. This follows from the open-endedness of physical realizations of a given computational function. Not only can such computational sequences be realized in any digital computer ever made or that will ever be made, but they can be realized in devices operating in any imaginable media—mechanical (as in Charles Babbage's Analytical Engine), hydraulic, acoustical, optical, or organic—even a group of pigeons trained to peck as a Turing machine!

The reader will have recognized the similarity between the discussion above and the parallel arguments for the independence of cognitive processes from their underlying physical instantiation. Both computation and cognition are appropriately viewed as *rule-governed* processes. Computation is rule-governed because, as noted, regularities in the sequence of states a computation goes through are not expressible in terms of nomological laws, inasmuch as they depend on the instantiation function IF that specifies the equivalence class of physical states which count as a particular computational state. In addition, since IF is systematically alterable, as is also noted above, the regularities of the system are not lawlike, but rather have a rule-governed character. Similarly, cognitive processes are viewed as rule-governed, since the regularity in the sequences mental states go through is also nonnomological; that is, although the process is physical, its cognitive regularities cannot be explained by appeal to physical laws (see chapter 1). Also, the regularities can frequently be altered systematically by providing information (an important point discussed in chapter 5).

One of the most important similarities between cognition and computation, however, is suggested by the observation that the explanation of how a computation (in the usual sense of the term) proceeds must make reference to what is represented by the various intermediate states of the process just as the explanation of cognitive processes must make reference to the content of mental states.[1] In other words, the

1. Note that, in this sense, computer science is concerned with more than mere computation. It is concerned with certain functional properties of classes of devices that *can* be used for computing. Thus, much of computing theory is concerned with certain formal properties of symbol-manipulation systems, not with computation in the sense intended here. Nonetheless, the main interest in these results is that they bear on the question of what interpreted computations can be performed. Here, we have a close analogy with formal logic. Although, in proof theory, one investigates properties of various, formal, axiomatic systems, the motivating concern is with the notion of truth and with transformations that preserve truth value. It would thus be correct to view logic the same way as we view computation, namely, as being concerned with interpreted-symbol systems, the only difference being that logic is concerned primarily with the class of truth-preserving transformations, whereas computation is concerned with a wider range of classes of transformations—though, in the end, they remain semantically specified classes.

answer to the question "What computation is being performed?" requires discussion of semantically interpreted computational states. This central point can bear detailed discussion. Notice that the operation of a computer, viewed as a physical device, can be described in terms of the causal structure of the computer's physical properties. The states of a computer, when it is viewed as a physical device, are individuated in terms of the identity of physical descriptions; and therefore, its state transitions are connected by physical laws. By abstracting over these physical properties we can give a functional description of the device, which, for example, might be summarized as a finite-state transition diagram of the sort familiar in automata theory.

If, however, we wish to explain the *computation* being performed, or the regularities exhibited by a particular computer programmed to carry out a specific function over, say, numbers or sentences, we must refer to objects in the domain that are the intended interpretation, or *subject matter*, of the computations. (See the discussion in chapter 2 concerning the relation of explanations to the taxonomy under which we view the events being explained.) Thus, to explain why the machine prints the numeral "5" when it is provided with the expression "(PLUS 2 3)" (with the symbols given their usual interpretation), we must refer to the meaning of the symbols in both the expression and the printout. These meanings are the referents of the symbols in the domain of numbers. The explanation of why the particular numeral "5" is printed out follows from these semantic definitions; (that is, it prints out "5" because that symbol represents the number five, "PLUS" represents the addition operator applied to the referents of the other two symbols, and five is indeed the sum of the numbers two and three). In other words, from the definition of the symbols, or numerals, as representations of numbers, and from the definition of "PLUS," as representing a certain abstract mathematical operation (defined in terms of, say, the Peano axioms of number theory), it follows that some state of the machine, after reading the expression, will correspond to a state that represents the value of the function and (because of a further definition of the implicit printout function) cause the printing of the appropriate answer.

In addition to being dependent on the instantiation function IF, computational explanation requires another interpretation function, one that might be called the semantic function (SF), which maps articulated functional states onto some domain of intended interpretation. These semantic interpretations cannot, of course, be provided capriciously if the computation is to follow a given set of semantically interpreted rules. What is special about computers is that they are designed to make easy certain, particular, consistent interpretations. One way they do this is to arrange for the initial state of the machine (that is, the hardware plus the operating system, or top-level language) to map in a straightforward way (via a simple IF) onto a variant of a Universal Machine. That way, the machine can be made to compute any function specifiable in its top-level language. Another way this is done is to have certain built-in regularities that allow substates of the machine to be easily interpreted in some generally useful domain, for example, numbers. The following example illustrates the provision of a simple SF in the design of symbol-manipulating mechanisms.

Syntax and Semantics in Computation

A Numerical Example

Suppose we have a certain IF that expresses a mapping from equivalence classes of physical states of a certain machine to symbolic expressions. The IF mapping might be defined by certain electronic circuits that cause the printing of strings of symbols on a printer, where the strings correspond to the states of certain parts of the machine called "memory registers." The states of the machine's memory registers could then be characterized in terms of certain symbolic expressions. Let us say that the expressions consist of the atomic symbols o and x arranged in strings of arbitrary length. In this example the states of the memory registers are designated by such expressions as o, x, ox, xo, xx, oox, oxo, oxx, xoo, xox, xxo, xxx, xooo, and so on; each expression designates some possible state of each machine's memory registers.[2] Let us further suppose that when a certain pattern (designated by the symbol "⊕") occurs in a portion of the machine called its "instruction register," the machine's memory registers change states according to a certain, specifiable regularity. For example, when the portion of the machine called register 1 is in the state that maps onto the string xox, and register 2 is in the state that maps onto the string xxo, then register 3 changes its state from whatever it was to the state corresponding to the string xoxx.

This regularity *might* be used to represent addition of numbers, providing we adopt an appropriate semantic function, SF, and that the

2. Note that, although I assume no bound on the length of the expressions, the points I will make hold as long as the length is sufficiently long that the expressions must be treated as though they were not atomic, something that is true in any useful computer. Therefore, there is a restriction on IF paralleling the restriction on how computational states are expressed, namely, that the expressions are instantiating *by means of* instantiating the elementary symbols o and x and the concatenation relation. We see below that another reason here is that the operation ⊕ (defined below) must also be defined over the individual symbols.

regularity meets certain requirements. Here, the required semantic function is easily defined; it happens to be the function that maps strings of o's and x's onto numbers, namely, the binary number system. Moreover, in defining the SF formally, we provide a way of stating the requirements the regularity must meet if it is to be consistently interpretable as addition of numbers. Before I define the SF, I must give a formal definition of the set of expressions consisting of x's and o's. Since I do not assume any bound on the number of states a register can take (hence, on the length of the strings of x's and o's), the definition of the strings must be given recursively as follows:

(1) o is a string
(2) x is a string
(3) if T is a string, then so is To (string T followed by o)
(4) if T is a string, then so is Tx (string T followed by "x")

A simpler way to express (1) to (4) is:

$$T \equiv o \lor x \lor To \lor Tx$$

(where $\equiv$ means "is defined to be" and $\lor$ means "or").

The semantic function can then be defined recursively as follows, using the definition of the strings provided above:

(1) $SF[\![o]\!] = 0$
   (the semantic interpretation of "o" is the number zero)
(2) $SF[\![x]\!] = 1$
   (the semantic interpretation of "x" is the number one)
(3) $SF[\![To]\!] = 2 \times SF[\![T]\!]$
   (The semantic interpretation of a string T followed by "o" is two times the semantic interpretation of T alone.)
(4) $SF[\![Tx]\!] = 2 \times SF[\![T]\!] + 1$
   (The semantic interpretation of a string T followed by x is twice the semantic interpretation of T alone plus 1.)

This is an example of a semantic function defined recursively on the structure of strings of symbols. It is analogous to Tarski's method of defining the semantics of sentences in some formal calculus in terms of their combinatorial properties. The mapping function is nontrivial; in fact, it defines the semantic interpretation of a *place-value* numeral notation.

For this semantic function to be useful, however, there must be regularities in the computer's state transitions that correspond to mathematical operations defined over the interpretations of the symbols in the domain intended. In other words, there must be state transitions that *preserve the intended interpretation SF.* I have suggested such a regularity, one associated with the occurrence of the symbol ⊕ in the instruction register. For ⊕ to correspond to addition or, alternatively, for it to be consistently interpretable as addition, state transitions must preserve the semantic interpretation of the symbol strings under the mathematically defined operation of addition (defined, say, in terms of the Peano axioms). In other words, something like the following must be true:

If the computer is in the state characterized by the description:

(1) register 1 "contains" (or IF maps it onto) string T'
(2) register 2 "contains" (or IF maps it onto) string T"
(3) instruction register "contains" (or IF maps it onto) the symbol, ⊕

then the computer goes into the state characterized by:

register 3 "contains" (or IF maps it onto) the string T, where

$$SF[\![T]\!] = SF[\![T']\!] + SF[\![T'']\!].$$

In other words, the mathematically defined sum of the semantic interpretations of the two register states must always correspond to the semantic interpretation of the state of the third register. Note that the interpretation is in the abstract domain of *numbers*, where such operations as additions are mathematically defined, whereas the symbols being interpreted (the domain of the SF function) are functional states, defined by IF as equivalence classes of physical states of the computer.

An interesting question remains: How is such an operation as ⊕ possible if the number of expressions is nearly unlimited? If the number were small one could imagine wiring up some sort of table-lookup (which is easy in a random-access memory). For a large or infinite number of expressions, however, that is not possible. What must be done instead is capitalize on the compositional nature of the semantic function and define simple rules that operate on individual x and o symbols.[3] That, of course, is precisely what people do when they learn

---

3. Here, for example, is a set of eight production rules that will suffice. They map 5-tuples into 5-tuples. The 5-tuples are to be interpreted as: position of symbol; symbol in register 1 at that position; symbol in register 2 at that position; symbol in register 3 at that position; and carry symbol. The symbol "-" indicates that the symbol is irrelevant, and the n going to n + 1 is simply a way of indicating that after applying the rule to column n, one moves on to column n + 1 (right to left); no actual counting is required, only moving over one column.

(n,o,o,-,o) → (n + 1,-,-,o,o)	(n,o,o,-,x) → (n + 1,-,-,x,o)
(n,o,x,-,o) → (n + 1,-,-,x,o)	(n,o,x,-,x) → (n + 1,-,-,o,x)
(n,x,o,-,o) → (n + 1,-,-,x,o)	(n,x,o,-,x) → (n + 1,-,-,o,x)
(n,x,x,-,o) → (n + 1,-,-,o,x)	(n,x,x,-,x) → (n + 1,-,-,x,x)

to add; they learn what to do with pairs of digits, then repeat the procedure indefinitely for larger numbers. Computers must do this, too, though there are some shortcuts for fixed-length expressions. That is why, as I have said, expressions are instantiated *by means of* instantiating the individual symbols and applying the concatenation operation. Biological instantiation of cognitive representations must also be realized by means of instantiation of component parts of the representation, so long as (a) there is an arbitrarily large number of representations, and (b) representations are transformed according to operations which, like the addition operation $\oplus$, respect semantical rules.

These ideas and distinctions, which arise in clear form in the case of conventional computers, are presented here because they help us keep straight what must be going on, since it becomes somewhat harder to think about these things when we take up the parallel case of mental processes in the next section. What we discover there is that we need all three distinct levels (physical, symbolic, semantic), just as we need them in the computer case. We need the syntactic or the symbolic level because we must preserve certain interpretations over mental operations, just as we must preserve the numerical interpretation given by SF in the example above, over the operation designated $\oplus$. This we can do only if we have a semantic function whose definition has access to the generative structure of the symbolic expressions (assuming that the set of thoughts is unbounded, just as the set of symbolic expressions was assumed to be unbounded in the example above). In the next section I will lead up to this by giving some simple examples of rules that must preserve their semantic interpretations.

Cognitive Rules and Syntax
In discussing the notion of a universal mechanism earlier, I spoke of interpretation, or *designation,* as being a key relationship into which symbols in a computer enter. Symbols can designate other symbols or primitive operations in the machine. To count as a computation rather than simply any functionally described physical system, however, it must contain symbols that are interpreted. In other words, the symbols must represent numbers, letters, or words, etc. (the slogan here is: "no computation without representation"). This is a different kind of designation because it is not wired into the machine (for which all symbol tokens are meaningless, except that certain ones can be made to cause the execution of primitive operations). The designation is provided by a person who takes the symbols to be about something—that is, the person gives the symbols a semantic interpretation. Of course, the task of remembering and communicating to others what interpretation of internal symbols a user has in mind is greatly simplified by labeling

keys with letters and numbers and wiring certain states to cause letters and numbers to be printed. Still, the interpretation typically is effected by the user, not the machine or the input-output terminal. (We have already considered the vexing question of whether this is a matter of necessity or whether machines can have "original" semantics.)

This quality of symbols and of computational states, whereby they can consistently be given a semantic interpretation, is not the only thing that makes useful computation possible; but it is one of the most important characteristics shared by computation and cognition. Any description of a cognitive process that characterizes the process as a rule-governed sequence of semantically interpreted states can be mapped directly onto a computational description of the process. Although computation may not be the only way to realize a semantically described process, it is the only one we know how to achieve in a physical system. Put another way, nobody has any idea how it might be possible, even in principle, to build a system whose behavior is characterized in terms of semantic rules without first describing the system in terms of operations on symbol structures.

Let us see how we might convert into a concise formal statement the sort of description of behavioral regularities we have been citing as putative examples of cognitive generalizations. The attempt to do this will help illustrate the nature of a computational account and at the same time suggest why a level of articulation of the representational states is necessary, hence, why a level of syntax or symbol structure is required to explain such regularities.

In chapter 2, I claimed that some regularities in behavior can be captured only in terms of a description that refers to the representational content of cognitive states. In the example given, I suggest regularities, which I now refer to as rule-governed, and which might roughly be conveyed by such descriptions as:

> R1: If you *perceive* an event E as an instance of the category "emergency" (call this cognitive state S_1), then create the goal to get help (call this S_2), and
> R2: If you have the *goal* of getting help, and you *know* that help can be obtained by telephone (call this combined state S_4), then create the goal of locating a telephone (resulting in state S_5).

These represent rules which hold among cognitive states. The first rule, R1, holds between S_1, the state in which you perceive the event as an emergency, and S_2, the state in which your goal is to obtain help. Rule R2 refers to mental state S_4,—which is a conjunction of two components, one being identical to S_2—and the other corresponds to the belief that help can be obtained by using a telephone. Rule R2 connects S_4 with state S_5, which represents the state of having the goal of locating a telephone. Such an account can, in fact, be made precise if not by providing operational definition of terms, at least by specifying the formal relationship that hold among the terms. Indeed, the account can be simply represented in a computer.

Two points should be noted about these rules. First, in this explanation of the behavior, we describe R1 as holding between S_1 and S_2 by referring to what S_1 and S_2 represent, in terms of their semantic interpretation or their content. At this stage it might seem that any pair of states connected by a transition rule can be made to represent this regularity merely by interpreting the states appropriately. From such a perspective the system can be described by the following two state-transition rules:

R1: $S_1 \rightarrow S_2$
R2: $S_4 \rightarrow S_5$

On reflection, that cannot be the case—and this is the second point. The cognitive rule, as stated, relates semantic *contents* and is dependent on the presence of component parts of these contents (for example, on having the goal of obtaining help and holding the belief that help can be obtained by using a telephone to dial a certain number). Hence, when we express the rule in terms of state transitions, all rule-relevant aspects or components of the content must be distinguished as well. For instance, R2 must refer to the S_2 component of the S_4 state in a way that identifies it as the same representational content that appears in R1. Thus, R2 cannot be expressed simply as a rule between S_4 and S_5; the inclusion of two distinct parts of S_4 must be explicitly represented in R2, and one part must be identified as being identical to the consequent state of rule R1. Similarly, we will find that even S_1 and S_2 are not sufficiently fine decompositions; the fact that S_1 is a state that results from perception rather than from inference makes a difference to some further cognitive processing, as does the fact that S_2 is a goal state rather than a belief state. Therefore, such distinctions must be encoded by some functional feature of the state.

The moral here is that, to represent the system of rules holding among interpreted states, we cannot continue to refer only to sequences of distinct states, as I have been doing. We must refer to the states not as atomic entities but as *expressions* in which all cognitive terms and relations are mentioned explicitly. Cognitive processes thus must be represented as sequences of symbolic expressions. The terms of the expressions correspond to aspects of cognitive states to which cognitive rules are responsive. We thus conclude that, to account for behavioral regularities we must have terms which (a) provide distinctions among cognitively distinct states, that is, states individuated in terms of their content; and (b) at the same time reveal the structure existing among distinct states, and show how various subsets of states share common features. For example, the term *goal* is necessary because goal states differ predictably from non-goal states, in that certain rules apply to certain states by virtue of the fact that they are goal states. This is true of such verbs as *see, believe, know,* and *hypothesize.*[4]

The situation here is similar to that which obtains in, say, phonology (a point first brought to everyone's attention by de Saussure, 1959). To account for the relationship among sounds when the sounds represent linguistic codes, it is necessary to analyze them into component parts called phonemes, each of which accounts for a potentially linguistic distinction. Phonological rules (which distinguish between well- and ill-formed linguistic sounds in a language and account for certain systematic relations among sounds, for example *contrite:contrition, ignite:ignition*) can then be stated over phonemic units. No such regularities can be captured if the rules must be stated over either unanalyzed whole utterances or sounds described in acoustical terms.

It is a general property of events and physical objects that if they are instances (token occurrences) of a *code* that designates something extrinsic to the physical system (that is, which is given a semantic interpretation), then, even though physical laws govern the properties of the *instances* (for example, their shape and succession if they are generated mechanically), the relationship among the events *as* codes must be stated in the form of rules that depend on what they are codes *for.* Anticipating an example used in chapter 7, I point out that patterns of Morse code follow rules of spelling because they are codes for letters. To express this, however, we must refer to what the codes represent: letters. Furthermore, the argument above is that this dependence of rules on interpretation means the codes themselves must explicitly

---

4. There is a question whether such verbs of "propositional attitude" as *believing, desiring, fearing,* and so on should be encoded as explicit symbols or whether they should be distinguished one from another in some nonsymbolic manner (for example, by storing their object clauses—the particular belief or desire—in different places). It seems that if such terms are symbolically encoded as in the examples above, they will behave differently from other symbols in the expression. For example, belief sentences do not allow existential generalization; from the fact that someone believes that "Bradford is a wise publisher," one may not infer that there exists someone who is a wise publisher (namely, Bradford), though, from "Harry believes Bradford is a wise publisher," one may conclude that Harry believes something, namely, that Bradford is. . . , etc., which shows there is something special about the verb *believe* itself that is not shared by other terms within its that-clause object. There are those who are much impressed by such facts. For the present, I think I will let the examples above stand as they are, since they provide convenient illustrations.

carry all relevant aspects of the interpretation as part of their intrinsic physical and functional *form*. This is exactly what is involved in the example given in the last section, where I describe an elementary computing system capable of going through state transitions that can be interpreted consistently as arithmetical operations. To characterize this constraint we mapped the substates of the system onto symbolic expressions. The expression-transforming operations were then given a finitary characterization so they could be interpreted, for instance, as adding numbers (as we do in our example). Here is the basic argument again, in a slightly more formal style. According to the computational theory of mind, two criteria must be met in providing an explanation of the behavior of an intentional or representational system.

(1) We must represent the rule-governed behavior of the system by giving formal rules holding among codes or among articulated cognitive states. In a formal system that is all the system has access to. It does not have the interpretations; only the theory provides that.

(2) As is argued above, though, if the system is representational, so that regularities in its behavior can be captured only by referring to the content of its representations, then the rules must have the property that those that apply to a particular code or state will appear to depend on what it is a code *for*, or, to cast it in the terms I used in speaking of the arithmetic example, they must "respect the semantic interpretation."

These two criteria place restrictions on the form the code (or the description of the state) can take. In particular, a formal distinction must be made among the codes that corresponds to each rule-relevant distinction among the codes' interpretations: codes must preserve rule-relevant distinctions. For example, suppose $C_1, C_2, \ldots, C_n$ are codes, and $I_1, I_2, \ldots, I_n$ are their respective semantic interpretations. Suppose, further, that a set of interpretations $\{I_i\}$ differs from another disjoint set $\{I_j\}$ by virtue of the former having some semantic property or satisfying some predicate P (in the domain of interpretation) not satisfied by the latter. If there exists a rule whose applicability depends on P (for example, the rule applies to some code just in case the interpretation of that code satisfies P), then the system must be able to decide for any C_i whether $P(I_i)$ holds, that is, whether the predicate is true of the interpretation of the code in question. Because the system has no access to the semantic interpretation, whether $P(I_i)$ holds must be decidable by examining the formal structure of C_i alone. If the cardinality of the set of C_i is finite, one way the system might be capable of deciding whether $P(I_i)$ holds is to look up the particular C_i in a table that indexed all the codes according to which P applies to them (there can be only a finite number of distinct P's in that case). This trick cannot be used, however, if the set of C_i is unbounded.

If the set of rule-relevant semantic discriminations is arbitrarily expandable (that is, if it is, in principle, unbounded), the only way the set of codes can reflect all rule-relevant distinctions, as required by the above condition, is itself to be expandable, that is, constructive or productive. We cannot have an arbitrarily expandable set of codes unless a procedure exists for constructing the codes from a finite set of elements. This, in turn, means that computational states must be structured so they correspond to syntactically articulated expressions, rather than being mere atomic names. The C_i must have a structure that makes it possible to formally distinguish (by virtue of the presence or absence of more elementary components or symbols, or by virtue of specifiable properties of their arrangement) those codes C_i for which $P(I_i)$ holds from the codes C_j ($i \neq j$) for which $P(I_j)$ fails to hold. This is true for each predicate P that discriminates among rules in the system.

Even where the set of semantic discriminations is bounded (a thoroughly unreasonable assumption in human cognition, where clearly we cannot place a bound on the set of distinguishable thoughts)— hence, in principle, the codes could be atomic—the assumption that they are not expressions would, in general, be implausible on other grounds. In this case, the paradigmatic relations among the codes reflecting the structure among the things represented (as inferred, for example, from generalization gradients, confusion matrices, and so on) would have to be accounted for in other ways. For example, they would have to be explained as arising from distinct families of rules applied to different codes. What this would amount to is, we would get the effect of structured codes by applying collections of rules which, in effect, re-created relevant syntactic structures solely on the basis of the code's identity. This redundant proliferation of rules, needed to accomplish something so natural in a system that assumes the codes themselves to be structured, would have to be independently motivated.[5]

Such considerations as these also explain why programs cannot be described adequately in terms of state-transition diagrams, for example, those used in the description of finite-state automata, which, among

5. Such motivation does sometimes exist. Occasionally, there is evidence that a representation behaves as though it were not articulated into component parts, although, in other respects, it exhibits a multidimensional generalization or a similarity structure. An example is the "word superiority effect," where there is evidence that a whole word is easier to recognize than any of its constituent parts. In such cases we might be inclined to adopt the view that the code is unitary or atomic and that the generalization structure results from the application of sets of rules (for example, the atomic code for a lexical item may be used to access other properties of the word, such as its spelling).

other things, show that when a machine is in some state S_i and receives input x, it will go on to state S_j; but if it receives input y, it will go into state S_k, and so on (see figure 1). As we have seen, the rule for adding numbers in a computer cannot be directly expressed in a finitary manner as a rule for producing a transition from state S_n to state S_{n+1}; rather, it must be expressed as a rule or set of rules for transforming an expression of numerals into a new expression (see the preceding section). A *semantic* rule such as that for addition applies to states with a particular semantic interpretation, say, as certain numbers. Changes in the machine's state, however, are the result of physical causes; that is, they are caused by certain physical properties of the machine. Consequently, the way the machine must work to be correctly described as following a semantic rule is, on every occasion in which the rule is invoked there must be physical properties of the machine's state capable of serving as physical codes for that semantic interpretation. In other words, for each distinct, rule-relevant semantic property a corresponding, distinct, physical property must be associated with that state. Distinct, semantic properties must be preserved by *some* distinct, physical properties; in fact, they must be exactly the same physical properties that cause the machine to behave as it does on that occasion. Furthermore, such articulation of states into distinct properties must correspond to the articulation of the semantic rule in terms of symbolic expressions. In other words, articulation of the states must be made explicit if we are to express the rules governing the computation and at the same time show how, in principle, such rules might be realized in a physical system.

Another way to state the above is to say that if, in order to express some computational regularity in a finitary manner, we must refer to a structure of symbols, then the structure of the expressions must be

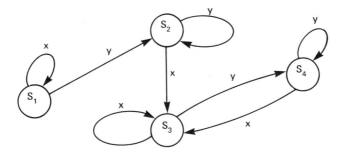

Figure 1. Diagram of a finite state automaton that reads strings of x's and y's. This automaton starts in state S_1 and stops in state S_4 just in case it reads a string containing one or more x's that are not part of either an initial or final run of x's.

reflected in the structure of the states of the system, as they were in our arithmetic example. Hence, it is not enough to describe the system as merely transforming state S_n into state S_{n+1}. That will not capture what is regular about the system's behavior in a finitary manner. Indeed, the machine itself must be designed so its physical operation will be governed not simply by the state of the entire device but by the substates of parts of the device exactly as described by the syntactic, or expression-transforming, description of the rules.

Thus: to capture the rule-governed quality of computation the process must be viewed in terms of operations on formal expressions rather than in terms of state transitions. Consideration of this view provides insight into why a computer (or a brain, for that matter) is more appropriately described as a Turing machine than as a finite-state automaton, though clearly it is finite in its resources. Notice that the finitude of the machine has a rather different status in the expression-transformation description than it does in the state-transition description. In the finite-state automaton case, the finiteness of the device is both intrinsic to that device and rigid, in the following sense: To increase the range of computation, one may increase the number of states. To do that in the finite-state automaton representation, however, one must, in effect, provide a new machine description, for example, a new finite-state diagram. In a "transformation on expressions" representation (or the more usual computer program representation), the device's finiteness is factorable from its computational process. To increase the range of computations or the range of expressions computed, one merely specifies an increase in the length of allowable expressions. The *procedure* and the *machine limits* are kept conveniently separate, as would seem desirable in view of the fact that altering the two is a fundamentally different kind of operation. In particular, changing the limits of either machine or brain can, in principle, be carried out indefinitely by providing more external storage (for example, magnetic tape or pencil and paper). (For more on this issue as it relates to the competence-performance distinction, see Pylyshyn, 1973a.)

A Note on the Notion of "Computing"
Above, I take a view of computation which, I believe, is the general view in computer science. I should point out that despite some 50 years of study (starting with Turing's famous paper on computability), there is still no consensus on just what are the essential elements of computing. Because I am concerned in this book with the computational view of mind, it is of some interest to try to understand what that commits us to. Clear cases of computing—in both practical computers and theoretical devices—differ in many ways. Even more significantly, there is

some feeling around that radically different kinds of "computers" may be possible that might fall outside the characterization I give here. Since some of this speculation has been gaining currency in cognitive science (where the problems are so difficult that people are continually desperate for a different technology), it may be worth a brief digression to consider just how chauvinistic and shortsighted is the view I have been presenting here.

It is my view that to understand what is essential about computing—or, at least, the aspect of it that is relevant to cognitive science—it is mandatory that we preserve a number of distinctions. In particular, we must distinguish between a machine and a program, and between a program and the "rules and representations" that the program uses. The second distinction is less important to the present discussion; it merely acknowledges that some symbols in the computer are semantically interpreted in some domain, whereas others are not, and that such semantically interpreted symbols alone are not enough to explain the actual behavior of the system (see chapter 2). We also need to know something about the control structure and about exactly how the rules and representations are turned into behavior by the architecture of the system—for example, how the operations are sequenced, if, in fact, they are carried out serially. In the sense I use the term, a *program* makes this distinction explicit, though such programming languages as PROLOG hide the control aspect from the user in order to keep the representations' semantics "clean" and mathematically tractable. Although I do not want to go into this distinction here, I should point out that it is closely related to the distinction discussed earlier in this chapter between the two classes of symbols on the tape of a universal Turing machine—one representing the inputs to the function, the other designating which Turing machine is to be simulated.

In my view, the other distinction—that between the program and the machine—is absolutely fundamental.[6] In this chapter, I try to make this point in a number of ways, but it deserves another try, since it is a distinction people frequently try to dismiss (cf. Anderson and Hinton, 1981).

The difference between an extremely complex device characterized merely as proceeding through distinguishable states (but not processing symbols) and what I call a "computer" is precisely the difference between a device viewed as a complex finite-state automaton and one

6. It does not matter here whether by *the machine* one means the device described in the manufacturer's manual or what is sometimes called the "virtual machine," consisting of the raw machine plus an interpreter for some higher-level programming language. That is merely a conceptual distinction, since the virtual machine is no less a real physical machine than the one delivered from the manufacturer; it just has a different initial state.

viewed as a variant of a Turing machine. I shall use the term *finite-state automaton* as a general way of talking about any device whose operation is described without reference to the application of rules to symbolic expressions. Thus, in this view, the "new connectionist" machines described by Anderson and Hinton (1981) are finite-state automata characterizations, as are various "network" or "planar circuit" characterizations of computers, such as those studied in complexity theory (for example, Pippenger and Fischer, 1979) or in VLSI design theory (Chazelle and Monier, 1983).

The difference between Turing machines and finite-state automata might seem to be merely that one is infinite and the other finite; but that isn't so, as I suggest a few paragraphs earlier. It is true that the class of functions that can be computed by these two machines depends on the unboundedness of the Turing-machine tape. As far as the relevance of the notion of Turing machine to cognition is concerned, however, the potentially infinite length of the Turing-machine tape serves to force a kind of qualitative organization on the process. Although certain cognitive capacities may be strictly finite, the fact that they apply over very large domains (for example, the number of sentences we can understand is very large) means they must be dealt with *generatively*. In mathematics, when the cardinality of a set is allowed to expand without bounds, for many purposes it becomes necessary to characterize the set *intensionally* in terms of some effective, finitary specification of its members or of conditions for membership in the set, since the elements of the set can, in principle, no longer be listed. Instead of simply referring to sets of infinite cardinality, mathematical methods typically consider some finitary procedure for, say, pairing elements of two sets.

Although the unboundedness of a Turing-machine tape does have consequences (such as undecidability results) whose relevance to cognitive science at present is not clear, it is the touchstone for the fundamental distinction that I also want to press, namely, the distinction between a strictly finite *mechanism* (the Turing machine's finite-state "control box") and a finite but unbounded string of *symbols*. If it weren't for that distinction it would not be possible to have a universal Turing machine. The finite characterization of machines that such a distinction gives us is crucial. Turing machines are individuated by their finite part—that is what allows them to be effectively enumerated. Similarly, a finite part is required for proof theory (the axioms and rules of inference must be specified in a finitary manner). Frege (1980, p. 6) points out that the notion of an infinite number of primitive axioms is incongruous because "it conflicts with one of the requirements of reason, which must be able to embrace all first principles in a survey."[7]

---

7. I am grateful to William Demopoulos for bringing this point to my attention.

As I have stated, it isn't the unboundedness per se that is important for our purpose, it is the form of organization the condition imparts. After all, one could extend without limit the number of states of a finite-state automaton; yet, without some finitary characterization of state-transition regularities, we would be right where we are in the case of an infinite-axiom logical system: Such a characterization would not allow us to understand (or, as Frege puts it, "survey") the function such a machine is computing. It is no accident that allowing the length of a Turing-machine tape to increase without bounds leads to a device that can be described in semantic terms, say, as computing some numerical function; whereas allowing the number of states of a finite-state device to increase without bounds does not.[8] A device possessing an infinite number of atomic (nonarticulated) states cannot be given an effective semantic interpretation because the mapping from states to a semantic model cannot be specified in a finitary manner. For that to be possible, the set of states would have to be characterized intensionally or generatively, as is the case with the arithmetic example described above.

It is important to understand that what is at stake here is the nature of the organization captured in a certain description. Clearly, an ordinary von Neumann-style computer can correctly be described as a finite-state automaton. Such a computer can also be given a true description at the circuit level and at what Newell (1982) refers to as the "register transfer level." It is only when the computer is described as *operating upon symbols* (and, in fact, only when it is viewed as processing the particular symbols that are interpreted semantically) that we can explain its input-output behavior in semantic terms, for example, in terms of doing arithmetic, playing chess, carrying out inferences, or whatever else the device may be doing. Describing the computer at the symbol level is to make the crucial distinction I have been arguing must be made: separate the finite mechanism from the (to a first approximation) arbitrarily expandable symbol structures.

---

8. Again, it must be emphasized that what is at issue here is the way a machine is characterized. An FSA, with unbounded states, can be made to simulate a Turing machine in some fairly standard ways. In doing so, however, the network simulation of the Turing machine must explicitly preserve the distinction between the finite control box and the symbols on the tape. For example, in Chazelle and Monier (1983), different parts of the circuit simulate the tape and the control box. My point here is not that an FSA with unbounded states is any less powerful than a Turing machine, only that the characterization of the machine must observe the distinction between symbol and control mechanisms, in order for a device to be both universal and a computer in the sense in which I am using the term, namely, a device that computes a semantically interpretable function.

Here is another example that illustrates the point that what is at stake is how well the description reveals the underlying processing regularities. Suppose we take a Turing machine and "truncate" it, modifying it by providing the machine with a *finite* tape marked at each end with a special symbol. We then slightly modify the machine's control box, or "program"; that is, we compose this particular Turing machine with another, simple one so that whenever it reads the special symbol, it lights up a sign reading "tilt," then halts. In a certain sense the new machine is formally equivalent to some finite automation; that is, it computes the same function. A description of the finite-state machine, however, loses all trace of the function computed by the original machine. This happens because, as I remark above, the source of finitary limitation is not factored out from the function computed in the finite-state-automaton characterization. True, the new truncated Turing machine computes a different function from the one computed by the original Turing machine; but it is equally true that there is *some* relation between the two. In fact, there is a rather close relation, but a finite-state characterization has no way of showing this.

Those who object to the conventional view of computation frequently have in mind the implausibility of the mind working like an IBM machine. I have much sympathy for this view, as I keep saying; that is why it is so important in cognitive science to discover the correct functional architecture of the mind. I would not be the least surprised to find that the mind's architecture is so different from that of a von Neumann machine that it might not be recognized as one of *our* computers. No doubt, the correct architecture will contain a great deal of parallel processing. Many people think that a substantial degree of parallel processing makes a fundamental difference in what is considered computing. The issue, however, is not whether the mind is a serial computer or a highly parallel one; it is whether the mind processes symbols, whether it has rules and representations. A highly parallel system can process symbols in at least two ways. One way is that the system may be parallel only in how it implements its primitive functions; that is, the functional architecture may be neurally implemented in a highly parallel way. That much, of course, is true of the von Neumann computer. Its random-access memory mechanism requires a great deal of simultaneous activity throughout the memory. The other way is that the primitive operations need not form a total ordering in time. For example, many rules might be applied at once, as in the production system designed by Forgy (1979). Since each rule is symbolic, there is no conflict with my sense of computing here. Even in an architecture as radically parallel as Hewitt's ACTOR scheme (Hewitt, 1977), there is no conflict with the sense of computing I claim must go on in the mind, because each actor processes *semantically interpreted symbols*.

My point here is, so long as cognition (human or otherwise) involves such semantic regularities as inferences, and so long as we view cognition as computing in any sense, we must view it as *computing over symbols*. No connectionist device, however complex, will do, nor will any analog computer; but that is the topic of chapter 7.

To summarize what I have said about computing: A computational process is one whose behavior is viewed as depending on the representational or semantic content of its states. This occurs by virtue of there being another level of structure—variously called the "symbol level" or the syntax or logical form—which possesses the following two essential properties. One, the formal syntactic structure of particular occurrences (tokens) of symbolic expressions corresponds to real physical differences in the system, differences that affect the relevant features of the system's behavior. Two, the formal symbol structures mirror all relevant semantic distinctions to which the system is supposed to respond and continue to do so when certain semantically interpreted rules are applied to them, transforming them into new symbol structures. For every apparent, functionally relevant semantic distinction there is a corresponding syntactic distinction. Thus any semantic feature that conceivably can affect behavior must be syntactically encoded at the level of a formal symbol structure. By this means we arrange for the system's behavior to be describable as responding to the content of its representations—to what is being represented—in a manner perfectly compatible with materialism.

The Role of Computer Implementation

Our discussion so far concerns information-processing theories which are cast at the symbolic, or computational, level. We have not specifically addressed computer-implementation or -simulation models. What is the significance of the computer itself to this endeavor?

What the computer enables us to do, at the most abstract level, is exploit certain facilities (in the form of wired-in operations and compilers or interpreters for "high-level languages"), for

> representing cognitive states in terms of symbolic expressions systematically related to their interpretation (that is, in a manner which preserves relevant distinctions);
>
> representing rules responsive to these symbols (and hence to the interpretations of the states); and then

mapping this system onto causal physical laws so the entire apparatus can run, or produce state-to-state or expression-to-expression transitions that preserve the interpretation's coherence.

Not only is this an important tool for the construction and empirical exploration of computational models, but it also provides a way of understanding the possibility of a physical basis for mind, or at least of seeing that physics and mentalism are compatible. It makes it possible as well to see the sense in which such mentalistic notions as "cognitive process" can be literally true descriptions of intellectual activity occurring in the human organism, since we have no trouble seeing programs as literally—not metaphorically—true descriptions of the computational processes occurring in a computer.

The existence of digital computers, however, has an importance to cognitive science that goes beyond merely providing an existence proof that certain types of semantically described processes are compatible with materialism. Digital computers have dramatically altered the criteria by which the success of theories of cognition is judged. In addition to requiring that the theory capture generalizations about behavior, the notion of *sufficiency* now permeates theory construction in cognitive science. The term *sufficiency* refers to the theory's ability to explain how actual instances of behaviors are generated. Further, the explanation of the generation of such behaviors must be constructive, that is, effectively computable or realizable by a formal mechanism, for example, a Turing machine.

Such notions as "constructive" and "effectively computable" are central as well to a movement in mathematics called constructivism or intuitionism; the latter term, however, carries philosophical assumptions not necessarily shared by constructivism in general. Though quite different in their goals and assumptions, constructivism in cognitive science (in the sense of the adherence to a mechanistic sufficiency condition) and constructivism in mathematics share common assumptions concerning the conditions under which a claim is considered meaningful. Both cognitive science and mathematical constructivism require that functions referred to in the theory be effective or mechanistically realizable. In constructivist mathematics, for example, existence proofs are acceptable only if they provide a method for generating the objects whose existence is being proved; it is not enough to show that the assumption of the nonexistence of such objects leads to a contradiction. Proof by contradiction is not acceptable; demonstration that assuming $\neg P$ leads to a contradiction is not considered a valid method of proving P, since the law of excluded middle is not a logical axiom in constructivist mathematics.

Correspondingly, in the cognitive-science approach, to demonstrate that a certain method or a certain set of principles can account for a particular intellectual skill, it is necessary to show constructively (by exhibiting an effective procedure) that the method or set of principles can generate instances of that skill. In both constructivist mathematics and computational psychology, *construction* means to realize by a formal mechanism, where the notion of mechanism, in turn, rests on the notion of effective computation, or Turing-machine realizability, that is, the notion of mechanism discussed above in this chapter. In cognitive science, however, much stronger constraints than effectiveness are applied in assessing theories.

Any symbolic function implemented on a general-purpose digital computer is, by definition, effectively computable; yet mere implementability means little in psychological theory, for a variety of reasons to be explored in the next two chapters. As noted, one reason is that we are concerned with a much stricter sense of equivalence than input-output equivalence or behavioral mimicry; at the very least, we are concerned as well with realizability within various independently motivated constraints, including, of course, some sort of bounded time and memory complexity (whatever precisely that comes to). (This question is examined in greater detail in chapters 4 and 5.) Another reason for this formal sense of realizability being of limited concern is that the functions we are interested in constructing frequently are neither well defined nor purely symbolic; that is, they are initially specified in terms of physical inputs from the environment and the behavior of the organism. Thus the further requirement—that we be able to implement the process in terms of an actual, running program that exhibits tokens of the behaviors in question, under the appropriate circumstances—has far-reaching consequences.

One of the clearest advantages of expressing a cognitive-process model in the form of a computer program is, it provides a remarkable intellectual prosthetic for dealing with complexity and for exploring both the entailments of a large set of proposed principles and their interactions. In the case of human cognition, there is every reason to believe that the underlying causal mechanisms are unique with respect to both the quantity and the quality of their complexity. While it is true that theoretical understanding involves discovering the most general, abstract principles underlying apparent complexity, and that every object of study is infinitely complex until we have a theory that focuses our attention on its causally relevant features, it remains true that, relative to certain boundary conditions we impose on the project, theories can differ radically in the sheer number of ineliminable principles they must appeal to.

A major factor in determining the complexity of the theory is the requirement placed on it of accounting for certain pretheoretically specified phenomena—for example, how we understand language, remember our past, decide what to do next in playing chess, what to say in conversational communication, how to plan a trip, and so on. Although such specification is crude, and though only the successes of our evolving theories can dictate exactly how we should formulate our questions and puzzles, pretheoretical specification is not arbitrarily malleable; the phenomena have features we *insist* the theory address. In addition, the theory itself will have features which we insist it should have (being constructive, mechanistic, compatible with materialism). Even if we assume that no initial presumptions are inviolable, such a background of pretheoretical requirements can still determine the minimum complexity a theory can get away with and remain an account of the original phenomena we wish to explain. Relative to a strong form of constructivism, a theory must explain how an arbitrarily large set of beliefs, goals, and utilities can be brought to bear in generating behavior and that is likely to require a large theoretical apparatus.

My point about complexity is not merely that a lot is going on—for, clearly, just as much is going on in the physical universe—but that, unlike the case in physics, all the complexity may potentially be relevant to the constructive explanation of *any* aspect of behavior. This point is related to the "maximal-plasticity" property of symbolic systems already discussed. I suggest that, given our metatheoretical constraints, there may be a principled lower bound on the complexity of the constructive process. We already know from certain mathematical results in recursion theory that functions exist whose computational complexity is arbitrarily great in *any* machine (Blum, 1967) and that there are theorems whose proofs are likewise arbitrarily long.[9] What we might well have in cognitive science is a case where the functions we have pretheoretically picked out (for example, those involved in intelligent action) do not admit of a simple, constructive realization, given the constraints on such realizations we require for independent reasons (which include more than that they be effective; see chapter 4).

Explanation, of course, is not the same as construction. In explanation, we need to factor apart various antecedents of behavior and provide general principles at various levels. Still, if the constructivist meth-

9. This follows from Church's undecidability theorem. The result may be stated more precisely, as follows: For any recursive function f, there exists a theorem ϕ for which no proofs of length less than the absolute value of $f(\phi)$ exist. For, if there were, we could use this fact to construct an effective decision procedure for the existence of a proof of ϕ, which is contrary to Church's theorem. I am indebted to Keewatin Dewdney for drawing this result to my attention.

odology is to be applied to anything resembling what we now call cognitive phenomena, then complexity may be endogenous to our project. It would be premature to draw sweeping conclusions from this possibility; surely it does not warrant the claim that human behavior is too complex to succumb to a constructivist analysis, as von Neumann (1966) and Shaw (1971) suggest. Yet that may be a reason why implementation of theories on real computers is more than a matter of convenience. The intrinsic complexity of the process, given our sufficiency requirement, may be more than could ever be accommodated without this prosthetic. There is an analogy here with the constructive proof of the four-color theorem in topology (see Appel and Haken, 1977): the only proof of this old conjecture that has ever been produced involves analysis of a large number of cases, and is so complex that, in all likelihood, it would not have been possible without the help of a computer. Similarly, it may be that the computer is indispensable to the realization of a constructivist theory of mind.

Ironically, one of the behaviorists' main criticisms of mentalism has long been that it is empty because it is all too easy to explain why people do things by appealing to their beliefs and desires: No problem; show me a pattern of behavior, and there is some obvious story based on the person's beliefs and desires that will explain it. If we now demand that the story be framed as an operational model—that is, as a computer program—this criticism no longer seems plausible. Not only isn't it easy to come up with a coherent cognitive story, it seems pretty nearly impossible to do so. Recent successes of artificial intelligence in building "expert systems" attests to both the complexity of the problem and how far one can go merely by building a lot of knowledge into some fairly conventional (by computer-science standards) systems.

Accepting the sufficiency condition on theories raises an entire, new set of issues. We are forced to understand the role of a new set of constraints on the theory-building enterprise, constraints that arise because the model must generate actual tokens of behavior. For example, the requirement that we bridge the gap between general principles and actual performance raises technical issues previously neglected in psychological theorizing concerning the notion of control.

The Control Issue

The commitment to construction of a model that actually generates token behaviors forces one to confront the problem of how, and under what conditions, internal representations and rules are pressed into service as actions are generated. These are questions that concern *control* of the process. Although a central topic in computer science, they have almost never been raised in a cognitive psychology not constrained by computational sufficiency. Indeed, one of the main criticisms leveled against the early work of such cognitive psychologists as Tolman is that their theories deal only with an organism's representations, or "mental maps"; having established something about the representations, however, they cannot say how the representations lead to action: the theories left the organism "lost in thought."

There is much more to understanding control structures than knowing how operations are sequenced. We are so used to thinking of procedures as sequences of instructions which continue on a fixed course until some conditional branch operation detects a specified condition that alternative organizations do not readily spring to mind; yet that is merely one type of organization of control, one in which control is *passed* along a linear sequence from operation to operation. When one operation finishes, it passes control to the next operation in line. In computer science and artificial intelligence, however, there is much interest in very different control schemes, schemes that may change psychologists' thinking about the range of possibilities available for converting representations into action. In what follows I briefly survey some issues that arise when one considers the problem of controlling the way in which processes unfold in response to representations, rules, and the contingencies of the environment. My purpose is not to describe the range of control structures currently being studied in computer science, but merely to provide an intuitive sense of some of the distinctions in this field and suggest that cognitive science has much to learn from this area of development. Such considerations are not likely to be raised without a commitment to realization of the process model on a computer. Also, because control issues are a major area of study in computer science, progress in developing computational models of cognitive processes very likely will depend on technical ideas originating in that field—and especially in artificial intelligence.

Historically, a major breakthrough in understanding the nature of control was the articulation of the idea of feedback through the environment. With that understanding, a certain balance of control was restored between a device or an organism and its environment. Although only the device is credited with having a goal, responsibility for its behavior is shared. At times, when the environment is passive, the initiative appears to come primarily from the device; whereas, at other times, the environment appears to intervene, and the initiative seems to go in the opposite direction. This notion of the responsibility for initiation of different actions is fundamental to understanding control. In most computer programs the most common idea has been that of control moving from point to point, or from instruction to instruction, in a largely predetermined way. This sequencing of instructions makes the notion of *flow* of control quite natural; branch instructions make it equally natural to think of *passing* or *sending* control to some other "place." When control passing is combined with a primitive message-passing facility—at minimum, a reminder of where the control came from, so it can be returned there later—*subroutines* become possible. And, because subroutines can be nested—that is, send control to still lower subroutines, and so on, with the assurance that control will eventually find its way back—the notion of a hierarchy of control emerges. Miller, Galanter, and Pribram (1960), who saw the psychological importance of the idea of hierarchical subroutines, called them test-operate-test-exit or TOTE units and suggested they be viewed as the basic theoretical unit of psychology, replacing the ubiquitous reflex arc. This idea has been highly influential in shaping psychologists' thinking about cognition.

There are several good reasons why a hierarchical system of control is so powerful (for a discussion, see Simon [1969]), one of the most important being that it results in "partial decomposability" or "modularity" of the total system. By keeping the interactions between routine and subroutine simple (in terms of when control is passed and the messages sent along with it), it becomes easier to think of each routine as a nearly independent subsystem, which makes the overall system easier to add to, modify, and understand. Moreover, each routine in the hierarchy can be viewed as defining some subgoal in an overall goal-directed system. Passing control to a subroutine amounts to activating or setting a subgoal; control is returned when the subgoal is achieved. So powerful is this idea that for years its shortcomings were largely overlooked. As early as 1962, however, Allen Newell (1962) pointed out some rigidity in this organization. So long as each subroutine is a narrow "specialist," Newell said, the minimal, rigidly prescribed communication between routine and subroutine works well. If it is a square-root extractor, you can just send it control and a number, and it will perform its function on that number independently of anything else in the data base. If, however, the subroutine is a less narrow specialist, it might help to be able to communicate each task in more flexible terms. Further, it might help to monitor the subroutine's progress along the way, to prevent it from consuming an unwarranted amount of time and resources (for example, memory) on some relatively minor task or on a task another process is in a position to determine is doomed to fail. Similarly, it would help for the subroutine to report its results more flexibly—especially if it could report "what went wrong" in cases of failure. How to convert these anthropomorphically stated desiderata into mechanical form, and how to do so without swamping the system in a bureaucratic nightmare of control messages, is a major design concern in recent artificial intelligence programming languages (for a description of some of these languages, see Bobrow and Raphael, [1974]).

Because differences in control structure can have implications for psychological theory, and because these implications are not always obvious, I shall outline some general aspects of the problem. The aspects are stated in terms of the notion of *locus of responsibility* for such actions as transferring control and passing messages. I make two particular distinctions between (1) *sending* control (where the initiative lies with the old locus) and *capturing* control (where the initiative lies with the new locus), and (2) *directing* a message to a specific recipient and broadcasting it to all routines, or "modules," at once, that is, "to whom it may concern." Various control structures can be characterized on the basis of these distinctions. In the standard subroutine-hierarchy case, for example, control is always sent (by the routine that already has it), and a message (containing parameters and a return address) is directed specifically to the routine being given control. When the subgoal is achieved, control is sent back, along with a result message. In PLANNER-type languages (see Bobrow and Raphael, 1974), when a task is to be done, a message describing the goal is broadcast, then control is captured by a module designed to respond to that particular goal message. Next, control is sent to another location, one that depends on how that execution terminated (for example, whether it is successful, or on what result it produces). In a "production system," another control scheme that is becoming popular in certain areas of artificial intelligence and cognitive science, messages are also broadcast and control is captured. When the module (or "production") finishes, however, it again merely broadcasts a message; rarely is control sent to a specific locus. We will return to some implications of these choices; first, let us see how they show up in some simple examples and in the design of certain computer systems.

Remembering often consists of arranging the environment to trigger appropriate processes at appropriate times. People used to tie knots in their handkerchiefs or set up unusual situations to act as general "meta-reminders." Whereas mnemonic cues such as those used to improve one's memory are usually content-oriented access keys, memories often are evoked by less specific signals from the environment. Such signals are called "interrupts," because the initiative for capturing control originates outside the process currently active—in fact, outside the organism. The distinction between an interrupt and a test is relevant to understanding transducers, and will be discussed again in chapter 6. In addition, the distinction between data-directed, or event-directed, processing responsibility (characteristic of what are called "demon" procedures, as well as of "if-added," "if-altered," or "if-examined" procedures evoked under various, special, recognized conditions) and process-directed control responsibility (characteristic of what are sometimes called "servant" or "if-needed" procedures) is an important, recurring theme in the study of control regimes.

Attempts to work out a balance between process-directed and data-directed procedure invocation is a major concern in the design of control structures for computational systems. Indeed, as the study of programming systems progresses, it has become apparent that the distinction between commands and other types of representation is more subtle than appears at first; the distinction rests on the role a particular symbol structure plays in the system. For instance, it is possible to have programming systems (for example, PROLOG) in which the notion of a command does not enter explicitly, in which everything takes the form of an assertion. In such cases it becomes apparent that the principal question is not whether something is a procedure or a datum but how information about control is represented, whether explicitly, so it is programmable, or implicitly (compare Kowalski, 1979). On the other hand, in some programming systems (for example, the ACTOR system of Hewitt, 1977), everything looks like a command or a procedure. In these systems control is completely decentralized, and the responsibility for initiating various procedures is distributed to the objects on which the procedures operate, instead of always coming from whatever procedure executed previously. People are just beginning to analyze in general terms these important issues in computer science. Clearly, the issues are relevant to an understanding of possible ways such knowledge systems as minds might be organized from the perspective of control.

As a final example of a novel control scheme, one that carries the idea of distributed control even further, I discuss a specific kind of system especially well suited for designing psychological models: the "production system" formalism developed by Newell (1973b). I mention it here briefly; my purpose is not to discuss the system's advantages and disadvantages in detail but merely to illustrate some benefits of thinking in terms of nonstandard control structures.

A production system has two main parts—a communication area, called the workspace, and a set of condition-action pairs, called productions. If the condition side of a production is satisfied by the current contents of the workspace, then that production is said to be evoked, and the action on its action side is carried out. The workspace resembles a public bulletin board, with the productions resembling simple minded bureaucrats who do little except look at the bulletin board. Each bureaucrat, however, is looking for a certain pattern of "notices" on the board. When it finds that pattern, the "bureaucrat" performs whatever its action is—usually merely posting a notice of its own (except that some actions are transductions and perform input or output operations). In Newell's (1973b) version of production systems there is, strictly speaking, no explicit control-transfer operation (called "go-to" in conventional programming languages) or subroutine; that is, no bureaucrat ever gives any orders nor delegates authority, nor even sends messages to any other bureaucrat. All messages are broadcast (the contents of the workspace are visible to all productions), and control is always captured by a production whose conditions happen to be satisfied by the current workspace contents. The system is completely homogeneous, distributed, and modular.

Even on the basis of this brief description, we can see that production systems have attractive properties from a psychologist's point of view:

1. The system is responsive to a limited number of symbols at a time, which may be thought of as being in its focal attention. The system is completely "data-directed," in the sense that nothing happens unless some symbols in the workspace initiate processing by evoking a production.

2. Since symbols in the workspace can originate either from an environmental interrupt or from the action of some production, data-directed and environment-directed effects are combined, thus permitting a uniform treatment of what psychologists call stimulus-bound and stimulus-independent activity.

3. The primitive operation is one of *recognizing* that the symbols in the workspace satisfy some condition. Such recognitions can be made as elementary or as complex as desired; choosing them, however, amounts to selecting the primitive operations of the functional architecture, which, for psychologists, is at least partly an empirical issue.

4. Because production systems are completely data-directed, whenever they are used as models they must *explicitly* model the process's control structure. That is, since no hidden control apparatus exists, the flow of control must be handled by putting appropriate symbols *in the workspace* to evoke the relevant actions. These symbols then identify goals. A typical production system contains many goal-setting and -consummating productions—with the interesting consequence that, at any moment, the contents of the workspace can be thought of as containing everything that occupies the system's attention, including all active goals, as well as the debris of recent processing.

5. Production systems are highly modular; therefore, they can be extended uniformly without making widespread alterations to the existing

system. Another benefit of this modularity is that individual productions tend to be meaningful components of the entire system, a characteristic that may make it easier to give them psychological interpretations in terms of beliefs and goals.

6. The workspace is the dynamic, working memory of the system; thus it is assumed to be small, constituting one psychological hypothesis about resource constraints on the processor. For example, in order to attend to more aspects, it is necessary to trade off space for time. A natural approach is to assign a single symbol to designate an entire group of symbols, which can then be reconstructed from that single symbol whenever necessary. This approach fits well with psychological evidence for the mnemonic process called "chunking" (see Johnson, 1972), and Newell (1972) has used it in a model for Sternberg's high-speed-memory-scan results.

The production system control regime, as well as some other schemes sketched above, represent just a few of the ways in which the strictly hierarchical organization of control is being challenged by the notion of dispersed responsibility; but there are many more issues surrounding the study of control structures. What these studies represent is an attempt to understand alternative types of functional architecture for computing. In chapters 4 and 5 we see that what processes are realizable in a system, and with what complexity, depends crucially on the system's functional architecture. New ideas, such as parallel-processing architectures and networks that can create new interconnections or perform such operations as set intersection primitively (for example, Fahlman, 1979), are broadening our horizon of conceivable ways to realize processes in physical devices.

Many problems encountered in designing new architectures can be reduced to the three questions: How can we enable flexible, effective communication among different processes or modules? How do we ensure that all relevant information (and as little irrelevant information as possible) is brought to bear in making decisions or inferences? How can the making of decisions be withheld and released until the appropriate time? The second question (sometimes called the reference window problem; Marr and Nishihara, 1977) has received a great deal of research, leading to some proposals for organizing knowledge so its relevance to particular topics can be determined easily (for instance, "frames," "scripts," "symbol-mapping" schemes, "label-propagation" schemes, and so on; see, for example, Nudel, 1983). The third question is of special concern to such psychologists as Bransford and Johnson (1973), who have demonstrated experimentally that many inferences are carried out in advance of being required for a particular task (for example, when utterances are heard). Occasionally, making decisions or executing procedures must be withheld until the appropriate context is available. Several proposals for dealing with such linguistic problems as referential opacity rely on the notion of withholding interpretation of parts of sentences pending the appropriate context. For instance, Davies and Isard's discussion (1972) of language comprehension places considerable emphasis on the importance of withholding evaluation of procedures that attempt to identify the referents of various parts of an utterance until the appropriate time. Thus there is growing recognition among investigators interested in the problems of cognitive psychology that a variety of questions related to control must play a more prominent role.

Often it is the necessity to provide a total running system that forces these issues to the fore. Without that requirement, people typically have focused on what are sometimes called "permissive" (or, in computer science, "nondeterministic") rules—for example, the rules of logic or of grammar—which specify the permissible relations among representations rather than on the issue of the conditions under which such rules are invoked. There is no denying that such permissive rules are fundamental. As I have argued in various contexts, it is essential that we know what they are, because that will tell us what the organism knows, which, in turn, determines the organism's behavior. Without the distinction between *performance* theory and what Chomsky calls *competence* theory, without what McCarthy and Hayes (1969) refer to as the distinction between the epistemological problem and the heuristic one, we could find ourselves simply mimicking the most frequent behavior rather than inferring the underlying mechanisms. Nonetheless, according to the computational view, understanding a process also requires having a theory of what makes the process unfold as it does on particular occasions—and that, in turn, requires that issues of control be addressed as well.

The real danger in following the sufficiency, or "performance," route is that it could lead to constructing ad hoc systems whose only virtue is that they can perform tasks similar to those performed by people, perhaps making the same sort of errors. (Various writers have cautioned about this hazard; see Marr, 1977; Pylyshyn, 1978a,1979c,1981.) Constructing such objects of mimicry, however, is not what psychology is about. Psychologists pursue the goal of explanation, which means that, although we pursue the constructivist program, we must make sure our use of computer models is principled. This, in turn, means that stringent constraints must be applied to the theory construction task to ensure that the principles are separated from the ad hoc tailoring of the systems to make them fit the data. To put this in more familiar terms, we must make sure we specify the constants of the model in order to determine whether there are fewer degrees of freedom than there are data points.

In chapter 4 we consider the application of constraints to computational models, in order to take such models literally as embodying the same processes as those occurring in the mind.

Chapter 4

The Psychological Reality of Programs: Strong Equivalence

Meeting a friend in a corridor, Wittgenstein said: "Tell me, why do people always say it was *natural* for men to assume that the sun went round the earth rather than that the earth was rotating?" His friend said, "Well, obviously, because it just *looks* as if the sun is going round the earth." To which the philosopher replied, "Well, what would it have looked like if it had looked as if the earth was rotating?"

Tom Stoppard, *Jumpers*

The Role of Functional Architecture

If a programmed computer, or even a formally specified computational process, is to be a serious candidate as an explanatory model of mental processing, one is owed as explicit an account as possible of the way the model relates to the domain of phenomena it is to explain. There are many levels at which we can interpret a computational system as a model. Specifying the empirical claims entailed by the model is the task of the theory instantiated by that model. Such a theory might, for example, simply claim that the model realizes the same input-output function as the organism being modeled. Although that is the weakest claim for it, the theory can still make a substantive contribution to understanding the task domain. Further, it represents a constraint on possible classes of mechanism considered adequate.

Consider the claim that the task of language comprehension involves, among other things, computation of a function given by a context-free grammar; that among the input-output functions which people can realize is the function that maps strings of words onto the categories "sentence" and "nonsentence," and that this mapping is of the type specifiable by a formal mechanism called a "context-free grammar." If this claim is correct, whole classes of theories are immediately excluded from those that could account for the function, among which are theories based on the principle of association (Bever, Fodor, and Garrett, 1968) or any other mechanisms formally equivalent to finite-state automata (Pylyshyn, 1973a). Providing a weakly equivalent model of some domain of intelligent behavior is, in general, a nontrivial task; it is an existence proof that the task has at least one realization that can be understood on mechanistic principles.

A stronger claim might be that the model realizes a particular function using the same *method* as the person being modeled. The notion of a method is neither well defined nor consistently used, even among computer scientists; but in general it entails something more specific than mere input-output equivalence. For example, we speak of the relaxation method of solving equations of interacting constraints, the Newton-Raphson method for finding the roots of an algebraic equation, the Fourier transform method of computing the effect of a certain filter on a waveform, and so on. All provide a more specific indication of the nature of the process than we would get merely by knowing the input-output function.

Specifying in greater detail the sequence of steps that the system went through would be to provide something resembling an algorithm for the process.[1] The notion of algorithm is somewhat better established in computer science than is the notion of method. For example, a variety of well-known algorithms exist for various numerical approximations to functions (which, in fact, are catalogued and published), for doing Fourier analysis (for example, the fast Fourier transform algorithm), and for parsing context-free languages, such as the Early algorithm. Algorithms for sorting and merging lists are another major area of study (Knuth, 1968), as are algorithms for table lookup.

An even more specific level of comparison for computational models is that of a *program*. A program is a piece of text; it is the encoding of

1. There has been some confusion outside computer science regarding the use of the term *algorithm*, resulting from Newell and Simon's (1972) well-known distinction between algorithmic and heuristic methods. Some now understand *algorithm* to apply only to those procedures guaranteed to solve a problem, whereas the term *heuristic* applies to more plausible but incomplete procedures. All computational procedures, even heuristic ones, however, are carried out by some algorithm. As Haugeland (1981a) has nicely put it, the distinction applies only when one wishes to emphasize the performance of the procedure with respect to a particular result one has in mind. With respect to the goal of executing a particular set of heuristic rules, surely the algorithm used is complete and deterministic. In fact, some heuristic methods (for example, the heuristics used by resolution theorem provers) are guaranteed even to be complete and exhaustive in solving a problem and are considered heuristic only relative to the most efficient possible method, since they do not necessarily solve the problem (albeit exhaustively) by the shortest path. I use the term *algorithm* here in approximately its standard computer-science sense, as any completely-specified procedure, regardless of whether it is guaranteed to produce some particular desired result.

a particular algorithm in some programming language. Thus we can have different programs for the same algorithm (one might be in FORTRAN, another in PASCAL, and still another in LISP). Because *algorithm* is a more abstract notion than *program*, in a variety of ways, it is possible as well to have different programs in the same language for a particular algorithm. In that case, programs are viewed as differing in inessential respects; for example, they may differ in the order in which they do certain minor operations—such as the order in which they take rows and columns in a matrix multiplication, the order in which they exhaustively search through a list, or the notation they use to represent certain equivalent expressions within the language, say, by using or not using parentheses in lieu of appealing to operator precedence.

Even finer levels of comparison between computational systems are possible when the systems are implemented on actual computers. We could, for example, have identical programs that run on functionally different computers, say, on a single-user variable-word-length machine such as the old IBM 1620, as opposed to a fixed-word-length machine with built-in floating-point, multiprocessing, and time-sharing capability, such as the Cyber 835. At a still finer level of resolution the same program might be run on functionally indistinguishable computers (say, both members of the same computer "family," for example, the IBM 370 or the DEC PDP-10) realized by different solid-state technologies, as is the case between the PDP-KA10 and the PDP-KL10, the latter of which uses LSI technology. In principle, a program could be run by entirely different media, say, optically instead of electronically.

Thus there is plenty of scope in the possible claims a theory might make about the level of correspondence between model and empirical domain or about the properties of the model that could be said to have "psychological reality." Clearly, if the computational system is to be viewed as a model of the cognitive process rather than a simulation of cognitive behavior, it must correspond to the mental process in greater detail than is implied by weak equivalence. On the other hand, it is equally clear that, because computers not only are made of quite different material than brains but, through details of realizing particular operations (for example, certain register-transfer paths or binary mechanisms and bit-shifting operations), differ from the way the brain works. The correspondence between computational models and cognitive processes appears to fall somewhere between these extremes.

I suggest that the appropriate level of comparison corresponds roughly to the intuitive notion of the algorithm. An algorithm is related to a program approximately as a proposition is related to a sentence. The two are in a type-token relation. There are at least as many ways of expressing a proposition by some sentence—or an algorithm by some program—as there are different languages. To specify what proposition or algorithm we have in mind, however, requires use of something like canonical notation. Thus a proposition is identified with a sentence in some formal language (for example, predicate calculus), whereas an algorithm is identified with a program in some canonical programming language. Not just any language can be used to express propositions; the language must be free, for instance, of both lexical and syntactic ambiguity, and it must be sufficiently rich to capture relevant distinctions, and thus must contain quantifiers and devices to mark their scope. Similarly, not just any programming language is appropriate for expressing a cognitive algorithm. Indeed, I argue below that providing an appropriate canonical language is crucial to the expression of mental processes at the required level of specificity.

I should point out that, although the notion of an algorithm, as an abstraction of a class of programs independent of both programming language and of the form of implementation on a particular computer system, is intuitively appealing, little progress has been made in formally defining the algorithmic equivalence of programs, or what I call the "strong" equivalence of programs. No one has yet produced a natural, uniform way of distinguishing essential from nonessential properties in programs that applies over a variety of domains and languages. Although this area is just beginning, some tentative approaches are being developed. The relevance of formal criteria to cognitive-science goals is marginal (we are not concerned with the task of comparing two *programs* but with comparing a program and set of empirical phenomena); the pursuit of strong equivalence in computer science is of interest because it reveals underlying conceptual issues. For that reason it may be worthwhile to outline a class of approaches that is closely related to the goal of specifying strong equivalence, namely, providing a "mathematical semantics" for programming languages (compare Scott and Strachey, 1971).

Providing a mathematical semantics for a programming language is important in proving that a program can compute a particular function, that is, in proving the program "correct" or that two programs are equivalent in that they can compute the same function. A variety of approaches to this goal are available, one of which is to define a formal model consisting of certain mathematical objects (for example, functions from states to states) and relations and an evaluation function that maps expressions in the text of a program onto the objects. By using this "semantic model"[2] it would be possible, in some usable notation,

---

2. Note that this is *not* the same sense of semantics discussed above. Here, the model is not the domain of interpretation of the symbols intended by the programmer. For example, it does not consist of people's ages or chess positions or dollars or whatever

to derive the mathematical function performed by the entire program in terms of the *significant* features of the functions carried out by more elementary parts of the program. Objects in the model define the appropriate level of specificity for this recursive analysis, just as a model in Tarskian semantics defines the significant features of a logical notation. If a mapping (or evaluation function) can be defined from two different programming languages onto the same abstract model, it becomes possible to prove the weak equivalence of programs written in the two languages. From our perspective, the important point about this approach is that the model defines what will count as "significant" changes: hence, it provides one approach to specifying the appropriate level or grain of comparison among programs. Within the mathematical-semantics approach, strong equivalence can be understood in terms of the equivalence of the processes at the level of the most elementary functions that produce differences in the model. In Scott and Strachey's terms the two processes would have the same "semantical equations."

Another approach to the problem of providing a semantical analysis of programs, the "operational approach," defines the programs' "semantics" operationally by translating them into another canonical programming language, frequently by providing a program for the interpreter of the target language. What such approaches as these can be viewed as doing is distinguishing—or, at least, providing a principled way of distinguishing—between significant and insignificant properties of programs by, in effect, defining an abstract virtual machine whose state transitions correspond, in well-defined ways, to the significant features of changes produced by commands, procedures, and other expressions in a program's text. The notion of a virtual machine is important for the concept of strong equivalence. Although the idea has not been formally developed to a high degree in the study of the semantics of programs, the general notion is sufficiently clear for our purposes, since I shall not be using this highly abstract technique in my more empirical approach.

In my view, two programs can be thought of as strongly equivalent or as different realizations of the same algorithm or the same cognitive process if they can be represented by the same program in some theoretically specified virtual machine. A simple way of stating this is to

---

else the program may be computing; rather, it is an abstract mathematical object, a set of ordered pairs with no real-world interpretations intended solely to prove certain theorems about the the input-output mappings carried out by a certain sequence of operations embodied in the algorithm. One might say it is a semantic model of the sequence of operations, and not of the data. The model-theoretic *method*, however, can sometimes be used for the other sense of semantics, providing we have a mathematical theory of the semantical domain. This we have in the case of arithmetic, which is why we can use the method for numerical algorithms (see the example in chapter 3).

say that we individuate cognitive process in terms of their expression in the canonical language of this virtual machine. The formal structure of the virtual machine—or what I call its *functional architecture*[3]—thus represents the theoretical definition of, for example, the right level of specificity (or level of aggregation) at which to view mental processes, the sort of functional resources the brain makes available—what operations are primitive, how memory is organized and accessed, what sequences are allowed, what limitations exist on the passing of arguments and on the capacities of various buffers, and so on. Specifying the functional architecture of a system is like providing a manual that defines some particular programming language. Indeed, defining a programming language is equivalent to specifying the functional architecture of a virtual machine.

Thus the way I address the issue of the appropriate level of comparison between a model and a cognitive process—or the notion of strong equivalence of processes—is to provide a specification of the functional architecture of a "cognitive virtual machine." Much of the remainder of this book is taken up with developing this idea, with providing constraints on an adequate functional architecture and showing its relevance to the computational view of mind. Throughout the rest of this section, however, I try to provide an intuitive feel for the notion of functional architecture by discussing the role the idea plays in computer science and by introducing the closely related—though, in many ways unique—role it must play in cognitive science. In the course of this discussion I make the point that *any* notion of correspondence stronger than weak equivalence must presuppose an underlying functional architecture, or at least some aspects of such an architecture. The question, therefore, is not whether we need to worry about the functional architecture of the mind in developing computational models but, rather, whether we can be content to leave it as an implicit assumption conditioned largely by the functional architecture of currently available computers, or whether we should make the architecture explicit and endeavor to bring empirical criteria to bear in constraining it.

3. It is unfortunate that the term *functional architecture* also has an established usage in neurophysiology (for example, Hubel and Weisel, 1968) that differs in important respects from my use of the term here. Although in both cases *architecture* refers to certain structures, the structures of interest in neurophysiology are anatomical or topographical ones—specifically, according to Hubel and Weisel, the columnar arrangement of related detector cells. In my usage the structures are functional, corresponding to, for instance, primitive symbol-manipulation operations, various buffers, and storage and retrieval mechanisms. I shall continue to use *functional architecture* despite its potential ambiguity, because the term's meaning in computer science so closely captures the idea I wish to convey.

Functional Architecture and Computer Programs

The concept of functional architecture has considerable utility in computer science, since it marks the distinction between what corresponds to the program of interest and the various incidental properties grouped under the general rubric "implementation concerns." As we have seen, this distinction is important in theoretical computer science, because such notions as the correctness and equivalence of programs rely on the distinction. The distinction is also important in practical computer science because it marks a level of computational resource or facility that is uniformly available to program designers. The discipline of writing clear, easily understood and modifiable programs requires that we respect the boundary between program and architecture.

A major concern in the design of computer languages is providing programmers with resources at the right conceptual level, so that, in writing programs for particular applications, they can concentrate on the problem's algorithmically significant features. Although this concern arises in the practical matter of writing programs for problem areas, it is, in fact, not entirely unrelated to the issue of the correct level of aggregation relevant to cognitive science. In both cases one is concerned to find the level at which the general principles of that domain can be stated so as to maximize the domain's apparent systematicity.

To the extent that a language has been well designed for a problem area, it is good computer science practice to view the facilities provided by the language as comprising the immutable, functional architecture of the machine on which the program is to be executed—that is, the *virtual machine* (a somewhat misleading term since, of course, this virtual machine is the *real* machine, but one with a particular initial state). We usually have ways to circumvent the restrictions imposed by this architecture, say, by making alterations to the language interpreter, going outside the language to other lower-level commands, even using special functions occasionally provided to make certain kinds of hardware-specific operations and programming shortcuts possible—for example, the *peek* and *poke* operators provided in some microcomputer languages that take actual hardware addresses as arguments. Nonetheless, such violations of the virtual-machine boundary should be viewed as a very special sort of intervention (such as changing a wire in the machine or, in the corresponding cognition case, altering one's cognitive process by judiciously inserting a probe in one's brain). Generally, use of facilities that fall outside the functional architecture of the virtual machine is discouraged. In computer programming this methodological principle is enforced, for both conceptual and practical reasons. Programs that do not respect the virtual-machine boundary tend not to be robust, generally failing to run on a different computer or with a different compiler or interpreter. This lack of robustness is symptomatic of a level violation, in which the operations in question are interventions at the wrong conceptual level. An important principle of software design is: A good programming language systematically suppresses details irrelevant to the algorithm for the task at hand.

The practical distinction between functional architecture and program is based on the fact that the notion of a program is tied to the existence of a language, and that typically there is a set of largely independent levels of language in a computer system. A language at one level in this set, or cascade, interprets the operations of the language at the level above it. Thus, if a program is written in, say, STRIPS (Stanford Research Institute Planning System), the language's commands can be interpreted by programs written in LISP, which, in turn, are interpreted by programs written in an assembler language, which may be interpreted by microprogrammed instructions stored in read-only memory; and so on. The regression may continue beyond that point, since one can view the circuits of the computer—even the function of individual transistors—in symbolic rather than electronic terms; indeed, that is how computer-design engineers view them.

Although computation can be viewed as involving many levels of symbol processing, the distinction between a program written using the operations provided by a certain language and the processes that implement the basic operations of that language is worth preserving. At least two considerations are involved in this distinction. The first is that the symbolic expressions at the program level usually are intended to represent something quite different from the expressions at the implementation or the interpreter level.

The following may serve to illustrate this point concerning the domain of interpretation of the symbols. Presumably, at the program (as opposed to the implementation) level, the symbols represent specific aspects of the domain which the computations are concerned with. In a STRIPS planning program the symbols might correspond to the robot's "knowledge" of its environment and goals. At the next level down, they might correspond to, for example, pointers; placeholders; bookkeeping counters; return-address stacks; save states; names of operations for constructing lists by appending new symbols to old lists or searching through a list for a token occurrence of a certain symbol; or symbols indicating the success or failure of such searches. At this level the symbols are treated either as formal tags carrying information for the internal use of the computational mechanisms or as references to LISP functions interpreted at a still lower level (though not necessarily as *planning* operations). In Haugeland's (1978) terms, different levels in this cascade of interpreters correspond to different intentional interpretations or to interpretations on different dimensions.

The second consideration that is involved in the distinction between a program written in a certain programming language and the symbol processes that constitute the interpreter of that language is that the two sets of processes respond to different interventions. In altering the program by varying the sequence of instructions, we are using resources (or basic operations) provided by the language itself. Conceptually, this is quite different from the kind of alterations we can make by going outside the resources of the language, say, by altering the operations the language itself provides by making changes to the command interpreter. In the latter case we are altering what I have called the virtual machine.

These two general reasons for wanting to preserve the distinction between a program written in a certain language and the processes that carry out the commands of that language (which may or may not themselves be symbolic processes) become even more important when we consider the issue of viewing mental processes literally as computations. I shall argue that—while the computer's operation may be viewed as consisting of various levels, each implying the existence of a program in some language, and a functional architecture that interprets the program—the situation is somewhat different in the case of cognition. There, rather than a series of levels, we have a distinguished level, the level at which interpretation of the symbols is in the intentional, or cognitive, domain or in the domain of the objects of thought. In addition, the criterion of being manipulatable in a specific way plays a role that is parallel to the more pragmatic role it plays in computer science practice.

Algorithms' Dependence on Functional Architecture
To the cognitive scientist the distinction between the mental algorithm and the functional architecture of the "cognitive virtual machine" is even more important than it is to the computer scientist, though the principle for distinguishing the two must be stated differently, since ultimately it depends on empirical criteria. As in the computer case, I view the functional architecture as part of the system that is fixed in certain respects (see the next section). Certain features of the functional architecture also may turn out to be universal to the species.

Mental algorithms, the central concept in computational psychology, are viewed as being executed by this functional architecture. According to the strong realism view I advocate, a valid cognitive model must execute the *same* algorithm as the one executed by subjects. Now it turns out (as we shall see) that *which* algorithms can be carried out directly depends on the device's functional architecture. Devices with different functional architectures cannot, in general, directly execute identical algorithms. Typical, commercial computers, however, are likely to have a far different functional architecture from that of the brain; hence, we would expect that, in constructing a computer model, the mental architecture must first be emulated (that is, itself modeled) before the mental algorithm can be implemented. In what follows I shall try to unpack this claim and make its implications clear.

Let us consider how we would go about using a computing system as a cognitive model. First, in order to describe an algorithm so it can be viewed as a literal model of a cognitive process, we must present the algorithm in standard, or canonical, form or notation. Typically this means formulating the algorithm as a program in some programming language; it might also include graphical presentation (as a flowchart) or even a discursive natural language description. What is often overlooked when this is done is the extent to which the class of algorithms that can be considered is conditioned by the assumptions made regarding the basic operations possible, how they interact, how operations are sequenced, what data structures are possible, and so on. Such assumptions are an intrinsic part of the descriptive formalism chosen, since it is that formalism which defines what I call the "functional architecture" of the system.

What is remarkable here is that the range of actual computer architectures, or even the theoretical proposals for new architectures, available for our consideration is extremely narrow compared with what, in principle, is possible.[4] Virtually every architecture that is widely available is of the type that many people refer to as von Neumann (though this name is sometimes used rather lossely to mean "conventional"). This architecture—which has been universal practically since the design of the Princeton I.A.S. Computer—is a register machine in which symbols are stored and retrieved by their numerical "addresses," control is transferred sequentially through a program (except for "branching" instructions), and operations on symbols are accomplished by retrieving them from memory and placing them in a designated

4. In saying this I do not mean to minimize the important and growing body of research devoted to the topic, in both computer science and more empirically oriented cognitive science (see, for example, Feldman and Ballard, 1982; Hinton and Anderson, 1981; and various papers in Anderson and Hinton, 1981). Yet this research represents the early stages of a program whose full importance cannot properly be assessed yet. Indeed, some proponents of this work do not view it as involving the study of functional architectures, but, rather, new ideas about cognition. In this, surely they are wrong, as I suggest in chapter 3 and will reiterate in chapter 7.

register, applying a primitive command to them, then storing the resulting symbol back in memory. Although there are variants on this pattern, the main idea of a sequential process proceeding through a series of "fetch," "operate," and "store" operations has been dominant since digital computation began. That is true as well for both hardware and software (for a discussion of the latter, see Backus, 1978).

Because our experience has been with a rather narrow range of architectures, we tend to associate the notion of computation, and hence of algorithms, with the particular class of algorithms that can be executed by architectures in this limited class. For example, we tend to think of the familiar flowchart as a neutral way to exhibit an algorithm. That is the idea behind the TOTE unit of Miller, Galanter, and Pribram (1960). Such flowcharts (and TOTE units), however, are totally inappropriate as a means of characterizing algorithms realized by unconventional (not von Neumann) architectures—for example, the less familiar architecture of production systems, PLANNER-like languages, or such predicate calculus-based programming systems as PROLOG. (See related comments on the importance of understanding the control structure at the end of chapter 3.) If we were to use a criterion of strong equivalence to individuate algorithms, we would find that the different architectures that resulted are, in general, not capable of executing identical algorithms directly.

This point is best illustrated by considering examples of several simple architectures. The most primitive machine architecture is, no doubt, the original binary-coded Turing machine introduced by Alan Turing (1937). Although Turing's machine is "universal" in the sense that it can be programmed to compute any computable function, anyone who has tried to write procedures for it will tell you that most computations on the machine are extremely complex. More important, the complexity of the sequence of operations the Turing machine must go through varies according to the task and nature of the input in ways considerably different from those of machines with more conventional architecture. For example, the number of basic steps required to look up a string of symbols in a Turing machine increases as the square of the number of strings stored. On the other hand, in what is called a "register architecture" (an architecture possessing what is usually called random-access memory, in which retrieving a symbol by name or "reference" is a primitive operation), the time complexity can, under certain conditions, be made independent of the number of strings stored. Because of this characteristic, a register architecture can execute certain algorithms directly (for example, the hash-coding lookup algorithm), something that is impossible in the Turing machine, despite of the fact that the Turing machine can be made to be weakly equivalent to this algorithm.

In other words, the Turing machine can compute the same lookup function, though not with the same complexity profile, hence, not by using the same hash-coding algorithm.

A Turing machine, of course, can be made to mimic the sequence of states the register machine goes through by a two-stage process. First, we arrange for it to compute the functions realized by each individual operation of the register machine, in short, to simulate each step the register machine takes in executing its algorithm. I call this stage *emulation*. Thus, the Turing machine first *emulates* the architecture of the register machine, then executes the algorithm in the emulated architecture, a far different matter from the Turing machine directly executing the algorithm.

The distinction between directly executing an algorithm and executing it by first emulating some other functional architecture is crucial to cognitive science, bearing, as it does on the central question: Which aspects of the computation can be taken literally as part of the model, and which are to be considered as mere implementation details? Naturally, we expect to need ways of implementing primitive cognitive operations in computers, but the details of accomplishing that goal may have little empirical content. Clearly, this level of empirically irrelevant implementation detail, or emulation of mental operations, is necessitated by the fact that at the level of actual hardware, the functional architecture of production-model electronic computers differs from that of the brain: they use different circuits and different media.

This distinction is important not only for theoretical reasons relating to use of the algorithm as a model; the difference between direct execution of an algorithm and its indirect execution via an intermediate stage of architectural emulation is significant from a strictly computational viewpoint, something that later becomes important in developing empirical criteria for strong equivalence. A Turing machine that emulates a register-machine architecture—and in doing so mimics the execution of, say, the hash-code lookup algorithm—still cannot do a table lookup with time complexity independent of the size of the table. It would take a time complexity at least of order 2; that is, the time or number of Turing machine steps increases at least as the square of the number of items in the table.

Other examples of the architecture specificity of algorithms are easily found. For example, a register machine with arithmetic operations and certain arithmetic predicates among its primitive operations (hence, which can use numerals as names, or, as they are more frequently called, "addresses") makes various additional algorithms possible, including binary search, in which the set of remaining options is reduced by a fraction with each comparison, as in the game "Twenty Questions."

The existence of arithmetic primitives as part of the architecture means it is possible to specify a total ordering on an arbitrarily large set of names, and thus primitively partition certain search spaces (as in an n-dimensional matrix data structure), so that search can be confined within a region while other regions are not considered (items in those regions are not even checked and discarded, as they would have to be if they were merely part of an unordered set of items). These algorithms cannot be executed directly on a Turing-machine architecture.

As we proceed to more unusual architectures, other, quite different algorithms become possible. Scott Fahlman (1979) has proposed a design for an architecture (realizable with highly unconventional hardware) which computes set intersection as a primitive operation in time independent of set size. Fahlman argues that many otherwise complex, combinatorial algorithms required for symbolic pattern-recognition—that is, for access to stored data through multiple descriptions—become simple in such an architecture. Because the architecture allows implementation of interesting new classes of algorithms, the locus of computational difficulty of certain tasks shifts dramatically. Fahlman argues as well that, in this architecture, the resulting complexity profiles of certain memory-retrieval processes more closely resembles that of "natural intelligence." Others have proposed new kinds of memory-access functions, which, interestingly, differ from that of location-addressable storage in ways that make them of potential psychological relevance (see, for example, the papers in Hinton and Anderson, 1981). Along the same lines Mitch Marcus (1979) has proposed certain general architectural features of the processor associated with grammatical analysis, which, at least arguably, has the interesting consequence of providing a principled account of certain linguistic universals in terms of general architectural constraints.

As I have remarked, even when information-processing theorists make no claims about the functional architecture's form, attempting merely to develop models of certain cognitive processes, they cannot avoid making certain tacit assumptions about the underlying architecture. Further, the adoption of a particular architecture implies certain other assumptions about the nature of mental functions. To see exactly what those "other assumptions" are when a certain architecture is adopted, it is useful to look at the architecture's properties more abstractly, asking what it is about the architecture that makes it possible to carry out certain functions in certain ways.

A fruitful way to approach this question is in terms of the formal, or mathematical, *type* of primitive operations built into the virtual machine. The primitive relation we call *reference* (the operation of retrieving a symbol, given another symbol which serves as its name) is of the formal type *asymmetric*. This relation can be used to construct operations for evaluating other relations. For example, the successor operation we might call AFTER, which is irreflexive, antisymmetric, transitive, acyclic, and connected over a specified set of names. Such a syntactic operation in the functional architecture can be interpreted freely as any relation in the semantic domain that is of the same formal type, for example, the relation of being of higher rank, being older, or being a superset of something (a relation frequently used in semantic hierarchies known as "ISA trees"—see, for example, Norman and Rumelhart, 1975).

In using such a formal operation in this way to realize an interpreted rule, we automatically inherit the formal properties of the built-in primitive relations. Thus we need not represent explicitly such properties of the relation as its reflexiveness, symmetry, transitivity, noncyclicality, and so on. In other words, if we choose to represent *older* by a primitive relation in the architecture that is of the appropriate formal type, we do not need an explicit symbolic representation of such a rule as "If X is older than Y, and Y is older than Z, then X is older than Z." The inference this rule sanctions can be obtained "free" as a by-product of using that particular primitive operation to represent *older*. Certain semantical properties of *older* are automatically preserved, just as the semantics of numbers are preserved by primitive arithmetical operations (recall the discussion in chapter 3).

In an architecture with what we call an "arithmetic unit" (which, as we saw in chapter 3, is merely a set of functional properties useful, among other things, for representing the syntactic rules relating numerals under certain mathematically interpretable operations), as well as an ordering relation over symbols, an even richer set of formal types is available for exploitation in constructing an interpreted system of rules. For example, certain formal properties of the Peano axioms for arithmetic, as well as metrical axioms, can be modeled in terms of these primitive "arithmetic" relations. This means that, in such an architecture, certain aspects of metrical scales are available without having to explicitly encode the metrical axioms. In fact, since the axioms of Euclidean geometry have a well-known Cartesian model over pairs of real numbers, this architecture allows us to choose an interpretation scheme that makes available certain geometric properties without the need to represent geometric axioms symbolically. For example, if we interpret pairs of numerical expressions as locations of points in space, and if we use the arithmetic operations of addition and subtraction to define components of distances and movements through this space, we do not need a representation of the Pythagorean theorem, since that theorem will always be respected by our interpretation of movements and relative distances in the representation. Thus, by semantically interpreting primitive (built-in) operations in this way, a variety of spatial and metrical properties can be represented and changed and the logical consequences of the changes inferred without the need for symbolically encoded rules to characterize properties of space or other quantities (for example, Euclidean or metrical axioms).

Functional Architecture and Mental Processes

The exploitation of the functional architecture of computational systems that we have been discussing is central to computer science. From the point of view of cognitive science, though, it not only is important that we choose functional properties of the computational architecture so as to accomplish certain tasks efficiently, it is equally important that we be explicit about *why* the resulting model works the way it does and that we justify independently the crucial assumptions about the functional architecture. That is, it is important in using computational models in an explanatory mode rather than simply a performance mode that we not take certain architectural features for granted just because they happen to be available in our computer language. We must first explicitly acknowledge that certain noncomputational properties originate with certain assumed properties of the functional architecture; then we must attempt to justify and empirically motivate such assumptions. Otherwise, important features of our model could be left resting on adventitious and unmotivated assumptions.

This issue frequently arises in connection with claims that certain ways of performing intellectual tasks—for example, the use of mental imagery—bypass the need for explicit representation of certain logical (or even physical) properties of the represented domain, as well as bypassing the need for such inefficient, combinatorially explosive processes as logical inference. The issue is often stated in terms of hypotheses that one or another mental function is performed using an "analogue" process. The entire issue of analogue versus digital will be raised again; for now, I shall consider only simple cases involving the claim that certain properties of mental imagery are not due to reasoning or other knowledge-dependent processes. This can be interpreted as the claim that some cognitive function is actually part of the functional architecture. At this point in my analysis I should point out some problems posed by these claims and briefly relate them to the notion of functional architecture. (Chapter 7 is devoted to a discussion of this issue, one in which functional architecture is of central concern.)

Consider a simple example. Occasionally people have suggested that subjects need have no knowledge of such relational properties as transitivity in making certain inferences in, for example, three-term series problems ("John is taller than Mary and John is shorter than Fred. Who is tallest?"). According to this view, all one has to do is arrange the three items (here, the names) in order, either in a list or in an image, and read off the answer; then one simply *notices* which object is first (or last) in the list. Of course, even if a problem can be solved this way, it does not follow that tacit knowledge of formal properties (for example, transitivity) of the relation *taller than* is *not* needed.

There are at least two reasons why one might have to postulate the active use of a knowledge of formal relations. First, the decision to represent *taller* by something like *further on the list* must be based on the implicit recognition that the two relations are of the same formal type; for example, a list is not suitable for representing the relation *is married to*. Second, although ordering three names in a list and then examining the list for the position of a particular name may seem straightforward and free from logical deduction, a little thought shows that the ability to do this operation mentally, as distinct from physically, presupposes a great deal about the available, primitive, mental operations. Specifically, when a theorist appeals to the existence of a "mental list" or similar structure, certain assumptions must be made about the properties such a structure possesses *intrinsically*. If say, a person has a mental representation of items A, B, and C, and reasons, according to the theory, by placing A and B in a certain order and then adding C next in the sequence, then such a theory must also be making certain additional unstated assumptions about the intrinsic constraints on the system's behavior, for example, that (1) placing C next to B leaves the relation of A to B unchanged, and (2) the relation of A to C (with B between them) remains the same with respect to the relevant aspect represented (for example, tallness) as that between A and B.

Assumptions such as these are justifiable only if there exists an operation in the functional architecture that has the same formal properties as (that is, behaves isomorphically to) the relations *taller* and *further on the list*. Even if this operation is part of the functional architecture, we still may not assume that the use of this capacity requires no further appeal to tacit knowledge of such logical constructs as transitivity, as the point about assumption 1 in the preceding paragraph shows.[5]

5. Some theorists, such as Fahlman (1981), speak of "implicit knowledge," by which they mean to the sort of property built into the functional architecture—for example, the transitivity property in the three-term series problem. The difficulty we encounter in calling this *knowledge* is, we thereby open the door to accepting every functional property as involving implicit knowledge—for example, the property *knowledge of temperature* possessed by a thermostat's bimetalic strip. What Fahlman appears to have in mind is that there are cases of apparent inference, such as the three-term series problem above, in which certain steps are not, in fact, carried out by a rule-governed process operating over representations. Of course, *some* representations and *some* rules are in-

To take another example, matrix data structures are often used to represent the spatial properties of images (Kosslyn and Shwartz, 1977; Funt, 1980). This is a convenient way to represent spatial layout, partly because we tend to think of matrices in spatial terms anyway. In addition, a matrix data structure seems to make available certain consequences with no apparent need for certain deductive steps involving reference to a knowledge of geometry. For example, when we represent the locations of imagined places in our model by filling in the cells of a matrix, we can "read off" such facts as which places are adjacent, which are left of, right of, above or below a given place, and which places are in between a given pair of places. Further, when a particular object is moved to a new place, its spatial relationship to other places need not be recomputed. In an important sense, this is implicit in the data structure. Such properties make the matrix a much more natural representation than, say, a list of assertions specifying the shape of objects and their locations relative to other objects.

As in the example of using a list to solve the three-term series problem, however, such properties of matrices arise from the existence of certain formal properties which are part of the functional architecture of nearly all contemporary computers. These properties, however, are not constitutive of computing. For instance, they are not available in a Turing machine's architecture. For a matrix data structure with the desired properties to be realizable, the architecture must provide at least the primitive capacity to address the content of a representation by place; that is, it must be possible to name a location and ask for the content of a named location. This itself requires a "register architecture" (or some other kind of location-addressable store).

In this architecture it must be possible as well to primitively generate the names of places adjacent to a given place; that is, it must be possible without appealing to other representations, a tacit knowledge of geometry, or anything else that involves intermediate inferential steps. This is necessary if we want to view such operations as "scanning" of the representation to be a primitive. There must also be primitive predicates which, when applied to names, evaluate the relative directions of places corresponding to those names; for example, such two-place predicates as *right of* must be primitive in the architecture—which, in

---

volved—just not those one might at first have thought are involved (if, for example, one were thinking in terms of a particular syllogism). This, however, just goes to show that an inference can be performed in more ways than one, that it is possible to be mistaken when one assumes a particular sequence of inference steps. What always remains moot are the precise primitive operations in terms of which the inference actually is carried out. Some operations can make the inference extremely short, even if not always valid. Nothing in this discussion, however, suggests that some sort of nonsymbolically encoded knowledge is involved.

turn, implies that there are at least two independent, implicit, total orderings over the set of names. In addition, if the relative distance between places is to be significant in this representation, further primitive operations might be required that can be applied to place names so as to evaluate, say, relative size (for example, the predicate *larger than*).

This array of formal properties is available in all common computer architectures, because all use numerical expressions for register, or place, names and all have built-in primitive arithmetic operations. These properties, however, are part of such architectures for reasons unrelated to the theoretical requirements of cognitive science. When these features are exploited in building cognitive models, we tacitly assume that such operations are part of the functional architecture of the mind—clearly, an assumption that must be justified. Arguments have rarely been provided for such proposals, though; the only suggestion of an argument that I am aware of is one made by Piaget, who was concerned with abstract formal characteristics of cognition, and Brouwer (1964) and Nicod (1970) who, for different reasons, proposed that *succession* be viewed as a cognitive primitive.

The general point concerning the intimate relationship between virtual-machine architecture and process is exactly the same as the observation that different notations for a formal system can lead to different expressive powers and even different axioms for the same system. For example, if we use conventional notation for algebraic expressions, we must explicitly state facts about the associativity and precedence of arithmetic operators, whereas in Polish notation we do not need to represent such properties explicitly because, in a sense, the properties are implicit in the notation. Similarly, propositional logic normally contains axioms for both commutativity and the complementarity expressed in de Morgan's principles. If, however, we use the disjunctive normal form for logical expressions, such axioms need not be stated because, as is true of the algebraic case, they are implicit in the notation.

Mechanical theorem-proving exploits a variety of such intrinsic formal properties of both notation (for example, using the disjunctive normal form) and virtual-machine architecture. For example, in certain domains these theorem-provers can be made more efficient and natural by representing sets of propositions in the form of "semantic nets" that exploit the formal properties of the reference relation available in typical register machines.

From the viewpoint of cognitive science the notation chosen is important for reasons that go beyond questions of efficiency or naturalness. Because we claim that behavior is governed by symbolically encoded rules and representations, the exact format or notation used to encode the representations constitutes a claim about mental structures; hence, the format is an empirical claim. Such claims about formats or about functional architectures become empirically decidable in principle, when the relevance of the criterion of strong equivalence is admitted and when appropriate methodologies based on this criterion are developed.

It is important to recognize that the greater the number of formal properties built into a notation in advance, the weaker the notational system's expressive power (though the system may be more efficient for cases to which it is applicable). This follows from the possibility that the system may no longer be capable of expressing certain states of affairs that violate assumptions built into the notation. For example, if Euclidean assumptions are built into a notation, the notation cannot be used to describe non-Euclidean properties, just as the disjunctive normal form cannot be used to express "logics" in which de Morgan's principles do not hold; and so on. The corresponding point is equally true of computation: The greater the number of primitively fixed formal properties of the functional architecture the system is forced to use in specified circumstances (as opposed to being allowed to contruct new functions from a more primitive basis of elementary operations), the more constrained is the resulting computational system. One no longer has the option of constructing arbitrary functions as they are needed or changing them at will.[6] In choosing a notation or architecture, one makes a commitment concerning the functions that are the free parameters which can be tailored to fit specific situations and the functions that are fixed over a certain range of influences or that are primitive subfunctions shared by all processes in a certain class (for example, the class of "humanly accessible processes"). Weakness of expressive power of a notation, or restrictions on the availability of new, primitive computational functions is a virtue if our goal is providing an explanation. The more constrained a notation or architecture, the greater the explanatory power of the resulting models.

This is precisely the problem of reducing the degrees of freedom

---

6. Of course, if the architecture is universal in the sense of being formally equivalent to a universal Turing machine, adding new primitives will not lessen the architecture's computational power, no matter how constrained the new primitives. Its computational power would, however, be lessened if there were, in addition, certain specifiable circumstances in which the new primitives *had* to be used—the system being prohibited from using other primitive operations. In effect, this is being claimed when certain cognitive functions are hypothesized as being used in, say, reasoning by using mental imagery (see chapters 7 and 8). Even where the computational power remains universal, the existence of particular primitive operations in the functional architecture makes a difference, for instance, when our concern is with *strong equivalence* rather than merely with the sense of equivalence involved in "computational power" or the set of functions that can, in principle, be realized by a certain computational architecture.

available for fitting a model to observations. In the model, each function that can be attributed to the functional architecture rather than the flexibly alterable program attains the status of a constant instead of a free, empirical parameter. (I shall have more to say about this topic in chapter 5). Such attribution provides a principled rationale for why, on a given occasion, the model takes a particular form, as opposed to others which, logically, are possible. It is precisely the lack of this rationale that renders some computational models ad hoc. Therefore, a goal in developing explanatory cognitive models is to fix as many properties as possible by building them into the fixed, functional architecture. Opposing this goal, however, is the need to account for the remarkable flexibility of human cognition. In Chapter 7 we shall see that this characteristic of cognition provides the strongest reason for attributing much of the manifest behavior of human cognition to tacit knowledge of various kinds rather than to the sorts of fixed functional properties that frequently have been proposed.

Chapter 5
Constraining Functional Architecture

The [benefit] which rhyme has over blank verse . . . is, that it bounds
and circumscribes the fancy. For imagination in a poet is a faculty
so wild and lawless, that, like an high-ranging spaniel, it must
have clogs tied to it, lest it outrun the judgment.

John Dryden, dedication of *The Rival-Ladies*

The Level-of-Aggregation Problem

Given the central importance of functional architecture, the question
we need to ask next is, How can one empirically constrain the functional
architecture adopted in constructing models of cognitive processes? In
approaching this question I shall concentrate on a particular aspect of
the architecture, namely, the "level of aggregation" of its primitive
operations. Beyond the sketch presented in chapter 3, no other aspects
are discussed, such aspects as disciplining the control of processes (Is
it serial or parallel? What constraints exist on the availability of resources,
for example, workspace buffers? What initiates different processing?
What controls are there over their sequencing? How transparent and
modular are various aspects of the control structure?). Although those
issues are also crucial to cognitive modeling, there is much less to be
said about them at the moment, except that various alternatives are
under investigation in computer science.

The *level of aggregation* defining the strong equivalence of programs
in the Scott and Strachey sense already outlined was dictated by the
abstract semantic model, particularly, what were considered the significant functions performed in the virtual machine. In the case of
cognition, choosing the appropriate level of aggregation at which to
model the process is one of the most difficult problems confronting
theorists. Newell and Simon (1972) discuss this problem in relation to
a study of human problem-solving. Their goal here was to account for
the regularities in a problem-solving trace called a "problem behavior
graph" constructed from an analysis of a "thinking out loud" protocol

recorded from a subject. Specifically, the problem was to posit a set of operators that would account for the transitions among problem states or *states of knowledge* about the problem. Newell and Simon (1972, p. 186) cite several pitfalls accompanying a too global or too microscopic choice of operator. In the too-global case:

> It may be that the essential problem solving is done "inside" one or more of these [operators]. If this were so, the problem graph would have to be termed *superficial*, since, although a true enough description, it would not explicate the important processing steps. Note that the basic issue is not how much selection is performed within the components . . . but whether the selection requires problem solving: either search in another space, or some other as-yet-unspecified intellectual process.

In the too-microscopic case:

> It may be that the analysis has gone too far—is too *disaggregated. . . .* Excessive disaggregation would reveal itself in the capriciousness of various selections, viewed in terms of the local context, whenever the next action was in fact (but not explicitly) determined by the structure of the higher-level plan or method.

These cases are quoted because they suggest several issues that concern us in this book. First is the suggestion of an appropriate level at which the greatest regularity is to be found (see the beginning of chapter 1). Second, the claim is made that a too-fine-grained analysis loses regularities because the explanation (or determination) of each component is found at a higher level; or if, as in verbal protocols, the hierarchy itself is flattened (so that higher-and lower-level descriptors are mentioned in a linear narration), the determiner of a particular behavior may be far away in the linearized sequence. This case also poses the problem "we will be led to analyze in detail subprocesses that are not problematic for the subject, hence amount simply to doing what the task environment demands . . . " (p. 189). The notion that processes which are not difficult or problematical for the subject need not themselves be explicated in detail also appears in the quotation for the first case. With it is introduced my third and most important point. Newell and Simon claim that an elementary operation can be as selective or complex as is appropriate, providing it is not an instance of further problem-solving. This sounds like Dan Dennett's requirement (Dennett, 1971) that the work of each homunculus be done by "committees of stupider homunculi." It is stronger than that, however, for *any* problem-solving activity hidden in an operator—even if the problem is substantially easier than the original one—would lead to superficiality in the account (and perhaps to loss of systematicity). We want to encapsulate as a basic operation nothing which itself involves nontrivial processing and which thus, in turn, must be explained.

Exactly what kinds of processes qualify as primitive (hence, explanatory) operations is a question to which the remainder of this chapter is devoted. Clearly, the criterion of being an instance of problem-solving is insufficiently precise; at least, it provides no methodological criterion, unless we already know when problem-solving is occurring or unless we know in advance what are the basic operators or states of the "problem space." It is equally clear that a number of fundamental distinctions hinge on there being such criteria, among these the ability to distinguish between an ad hoc model (with numerous free, empirical parameters) and a principled model (in which independently motivated constraints are imposed to decrease the number of free parameters), between a computational or representation-governed process and a process whose operation can be explained physically, and between weak and strong equivalence. Thus it becomes crucial to make the criteria for primitiveness as precise and as principled as possible.

Several criteria have already been discussed in various contexts, particularly in chapter 4. One criterion might be that no cognitive operator is considered primitive unless it can be realized on a computer. Surely this criterion, or condition, is, in principle, necessary. As I have argued, mechanical realizability is the sine qua non of noncircular, mechanistic explanation. Without a demonstration of the constructibility of the behavior in question by a mechanistic process, we have not, as Dennett puts it, discharged all the homunculi and repaid our explanatory debt. Yet the condition clearly is not *sufficient*, since it relies on the realizability of the process on a functional architecture we have no reason to believe is the correct one, a functional architecture responsive primarily to commercial and technological considerations rather than empirical ones.[1]

---

1. This is somewhat of an oversimplification. Even in work apparently unmotivated by cognitive science concerns, several empirical constraints are implicit. For example, there are general constraints on the material realizability of certain complex, information-processing functions. While these constraints are not clearly understood, they appear to include the need for autonomous levels of organization. No complex information processor (especially no "universal" processor in the sense discussed in chapter 3) has yet been designed that does not have several distinct levels of organization, one of which is a "symbolic level" (for more on this claim see Newell, 1982), where tokens of physical properties of states function as codes for something else. Another way that empirical constraints are implicit even in work concerned purely with technical computer implementation problems, is that empirical facts about the structure of tasks, as well as human understanding of classes of tasks, is smuggled in whenever machines are designed to do "intelligent" things. I discuss this topic in some detail in Pylyshyn (1978a).

Unless the functional architecture has been independently constrained, the program or model cannot be viewed as strongly equivalent to the cognitive process.

Another criterion implicit in the discussion of informal examples in chapters 1 and 2 is that of capturing generalizations. One might want simply to maintain that the appropriate level of aggregation depends on how useful generalizations turn out to cluster. It might be that for a particular set of generalizations one would adopt a certain level of aggregation, whereas for another set, another level is more appropriate. This much is true: Behavior can and should be described over a variety of levels, each of which captures some generalizations. We cannot be content, however, merely to set our sights on what seems the most convenient level of abstraction available at the moment for dealing with each phenomenon—for several reasons, which arise primarily from our desire to achieve explanatory adequacy.

In cognitive science, as in all theory-motivated sciences, the goal is not merely to describe the regularities of behavior but to relate these regularities to causal mechanisms in an organism. Thus generalizations of such a nature that no one has any idea (however sketchy) how they can possibly be realized by some mechanism are interpreted as *descriptions* of phenomena, not *explanations*. Among the examples of such generalizations are those that seem to require nothing less than a full-blooded, intelligent homunculus inside the model to make it run (the old telephone-switchboard model comes to mind). Also included are generalizations stated over properties of the represented domain, with no indication of the functional (that is, symbol or physical-level) properties of the organism that can give rise to them (several examples are mentioned in chapter 8).

Once one accepts the need for an explanation that is couched at least partly in terms of properties of some mechanisms, the questions arise: Which principles or which aspects of the observed regularity can be attributed to intrinsic functional properties of these mechanisms? Which ones reflect the rules and representations symbolically encoded in the system? I have argued that these different aspects not only involve two fundamentally different forms of explanation, but the assumptions made about the available functional architecture severely constrain the algorithms that can be realized. Furthermore, as I have been at pains to point out, there is no neutral way to describe a cognitive process: every algorithm implicitly presumes some functional architecture. Thus, even though the primary concern is to express generalizations at various levels of the abstraction hierarchy, the need to relate these generalizations to an explanatory causal mechanism makes essential a principled way to choose an empirically constrained *basic level* that is realizable by the available functions of the architecture.

Some Methodological Proposals

How can we distinguish between regularities that are attributable to properties of the functional architecture and those that are attributable to the nature of the cognitive process and its representations? No "simple and sovereign" method is available that will ensure the correct, basic architectural functions have been hypothesized. Not only that, there are no necessary and sufficient conditions for a function qualifying as primitive. Primitiveness is a theory-relative notion. Although we have a sketch of the theory—or, more accurately, some metatheoretical conditions on a theory, together with a set of fundamental, empirical hypotheses—there is still plenty of room for maneuver. Twenty-five years ago many of the techniques (for example, "mental chronometry") for assessing strong equivalence were not available, or, rather, their use in this context was not understood. If, at that time, someone had undertaken to analyze the notion of strong equivalence, much of what we now believe is germane would not have been included. Similarly, it would be foolhardy today to lay down a set of necessary and sufficient conditions to be met by a strongly equivalent model (and, in particular, by the functional architecture). Nonetheless, I shall develop a few provisional ideas because they are already implicit in the work of information-processing psychologists (even if some might not agree with my way of putting it; compare Anderson, 1978; Wasserman and Kong, 1979), whereas others are simply entailed by the theoretical position outlined here.

As an example of the latter idea, recall that strong equivalence requires that a model be expressed at a level of aggregation such that all basic representational states are revealed, since each of these states is essential in the representational story; that is, each cognitive state plays a role in the explanation of behavioral regularities. Thus the transition from one representational state to another must itself involve no representational states; it must be instantiated in the functional architecture. Hence, any evidence of the existence of such intermediate representational states is evidence of the nonprimitiveness of the subprocess in question. Various methods for obtaining such evidence are available. One of the earliest methods for discovering intermediate states in problem-solving involves recording subjects' expressed thoughts while solving the problem (Duncker, 1935). Newell and Simon (1972) developed this technique, which they call "protocol analysis," to a high level of precision (parts of it have been automated in a system called PAS-II; Waterman and Newell, 1971). Although the method can be used only with certain slow, deliberate types of problem-solving tasks (including problems involving visual imagery; see, for example, Baylor, 1972; Farley, 1974; Moran, 1973), it provides evidence of intermediate states that otherwise might not be available for constraining the model. When combined with additional, intermediate observations—for example, protocols of hand movements obtained from video recordings (Young, 1973) and records of eye movements (Just and Carpenter, 1976)—the method can yield extremely useful data.

Possession of intermediate representational states is sufficient reason for the operation not being a primitive one. Protocol analysis has the usual caveat about methodology: Subjects cannot be relied on to provide evidence of only authentic intermediate states; they may provide retrospective rationalizations as well. Furthermore, subjects are highly prone to miss some states; thus the protocol's failure to indicate intermediate states in a certain subprocess is insufficient evidence that such a subprocess is primitive. In the quotation near the beginning of this chapter, Newell and Simon indicate the general strategy for inferring the best set of operations from a summary of the protocol, called the "problem behavior graph". This strategy consists of searching for the smallest set of hypothetical operators to account for the largest number of transitions in the problem-behavior graph.

The existence of intermediate representational states sometimes can be inferred in more indirect ways. A good example occurs in psycholinguistics, in the study of real-time sentence processing. Some indirect evidence exists of certain components of syntactic analysis becoming available during sentence comprehension (Frazier and Fodor, 1978; Marslen-Wilson and Tyler, 1980; Forster, 1979). Any evidence of the availability of intermediate states of a process to any other process (that is, evidence that the workings of the process are "transparent" to another part of the system) can be taken as evidence that such a process is not primitive but has a further cognitive decomposition.

Occasionally the argument that an operation is not primitive must be extremely indirect, because intermediate states are not observable and other relatively direct methods (to be discussed next) are not applicable. In such cases we can resort to the oldest, most venerable method of all: the hypothetico-deductive strategy. If hypothesizing a particular theoretical construct allows us to account for a greater range of phenomena, with fewer assumptions than some other alternative, then we can conclude—always provisionally—that the hypothesis is true. Thus some interesting work has been done that establishes elaborate, detailed models of apparently simple processes such as subtraction without using protocols, reaction time, or many other more common measures of strong equivalence. One example is the BUGGY model described by Brown and Burton (1978), and Brown and Van Lehn (1980), and further developed by Young and O'Shea (1981). This and similar research is based entirely on observation of errors children make in doing arithmetic problems, primarily subtraction. In a task that might otherwise appear quite straightforward, these authors have found it necessary to postulate a large number of extremely detailed subprocesses and rules in order to account in a systematic way for what might otherwise appear to be a random scatter of "silly mistakes" children make. Thus, such an indirect analysis, which involves a much longer deductive chain than other methods, provides evidence of more elementary operations than might otherwise have been hypothesized, as well as providing evidence of the role of various individual rules in explaining regularities in the process.

The preceding brief discussion should serve as a reminder that our ability to discern whether a certain process goes through intermediate representational states is limited only by the theorist's imagination. Whereas there are a number of techniques that, when properly used and independently verified, are sufficient to demonstrate that a process is not primitive but instead involves more microscopic *cognitive* steps, the ability to demonstrate that even smaller steps exist is largely a matter of being clever.

In the remainder of this chapter we consider two empirically based criteria for deciding whether certain aspects of behavioral regularities should be attributed to properties of mechanisms—that is, to the functional architecture—or to the representations and processes operating on them. As I have already suggested, both criteria ideally can tell us when a function requires a more complex cognitive analysis, though they cannot tell us that we have gone far enough, since, as was pointed out, there may be various sources of indirect evidence of the need for further decomposition. The first criterion derived from computational considerations, defines a notion of strong equivalence of processes which I refer to as *complexity equivalence*. This notion of equivalence—while it appears to be similar, though perhaps somewhat weaker, than the intuitive notion of the "same algorithm"—has the advantage of being related to a set of empirical indicators that have been widely investigated in recent cognitive-psychology studies, for example, reaction time and attention-demand measures.

The second criterion is more subtle. It assumes that what I have been calling cognitive phenomena are a "natural kind" explainable entirely

in terms of the nature of the representations and the structure of programs running on the cognitive functional architecture, a claim we have
already considered informally. If that assumption is found to be true,
then the functional architecture itself must not vary in ways that demand
a *cognitive* explanation. In other words, the architecture must form a
cognitive "fixed point" so that differences in cognitive phenomena can
be explained by appeal to arrangements (sequences of expressions and
basic operations) among the fixed set of operations and to the basic
resources provided by the architecture. Although the architecture might
vary as a function of physical or biochemical conditions, it should not
vary directly or in logically coherent or rule-governed ways with changes
in the content of the organism's goals and beliefs. If the functional
architecture were to change in ways requiring a cognitive rule-governed
explanation, the architecture could no longer serve as the basis for
explaining how changes in rules and representations produce changes
in behavior. Consequently, the input-output behavior of the hypothesized, primitive operations of the functional architecture must not
depend in certain, specific ways on goals and beliefs, hence, on conditions which, there is independent reason to think, change the organism's goals and beliefs; the behavior must be what I refer to as
cognitively impenetrable.

Both criteria are developed in the following sections of this chapter.
It should be pointed out, however, that there is no way to guarantee
in advance that both criteria pick out the *same* level of functional architecture. In fact, it is an interesting empirical question whether they
do this. Since we are interested in the strongest possible sense of the
psychological reality of programs—hence, of the strong equivalence of
processes—we should screen our models by all available criteria, together with such general scientific principles as maximizing the range
of generalizations that can be captured by the theory.

Complexity Equivalence

In discussing the dependence of possible algorithms on the functional
architecture of the underlying virtual machine, I have presented some
examples of algorithms I claim cannot be executed directly on certain
types of architectures. For example, I claim that such algorithms as the
hash-coding table lookup algorithm, which relies on the primitive capacity of the underlying architecture to retrieve a symbol when given
another symbol (called its "name" or "address"), cannot be executed
on a primitive machine of the type originally described by Turing (1937),
that is, a machine that stores symbols as a linear string on a tape.
Similarly, I claim that a register machine that can retrieve symbols by

name cannot execute a binary-search algorithm of the kind involved in playing "Twenty Questions" unless it has a way to primitively determine something like an interval measure over the set of names, as would be the case if the names were numerals and the functional architecture contained primitive operations corresponding to the operations of arithmetic.

If we know the architecture—that is, if we are given the set of primitive functions—we can determine whether a particular algorithm can be made to run on it *directly*. For an algorithm to run directly on a certain architecture, the architecture must contain primitive operations whose behavior is formally isomorphic to each elementary step required by the algorithm. In other words, for each elementary operation in the algorithm there must already exist some operation in the functional architecture whose input-output behavior is isomorphic to it. If, to get the algorithm to execute, we must first mimic the input-output behavior of each elementary step in the algorithm, using a combination of different, available operations, we would not say the algorithm is executed *directly* by the available operations, that is, by that virtual machine. We would say that it is the emulated functional architecture rather than the originally available one that directly executes the algorithm in question. The reason I insist on examining the direct execution of algorithms by the relevant functional architecture is that the whole point of specifying a functional architecture is, the architecture is supposed to pick out the correct level of aggregation for the purpose of defining the notion of *same algorithm*, hence, of defining the strong equivalence of programs.

My goal in this section is to work toward a notion of strong equivalence that will serve as a methodological tool for deciding whether a proposed mental function is at the correct level of aggregation, so the program can be viewed as an explanatory model. I shall do this in two stages. In the first stage I suggest a number of properties that are shared by distinct realizations of what intuitively would seem to be instances of the same algorithm. Based on the preceding discussion, it then appears that such properties probably are not preserved if the algorithm's input-output behavior is simulated on the "wrong" functional architecture—even if that is done by emulating each step of the algorithm. On the other hand, these properties should allow for quite different implementations of the same algorithm, so long as the differences are ones that seem inessential to the algorithm's identity. Since, as I have indicated, there is no well-developed theory of algorithmic equivalence in computer science, these ideas must be developed without benefit of an existing body of analysis.

In the second stage I discuss some additional assumptions needed to make these general properties or conditions serve as methodological tools. As an example of the property I have in mind, recall that I have already suggested at least one property of the hash-coding algorithm that must be preserved by any strongly equivalent process, which would not be preserved if the same function were realized on a traditional Turing machine. That property is the relation between (or the form of the function that *characterizes* the relation between) the number of steps it would take to look up a symbol in a table and the total number of symbols stored there. The hash-coding algorithm, implemented on a machine with a primitive facility to retrieve symbols by name (commonly referred to as a random-access or register architecture), can look up symbols with a number of steps that, to a first approximation, is independent of the number of entries in the table. By contrast, if this algorithm were emulated on a Turing machine, the number of steps required would increase as the square of the number of strings stored on the tape (so that the function relating the number of steps and the number of items stored would be a polynomial of order 2). Whereas the exact number of steps required depends on what one decides in advance to count as individual steps, the shape (or order) of the function relating the number of such steps to the number of entries in the table (subject to a qualification concerning what is allowed to count as a single step) does not.

The relation between the number of primitive steps taken and certain properties of the symbolic input (where, in the example above, the entire stored table counts as an input) is generally considered an essential invariant property of what one intuitively regards as different realizations of the same algorithm. For example, clearly we would not count two processes as realizing the same algorithm if one of them computes a function in some fixed time, regardless of its input, whereas the other is combinatorially explosive, so that the time it requires increases without bound as some property of the input (for example, length) is varied. The total time or total number of steps taken is not important in assessing the equivalence of algorithms, since these depend on the particular machine the algorithm is running on. What is important is the nature of the relation between such aspects as time or number of steps taken, and properties of the input, such as its length. Thus, certain differences among programs do not matter for purposes of what I call their *complexity equivalence*. For example, two different programs are viewed as instantiating complexity-equivalent (CE) algorithms if there exists a certain kind of topological relation between them. If every linear series of nonbranching operations in a program can be mapped into a single operation with the same input-output function in the second program, then the programs are complexity equivalent. The second program thus has more powerful primitive operations; but the operations lead to the same complexity profiles, to the same systematic variation in the number of steps or the time taken as the input is varied, *provided only that the number of steps or time taken by each operation is independent of the inputs.* If this provision is the case, then the two programs are indiscernible from the viewpoint of the complexity-profile criterion. Thus, if a program contains the sequence of operations illustrated in figure 1a, it counts as complexity equivalent to a part of another program with only one operation, O_1', which computes the same input-output function.

In this example I am speaking of the length of time or number of steps as a measure of relative execution complexity. A more general notion is one of "amount of resources used," the general idea of computational resources being that of some independently measurable index of the amount of processing being done. In the case of computers, the notion includes the number of basic machine cycles, length of time, amount of memory used, and so on. There are several reasons for considering *amount of resources used* an index of computational complexity. First, in the computer case, it comports well with intuitions concerning *how much computation* a process does. Furthermore, some interesting results have been achieved in computer science, using "time complexity" and "space complexity" (that is, the amount of memory used for intermediate results), though these have been too coarse-grained for distinguishing the kinds of differences we are interested in when we speak of strong equivalence. Second, as we shall see, there is some hope of finding empirical measures of on-line resource use in human cognitive processing, hence, of using these ideas in the empirical enterprise.

Figure 1b, in contrast, illustrates the case of a program *not* considered complexity equivalent to a program with only one operation that computes the same input-output function In the figure, the diamond-shaped box indicates a branch operation. The loop back to the previous operation, O_1, is taken whenever P(n), which is a predicate of, say, the length of input x, evaluates to "true". The reason this program segment does not count as equivalent to the one-operation subprogram O_1', *even if O_1' had the same input-output function as the segment above,* is that the number of O_1 steps it takes in the above program would be a function of n, whereas the corresponding O_1' has complexity independent of n. Thus any function that can be represented nontrivially with the same flowchart topology as the above segment does not qualify as a computational primitive. Similarly, a subprocess called recursively (for example, on the PUSH arcs of an augmented recursive transition network, or ATN, parser) does not qualify as a primitive operation,

118   Chapter 5

(a)

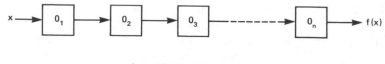

is complexity - equivalent to

(b)

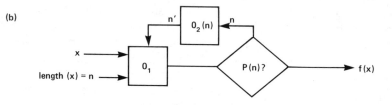

is not complexity - equivalent to

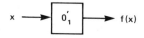

Figure 1. Graphical illustration of equivalent and nonequivalent program segments, using the *complexity-equivalence* criterion.

since its resource use, measured in terms of both time and memory, vary with input. Such formal methods as the graph-minimization methods described by Fosdick and Osterweil (1976) are available for deriving something like a canonical flowchart representation of an algorithm based on topological properties of flowcharts. Indeed, complexity equivalence can be viewed as a special topological relation between two flowcharts, in which the nodes in the flowchart are restricted to those that correspond to fixed-resource processes.

The set of programs that are equivalent, with respect to the way their resource use varies with properties of their input, clearly represents a refinement of the class of programs that compute the same input-output function, and hence, a restriction of the weak-equivalence relation. Although complexity equivalence captures an important aspect of the intuitive notion of *same algorithm*, it alone is not sufficient to define strong equivalence. In other words, it is a necessary but not sufficient condition for strong equivalence. It may not even be strong enough to correspond precisely to the intuitive notion of algorithmic equivalence, for reasons that will soon become clear.

Although the study of computational complexity is an active area in computer science, interest has been confined to study of the way in which the need for such resources as amount of memory and number of steps varies systematically with certain, special properties of the input. For example, the efficiency of sorting algorithms (which in some way order a set of symbolic expressions) is often expressed in terms of the order of the polynomial function that, under worst-case conditions, relates the number of items to be sorted to the maximum number of elementary steps required. There are, however, numerous, different algorithms that can sort n items using a number of elementary steps proportional to $n\log n$. Whereas all such algorithms are equivalent from the point of view of their *time complexity*, they are not complexity equivalent in our sense, because their resource use varies in different ways with change in *other* properties of the input—for example, with the degree of dispersion (along the ordering dimension) of the elements of the set being sorted or even with the addition of certain items to the list being sorted. From the viewpoint of the particular complexity-equivalence relation we are interested in, we can examine the function relating *any* resource-use parameter to *any* property of the input symbols, down to the properties of individual symbols. If two algorithms yield a different resource-use function for any pair of inputs (for example, if they have an interactive effect on a resource-use index), then the two algorithms do not count as equivalent.

Note that at least one pair of inputs is required, since the absolute resource usage means nothing in the case where different machines are involved; we can assess resource use meaningfully only up to a linear transform. Another way of stating this is to recall that collapsing over arbitrarily complex but constant-complexity operations is permitted; thus comparisons can be made only for the form—and, particularly, the polynomial order—of the complexity function.

Because there has been little study of such fine-grained notions of complexity equivalence in computer science, the precise equivalence class thus picked out is not known in detail. We can see already, however, that this criterion is much stronger than the one captured by such notions as the time complexity of algorithms already discussed. For example, both *merge-* and *insertion*-sorting algorithms have time complexity of the order of $n\log n$; yet the number of steps required for a merge algorithm to sort an item is independent of the exact interval value (on the scale along which the elements are ordered) of the element being sorted, whereas the complexity of insertion algorithms depends on the interval values of the elements. Conversely, our strong complexity-equivalence criterion distinguishes between two cases of a linear-search algorithm that differs only in the order in which the two linear-search algorithms scan a list, whereas many theorists count these as instances of the same algorithm (thus treating the order of the stored list as a nonessential property that can vary with different implementations of what would otherwise count as the same algorithm).

The notion of complexity equivalence is important in cognitive science. Whether it corresponds exactly to the intuitive notion of *same algorithm* is of relatively minor concern; what is important is that the notion provides a way to approach the relation of strong equivalence of programs in terms of functions from properties of inputs to a certain, uniform, aggregate property of the process (which, I argue, we stand a chance of being able to measure empirically). Note that, in this form, the relation of strong equivalence is expressed without the requirement that we know in advance what the functional architecture is. From our point of view, this is exactly the right direction to take, for eventually we want to determine the functional architecture from observed behavior. Thus the next question to ask is: In view of this discussion of complexity equivalence, is there any conceivable, observable behavior that can help fix the functional architecture, and hence, establish strong equivalence?

Strong-Equivalence and Reaction-Time Measures
In this section we need to make a short digression, approaching this question by way of dealing with a frequently heard lament that strong equivalence is, in principle, not possible in psychology, or that it can be achieved only by appealing to the facts of biology or by the gratuitous

importation of esthetic or other forms of subjective judgment. The lament might begin with a remark such as: Because weak equivalence is, by definition, equivalence with respect to input-output behavior, and because all we have to go by in psychology (if we exclude physiological psychology) is observed behavior, it must be the case that, leaving aside neurophysiological data, the best we can do is construct a model that accounts for the behavior, hence, that is weakly equivalent to the real mental, or brain, process. After all, how could we ever tell whether our model reflects the "true" process at a finer grain of detail than is exhibited as a difference in overt behavior? Because our notion of strong equivalence explicitly sets out to define a level of correspondence more refined than what appears to be behavioral equivalence, this objection merits discussion, especially in view of the widespread acceptance of the view that there is an inherent indeterminacy of information-processing theories arising from their commitment to behavioral data alone, hence, according to this view, to a weak-equivalence criterion (see, for example, the claims in Anderson, 1978; Townsend, 1974).

The apparent paradox of the behavioral indeterminacy of information-processing models has led to responses from various schools of theoretical psychology. Behaviorists frequently advert to this point in justifying their empty-organism view. If all we have to go by in building *functional* theories of behavior is a record of observations of behavioral movements, together with the environmental contingencies of their occurrence, how can we distinguish among behaviorally equivalent theories except in terms of preconceived, mentalistic ideas? In the case of information-processing theories, Anderson (1978) has developed this conundrum into an "indeterminacy of representation" thesis. The claim of this thesis is that, as long as we attend only to behavior we cannot, *in principle*, tell which of two behaviorally equivalent models (which might differ, for example, in the form of representation they use) is the correct one.

Before looking into these claims in detail, we should note that, as far as this thesis is concerned, there is nothing special about psychology. It can be argued with equal validity that all we have in *any* science is behavior of one kind or another; yet no one has ever suggested that physical theorizing is, in principle, indeterminate, that we cannot, in principle, discover, for instance, the earth's true shape. After all, it *could* be argued that the earth actually is flat and that the physical laws we have discovered are incorrect. In principle, one could have an entirely different set of laws that are compatible with every empirical observation made up to this time, together with the assumption that the earth is flat. Indeed, an unlimited number of models are compatible with any finite set of observations; that is why we have the well-known problem of explaining how induction works. On the face of it, though, the claim is absurd. It is absurd because merely matching a body of observations is not the goal of science; the purpose of theories is to cast light on what seems like chaos by finding the most general and revealing, *lawlike generalizations* that lie behind the observations. To be explanatory, a theory cannot have as many free parameters as there are data points. Put another way, we would not be content with a theory that must be changed each time a new observation is made even if, at any given time, the theory accounts for all available observations (that is why the *pre* appears in the word *prediction*).

The requirement of explanatory adequacy—that theories should capture the most general and revealing, lawlike (counterfactual supporting) generalizations—is itself enough to ensure that the criterion of matching a set of behaviors does not allow proliferation of weakly equivalent theories, among which science should be indifferent. There is a more specific way to approach the indeterminacy thesis in information-processing theories. I have argued (Pylyshyn, 1979c) that the answer to the sort of counsel of indifference one finds in Anderson (1978) and elsewhere is this: While, in a sense, all we have is behavior, not all behavior is of the same kind, from the point of view of theory construction. By imposing an independently motivated partition on a set of behaviors, and by interpreting the partitioned behaviors in different ways, we can do much better than weak equivalence.

As an example, consider modern linguistics. It is true that all we have are the linguistic utterances of speakers. It does not follow, however, that the best we can do is analyze a corpus of utterances and, perhaps, develop a taxonomy and tables of co-occurrence relations. Even within the narrow goal of describing the syntactic structure of a language (as opposed to, say, explaining when and why certain utterances occur in relation to other factors), we can do much better— as Chomsky showed in the early 1950s (see, for example, an early monograph reprinted as Chomsky, 1975). To do that, we must distinguish two classes of utterances (ignoring, for now, the question of developing appropriate idealizations rather than taking actual observed behavior). The utterances in one class are those sentences whose structure we wish to describe. Together with their structural descriptions, they constitute the output of our grammatical theory.

The utterances in the other class, by contrast, are *judgments*; they are not part of the output of any theory. Rather, they are interpreted as judgments reflecting the speaker's perception, or tacit knowledge, of the structure of sentences in the first class. In other words, it is the semantic content of the latter group of sentences, or what they *assert*, that matters. In contrast with the primary data sentences, these sentences are taken as asserting something the theorist chooses to believe or not to believe, depending on the theorist's methodological bent. The sentences provide secondary data of a metalinguistic sort (in the sense of their not being among the outputs of the model, not in the sense of their being less important), from which the theorist typically infers the structural properties of the primary data sentences.

A parallel distinction is made in experimental cognitive psychology. Here, the investigator collects primary observations in a certain domain—say, those concerning the behavior of a person solving a problem. These are observations which a constructive theory of the domain might be expected to generate as output. In addition, the investigator typically collects secondary observations, or what might, without overly distorting the terminology, be called metabehavioral observations, from which certain properties of the intervening process are inferred. Sometimes such observations are taken to be truth-valuable assertions, or judgments about the primary behavior, similar to the linguistics case. This is the case, for example, when subjects provide "thinking-out-loud protocols" of the kind studied extensively by Newell and Simon (1972). At other times, such secondary observations are interpreted as *indices* of, for example, processing complexity or what I have referred to as "resource use." In this case, it is not expected that a theory or a model actually generate such behavior as part of its output. Rather, the model should generate the primary (output) behavior in a manner that reflects certain real-time processing properties assumed to be indexed by observations in the secondary class.

Consider the following example in which the developing methodology of cognitive science has led to a gradual shift in the way an important aspect of observed behavior is interpreted. The example involves what may be the most widely used dependent measure in cognitive psychology: reaction time. On occasion this measure has been interpreted as merely another response to be accounted for by a cognitive model just as the model accounts for such response properties as the record of buttons pressed. Since Donders' pioneering work (in the 1860s; reprinted as Donders, 1969), the measure has been widely interpreted as a more or less direct measure of the duration of mental processes (Wasserman and Kong, 1979). In commenting on the Wasserman and Kong paper, I argue (Pylyshyn 1979a) that neither interpretation essentially is correct, that, in general, reaction time can be viewed as neither the computed output of a cognitive process itself nor a measure of the duration of a mental-event type.

If reaction time were viewed as simply another response, it would be sufficient for our computational model to calculate a predicted value for this reaction time, given the appropriate input. That would not be sufficient, however, if the computation is viewed as modeling the cognitive *process*. Contemporary cognitive theorists would not view a system that generated pairs of outputs, interpreted as the response and the time taken, as an adequate model of the underlying process, no matter how well these outputs fit the observed data. Instead, they wish to interpret the model as computing the output *in the same way* as the subject that is, by using the same algorithm.

It has become customary in cognitive science to view reaction time in the same way that measures such as galvanic skin response, or plethysmograph records, and distractibility (as measured, say, by Brown, 1962) are viewed, as an *index* or an observable correlate of some aggregate property of the process. Frequently, reaction time is viewed as an index of what I call "computational complexity", usually considered as corresponding to such properties of the model as the number of operations performed. A process that merely computes time as a parameter value does not account for reaction time viewed in this particular way, since the parameter does not express the process's computational complexity.

This view of the role of reaction-time measures takes it for granted that such measures are not interpreted as a direct observation of the duration of a certain mental type. True, reaction time may be a measure of the duration of a particular episode of some mental event; to interpret it as the duration of a mental-event type, however, is to assume that, in other circumstances (on another occasion, in another subject, in another part of the brain), the same event type would always require the same length of time. If we were considering a type of physical event, we would know that if something which counts as the identical physical event occurred on a different occasion, it would indeed require the same length of time—because taking a particular length of time is part of being a particular physical event; that is, it is an intrinsic property of a physical event (something that took a different length of time is, by definition, a different physical event). It is helpful to remind ourselves that a mental process does not possess the intrinsic physical property of duration any more than it possesses the property of location, size, mass, electrical resistance, or concentration of sodium ions. Since this statement often causes eyebrows to be raised, it might be useful to pause and consider why that must be true, as well as why we find it so natural to ascribe duration to mental events even when we are not similarly tempted to ascribe volume or some other physical property to them.

The distinction that must be kept in mind is the one I devote considerable attention to in chapter 1, namely, that between types and tokens of events. Every mental-event type (for example, thinking that $2 + 3 = 5$) is realized by a corresponding, token brain event, or so goes the "supervenient," or conservative, version of the materialist story. Naturally, this token brain event has various physical properties, including mass, volume, temperature, and duration. As I have argued though, there is no a priori reason for assuming that the entire class of brain events that could ever conceivably constitute the same mental event (identified by whatever criteria for sameness of mental-event type we are disposed to adopt—for example, functional or semantic) has any physical property in common. Clearly, in a machine, all tokens of the same computational event type (such as adding two numbers) need have no common physical property—at least, not in the ordinary sense of physical property, such as those found in physics texts. Thus there is no reason to assume, a priori, that all instances of brain events corresponding to a certain cognitive event have certain physical properties in common. We would certainly not expect all brain events corresponding to thinking $2 + 3 = 5$ to have a common temperature or volume.

It does not seem at all implausible, however, that every occurrence of a brain event corresponding to certain elementary cognitive operations might turn out to require the same length of time, to a first approximation. If that contingent empirical fact turns out to be true, then we will have discovered an important feature of the cognitive system, in which case we could make important inferences from measurements of the duration of token brain events. Strictly speaking, we would still not be measuring the duration of the mental event—that is, of an independently defined class of biological events—only a property of a brain event we have discovered to be invariant over the class. In other words, we would be measuring an empirically valid physical correlate of the mental event.

Although the use of reaction time and other, similar measures is crucial in the empirical assessment of complexity equivalence, it is equally important to understand the way in which these measures serve this methodological goal. Let us suppose we have an observation (for example, duration) of a property of the algorithm's physical instantiation. I have already argued that this observation cannot be interpreted as the direct measurement of a property of some mental or computational event. Nonetheless, the question remains: Under what conditions can such observations provide evidence in favor of one proposed algorithm over another?

We have already considered several cases in which it is possible to decide which of two radically different algorithms is executed by examining the relative number of primitive steps (or single operations in the functional architecture) they took when given different inputs. Now, if we have some reason to believe that the amount of real time required is proportional to, or at least is a monotonically increasing function of, the number of such primitive steps of the algorithm, then measures of relative time taken might provide the evidence needed for deciding between the putative algorithms. In this case, however, we need an independent reason for believing that reaction time is a valid index of an algorithmic property—namely, the number of primitive steps in the functional architecture. Such independent reasons as these frequently are available, for example, when regularities inferred on the basis of the assumption that reaction time is a reliable indicator of processing complexity are corroborated by other methods. When such patterns of consistency keep showing up under converging methodologies, we have a prima facie reason for expecting the methods to be valid, all else being equal (for examples of much convergence, see Posner, 1978).

Nonetheless, it should be kept in mind that inferences drawn about the nature of the algorithm from reaction-time data (or any other *physical* measurement) always depend on the validity of an ancillary hypothesis. Such a hypothesis could, in principle, be false. There are many situations in which measurements of properties of the underlying physical events tell us little about an algorithm. Instead, they might tell us (1) about the way a process is physically (that is, neurophysiologically) instantiated on some occasion, in some individual, or (2) about subjects' tacit knowledge, or about the nature of the task itself. Here, I digress briefly and consider these two cases, since they reveal an important, general point concerning the relationship among cognitive phenomena, the task being carried out, the method a person uses, the fixed, functional properties (or functional architecture) of the cognitive system, and the biological or physical properties of a particular, token instantiation of the solution process.

The possibility that such measurements as reaction time tell us little about the underlying biological mechanism is of special concern in "higher-level cognitive functions," where processing is not tied as closely to anatomical structures as it is, say, in certain areas of perception or motor coordination. In such cases, we are not as likely to find physical properties that are invariant over all instances, or token occasions, of cognitive events. Whereas, often there is a correlation between the duration of an observable physical event and such purely algorithmic properties as the number of steps taken, the particular steps taken, whether parts of the algorithm are performed serially or in parallel, and so on, that is not always the case. There are certainly cases in which time differences arise from properties of the physical realization that are unique to the particular occasion or instantiation (for example, a particular individual) and therefore are, in general, irrelevant to the algorithmic, or process, explanation. Such duration data may not validly discriminate among putative algorithms.

Using a computer as an example, we can see that some time differences might arise because a signal has farther to travel on a particular (or token) occasion because of the way the machine is wired or the way the algorithm is implemented in it, or that some differences might arise from variable-delay effects unique to specific occasions. An example of the latter case is the delays caused by the distance a movable arm must travel in making a disk access in some implementation and on certain occasions, unrelated to the content of the memory or the algorithm used. Other delays may depend on physical properties of the noncomputational environment, as would be the case if real-time interrupts were to occur. None of these observations bears on the nature of the algorithm, since they could differ considerably on another occasion or for a different realization of the same algorithm. Consequently, in this case, measuring the times involved does not help us distinguish different candidate algorithms. That is why, in the computer case, time measurement alone cannot be taken as measurement of a property of the algorithmic process. For precisely the same reasons, time measurement cannot be taken literally as a measurement of mental duration—only as indirect (and, possibly, false) indicators of such things as processing complexity, to be used judiciously with other indirect sources of evidence in inferring underlying mental processes.

The other case in which observations may tell us little about the cognitive process itself arises when the primary determinant of the behavior in question is what Newell and Simon (1972) call the "task demands". Consider the various observations associated with certain operations on mental images. Many such investigations (for example, Shepard and Feng, 1972; Kosslyn, 1980) have measured the time it takes to imagine a certain mental action, for instance, mentally folding a piece of paper according to certain instructions, or scanning your attention between two points on a mental image. What these experiments consistently fail to do is distinguish between two different tasks demanded by the same general instructions to a subject. The first task is simply to use a certain form of representation to solve the problem; the second is to imagine *actually seeing* certain problem-solving events take place. In the latter case, we would, of course, expect the subject to attempt to duplicate—while imaging—various incidental properties of the events they believe would occur if they were to watch the corresponding, real events unfold, for example, the order and duration of particular component events. If the second task is the one subjects are performing, the fact that certain temporal patterns are obtained tells us nothing about the process used, only that the subjects can generate actual time intervals corresponding to those they believe would have occurred if the event had actually taken place. I have argued that this, in fact, is the task being performed by subjects in many such experiments. These and similar examples are discussed in chapter 8.

One more point needs to be made about reaction-time measures before we turn to the second major methodological principle. Whatever the human, functional architecture turns out to be, clearly it is capable of carrying out Turing-machine computations within the limits of its resources (limits which, in fact, humans can increase artificially by getting a piece of paper or writing a program for another machine). Like the universal Turing machine, not only can a person carry out any computable function, that person can *emulate* any conceivable functional architecture, perhaps to the extent of generating the appropriate time intervals or latencies (all the person would have to do is simulate the other functional architecture and, in doing so, arrange to take a constant length of time for each primitive operation of the functional architecture being emulated). If that is the case, though, how can we know that when we do experiments using reaction time as our dependent measure, we are not, in fact, getting measures of an emulated functional architecture? If we *were* getting such measures, the point of the reaction-time measurements would be destroyed, since we would be learning nothing about the person's native, or biologically endowed, capacities.

The reply to this concern is the same as that to most other such concerns: All methodologies are based on assumptions. The proof of the correctness of these assumptions is the continued success of the methods in revealing interesting, general properties of the system under study. Many assumptions underly the use of reaction-time measures in cognitive psychology. One is the assumption that in the range of times where many of the reaction-time regularities appear (on the order of 20 to 100 milliseconds per operation), only the operation of the primitive level of the functional architecture is being tapped. Even the highly complex operations involved in grammatical analyses of sentences appear to take place in time spans less than the duration of a syllable (a few hundred milliseconds). Much longer mental operation times have been observed under certain conditions (for example, the time required to generate a mental image appears to be more than 1 second). In these cases one must be wary of the possibility that more complex cognitive processes may be occurring. Even here, though, we *may* have reason to believe that primitive operations are being observed, only that they are slower operations. In other cases one may have good reason to think an operation one is measuring is not primitive but that the conditions have been set up so the variation in reaction times occurs primarily from the iteration of primitive operations. This assumption is made in explaining the results of the Sternberg short-term memory-scanning experiment (Sternberg, 1966).

On the other hand, an example of a widely used measure which theorists have begun to suspect is actually tapping a more complex decision process is the "lexical decision task" used to study access to the mental lexicon in such performances as reading (West and Stanovich, 1982). The lexical decision task requires subjects merely to state whether a designated string of characters is a word. Because of its sensitivity to various interesting manipulations (for example, it is shortened significantly by priming the subject with a semantically related word), this task has been studied extensively. Although reading time for words is only a few hundred milliseconds, lexical decision time is considerably longer. Thus the task may involve a complex decision (such as double-checking). In that case, it may be the decision component that accounts for the way reaction time varies with such things as the semantic similarity of the target item. This is a case where length of reaction time alerts investigators to the possibility that they are studying a complex composite process.

Then there is the converse concern. The question sometimes arises whether it is possible, with practice, for an operation that was once slow and complex to become a fast, primitive operation. It is certainly a well-known phenomenon that with a great deal of practice, a process that was once a deliberate and slow sequence of operations becomes automatic and very fast. Nothing in what I have said so far prevents the creation of new, primitive operations (analogous to running part of a program through an "optimizing compiler," creating an efficient subroutine). As we see in the next section, primitive functions of the functional architecture *can* change. They cannot change in certain ways, however; to do so would violate basic constraints on the functional architecture without which the notion of functional architecture, as a theoretical construct, is powerless to explain the cause of certain generalization in behavior. Whereas the functional architecture might change in systematic ways in response to biological, physical, or chemical causes, and perhaps to repetition, it must not change the way behavior changes when people find out new things and acquire new beliefs and goals. Those are precisely the regularities the cognitive process, realized by the symbol-processing facilities of the functional architecture, is meant to explain. Hence, those changes must not be internal to the functional architecture. All kinds of other causes of change can occur, however, and can alter the functions instantiated in the functional architecture. Presumably, that is what happens when infants mature and people become ill or depressed or, perhaps, when performance changes in response to prolonged, repetitive practice (see chapter 9).

To conclude this section, it should be noted that despite the caveats concerning the fallibility of using such indices as reaction time, these measures have been instrumental in allowing psychologists to begin taking seriously the notion of strong equivalence. To the extent that the methodology for determining strong equivalence stands up to repeated scrutiny and continues to yield new insights concerning the structure of cognitive processes, the skeptics' claim of indeterminacy will be just as empty in psychology as it would be in any other science.

Cognitive Penetrability

The second criterion for determining the appropriate level of aggregation is in many ways the more fundamental one. It relies on the distinction, already discussed, between phenomena that can be explained functionally and those that must be explained by appeal to semantically interpreted representations. The second criterion I will propose consists of little more than an application of this distinction to individual subfunctions of the model. What makes the difference between phenomena explainable functionally and those explainable in terms of rules and representations is exactly what makes the difference between subfunctions that must be further analyzed in terms of a cognitive process and those whose operation can be attributed to the functional architecture of the underlying virtual machine. Thus, *whatever* the reasons for deciding to give a cognitive, or representational, explanation for some phenomena, these reasons should apply, mutatis mutandis, in deciding whether also to give any hypothesized subfunction in the analysis a similar cognitive explanation, as opposed to assuming that it is an instantiated function of the architecture.

The need to distinguish between regularities that can be explained by appeal to intrinsic biological and physical properties of a system and those requiring appeal to what the system represents (its beliefs and goals) is a central concern of this book. Paralleling this distinction is the closely related distinction between processes governed by semantic principles (which I call "cognitive processes") and those realized in what I call the "functional architecture" of the system, the latter being a term borrowed from computer science, where it is used to refer to the basic set of resources of a computer system (either hardware or software) available for creating programs. According to the position I have taken, processes carried out in the functional architecture are processes whose behavior requires no explanation in terms of semantic regularities—that is, in terms of rules and representations. That position, examined indirectly in this section, provides the basis for a criterion I call "cognitive penetrability."

Because of their centrality, these distinctions, raised and discussed in a number of places, are examined at greater length in chapter 7 in connection with the distinction between analog and digital processes. In this section, I take the importance of these distinctions for granted, worrying instead about how we can provide principled constraints on what counts as functional architecture. Such constraints are necessary in order to prevent the trivialization of explanations one gets if the presumed basic operations of the functional architecture are allowed to range over, for instance, "decide whether P is true," "find the winning move," or "solve the problem" while at the same time preventing the architecture from being tied to the psychologically unrealistic but widely used operations of a von Neumann computer architecture. The criterion proposed in this section is a direct consequence of a view that might be called *the basic assumption of cognitive science*, the assumption, already discussed, that there are at least three distinct, independent levels at which we can find explanatory principles in cognitive psychology. Classically, they represent the principal approaches to psychological explanation —biological, functional, and intentional. Newell (1982), who recognizes many more levels than are relevant to the present discussion, refers to these particular levels as the device level, the symbol level, and the knowledge level. These are probably the most revealing names, though *symbol level* implies something more specific than *functional level*, and the term *knowledge* raises philosophical eyebrows (strictly speaking, it should be called *belief*). By implication, the term *knowledge* also suggests that one is ignoring other representational states, such as goals, as well as such propositional attitudes as fears and hopes. By the same token, *intentional*, as a term of art of phenomenology, carries too many superfluous connotations. That is why, in chapter 2, I use the term *representational* or *semantic* for this level and will continue to do so here.

If one accepts this trilevel characterization of cognition, then attempts to explain certain empirical regularities should proceed as follows. First priority goes to explaining the regularity in question in physical or biological terms, that is, at the physical level. If, under a description of behavior that captures the regularity in question, that regularity can be subsumed under biological or physical principles, we need go no further; we do not posit special principles when the universal principles of physics will do. This application of Occam's razor prevents us from ascribing beliefs and goals to streams, rocks, and thermostats. Of course, if the system is a computer, there will be some description of its input-output behavior (namely, the description under which the system is seen as executing a program) that will not be explainable by appeal to physical laws. The explanation of the machine's production of a certain output symbol when the machine is given a certain input symbol is not explainable at the physical level, for numerous reasons already discussed; for example, because of the failure of type-type equivalence of the physical and computational vocabularies, a different physical explanation holds for each distinct way of "inputting" a particular symbol, of "outputting" another symbol, and of physically instantiating the same program, despite the existence of a single explanation at the symbol level. In other words, a single program captures all the regularities that otherwise would have to be covered by an arbitrarily large disjunction of physical explanations. Hence, in this case, a symbol level explanation would have to be given.

Similarly—again, if the assumption about levels is correct—if regularities remain that are not explainable (under the description that best captures the generalizations) at either the physical or the symbol levels, appeal must be made to the semantic level. But what sort of regularities can these be? The answer has already been given: precisely the regularities that tie goals, beliefs, and actions together in a rational manner (S wants G and believes that G cannot be attained without doing A; therefore, everything else being equal, S will tend to do A). Just as physical-level principles provide the causal means whereby symbol level principles (embodied in the rules or the program) can be made to work, so symbol level principles provide the functional mechanisms by which representations are encoded and semantic level principles realized. The three levels are tied together in an instantiation hierarchy, with each level instantiating the one above.

It is clear that certain systems (humans, chimps, robots) exhibit regularities at all three levels. Now, suppose we have a hypothetical model of the cognitive processes of such a system. At the symbol level the model contains component subprocesses with subsubprocesses, and so on, which, in turn, are composed of basic operations, the primitive operations of the functional architecture (recall that that is where the symbol explanation stops). The question arises: How can we tell whether the hypothesized primitive processes are actually primitive? In other words, how can we tell whether they are instantiated in the functional architecture or are themselves the result of representation-governed processes?

Being instantiated in the functional architecture merely means being explainable without appeal to principles and properties at the symbolic or the semantic level. An operation whose behavior (under the description required of it by the model) *must* be given an explanation at the symbol level does not qualify, nor would an operation whose behavior (again, under the relevant description) must be explained at the semantic level. The first exclusion is discussed in the preceding section, where a general characterization of a computational primitive is given in terms of resource use. What, then, is a general characterization of a primitive operation from the perspective of the semantic level? The answer is obvious: The behavior of the putative, primitive operation must itself not require a semantic level explanation. In other words, in explaining the behavior of the hypothesized primitive, there must be no need to appeal to goals, beliefs, inferences, and other rational principles, as presumably there is in the case of explaining the behavior of the original, complete system. Thus (to use the terminology introduced by Dennett, 1971), not only must the reduced homunculi be increasingly "stupid," but at the most primitive level they must no longer be "intentional systems." The most primitive level must not behave in a manner that requires a cognitive (rules and representations) explanation.

In discussing the reason for appealing to the semantic level, I made the following observation. An outstanding characteristic exhibited by systems governed by rules and representations or by semantic principles is an extreme degree of holism and plasticity. If what goes on in such systems is, among other things, a process involving *inference*, then such holism and plasticity is just what one would expect. In general, whether a particular "conclusion" is permitted can depend on *any* premise. Further, changing a premise can have arbitrarily far-reaching effects. If behavior is determined by beliefs inferred from other beliefs and goals, then changing a belief (equivalent to changing a premise in an argument) can change the behavior in radical, albeit coherent and rationally explicable, ways. This plasticity of behavior, wherein regularities can be changed in rationally explicable ways by changing beliefs and goals, is seen as a prime indicant (though not the only one) of representation-governed processes. Consequently, it becomes a prime counterindicant of a function or component that is part of the functional architecture. The rationally explicable alterability of a component's behavior in response to changes in goals and beliefs is what I refer to as *cognitive penetrability*.

The essence of the penetrability condition is this. Suppose subjects exhibit behavior characterized in part by some function f_1 (say, a relation between reaction time and distance, angle, or perceived size of an imagined object) when they believe one thing; and some different function f_2 when they believe another thing. Suppose, further, that the particular f the subjects exhibit bears some logical or rational relation to the content of their belief. For example, they might believe that what they are imagining is very heavy, that it cannot accelerate rapidly under some particular applied force. The observed f might then reflect slow movement of that object on their image. Such a logically coherent relation between the form of f and their belief (which I refer to as the "cognitive penetrability of f") must somehow be explained. My contention is that, to account for the penetrability of the process, the explanation of f itself must contain processes that are rule-governed or computational—for example, processes of logical inference—and which make reference to semantically interpreted entities, or beliefs. The explanation cannot state merely that some causal (biological) laws exist that result in the observed function f—for the same reason that an explanation of this kind is not satisfactory in the examples examined in chapters 1 and 2 (for example, dialing 911 when an event is perceived as an emergency, or leaving a building when one has interpreted an event as indicating the building is on fire); the regularity in question depends on the semantic content (in this case, of beliefs) and the logical relations that hold among the contents. Although, in each case, some physical process causes the behavior, the explanation must appeal to a generalization that captures the entire class of such physical processes. As Fodor (1978a) puts it, there may be token reduction but no type reduction of such explanatory principles to physical principles.

A process that must be explained in terms of the semantic content of beliefs typically contains at least some inferential processes, or some processes that preserve semantic interpretation in some form (for example, such quasi-logical principles as heuristic rules). Thus the term *cognitive penetrability* refers not merely to any influence of semantic or cognitive factors on behavior but to a specific, semantically explicable (that is, rational or logically coherent) effect. The examples I shall describe in connection with a discussion of imagery are clear cases of this sort of influence (for more on this particular point, see chapter 8). It should be noted as well that being cognitively penetrable does not prevent a process from having *some* impenetrable components that are part of the functional architecture. Indeed, in my view, this *must* be the case, since it is the functional architecture that makes the thing run; it simply says that the behavior (or the particular phenomenon in question) should not be explained solely by appeal to the functional architecture or to analogue media (see chapter 7), with no reference to tacit knowledge, inference, or computational processes.

A good example occurs in perception. Without doubt, the perceptual process is cognitively penetrable in the sense required by our criterion. What one sees—or, more accurately, what one sees something to be—depends on one's beliefs in a rationally explicable way. In particular, it depends in a quite rational way on what one knows about the object one is viewing and on what one expects. This, the point of numerous experiments by the "new look" school of perception (see, for example, Bruner, 1957), clearly shows that, by and large, perception involves semantic-level principles—especially those of *inference*. Nonetheless, as Fodor and I have argued (Fodor and Pylyshyn, 1981), a clearly noninferential component is required as well, one that is part of the functional architecture. This component, called a transducer, may well be extremely complex by biological criteria, yet it counts as a cognitive primitive (I shall have more to say about transducers later in this chapter and in chapter 6). Furthermore, the transducer component is cognitively impenetrable (though, in the case of vision, its sensitivity can be dampened, as happens in pupillary dilation; or it can be redirected, as happens when the direction of gaze is changed—neither of which count as instances of cognitive penetration).

Although cognitive penetrability is an extremely simple idea, its use as a methodological criterion can on occasion be less than straightforward. This should not be surprising, since the practical problem of applying a principled distinction is always difficult, even when the distinction itself is simple and clear—for example, the distinction between a causal connection and a mere correlation. Following are three major reasons why the *practical* application of the criterion requires care and ingenuity.

1. The first problem in applying the cognitive-penetrability criterion in practice is that, while we want to draw conclusions about a hypothetical *subprocess*, all we have direct access to is the behavior of the entire, intact organism, which, we already know, is cognitively penetrable. The problem can occur even in the simplest demonstration of cognitive penetrability, for example, the f_1 and f_2 examples already mentioned. The question can always be raised: How do we know that the same relevant component was used in the f_1 and f_2 conditions? Even if it was used, how can we be sure that the difference in functions is due to the direct influence of instructions (or whatever is the cognitive manipulation) on the component of interest, rather than some other component? Perhaps the component in question (the putative, primitive operation of the functional architecture) actually was cognitively impenetrable, and the effect on the observed f came from some other component. That the difference in an observed function may have come from a component other than the one under scrutiny remains a problem. Note, however, that it is by no means unique to the application of the cognitive-penetrability criterion. In fact, the problem occurs every time one wishes to test an information-processing model. For this reason, it has led to the development of various sophisticated strategies for analyzing information-processing components, or "stage analysis" (see, for example, Sternberg, 1969; Massaro, 1975; Posner, 1978). Since there

is nothing special about this aspect of the problem, relative to any model-testing task, I have little to say about it except to recognize that it is something that must be taken into account.

2. The second problem is that a principle such as that of rationality is not directly observable in behavior. The principle represents an idealization needed to distinguish importantly different classes of principles. Particular instances of behavior may manifest this principle, but they will at the same time also manifest the effects of a variety of other factors. Just as symbol level principles (say, those embodied in a computer program) do not account for *all* aspects of a computer's input-output behavior (even under the relevant description of this behavior), because of the intrusion of physical level properties (for example, components may fail, physical memory or disk resources may be exceeded, real-time interrupts may occur, there may be spikes on the power line, and so on), so also does the semantic level not account for all aspects of behavior that fall under its principles. In particular, not all inferences permissible under the rules *can* be made, for the following reasons: not all beliefs are accessible at all times (*that* depends on the access key used), beliefs can become entrenched and may not change even when it would be rational for them to do so, people do not bother to consider all relevant factors, they get misled by surface cues, they cannot keep track of complex arguments or derivations, and so on. These are deviations from logical omniscience or rationality that reflect the intrusion of such symbol level principles as control structure, limited resources, time and space constraints on various information-handling mechanisms, as well as, possibly, physical-level principles. Consequently, deciding whether a certain regularity is an instance of the application of a rational principle or rule is not always straightforward—though sometimes it is, as we see in the examples taken from studies of mental imagery, in chapter 8.

3. The third reason for difficulty raises certain questions that need to be sketched in some detail, because the difficulty has been the source of many objections to the cognitive-penetrability criterion (for example, those in the responses to Pylyshyn, 1980a; but see Pylyshyn, 1980b). The difficulty is illustrated by the following observation. In addition to intrusions that prevent the observation of "pure" cases of semantic level principles, there are certain systematic relations that hold between principles at different levels. Far from being intrusions, they are the necessary links between semantic principles (and representations) and the physical world. When, on the basis of my goals, beliefs, and utilities, I decide on a certain action, certain behaviors ensue whose subsequent unfolding may be explainable only under a physical description. For example, if I am playing baseball and I infer, on the basis of my knowl-

edge of the rules of the game and my interpretation of the behavior of an opposing player, that the player is about to steal third base, I may decide to throw the ball toward the third baseman. Much of what happens after I initiate this action cannot be explained in terms of my beliefs and goals or those of anyone else; most of the relevant regularities first come under the generalizations of physiology, then under the laws of physics. Similarly, when I perceive the world, the relevant generalizations for explaining what I see begin with the laws of optics, then the principles of biophysics and biochemistry. Only later do they involve semantic principles (that is, at the point where perception involves inferences; see Fodor and Pylyshyn, 1981).

Now, the existence of obvious, causal connections between semantic principles (or, more particularly, semantically interpreted representations) and physical properties suggests the possibility of "mixed vocabulary" principles involving both semantic and physical terms. If true in the general case, this might undermine the thesis of autonomy of the semantic level, hence, the basis of the cognitive-penetrability criterion. Indeed, the criterion might have no point, since the distinction between functional architecture and symbolic processes would disappear. Clearly, however, this concern is premature. The existence of some causal interface between semantically and physically explainable regularities does not undermine the distinctions I have been pressing as long as there are principled constraints on this interface. But there must be such constraints; thoughts cannot have just any kind of direct effect on physical properties. (Of course, they can have almost unlimited indirect effects, since they can result in someone deciding to go and do something about changing some property in the world, say, by setting up the right physical conditions to induce the desired change.) If thoughts did have such direct effects, life would be a lot easier than it is. On the other hand, the notion that there must be *some* such bridging principles makes the application of the criterion of cognitive penetrability less straightforward, since we can expect that some effects of beliefs on behavior will always be mediated by such mixed-vocabulary principles, especially since both *internal* and external properties may ultimately be affected by goals and beliefs.

Several examples have been cited by way of suggesting that semantic principles and physical or biological principles can interact freely. What I shall do in the following is describe a few of these examples and suggest that, as far as the purpose of the cognitive-penetrability criterion is concerned, they represent effects of the wrong kind to count as cases of cognitive penetration, either because they are not instances of content-dependent regularities or because they are "indirect" effects (such as those mentioned in the preceding paragraph). First, I simply argue that the cognitive-penetrability criterion remains useful because one can see intuitively that a different effect is responsible for these examples and that clear cases of cognitive penetration (involving rational or inferential processes, as in the case of perception) are easily discerned. Thus I conclude that, in practice, this kind of example presents no problem. In a subsequent section I take up the more fundamental question of whether such examples threaten the autonomy principle behind the distinction.

What theorists have worried about in connection with the cognitive-penetrability criterion apparently are counterexamples of the following classes.

1. The first class involves clearly noncognitive or nonsemantic processes which, nevertheless, appear to be systematically altered by the contents of beliefs. For example, beliefs about an imminent threat cause the heart rate to increase and an entire set of physiological reflexes to occur. The digestive process can be altered, causing one to become distracted. Surely, however, these processes do not follow semantic-level principles; they are not cognitive processes.

2. The second class of counterexample is closely related to the first, except that in this case the effects are under voluntary control. The class includes not only such voluntary actions as extending one's arm but control over normally involuntary processes such as heart rate and alpha rhythm, something which, to a limited degree, can be achieved through biofeedback and other training methods. Once again, it appears that we can cognitively influence noncognitive processes.

3. The third class involves what I call the "indirect" influence of goals and beliefs on both cognitive and noncognitive processes. As Georges Rey (1980) points out, *any* process humans have learned to tamper with (from the reproductive cycle of chickens to other people's feelings and, indeed, to more drastic cognitive alterations produced through psychosurgery) constitute cases in which beliefs and goals influence something (sometimes cognitive, sometimes not), although, as Rey concedes, it is clear that the "paths of influence are [not] of the right sort."

These examples were presented by various people to cast doubt both on the usefulness of the criterion of cognitive penetrability as a methodological principle and on the assumption of the autonomy of the semantic level and, hence, on the distinction between functional architecture and symbolic process. Worries about the methodological usefulness of the criterion (on the grounds that its use depends on an ability to discern "paths of influence of the appropriate sort") are the less serious of the two. General methodological criteria *always* require judgment in their application; indeed, no psychological experiment has ever been performed whose interpretation did not depend heavily on making *the very judgment* questioned in these examples: whether certain effects are caused by "influences of the appropriate sort." That is because every experiment involves instructing subjects to, for example, attend to certain stimuli and ignore others. The assumption is always made that the semantic content of the instructions is communicated to the subjects and that that is what determines their understanding of the task. In other words, it is assumed that at least instructions have their effect through "paths of influence of the appropriate sort," namely, those governed by semantic-level principles rather than, say, by causally affecting the subjects according to physical principles that take the instructions under a physical description, for example, according to their intensity or duration.

One must remember that cases in which the criterion is used (for instance, the perception examples and the examples concerning models of mental imagery, discussed in chapter 8) involve applications as clear as those in the instruction example. Indeed, in most cases, the manipulations are precisely instructional differences designed to alter subjects' goals and beliefs in the most straightforward manner. Questions that arise about the interpretation of the results invariably are concerned with such issues as those outlined several pages ago under problem (1), where there may be a dispute over which component is being affected by differences in beliefs; or under problem (2), where one might want to attribute certain regularities to beliefs and goals, despite the fact that the relevant beliefs are extremely difficult to change (sometimes for good reason; changing one's beliefs can have wide ramifications and may disrupt many intimately related, deeply held existing beliefs, which is why it takes so long to change scientific beliefs).

One way to view the penetrability criterion when it is used as a methodological principle is as a method that allows us to exploit some of our most reliable and stable intuitions, those concerned with the description under which certain regularities should be addressed. This, in turn, allows us to drive a wedge between cognitive processes and the part of the cognitive system fixed with respect to cognitive or semantic influences. Thus intuitions concerning which phenomena are cognitive in the requisite sense (as in the case of the effects of instructions) are used as a "forcing function" to spread the underlying constraint into the details of operation of a system where our intuitions are notoriously suspect and where, for example, our intuitions are susceptible to such traps as those involved when we reify the objects of our thoughts and images as though such properties actually were properties of the mental processes (see chapter 8). This methodology is similar to that involved in the study of grammar, where intuitions of clear cases of well-formedness are used to help infer the deeper structure of the language code where we have few valid intuitions.

Seen this way, the cognitive-penetrability condition, *qua methodological principle*, amounts to nothing more than a closure principle for the domain of phenomena explainable in terms of rules and representations, a way to capitalize on the original conception of a semantic level explanation, by applying the distinction consistently throughout the model-building task. The deeper issue of whether a distinction is obtainable at that juncture is one that must be addressed separately. In the end, the only verdict is the one issued by the success—or lack of it—of attempts to build theories based on these assumptions. For now, all I offer are some arguments that the view is at least plausible, given what is known about psychology and what is internally consistent. It is to this task that I now devote a brief aside.

Is Everything Cognitively Penetrable?

Whether the alleged cognitive penetrability of virtually any process, as implied by the examples we have considered, threatens the autonomy (or "level") thesis depends on the nature of the interaction between levels. It is a question of whether the "mixed vocabulary regularities" observed involve the same sort of explanatory principles as those at the physical or symbol level, on the one hand, or the semantic level, on the other. If they do, then it would seem that there is nothing special about the distinction between these principles beyond any other differences that might mark off subsets of explanatory principles in psychology.

The examples presented in the preceding chapters make it clear that such semantic level principles as inference, though carried out by symbol-level mechanisms, differ considerably from either the nomological laws that govern physical-level properties or the symbol-level mechanisms themselves. For one thing, they are interpreted semantically, which is to say, certain regularities among representations such as beliefs and goals are captured only in terms of the meanings of the symbolic expressions. In other words, there are regularities over equivalence classes of symbol structures that are not necessarily expressible in terms of the properties of the symbols—for example, the principle of rationality (*Why that particular rule?—Because, given what I know, it is likely to enable me to achieve my goal.*). Even more obviously, however, semantic level principles differ considerably from physical laws; the latter must be stated over bona fide physical properties (or, at least, projectable properties), whereas the former apply to open-ended classes of physical properties. There is no limit on the combinations of physical properties that can be used to instantiate, say, modus ponens. Consequently, the categories of both semantic level and symbol level generalizations cross classify those of physical level generalizations. That is why the two sets of principles have nothing in common; they are merely related by the happenstance of design or instantiation.

If that is the case, how can it be that there are "mixed-vocabulary principles"—or laws at all? There must be an interface between semantically interpreted symbols and physical properties; that's what perception is. On the other hand, the attempt to explain perception by linking percepts directly to the perceived properties of the world (as was Gibson's goal) clearly fails, for reasons not irrelevant to the issue at hand. It fails because the causally characterizable link must be highly constrained. This causal link is a very small part of the relation between percepts and the world. The rest of the relation is mediated by inference, or semantic level principles, which is also true of putative "mixed vocabulary principles," and for exactly the same reasons. To introduce these reasons, I briefly anticipate some of the arguments developed in chapter 6.

The interface between physical and semantic principles is a special, functional component (instantiated in the functional architecture) called a *transducer*. A transducer is not a particular organ; rather, it is identified functionally. Its exact location, if it is locatable at all, is no more a matter of cognitive theory than is the location of various codes or other encoding functions in the brain. A transducer, however, is one of the more important basic functions, because one's cognitive theory depends to a great entent on assumptions made about the transducer. For that reason the entire chapter 6 is devoted to an analysis of transduction.

In analyzing transduction I conclude that what can count as a transducer must be strictly constrained in several ways. Following are two central constraints. The input (or output, depending on whether it is an efferent or afferent transducer) must be described in physical terms; and the transducer function must be input bound (in the case of an input transducer, this is referred to as being "stimulus bound," whereas, in the case of an output transducer, it must be "symbol bound"), which means it must produce a particular output *whenever* it receives a certain input, regardless of its state or the context. Now we see that the problem with the view that everything is cognitively penetrable is that it is exactly (though in the reverse direction) the Gibsonian view that everything we see is "directly picked up." The reason Gibson's view cannot be sustained is that very few properties (in particular, only certain functions over physical properties) are directly picked up (see Fodor and Pylyshyn, 1981). The other perceived properties are inferred. The same holds in the case of output transduction.[2]

2. In the visual-detection case, only those properties qualify to which the system is stimulus-bound, and of these, only properties converted to symbolic form by the transducer

Consider now the claim that believing, say, that the Internal Revenue Service has scheduled an audit of your books causes certain acids to be secreted in your stomach (a plausible claim, I suppose). This cannot be one of those mixed-vocabulary explanatory principles, because it is not counterfactual supporting. Specifically, it is not a possible transducer function because it is not input-bound. Even though the relation between belief and reaction may be quite common, it is surely the case that under different conditions of subsidiary beliefs the principle claimed would not hold. For example, if you had been scrupulous about keeping your books, if you had had no income that year, if you believed (erroneously) that the IRS does audits in order to award prizes for the best-kept books, and so on, it would be unlikely that the acid secretions would occur. Evidently, the function from the belief under consideration to the physiological reaction is not transducible.

Perhaps, I have simply not put the principle precisely enough. Maybe it's not *that* belief but the belief in the imminent threat of being fined that is transduced. Whereas that belief, too, seems penetrable by other beliefs (you might believe you have so much money that such a fine would be immaterial), this suggestion seems on the right track. What we need is to identify basic, transducible, cognitive states. The apparent empirical fact is that there are few of these, certainly very few in comparison with the number of possible beliefs. If that is the case, then beliefs have their physiological effect in the same way percepts are generated from optical inputs (except conversely). They take part in inferences, the end product of which is a special, cognitive state that happens to be causally connected to a physiological state of special interest (because, say, it causes ulcers). The last link is completely reliable, since the cognitive state in question happens to be type-equivalent to a physiologically described state. This, at least, is a possible explanation why so few beliefs appear reliably to cause identifiable physiological changes: very few cognitive states are type-identical, or even largely coextensive with, physiologically described states.

Another consideration should be kept in mind in connection with

---

are said to be transduced. What this means is that it is not enough for some part of the organism merely to respond to a certain property P for there to be a transducer for P; it must also be the case that the response to P is in a class of properties that are *functional* for the organism. In other words, it must lead to an endogenous property that corresponds to a distinct, symbolic or computational state. That is what it means to say that the transducer "generates a symbol." In the case of an output transducer, only the subset of states corresponding to distinct symbols or computational states count as potential inputs to a transducer, and there may be transducers only for a small subset of potentially transducible states. This could mean that only a small subset of the system's symbols are transduced.

such claims as that particular beliefs affect, say, the digestive system, therefore, that the digestive system appears to be cognitively penetrable. This example, and many others like it, trade on a natural ambiguity concerning the system we are referring to when we mention digestion. As I have emphasized, when our concern is with explanation, the notion of system carries with it a presumption concerning the taxonomy under which we view the system's behavior. The system under scrutiny when we are concerned with the chemical interactions among substances in the digestive process is not the same system as the one we examine when we are interested in the effect of beliefs, even though the two may be partly or entirely coextensive; that is, they may be located in the same place in the body.

The system that takes nourishment, hydrochloric acid, and other fluids as input and provides glucose and other substances as output is a different system from one which, in addition, has as input the belief that the IRS is about to arrive. For one thing, the latter process must have access to other beliefs that make this news threatening, for example, *I did not keep all my records; I read somewhere that someone was fined a substantial amount of money as a consequence of an IRS audit.* The latter system *is* cognitively penetrable and *does* have to appeal to rule-governed processes, whereas the former does not.

If you have such a biological process as digestion, whose inputs and outputs are under a biochemical description, rather than being under some cognitive interpretation, say, as codes for something, the only way to explain how this process occurs, hence the only way to explain how it can be systematically changed, is to consider all its inputs and intermediate states under a biochemical description, or, at least, a non-cognitive one. If you take the inputs and outputs of a system under a biological description, then, by definition, its regularities will be sub-sumed under biological generalizations. No lawlike (counterfactual supporting) generalizations contain both cognitive and biological de-scriptions, not, that is, unless the cognitive categories happen to be coextensive with the biological categories.

The claim here is not that cognitive states do not cause biological states. Indeed, every state of a cognitive system is simultaneously a biological state and a cognitive state, since it is an element of both a cognitive- and a biological-equivalence class. Since, however, the classes are distinct (that's why they are described using distinct vocabularies that typically cross classify the states), and since biological regularities are stated over biological descriptions (that's what makes the descrip-tions biological), any explanation of how a biological input-output function can be altered must do so under a biological description of the influencing event. Thus, if we want to explain the influence of

some event taken under a cognitive or semantic description, on a biological process such as digestion, we must first do something like discover a relevant biological property that happens to be coextensive
with a certain class of cognitive descriptions.

The explanation of such cases as how digestion is affected by beliefs
must proceed in three stages. First, we must explain how the variation
in some biochemical or physical property (say the concentration of
hydrochloric acid) causes digestion to change in theoretically predictable
ways. Second, we must show that all the beliefs in question are related
by a rule or cognitive generalization to a certain, specifiable class of
cognitive states. Third, we must show that this last class of states is
coextensive with—or causally connected to properties that are coextensive with—the biochemical or physical property mentioned in the
first stage. (The last stage provides a description of the operation of a
transducer.) My point here is that, to provide an explanation of the
way in which what *appears to be* cognitive penetration occurs in such
cases as this, where the function in question is given under a physical-
level description, we must identify a system which contains a component
that responds in a principled way to events under a cognitive- (or
semantic-level) description, together with a cognitively impenetrable
function, such as digestion itself, whose variations can be explained
by biological and physical laws.

To make this point more concretely, let us consider a comparable
case involving a computer. Suppose a robot is provided with the capability of altering its own hardware architecture, say, by mechanically
removing an integrated-circuit chip when it is faulty and replacing it
with a new one from a storage bin. Clearly, an account of how this is
done requires both a description of the computational process, in terms
of the program and data structures, and a description of the physical
manipulation process. The first part of the account is entirely symbolic,
whereas the second is physical and mechanical. The overall account
of altering the hardware architecture by symbolic processes involves
showing how the symbol structures affect transducers, which affect
the behavior of the manipulators (here, the regularity is explained under
a mechanical description), which, in turn, affect the architecture by
changing the circuitry.

Note that, in this case, we cannot explain the change in architecture
in terms of the program alone—even if we do not know independently
that physical manipulation is involved—for the same reason that we
cannot explain the particular changes in beliefs that result indirectly
from deciding to take a drug or conduct self-psychosurgery. In both
cases, the nature of the changes produced are, in an important sense,
not accountable in terms of the content of the cognitive influence,

because the nature of the changes depends crucially on physical properties of the world (for example, to provide an explanation of the changes that took place, we must specify what chips were previously placed in certain, actual physical locations), whereas content is independent of such physical properties, inasmuch as the same content can be conveyed in arbitrarily many physical ways. Therefore, in cases such as this, a description of nonsymbolic physical activity and the relevant physical laws must occur as part of the explanatory account, as well as a description of the noncomputational environment—for example, the location of various integrated circuit chips in the vicinity. Such factoring of the process into a symbolic stage, a nonsymbolic (nonpenetrable) stage, and transduction stages is precisely what is required in such examples as digestion. Note that, while decomposition into stages is required for the independent reason that different regularities hold at each stage, decomposition also leads quite naturally to separation of the process into computational and noncomputational modules, together with well-defined and motivated interfaces between them.

The conclusion I come to is that examples of mixed-vocabulary regularities must be explained by decomposing them into components. For reasons independent of the problem of dealing with the cognitive-penetrability criterion, we find that by explaining such cases we go back to making a distinction between functions that operate on the basis of semantic-level or symbol-level principles and functions that must be explained in physical-level terms. We return to this recurring theme when we discuss perception (chapter 6), analogue processing (chapter 7), and imagery (chapter 8). Thus the threat that everything will turn out to be cognitively penetrable seems remote in light of such considerations, while the distinction of levels remains a basic working hypothesis of cognitive science.

Chapter 6

The Bridge from Physical to Symbolic:
Transduction

In a word, *insensible perceptions* are of as great use in Psychology as insensible corpuscles are in Physics, and it is equally as unreasonable to reject the one as the other under the pretext that they are beyond the reach of our senses. Nothing takes place all at once, and it is one of my great maxims, and one of the most verified, that *nature never makes leaps....* *Noticeable perceptions* also come by degrees from those which are too minute to be noticed.

Leibniz, *New Essays on the Understanding*, 1704

Introduction

In the preceding chapters we considered the fundamental notions of a symbol or the symbolic level of analysis and that of the important distinction between symbolically described (intentional) processes and those that occur in what I call *functional architecture*. I noted that not everything pertaining to an organism is appropriately described at the symbolic level, at the level of symbol structures and information; some aspects of the system are more appropriately described in the vocabulary of physics, chemistry, biology, electrical engineering, and so on. A fundamental issue in cognition—one that has scarcely been broached by cognitive scientists—is: Which phenomena of interest to cognitive psychology can be explained without using physical or biological terms, that is, without reference to structural material properties of the organism or its environment? As I noted in chapter 2, this is actually a question of what constitutes the natural domain of representation-governed processes, a question whose ultimate answer awaits the successful development of cognitive theories.

Although it seems fairly clear that some things (for example, aspects of the structure of the environment) must be addressed in physical terms (even here, however, the details are not without contention), the penetration of these terms into a description of the organism's functioning is unclear. A major thesis of this chapter is that the often implicit stand one takes with regard to the question of the bridge between physical and symbolic descriptions determines in a fundamental way how one views the problems of cognition.

A primary question here is, Exactly what kind of function is carried out by that part of the organism which is variously called the sensor, the transducer, or, in the case of Gibson, the "information pickup"? One's answer to this question determines the shape of any theory of perception and cognition one subsequently constructs. As I shall argue, unlike the symbolic processes that characterize cognition, the function performed by the transducer cannot be described as a computation, that is, by a purely symbol-manipulation function. Like all primitive operations of the functional architecture, the transducer fundamentally is a physical process; that is, its behavior is explainable (its regularities can be captured) in terms of its intrinsic properties—physical, chemical, biological, and so on. Thus, typically it does not come under study by cognitive psychologists who simply *presuppose* that an organism is equipped with certain transducer functions. The task of discovering these mechanisms is left for others, for example, "sensory encoding" neurophysiologists, biophysicists, and engineers.

It turns out that the cognitive theorist enjoys considerable latitude in deciding which functions to attribute to the transducer and which to the symbolic processor. The boundary between transducer and symbolic processor can be shifted about, but this shifting carries with it profound implications for cognitive theory. It is possible to assign the deepest mysteries of perception and cognition to different places, and consequently to make the part one is concentrating on at the moment appear either surprisingly simple or unfathomably complex. While explication of this point takes up most of this chapter, I might note here that the "allocation of complexity" phenomenon is a ubiquitous one in psychology (see Pylyshyn, 1980c). For instance, both Simon (1969) and Gibson (1966b, 1979) have argued that cognitive processes can be simplified considerably by attributing much of the complexity of an organism's behavior to the structure of the environment. Cognitive processes can also be simplified by attributing complexity to the functioning of the transducer, but a price must be paid for this shift. The price, as Fodor and I argue in our review of Gibson's program, is that one can trivially explain anything that way. Unless what counts as transduction is constrained in a principled manner, the simplification of the problems of perception gained by postulating certain transducers has, as Bertrand Russell is reported to have said once, all the virtues of theft over honest toil.

In the more general issue of the relation between physical and symbolic levels, there are closely related questions as well concerning the output, or motor functions, and even deeper questions concerning the relation between symbolic and physical properties in such functions as memory and thought. In chapter 5, I briefly discuss the need for "internal transduction." Here, only the case of input transduction is considered in any detail, though the case of output, or motor, transduction is similar in many respects. I begin by examining some reasons for studying the transducer.

Contact between Mechanism and Environment
In chapters 1 through 5, I spoke of the independence of physical and computational, or symbolic, descriptions of a process. One can describe the symbol-manipulation processes being performed without committing oneself as to the physical properties of the device performing it. If, however, the symbols are to represent anything outside the symbol system—if they are to have a semantics—there must be some connection between the symbols and the events outside the symbol system. This, in part, is how the symbols come to *refer* to things. (Note, however, that not all relations between symbols and events are relations of referring, and that not all cases of reference need be directly traceable to transduction, since we can refer to things with which we have not been in sensory contact but with which we may only be related through a chain of what might be called "informational contacts".)

Suppose that, to set out some issues, we transpose the question of transduction from the domain of organisms to that of computers. In the typical computer application, the relation between a machine and the things in its environment that it represents usually is not established by connecting the machine directly to its environment through sensors but by making the connections via a human link. The human user completes the connection by providing a symbolic input to the device. In practice, what the person does is convert the intended input (a number, a word) into some discrete, symbolic notation, then, through a suitable interface device such as a keyboard, induces an internal state in some part of the computer that corresponds to the symbol intended.

Although the distinction between direct sensing, or transducing, and human intervention is a useful one, we must look more closely at what is implied in order to set the scene for a more detailed examination of the notion of transduction. The description already given is imprecise, since a human does not literally provide a symbolic input. A key press is not yet a symbol; it must be converted into a symbol by a process which might also be thought of as a form of transduction. What is the difference between this case and that of direct connection with a physical environment? Although human behavior does constitute an environment (indeed, for both people and machines, it is one of the most important types of environment), there are two distinct ways in which the behavior can be related to that of a machine. These ways are represented paradigmatically by, on the one hand, using unconstrained speech as input, and, on the other, using key presses. The first is a case in which the behavior must be accepted in the natural form in which it occurs, whereas the second is a case in which the behavior has in some sense been constrained by a design that takes into account the physical properties of the computer.

Let us examine several apparent differences between receiving input directly from the natural environment and receiving input through what might be characterized as an engineered environment. One of the criteria in designing input devices such as keyboards is that they constrain the variability of the input to within strict tolerances. Thus one difference seems to be that the variability of the input is greater in the case of the natural environment. A moment's reflection, however, reveals that we cannot speak of variability without presupposing dimensions along which the variability is to be assessed. From one occasion to another, the typing of a particular word is done with quite different timings, with different vertical and horizontal forces, accelerations, dwell times, and musculatures. Thus, when we say that the variability of a spoken word (a natural input) is greater than that of a typed word (an engineered input), we have in mind such dimensions as the distribution of energy over frequency and time in the speech case but only the identity of the depressed key in the keyboard case. What makes keyboard input seem less variable than spoken input is that simple technological devices exist that respond differently, depending only on what key was depressed, regardless of how hard the key was depressed, whereas there are no simple technological devices that respond to what phones are uttered, regardless of how loud, with what average pitch, and so forth they were produced.

Lack of such devices is no accident, of course. Physical devices respond to physical magnitudes (that is, the basic dimensions of physics—force, time, length). The development of technological tools for mechanical or electrical tasks is intimately related to the development of physical theory. What makes speech seem highly variable is that we lack physical dimensions that correspond to phonetic similarity; in other words, we lack a description, in physical terms, that will group sounds into perceptually similar classes. It is the ancient problem of stimulus equivalence or, more accurately, giving a physical characterization of a psychologically defined equivalence relation.

The difference between the case in which a computational system is connected directly to a naturally occurring environment and the case in which it is connected to an engineered environment is that in the latter case the stimulus equivalence problem (at least, up to some level of specificity) is solved by the human user. The user does this by converting an event to a category symbol and transmitting the identity of the symbol to the computer, using a special device for which equivalence classes have been specified in simple physical terms. In the next section we consider what must be done in cases where a naturally occurring environment is to be interfaced to a computational system, using a transducer.

The Transducer Function

In its most general sense, as used, for example, in electrical engineering, a transducer is a device that receives patterns of energy and retransmits them, usually in some altered form. Thus a typical transducer simply transforms or maps physical (spatiotemporal) events from one form to another in some consistent way. In describing what makes a transducer especially important in cognitive science, I review some ideas introduced in chapters 2 and 3 concerning the functional level of description; and by showing how a transducer operates in a computer, how it mediates between functional and physical levels, I hope to provide a solid basis for discussing the psychological case.

Although a computer is a physical device with many properties measurable by physical instruments and with as many potential physical states as can, in principle, be discriminated by these instruments, only a tiny fraction of these properties and states are relevant to its functioning as a computer. In other words, its *computationally relevant* states are a tiny subset of its physically discriminable states. Not only are there fewer computationally relevant states than physically discriminable states but the former are typically a complex function of the latter. This simply means that there need be no natural, or even finite, description that, in general, specifies all the physical states that form an equivalence class corresponding to a particular computational state. On the other hand, aspects of the physical environment to which the computer may be called on to respond—say, in a machine vision or speech recognition system—generally are not the same as the aspects that define computational states. Indeed, rarely is a physical event outside a computer's mainframe considered a computational event (though, with distributed computation, the boundaries of the "computer" become less well defined). Computational events invariably are highly specific equivalence classes of electrical events within the machine's structure. If, however, we have a device that systematically maps interesting equivalence classes of physical events into classes of computationally relevant internal events, we encounter the possibility of coupling the machine—as computer—to a noncomputational environment.

This, then, is the importance of a transducer. By mapping certain classes of physical states of the environment into computationally relevant states of a device, the transducer performs a rather special conversion: converting computationally arbitrary physical events into computational events. A description of a transducer function shows how certain nonsymbolic physical events are mapped into certain symbol systems.

This much is conceptually straightforward, but as soon as we speak of physical events (as we must in characterizing the transducer function), we have to use descriptive terms. If the choice of such terms were unconstrained, the function of a transducer could be trivially reduced to an identity mapping. All we need do in that case is describe the physical event in terms that correspond one for one with the computational symbols. For example, we could describe a transducer for converting speech into symbolic form as follows:

(1) The device maps the acoustical event /a/ onto the symbol 'a', the acoustical event /b/ onto the symbol 'b', and so on.

Note that, as far as what I have said about transducers up to now goes, this is a perfectly legitimate description of a transducer function. It shows how physical, or acoustical, events are translated into symbolic events. (There can be no disputing that a term such as /b/ describes a *physical* event as surely as the term "550 Hertz.") One thing that may occur to the reader about this description is that it says nothing about how one could build such a device. The difficulty arises because the input side of the transducer is not described in the language of physics or in any other natural science that contains causal laws[1]— that is, the language that would be used to specify the design of an electroacoustical apparatus. In contrast, the following description characterizes a transducer that is easily built:

(2) If an acoustical frequency of f Hertz occurs with energy level e at time t, output the string of symbols 'f, e, t' (where the latter are replaced by certain symbolic codes, such as strings of numerals).

1. A more precise way to state this is that the transducer thus described is responding to *nonprojectable* properties of the events in question or to properties that do not occur in nomological laws. Responding to nonprojectable properties is taken by some (for example, Fodor, 1984) as the definitive criterion for the system in question being representation-governed and involving inferences. In chapter 7, I make the claim that this is too strong a position, that all that is needed is the kind of consideration that goes into determining properties instantiated in the functional architecture. In this view, the projectability criterion, though not always necessary, is sufficient.

The problem with this description of a transducer is that, though it can be constructed, the description leaves unspecified how the occurrence of such classes of physical events as the utterance of certain words is to be identified using these output symbols. Further, it is an empirical question whether the human transducer responds in the way specified by (2), that is, in terms of, say, instantaneous spectral distributions. It has been argued that the basic properties of speech perception are spread over temporal events corresponding to something resembling syllabic units, rather than being continuous. Other arguments against an "instantaneous pattern" transducer have been made, for example, Gibson (1966a). I shall return to the problem of choosing the right temporal extent after discussing some of Gibson's proposals.

What is needed are some general criteria for constraining what counts as the description of a transducer function. Otherwise, both (1) and (2) are acceptable transducers. Although both leave major problems unsolved, the problems in the two cases are radically different. In fact, without strong constraints, the entire cognitive system can be viewed as a transducer that converts physical events in the world into behavior! What we need is a principled way of blocking such trivializations of the transducer function. Because whatever is not transduced must be explained in terms of psychological processes operating on the output of the transducer, what we take the psychological process to be doing is intimately connected with what we take transduction to be.

Criteria for a Psychological Transducer

In what follows I shall raise some central issues involving the specification of transducers and indicate what I consider the stand of the computational approach on these issues. My assumptions are listed as a series of design specifications. Of course, alternative ways are available in which to try to develop a science of cognition. The point here is that the stand taken on these issues constitutes the choice of a foundation for one's cognitive theory. Nor are the choices independent; the assumptions made concerning what can serve as a transducer has far-reaching implications for the rest of the cognitive theory. This task, therefore, should be performed in a principled way with full knowledge of the relativity of one's subsequent theories to these choices and with a clear picture of the alternatives.

The principal criteria to be met by a transducer are listed and are subsequently discussed and defended.

• The function carried out by a transducer is *primitive* and is itself *nonsymbolic*. At least, the function is not described as carried out by means of symbol processing; it is part of the functional architecture.

- A transducer is, to a first approximation, a stimulus-bound component operating independently of the cognitive system. It is also *interrupt-* or *data*-driven by its environment.
- The behavior of a transducer is to be described as a *function* from physical events onto symbols:
    (a) The domain of the function must be couched in the language of physics.
    (b) The range of the function must be computationally available, discrete atomic symbols.
    (c) A transducer can occur at any energy transfer locus where, in order to capture the regularities of the system, it is necessary to change descriptions from physical to symbolic. The only requirement is that the transformation from the input, described physically, to the ensuing token computational event, also described physically, follow from physical principles.

In the remainder of this chapter I elaborate on some of these points.

The Function of a Transducer Is Nonsymbolic

Chapters 4 and 5 introduced the central idea of functional architecture. The operations of this architecture are computationally primitive in the sense that their internal operation is not considered a rule-governed computation; they are simply performed, or, "instantiated", by properties of the biological substrate in a manner not requiring the postulation of internal representations. To ask how a primitive function is carried out is to ask for a functional or perhaps a physical (or biological) description. Furthermore, a primitive operation is opaque. A cognitive process cannot examine intermediate states in the function of a primitive operation; if it could, we would no longer count the operation as primitive. My proposal, then, is that since the transducer is part of the functional architecture, the same requirements apply to it. A transducer is just another primitive operation, albeit one responsive primarily to the environment rather than the cognitive process. Just as one does not generally consider a thermometer, voltmeter, analog-to-digital converter, or any other piece of equipment connecting a physical environment to a computer as performing a computation, so a psychological transducer is considered nonsymbolic in its internal operation.

In addition, as is required of other operations constituting the functional architecture, transducers must be of constant resource use or computational complexity. Otherwise, paralleling the case discussed in the preceding paragraph, we would have to posit even more elementary operations to explain how resource use varies with inputs. This and the opacity condition are both instances of the principal criterion primitive operations have always been required to meet—that no explanations of strictly cognitive phenomena should require that we know the internal workings of a primitive operation. This, in turn, means that all the generalizations in the natural domain of cognition can be captured by describing processes carried out, using the primitive operations of the functional architecture and operating on representations encoded by symbol systems provided by the functional architecture.

Of course, what is considered a psychological transducer may—as in the case of other cognitive primitives—have to be implemented in complex ways in an actual computer model, because of the architecture of current, general-purpose computers and because of the commercial transducers generally available (such as television cameras, in the case of vision). Such complexity is irrelevant from a psychological viewpoint. The neurophysiological implementation is doubtless even more complex and is vastly different in detail from the computer implementation. The only psychological isomorphism claims made are, as usual, independent of the implementation details or the way the functional architecture is realized in some organism or artifact.

A Transducer Is Primarily Stimulus-Bound

The influence of cognitive processes over a transducer's operation must be extremely limited. At some level the following *must* be the case: An organism's contact with the environment must, at some level, be decoupled from its cognitive processes; otherwise, the organism has no stable base of causal interactions with the world from which to develop veridical perceptions. If it were not for this decoupling the organism would be in the position of a despotic leader whose only contact with the world is through compliant servants who, in their eagerness to please, tell their leader whatever he wants to hear, thus ensuring that he remains confined in the world of his wishes.

If the transducer function were arbitrarily "programmable" from above, it would be "cognitively penetrable" and hence not meet our criterion of being a primitive part of the functional architecture. An indication by empirical facts that our hypothesized transducer is arbitrarily modifiable by higher-level processes would be taken as evidence that we have not found the appropriate transducer (because arbitrary modifiability implies recombination of more elementary operations). In that case, we would seek to redescribe the function in terms of processes that operate on the outputs of more primitive transducers. This procedure would continue until a set of transducers is found that is relatively independent of subsequent, cognitive processing, that is, a set whose influence is primarily unidirectional from the environment inward.

The qualifying phrase *relatively independent* is used because I do not wish to exclude such gross influences as are involved in changing direction of gaze or such relatively slow acting and physically describable "tuning" phenomena as might be involved, say, in ocular accommodation and sensory adaptation or in the acoustical impedance matching mechanisms in the middle ear. Such influences from higher levels are relatively gross in nature and are generally on a much longer time scale than normal transducer latency. Further, in these cases, generally there is independent evidence that the regularities which govern such dependencies can be explained in terms of physical-biological laws or generalizations, with no need to appeal to representational processes. Hence, they are not treated as cases of cognitive penetration or arbitrary programmability from above.

It is important to note that this view of transduction has nothing to do with the view that perception is constructed from sensations or sense data; it is merely an attempt to derive some conditions on the lowest acceptable level of translation from the physical to the symbolic. It may be a long way from the output of transducers to a percept, but the process must begin somewhere. I have argued that at the most basic level, the process begins when an exogenous physical event initiates a chain of events causally connected under a physical description, which results in a computational event. This primal conversion must then proceed without substantial intervention of the computational process itself. For our purposes, whether the resulting computational event has conscious content (as is implied by the sense-data view) is irrelevant. There seems to be overwhelming evidence that at least some properties of the environment to which we react in a stimulus-bound manner are properties to which we have absolutely no conscious access, for example, derivatives of light intensities, eye movements made during tracking and saccades, the ratio of the velocity of feature movements on the two retinas (Regan and Beverley, 1980), the ratio of the difference in light intensity across some region boundary to the average intensity in the surrounding region (as in the perception of light sources; see, for example, Ullman, 1976), and numerous other properties studied routinely by psychophysicists.

The discussion so far characterizes the transducer as a mechanism whose operation is largely independent of any subsequent use to which its output is to be put; but there is another way to view the "direction of influence" phenomenon, one that brings it into contact with some useful computational ideas. Organisms can be thought of as making contact with their environment in one of two ways: actively, by probing and inquiring, or passively, by allowing themselves to be informed, that is, through the capacity to have their states changed willy-nilly by the environment. In computational terms the parallel distinction is that between a *test* and an *interrupt*, or, as it is sometimes put, between process-driven control and data-driven control. According to this dichotomy, transducers are clearly interrupt-, or data-driven.

In computer science there is a fundamental difference between a test and an interrupt. A test is an active operation; for one to occur, some currently active process must contain an operation that tests for some special, computational (that is, symbolic) state. For this reason, a test may occur only in fixed relation to the process. Furthermore, a test involves utilization of some computational resource; in fact, it is generally the case that the greater the number of alternative possibilities the process is prepared for, the greater the amount of resources required (since each alternative must explicitly be checked for). In contrast, from the point of view of the computational process, an interrupt is a passive operation. The occurrence of some internal or external event (not necessarily a computational event) *causes* a certain state change to occur or a new process to be activated. Hence, unlike the case of the test, the occurrence of an interrupt is not fixed in relation to the process, nor does it consume computational resources. Since an interrupt consumes no computational resources, it makes no difference how many distinct types of events can cause an interrupt, although when the number of interrupt types is increased, additional resources may be used by processes occurring after the interrupt.

Test and interrupt functions are indistinguishable from the point of view of what they accomplish, that is, from the point of view of their weak equivalence. They are, however, distinguishable by such criteria as the way in which they can be altered (test functions of the form, "If P then A1 else A2," are programmable; hence, they can be changed within the range of effects under symbolic control) or by their variable resource use or computational complexity profile. These criteria are precisely the ones that distinguish representation-governed, or computational, processes from processes instantiated in the functional architecture. Thus the difference between *test* and *interrupt* is: An interrupt, but not a test, is realized directly by the functional architecture; It is, in fact, a transducer function.

We can think of transducers as demons (to use a notion from Selfridge's pandemonium model of pattern recognition; see, for example, Lindsay and Norman, 1977) that wait passively to be activated only by physical events which meet the proper physical description, that is, events for which they are transducers. Thus activated, and at the initiative of the environmental event, they generate a computational event or symbol structure. What happens afterward depends on whether there are also cognitive demons which respond to the symbol structure generated by transducers, or whether such structures are sought actively by test operations. It seems overwhelmingly likely that both will be required. A view with only demons (for example, the feature detector hierarchy discussed by Barlow, 1972) always leaves the organism stimulus bound, whereas the view with only tests allows little room for the perceptual system to provide surprises and discoveries.

A Transducer Output Is an Atomic Symbol (or n-tuple)
Neither the specification of a transducer's input nor of its output is unproblematic. First, we consider what a transducer should provide to the rest of the cognitive system. Because the output is to serve as the basis for the only contact the cognitive system ever has with the environment, it should provide all (and only) cognitively effective information. It should not provide information that could never serve as the basis for a cognitive distinction (a point we return to in considering the relevance of neurophysiological evidence for discovering transducers). On the other hand, the output must provide the basis for all potential distinctions that could show up in cognitive phenomena— for example, in any perceptual effect, whether conscious or not. Consequently, the output of the set of transducers available to an organism *must preserve all distinctions present in the environmental stimulation that are also relevant to the explanation of some behavioral regularity.*

This requirement, straightforward as it appears, is not easy to meet when placed alongside other requirements of transducers, notably, the requirement that transducers be primitive operations of the functional architecture (as this notion is understood in chapters 4 and 5). Consider, for example, that transducers must provide the basis for the organism to uncover the paradigmatic structure existing among the objects of perception. In other words, transducers must preserve the information that two events or stimuli are, in certain respects, similar while differing in other respects. Moreover, the respects in which objects are perceived as the same or different are often global and topological rather than specifiable in terms of the presence or absence of local (region bounded) features. It would not do, for instance, to have a weighted list of all local, geometrical properties (features) in a display, since, as Minsky and Papert (1969) have shown, this causes information to be lost that is essential for distinguishing pairs of figures such as those in figure 1—a task we are clearly capable of.

In addition, the information provided by transducers must somehow preserve information about stimulus *magnitude*, it must at least make possible recovery of certain magnitude information, since people obviously can respond to magnitudes (for example, intensity, distance, and other ordinal or even metrical properties) in various ways, including

Figure 1. An example of forms that cannot be distinguished solely on the basis of an inventory of their local features.

making magnitude-estimation judgments, as well as judgments that reveal the multidimensional nature of perceived stimuli (for example, Shepard and Chipman, 1970). Later in this section I examine the proposal that transducers output numerals of some sort as a code for magnitude. This proposal, though attractive in many respects, is rejected on the grounds that it is incompatible with constraints on transducers to which we must adhere.

The requirement that arbitrarily many patterns or relational distinctions—as well as some form of metrical or dimensional properties—be recoverable from the outputs of transducers suggests that transducers provide some sort of symbol structures to the cognitive system. For example, the only general way anyone knows to encode metrical information is to use a notational device corresponding to a number system.[2] Such an encoding scheme allows an unbounded (that is, potentially infinite) set of magnitudes to be encoded finitely. It does this by specifying a set of rules whereby arbitrarily many expressions can be generated in a systematic, finitary manner from elements of a finite,

2. It is sometimes suggested that metrical information is encoded in an "analogical" way by some continuous form of representation. Several interpretations of such a claim are possible. The most coherent one is that there is some internal magnitude that serves as an analogue of the external one, say, the frequency of neural firing or the concentration of some biochemical substance. As far as the point at issue here is concerned, however, the fact that this new magnitude is located inside the organism's skin does not make it cognitive. It remains a physical magnitude until it maps onto properties that serve as codes in such cognitive processes as reasoning and inference; or, in computational terms, until it maps onto computationally relevant physical states. Otherwise, a stage of transduction is still required, even though the transducer may be internal. Another interpretation, occasionally suggested, is that the analogue is a continuous symbolic or mental entity—an element of what Goodman (1968) calls a "dense symbol system." The main problem with this interpretation is, nobody really knows what such a claim amounts to; no one has the faintest idea how to reason or compute over such a set of symbols, nor, in general, what postulating such entities gains us. In any case, when the time came to reason, solve problems, or make decisions in such a system, the symbols presumably will have to be converted into some sort of conceptual entities or truth-bearing expressions—which seems to bring us back to the same magnitude-transduction problem we started with.

discrete vocabulary of symbols, thus allowing the mechanism to, in Humboldt's words, "make infinite use of finite means."

Since the precision needed by a psychologically realistic encoding scheme is variable, a natural candidate for this notation is an expandable one, such as the Dewey decimal classification system used in libraries, which can be expanded for arbitrary precision and which provides a unique notation for any new item or magnitude. Because of the systematic relationship between the structure of the expressions in such systems as these and the magnitudes they represent, these systems make it possible to represent any physical magnitude to any degree of precision and to recover the ordinal and metrical relations among stimulus properties in an algorithmical or computable manner, hence, to explain the possibility of performing tasks requiring that magnitudes be encoded.

It might be noted in passing that the right kind of metrical information is not provided simply by quantizing the relevant physical magnitude and having a transducer generate a unique symbol to encode the identity of each quantum. Because the entire range of the dimension in question would have to be quantized in this way, we would have to have either an extremely large number of quanta or a coarse-grained quantization. Although resolution of our ability to discriminate magnitudes may be limited, there is no evidence that it is coarsely quantized; indeed, there is no evidence that it is quantized at all.

Contrary to a common misconception, the fact that our perceptual resolution is limited along certain dimensions does not demonstrate that the input magnitude is quantized into a finite set of categories by our transducers. Limited sensory discriminability does not entail that a fixed number of sensory magnitudes is encoded, and hence, is cognitively distinguishable. The mere fact that two stimulus magnitudes, S_1 and S_2, are separated by less than one just-noticeable-difference (*jnd*)—and hence, are pairwise perceptually indiscriminable—does not mean they are indistinguishable in *every* way to the cognitive system. For example, in a limited resolution system, as opposed to a truly quantized one, there will always be a third magnitude, S_3, such that, whereas S_1 and S_3 are pairwise indiscriminable, S_2 and S_3 can be pairwise discriminated. This shows that S_1 and S_2 behave differently in some situations; hence, they are not cognitively indistinguishable, and must have distinct, cognitive representations. The same is true for all pairs of values of S_1 and S_2 down to the finest grain, where real neural quantization presumably holds.

Note that, if no point S_3 can be found with the required property, then, at that grain, indiscriminability would be transitive; that is, if S_1 is indiscriminable from S_2 and S_2 is indiscriminable from S_3, then S_1

must be indiscriminable from S_3. In that case, indiscriminability would be an equivalence relation and—assuming some pairs of stimuli on that dimension were, in fact, discriminable—would indeed partition that stimulus dimension into equivalence classes or quanta. It is an empirical fact that this is not true in general until one gets to the very fine grain of neural sensitivity, and even there, spontaneous neural noise blurs the quantal boundaries.

Although such reasons as those outlined here might lead one to the view that the output of at least some transducers is a syntactically structured expression corresponding to a global, relational description, or to a numeral in some number system, I shall argue that such a view is inconsistent with the requirements I have placed on transducers. In addition, I shall suggest that the psychophysical facts concerning magnitude judgments, as well as other evidence of the preservation of metrical information by representations, is compatible with the view that transducers produce atomic—that is, noncombinatorial—symbols as codes.

According to the view I have been defending, a transducer is a particular kind of primitive operation in the cognitive functional architecture. According to the present view, the functional architecture represents the finest-grained decomposition of the cognitive process into subprocesses that are still cognitive. Thus it embodies the finest-grained operations that transform cognitive representations into cognitive representations or, in the case of input transducers, physical events into cognitive representations. As the boundary between processes requiring a cognitive or rule-governed explanation and those explainable in terms of physical-biological laws, the operation of such primitive units as transducers must itself not require a cognitive or rule-governed explanation. Hence, primitive operations are, from the viewpoint of cognitive processing, one-step operations. There is no sequence of cognitive states mediating the function realized by a primitive operation; there is only a physical-biological process whose regularities are captured in terms of physical-biological laws.

The generation of numerical or other structured symbolic expressions, however, must be carried out by a system of rules. There is no law of physics, chemistry, or biology that connects physical magnitudes to an arbitrarily extendable set of *arrangements* of symbol tokens; only a system of rules or a generative algorithm can do that. Thus operation of such an expression-generating transducer would have to be explained as a rule-governed, or computational, process. Even if such a process is not cognitive (a possibility already hinted at), it nevertheless fails to qualify as a primitive operation of the functional architecture. It would have to be combinatorial, and, consequently, would have intermediate states and (because the expressions must have variable size) would not be constant in its resource consumption over different inputs. This statement is not true of a transducer whose output consists of an atomic symbol, nor is it true if the output consists of expressions drawn from a finite prearranged set. Such a mechanism would merely convert one physical state into another according to their causal connection, except that the second would also correspond to a computational, or cognitive, state.

If, however, a transducer maps from physical properties into atomic symbols (or, for reasons to be discussed shortly, into n-tuples of symbols), would that not fail to preserve essential stimulus information? Would it not lose configurational or metrical information? The answer is, it need not, providing (a) the range of available transducers is large enough, and (b) the identity of the transducer (including, perhaps, a local neighborhood code from which its location can be derived) is also part of the output code.

For metrical information to be recoverable, all that is needed is a systematic pattern among the transducer outputs, making it possible to define a property over the outputs that meets the metrical axioms. In other words, it must be possible to define a metric over sets of transducer outputs. Of course, a metric defined in this way must also reflect the particular magnitude being transduced.

As an example of how such an interpretation of transducer outputs might work, consider the proposal made by Restle (1959) of a way to define a metric and an ordering on sets. Assume some measure function *m* over sets obtained by some procedure such as counting the elements of the set or taking a weighted sum of the elements, or, in general, any function that yields the value 0 for the empty set and which yields the sum of the values of individual sets as the value for their union when the sets are nonintersecting. The *distance* metric that Restle proposed between two sets consists of the measure of their symmetric set difference; that is, the "distance" between the two sets is found by obtaining the measure of the set consisting of all elements that are in one or the other but not both sets. Similarly, Restle also defines an ordering on sets in terms of such set operations; he shows that when the sets are nested this metric and ordering constitutes a Guttman scale. Restle also argues that such an ordering has interesting psychological properties; for example, the "betweenness" relation used to define the ordering fails to be transitive in certain cases that have empirical analogues in psychophysics.

What is interesting about Restle's proposal is, it shows a simple way in which metrical information can be recovered from *sets* of transducers, each of which produces nothing more than an individual, unique symbol. If, for instance, transducers in a certain class that fired when a signal of a certain magnitude was present formed a nested set (for example, additional transducers fired when the magnitude increased), metrical information could, in principle, be extracted in a simple way by later computational stages.

Similar results are to be expected in the multidimensional case. Here, the multidimensional structure of the stimulus space can be extracted by use of pairwise similarity metrics, which themselves can be based on an encoding such as the one already outlined. Shepard (1964) showed that a set of such pairwise distance measures allow recovery of a multi-dimensional similarity space. Again, it is not my intention to propose that this, in fact, is the process by which the cognitive system makes psychophysical judgments from primitive transducer outputs, only to show that preservation of such information can be achieved in relatively rudimentary ways. Hence, the ability to make metrical judgments does not entail obtaining anything additional from primitive transducers other than a code selected from a finite set; that is, such primitive transducers can remain noncombinatorial, as required by our general conditions on operations of the functional architecture.

In principle, only slightly more is required from transducers for them to preserve global distinctions, such as the topological property illustrated in figure 1. In that case, either there must be global-property transducers, or it must be possible, in principle, to compute relational properties among particular, primitive, region-bounded transducers. While there may be some global-property transducers, they cannot, in general, be the detectors. Because there is no bound on the number of global patterns we can discriminate, it must be true that these patterns are, in general, combinatorial, that is, recursively constructed from elementary subparts. On the other hand, to allow relational properties to be computed over region-bounded transducers, the location (or other unique identifier) of the source of a local code must be available. This is why I have added the requirement that the transducer signal its identity as part of its output. In the case of signaling its spatial location, the transducer need not provide coordinates or any other global index; all that is needed is local or relational information, for example, the identity of its immediate neighbors. This information might even be signaled topographically, by the actual location of the neural connection from the transducer in relation to the location of neural connections from other transducers.

The requirement that transducers signal their identity or their relative location has several interesting consequences which suggest possible points of contact with known empirical phenomena. Indeed, the requirement is reminiscent of Muller's doctrine of "specific nerve energies," which states that the sensation appropriate to a particular receptor is specific to, or is signaled by, the specific nerve fiber that carries information from it. The idea that a region-bounded transducer signals its identity (hence, that something about its location might be recovered) in the form of a symbolic code conforms closely with the independently motivated, theoretical hypothesis that the *place* and *identity* of a feature are encoded separately. This hypothesis arises in low-level vision work, where the notion of a "place token" (Marr, 1976) is needed to explain how the perception of the same higher order pattern can often be produced by arrangements of various elementary features, where it makes little difference what elementary features exist (for other examples, see also, Hochberg, 1968). The notion of a place token (or, as Pylyshyn et al., 1978, call it, an "instantiation finger" or "finst") has also been used to explain certain empirical phenomena involving the superposition of mental images on perceived scenes (see chapter 8).

Such a hypothesis is given strong support by evidence of the existence of "conjunction illusions" (Triesman and Schmidt, 1982), in which subjects misperceive the combination of place/color/identity of stimulus elements, for example, seeing a display consisting of the red letter "A" and the blue letter "B" as having a blue A and a red B, thus mislocating one or the other feature. There are also cases (the "odd man out" phenomenon) in which subjects correctly report whether a display contains a certain feature (say, a gap or end point in a display filled with continuous lines) without being able to report, even roughly, where the feature is found in the display (see Ullman, 1983). In texture perception (for example, Julesz, 1975), use is made of the notion of place as possessing a distinct code.

It may occur to some that the requirement that primitive transducers be nonconstructive or noncombinatorial is too restrictive. That need not be the case, however. No limit is placed on how "complex" a mapping from signal to symbol can be induced by a transducer (in the sense, for example, of mapping exotic classes of physical events onto the same symbol), so long as the complexity is not of a certain kind, namely, a combinatorial complexity that makes "infinite use of finite means."[3] In other words, the mapping must be realized without use of recursive or iterative rules, as is done in the case of all functions performed by primitive operations of the functional architecture. This basic requirement must be adhered to if we are to maintain a principled

3. Although I have not examined the case thoroughly, I would guess that the kind of process that produces what Marr (1976,1982) calls the "raw primal sketch" is a likely candidate for a primitive transducer function, even though it appears to be quite a complex many-one mapping from the proximal retinal stimulation to a (arguably non-combinatorial) data structure (see chapter 7).

interface between processes to be explained in terms of rules and representations and those to be explained in terms of intrinsic (physical, biological, structural) properties of the mechanism carrying out the rules or implementing the algorithm.

Transducer Inputs Must Be Stated in the Language of Physics
Requiring that transducer inputs be described in physics terminology is one of the strongest constraints imposed on what qualifies as a transducer. While most theorists acknowledge that organisms have devices for sensing the physical environment, and that the function we ascribe to such devices is an important part of psychological theory, many are unwilling to restrict such devices to those for which a description can be couched in the language of physics. What exactly does this requirement entail? In the first place, it says the terms of the physical sciences are, in an important sense, the primary terms for describing the physical world, including environments, brains, computers (as physical objects), but not, of course, mental, symbolic, cognitive, computational, or psychological phenomena. The requirement is orthogonal to any belief in philosophical dualism or material reductionism. Whether you hold that mental or cognitive events are reducible to, or independent of, physical laws, you might maintain that when one speaks of physical objects or events, they should be described in the only terms for which causal laws have been formulated in that domain—the terms of physics.

In this context *physical terms* means what philosophers call a "projectable vocabulary," only those terms (words, concepts) that enter into, or could conceivably enter into, laws of physics (and, by extension, laws of chemistry, biology, and so on). Thus, *physical terms* includes not only the basic terms *length, time, mass,* and *force,* and the derivative terms *energy, momentum, speed, charge,* and *temperature,* but more complex terms, such as *cellular discharge, potential gradient, contrast boundary,* and *reverberatory circuit,* which, in principle, are composites of (that is, are described in terms of) basic, physical categories. Not included are such informal class terms as *table, chair, people;* such psychological terms as *thought, decision, belief,* nor formal abstractions such as *symbol, information.* Although specific instances of the last group clearly are physical events or objects (after all, a chair is fairly palpable), they are not those categories that occur in the laws of physics; they refer to things that play a role in descriptions of functions or various statements of nonphysical generalizations, and hence, typically classify objects in a different way from the way they need to be classified for purposes of stating physical laws—as noted in chapter 1.

This informal characterization of what it means to require that inputs to a transducer be stated in a physical vocabulary suffices for our pur-

poses, though in other contexts a technically more precise characterization of *projectability* may be needed (for example, Goodman, 1954).
In fact, here, I continue to use the phrase *physical description* to mean
any description couched in the vocabulary used in physics and the
allied natural sciences. To understand the force of this requirement,
we first consider some possible reasons for *not* using physical-term
descriptions of the environment. As we have noted, the primary reason
is it is highly unlikely that there exists a finite, physical description
invariant over the entire set of objects corresponding to a typical, psychologically relevant category. For example, what can serve as a "reinforcer" is sufficiently open-ended and dependent on a subject's beliefs
that it is inconceivable that there exists a finite, physical description
covering the entire class of potential reinforcers. Even if such a description existed, it would be such a garrulous disjunction that it would
fail to capture the relevant psychological generalizations.

This is an extremely serious problem for a naturalistic psychology
attempting to find generalizations that hold between organisms and
the physical world and that attempts to do so directly by appealing to
a transducer that senses only physically describable aspects of the environment. Relevant aspects of the environment, it turns out, are generally not describable in physical terms. As Hochberg noted (see chapter
1), there are good reasons for doubting that a physical description exists
capable of defining "the stimulus configuration to which a subject is
responding, or by which we can decide what it is that two different
patterns, which both produce the same form percept, have in common."
Psychological regularities are attributable to *perceived*, not physically
described, properties. I have already discussed the reasons for believing
that regularities in psychology are best captured by using cognitive
terms. Thus cognitive generalizations require cognitive categories. We
can save ourselves a lot of trouble if we avoid imposing the restriction
that transducers must operate only over physical properties.

The temptation to avoid physical terms is intensified when we notice
that we *don't need* to define percepts in physical terms in order to
develop theories of certain aspects of "perception." A number of important areas of progress in cognition were possible because investigators
did not feel bound to describe the "stimulus" in physical terms. For
example, the science of phonology has made great progress despite the
failure of acoustical phonetics to provide an adequate description of
the units of analysis in physical terms. The units were simply defined
functionally as the minimal, discriminative elements in a linguistic context. Although no instrumental methods were available, an elaborate
methodology was developed to make such identifications reliable.

Similarly, there is a well-developed tradition in artificial intelligence that studies scene analysis using perceptual rather than physical descriptions as its starting point. That is, input typically consists of "line," "vertex," "shadow edge," and other perceptual categories provided by a human encoder, though it is not clear that, in general, identification of such categories by a perceptual system can occur in this order, with the identification of these categories preceding the recognition of more global patterns, any more than they can in phonetics. Nonetheless, the work of Guzman (1968), Huffman (1971), Clowes (1971), Mackworth (1973), and Waltz (1975) shows that much can be learned about what might be called the syntactic constraints in certain visual scenes without requiring that the input be described in physical terms. While much of the work in the psychology of perception shuns physical descriptions of the input (see the remarks by Hochberg, the work of such neo-Gestaltists as Attneave (1974), and especially the work of Gibson, 1966b,1979), it nevertheless has provided useful insights into the functioning of human perception.

Given the general failure of perceptual psychology to adequately describe stimuli in physical terms, and given the relative success of systems operating on functionally or phenomenologically defined objects (that is, definitions requiring human judgment and perceptual reactions), why is it necessary, or even desirable, to restrict transducer inputs to physically described patterns? Why not concentrate on discovering the properties of physical events that form part of a regular system of behavior and allow phonemes, edges, colors, melodies, even words and faces, to form part of the input to the perceptual system? Would it not be prudent to look for laws wherever we can find them without imposing the additional burden of requiring that some part of the system mesh with a science whose history goes back several millennia?

These questions constitute a serious challenge, to which one might wish to make several different replies. First, though, the requirement that the transducer input be described in physical terms should be clarified in light of the discussion thus far. There is nothing in this requirement which implies that cognitive principles or cognitive processes must be couched in physical terms; indeed, the burden on the transducer arose because all processes past the transducer, including the bulk of the perceptual process, are to be symbolic. The requirement we are discussing is not that the entire stimulus be described in physical terms, only that the input to computationally primitive transducers be so described. Subsequent processing, in which the centrifugal influence of higher cognitive processes figures prominently, will determine how the stimulus is perceived. Furthermore, the requirement is not equivalent to the claim that perceptual patterns (at least, those in vision) are constructed from a two-dimensional array of color-intensity dots, as Gibson thinks cognitivists assume. *Any* arbitrary function of the proximal stimulation, taking in an unspecified slice of space and time, and even including what Gibson calls "higher-order invariants of the ambient optic array viewed from a moving observation point"—are permitted in this formulation, provided only that the domain of the function eventually is given in terms of a physical vocabulary, that is, providing the arguments of the function are terms of physics. Of course, if such a function were specified in the desired manner, it would be possible as well to implement it, using an array of color-intensity sensors and a suitably programmed, general-purpose computer. In that case, the whole system can be considered the virtual transducer for theoretical purposes.

Even granting that the physical-description condition under discussion does not restrict one in certain ways, as some have assumed, it nevertheless is severely restrictive. We have only to note the relative scarcity of proposals for transducers that meet the condition, compared with the range of purely symbolic systems, for example, those of phonology, syntax, and much of both behavioral and cognitive psychology. Then, what virtue is there to our condition? I shall suggest that if we do not subscribe to this criterion, we stand little chance of systematically relating behavior to properties of the physical world.

The Descriptive-Coherence or Unity-of-Science Criterion   In the view of practically everyone, a transducer is a function from usually external physical events to cognitive events or, in our terms, to symbols. To describe this function, we must be able to describe the physical events. Now, as many investigators have recognized, there is no such thing as a neutral description of a physical event; there is no innocent eye, no disinterested observation language. As Hanson (1958) put it, every description is "theory laden." Just as there are better and worse theories—theories that account for larger or smaller segments of the physical world—so there are better and worse descriptions of physical events.

Physics is the basic science because it has provided the most general and most successful set of concepts for describing the physical world. Because of the particular choice of categories physics adopted long ago, it was able to state the laws of physics. We have little reason to think that a science of the physical world is possible with another, entirely different set of categories. Whereas, in the last 2,000 years the basic categories of physics have been refined, they have changed remarkably little. We should be impressed by the fact that there has not been a single serious proposal for reconstructing physical laws on a radically new basis, say, without such concepts as mass, length, time, location, force, energy, and so on.[4]

It is the vocabulary of contemporary physics that makes it possible to capture the natural laws we know. If we were to ignore the vocabulary of physics, and described the physical events that cause cognitive state changes using some other set of terms, say, *only* terms that refer to *perceived* properties such as Gibson's "affordances," we would lose the only coherent way we have of talking about *all* aspects of the physical world. We might simplify considerably our description of certain aspects of perception, but at enormous cost, the cost being that we would then have myriad, independent ways of describing physical phenomena but no way of interrelating them. For instance, we would have a set of terms for perceived speech sounds, perceived musical tones, perceived natural sounds, and so on, with no unifying general laws; for there are no laws about such categories. These categories do not pick out what I have referred to as "projectable properties." The laws of physics hold over such terms as energy, frequency, and time but not over phones, chirps, words, bangs, and the like.

The laws of physics are needed to unify and give coherence to our description of the physical world. Thus we are not at liberty to stop using physical terms to describe that world. On the other hand, as we have seen, we also need functional or perceptually defined terms to capture relevant, cognitive generalizations. In theories of perception both physical and cognitive domains are necessarily involved; thus our only alternative is to retain both physical and functional terms. We need to keep both because otherwise we could not connect our theories of perception with physical regularities. We could not, for example, understand how refracting lenses help some people see clearly, since the explanation of what these glasses do can be provided only by the laws of optics. Similarly, even if phonetics provided the correct description of speech sounds, if we do not connect the categories of phonetics with the categories and terms of physical acoustics, we could not predict what effect various filters have on the perception of speech;

---

4. This in spite of the fact that there would be much to gain if such a reformulation could be achieved. Such an achievement might, for example, resolve certain fundamental difficulties in the foundations of quantum mechanics. Quantum mechanical phenomena have placed considerable strain on our view of the physical world because they make it impossible to maintain a belief in three deeply held principles: the determinacy of physical laws, the validity of classical logic, and the primacy of traditional physical categories. Giving up any one of these principles could, in theory, resolve the impasse. As it happens, some physicists have been willing to discard determinacy and have even considered abandoning standard logic (for example, the law of excluded middle), but so far as I know nobody has ever seriously contemplated giving up the basic physical categories.

nor could we understand how the speech signal is transmitted by radio. And so the list goes. All of these processes require that we describe light and sound in terms of such basic categories as frequency, wavelength, energy, and so on.

Thus the requirement that the transducer function relate both physical and symbolic descriptions is not merely an appeal to keep cognitive science in harmony with physics, nor a wish to describe perceptual systems so they can be built; it arises because an essential part of what is meant when we say something is a physical event is that it can be described in a way that involves the laws of physics. Only a description in physical terms can accomplish that goal. Any other description of physical events deprives those events of physical structure—they can no longer be lawfully related to one another.

Note that I am not implying that the function of *all* primitive, cognitive operators must be described in physical terms. The need for a physical description arises in the case of transducers because they must deal with certain, special categories of physical events—namely, events that organisms can transduce—not just computationally relevant ones. Computational operators deal only with computational events. Although there are physical-event tokens which underlie instances of computational events, the regularities among the computational events are not captured by physical laws, but by computational rules instead. In other words, operators map computational states onto computational states, or symbols onto symbols, but not physical descriptions onto physical descriptions. That is why physical *descriptions* are irrelevant in characterizing computational operators, though, of course, they are relevant to showing how primitive operators are realized in a particular system.

A Note Concerning the Realizability Safeguard   The main purpose in requiring the domain of the transducer function to be stated over a physical vocabulary is to ensure a coherent, noncircular explanation of behavior—not to enable us to build perceptual systems. Still, the capability of building a general perceptual system would assure us that our assumptions about the transducer are not circular, that transducers of this type do not incorporate hidden, unexplained, cognitive processes. Thus, an important benefit of building a perceptual system, or at least using the constructibility criterion to evaluate proposals for transduction, is that the activity helps keep the theorist honest just as, in general, the requirement of computer implementation of cognitive theories can help keep the theorist honest. It is tempting to posit a process that accomplishes some task (for example, playing master-level chess) without realizing that important elements of one's understanding are missing or that the process stated is not mechanically realizable as described. A vital check is imposed by requiring a demonstration that such a task can be accomplished, or that there exists at least one material way to realize the hypothesized function, either by actual implementation or by some attempt to show that it is possible, given the assumptions embodied in the theory.

Demonstration that a process so described is mechanistic may take the form of providing an algorithm for it in a vocabulary of primitive operations, then demonstrating that the primitive operations can be realized physically. Because transducers are special-purpose, primitive operations, this requirement amounts to nothing more than the old criterion of mechanism discussed in chapter 3, now in a new guise. It may seem different because, in practice, one rarely starts off by specifying a process in just any manner that happens to be convenient for the theorist, then trying to show that the process can be mechanized. Although that sometimes happens, a more common course is to start with primitive operations intuitively known to be mechanically realizable, then try to describe a process in terms of those operations.[5]

In the case of transduction, the reverse often occurs. Theories of perception are often constructed on the assumption that certain primitive, transducer functions are available (for example, for the detection of phones, edges, texture gradients, or operands), because, by doing so, we can capture a system of internal regularities. Thus, in specifying transducers we bear a special burden of responsibility to show that such operations are mechanically realizable. The construction of a working perceptual system would go a long way toward assuring us that assumptions about what was being transduced are neither vacuous nor unrealizable. Attempts to develop such a perceptual system frequently have provided important insights into which features of the stimulation play the causal role, and they have led to important discoveries concerning the existence of certain natural constraints of the environment that make it possible for transducers to provide a highly reliable basis for perception. (See, for example, the work of Marr, 1982, and others described in Hanson and Riseman, 1978, or Ballard and Brown, 1982.)

Additional Constraints on Transducers

Can Transducers Be Identified by Neurophysiological Methods?
Many of the problems we have discussed do not arise if we take a

---

5. In a sense, this is what Turing did in attempting to justify informally the idea behind his abstract automaton. He argued that his primitive operations were intuitively basic

purely neurophysiological or biological view, since, in that case, all inputs and outputs of anatomically identified sensor organs consist of causally linked physical or biological events (for example, one studies the physical stimuli sufficient for causing certain cell firings). Problems arise in a cognitive account because one must cross a boundary between a physical vocabulary and a symbolic, or cognitive, one. The principles that govern the relationship of physical terms differ from those of symbolic-psychological terms; the former enter into physical laws, whereas the latter participate in such cognitive processes as inference, problem solving, and thinking—processes I shall henceforth call *computations*, since I take the parallel to be exact for our purposes in discussing transduction.

As we have noted, only a small fraction of the physically discriminable states of a system are computationally, or cognitively, distinct. Furthermore, the computational states consist of classes of physical states that may have no natural, or even finite, physical characterization. This fact has the following far-reaching implication: *The mere fact that an organism can be shown to respond neurophysiologically to a certain physically defined stimulus property such as wavelength does not mean this property is cognitively or computationally relevant.* If a neurophysiologist discovers that presenting a stimulus with property P (for example, an optical-contrast-boundary) causes a physiological event, E_p, then we cannot conclude, for the purpose of constructing a psychological theory, that the organism has a transducer for property P, because E_p may be computationally irrelevant. In fact, P may cause a change in some neurophysiological property that either cuts across cognitive states or leaves the cognitive state unchanged. Uttal (1967), in trying to make a similar point, differentiated between *codes* (which, in my terms, are computationally relevant events, a subset of E_p) and *signs* (E_p events, which are not computationally relevant).

Conversely, just because neurophysiological research has failed to reveal a unique neurophysiological response to physical events of a certain type (for example, the acoustical events corresponding to utterances of the syllable /ba/) does not mean there is no transducer (and thus no internal symbol) for /ba/. To be sure, there must be some internal neurophysiological event that corresponds to the perceived event /ba/ on each occasion; but, as has been argued, the class of such events need have no natural or finite description in the languages of physics or biology. Thus, irrespective of progress in neurophysiology, there will continue to be a problem in characterizing transducers.

This does not mean biological data of various kinds are irrelevant

---

and mechanical in the sense that they did not presuppose an intelligent agent for their execution.

to decisions about the transducers an organism has. Although it is neither necessary nor sufficient that we discover neural loci for particular transducers (no particular empirical data by themselves are ever necessary and sufficient to establish a theoretical construct), such evidence is often useful, especially when it is considered along with psychophysical and behavioral data. In addition, general neurophysiological considerations often can be used to narrow the set of possible mechanisms likely to be satisfactory. For example, general facts about the structure of retinal receptors provide constraints on reasonable hypotheses about mechanisms of color vision, as well as favoring local-interaction mechanisms over global mechanisms—that is, region-bounded as opposed to holistic primitive transducers, though they do not rule out the latter. Despite the relevance of this data, it is important to keep in mind the pitfalls of taking receptor physiology as a direct route to a determination of the nature of available transducers.

Can Transducers Be Identified by Psychophysical Methods?

The branch of psychology one might expect to provide the most direct evidence of the nature of transducers is psychophysics. Psychophysics traditionally has been concerned with relating physical and psychological (perceptual) properties. Traditional psychophysical experimentation, however, has run into considerable difficulty in the past, principally because it tended to treat the entire perceptual system as though it were a transducer. Thus, attempts to relate physically described events to judgments have foundered on two fundamental difficulties. One difficulty is the problem of choosing the appropriate physical description of the event—a problem we have already discussed. The other arises from the fact that most perceptual phenomena (certainly those involving judgments) are under the control of high-level cognitive processes. Of the two, the first difficulty has been of central concern to a group of perceptionists led by the late J. J. Gibson. The work of this group is more or less outside the mainstream of psychophysics (indeed, of psychology), but many of their findings bear directly on classic psychophysical questions. I take up some aspects of this approach in the next section.

The second difficulty has been surprisingly slow in coming to the attention of psychologists. Its first symptom was the constant difficulty of finding robust psychophysical measures, that is, measures which cannot be disrupted by contextual factors. One of the first casualties of this problem was that bastion of psychophysics, the psychophysical threshold. The success of the theory of signal detectability caused a minor revolution in psychophysics by demonstrating that an observer not only detects the presence of a signal (presumably a pure transducer function) but also must make a decision in the face of natural uncertainty about how to respond.

The difficulties in psychophysics go deeper than the mere neglect of response-selection processes, however. Virtually every psycho-physical experiment requires that a subject selectively attend to a par-ticular experimenter-defined stimulus feature, that the subject treat certain sensory qualities in isolation and perform certain comparisons, discriminations, or judgments, based on isolated elements of the total stimulus event. In other words, the subject must abandon the normal operation of the cognitive system and tap directly into what is assumed to be a single transducer.

The assumption that it is possible to access individual transducers is consistent with nineteenth-century British empiricist views of per-ception, which assumed that percepts are constructed from what were called "sense data," or elementary sensations that can be experienced in isolation. We now know that such sensations as the conscious ex-perience of redness, of roundness or brightness, are, in fact, cognitive *constructs* not determined solely by the nature of the stimulating event but by the *pattern* of stimulation as well, as Gibson (1966b) persuasively argued. Further, the phenomenal properties of perceived objects are affected by what people believe they are looking at (see, for example, Rock, 1983). The color you see something as possessing depends on what you take the object to be; red looks different on an apple than on an orange (for example, Delk and Fillenbaum, 1978). In other words, sensations are not stimulus-bound; they can be affected by context, memory, expectation, and inference. Sensations are not the basis of perception but, rather, the result of it. In the present view, perception begins with the output of transducers, not with sensations. Transducers provide the initial information, though this information is not necessarily available to consciousness (indeed, probably it almost never is). Many examples can be found showing that the operative information typically is not noticed by an observer, in the sense that the observer is *aware* of its having been in the input. For example, Hess (1975) has shown that various impressions about a person are reliably communicated by pupil diameter, though people are unaware of the role played by this cue. At some level beyond the transducer, where what is perceived may become available to consciousness, perception is largely symbolic and knowledge-based. That is the burden of the demonstrations con-stituting the "new look" movement in perception research (for example, Bruner, 1957). Thus, although transducers provide symbolic input to the complex, cognitive processes involved in perception, a psycho-physical experiment cannot bypass the cognitive system and directly examine the output of the transducers.

There is one class of psychophysical experiment, however, that re-quires a minimum of cognitive intervention, and which therefore pro-vides relevant data on transducer functions. The most sensitive possible measure of transducer operation is a *null* measure. If we can demonstrate that two physical events are perceptually equivalent over a range of contextual variation, we can be reasonably confident that the descrip-tions of the events are mapped onto the same symbol structures at some extremely low level of the perceptual system—possibly, the transducer output. Although the question of which physical descriptions are relevant is not solved, the null-detection task minimizes the problem, since the fact that two events are indistinguishable (in the special sense that they do not result in a perceptual discontinuity) implies that *all* physical descriptions of one event are cognitively equivalent to all physical descriptions of the other event. Thus that will be true of the particular description we choose. Of course, this holds true only as a first approximation, since, in practice, certain methodological assump-tions must be made in defining perceptual equivalence.

Data of the type already alluded to come from what Brindley (1970) has called class A psychophysical experiments. In these experiments subjects are required only to indicate whether they perceive a discon-tinuity in a visual field. Discontinuities can, for instance, involve a light in a dark field, a boundary between two halves of a field, or a break in a vernier line. These measures are the most sensitive psychophysical ones possible for revealing some of the physical descriptions that map into identical computational states. Ian Howard (1974) explains this sensitivity by pointing out that in class A experiments virtually all ambiguity is removed from both the stimulus and the demands on the subject, who, in effect, acts as a null-reading instrument. As soon as the subject is required to isolate the stimulus features being judged from among other features, the subject's entire repertoire of sensory, perceptual, and linguistic functions and skills is brought to bear—in which case we no longer have a null instrument but a conniving, guess-ing, knowledgeable strategist.

Where applicable, class A methods can be used to infer certain psy-chophysical functions, such as the mapping from mixtures of light of different wavelengths onto perceived colors. These functions place an upper bound on the discriminative power of a transducer. To the extent that the methods are maximally sensitive to psychophysical discrimi-nability, or that they provide evidence of maximal discriminative ca-pacities, they may be as close as we can come to tapping the outputs of primitive transducers. Even here, though, we cannot assume we are getting a direct reading of transducer outputs without independent confirmatory evidence; always in psychological investigations the whole cognitive system is involved, so one can never guarantee that the results are not directly attributable to some higher-level decision. In chapter 8 I consider some examples in which robust, reliable observations tell us more about the typical subject's understanding of the task and knowledge of certain topics than about the functions realized by the functional architecture.

Can Transducers Be Identified by Functional Analysis?
The most common way of inferring the functions carried out by transducers is simply to invoke the time-honored hypothetico-deductive strategy. If positing the existence of a transducer for some class of events E (where E may not be given in terms of a physical description) greatly simplifies explanation of some domain of cognition, then an E-transducer certainly becomes a plausible empirical hypothesis, though the correct way to describe the transducer (that is, how to characterize its input-output function so as to respect the conditions already discussed) remains an open research question. Such is the case, for example, for the concept of the phone in phonology.

By itself, functional analysis of some part of the cognitive system provides no more secure a basis for inferring the existence of particular transducers than does either psychophysical or neurophysiological observation. Recall that in psychophysical or neurophysiological observation the problem is lack of a purely neurophysiological basis for distinguishing between physical and computational events—between *codes* and *signs*. Similarly, a functional analysis may yield a useful taxonomy for some appropriately circumscribed subset of cognition (for example, the subset dealt with in phonology). This taxonomy, however, is extremely sensitive to the particular way in which the subset is delineated. Since other processes besides those covered in the chosen domain might also use the same transducers (for instance, in the phone example, processes dealing with the perception of intonation, accent, and suprasegmentals might well use the same acoustical transducers), the functional analysis (here, phonetic analysis) gives only part of the story. Demands imposed by the more general perceptual needs might cause us to change our idea of the transducer functions required.

This cautionary note is in part a consequence of the general principle which states that the taxonomies or theoretical entities that yield the greatest economies depends largely on how one assesses economies and what one chooses as the domain of explanation; a good choice is said to "carve nature at her joints." It is a consequence as well of a more directly appropriate, artificial intelligence principle known as the principle of least commitment, discussed by Marr (1976) in relation to the design of a vision system. Transduction must be a one-shot process;

moderately new interpretations should not require that the physical event be transduced again, this time with different transducers providing the information. Thus, either the symbols from all transducers continue to be available for some time after the event, or the transducer output must be sufficiently general purpose to allow its use in a reasonably large cognitive domain. Of course it *may* turn out that some transducers are extremely special purpose (there is some evidence that this is so in the case of speech perception). Clearly, the details of particular cases depend on theoretical and empirical progress. Nonetheless, such considerations suggest caution in accepting the result of functional analysis as setting the sufficiency requirements for transducers.

Functional analysis can be misleading in other ways. Because the analysis is based on judgments or perceptions involving the entire cognitive system, we cannot be confident that the units posited are stimulus bound in the sense discussed. That is, we do not know whether the elements are the outputs of transducers or the result of processes that depend strongly on events at higher cognitive levels. For example, phonetic studies have suggested to linguists that there are three distinguishable levels of stress in sentences. Trained linguists were able to mark these levels with reasonable reliability on transcriptions. However, Lieberman (1965), using acoustically modified speech that retained most of the supersegmental information but which destroyed intelligibility, was able to show that linguists can no longer reliably identify stress levels and locations. It appears that accurate perception of stress requires understanding of the utterance.[6] The influence thus is primarily from higher cognitive processes; thereafter, the functionally defined term *stress* is not stimulus bound. It may be that no physical description exists that can serve as the input to an appropriately constrained transducer function for phonetic stress.

To avoid pointless argument, we should avoid claiming that stress information is not in the physical event corresponding to a token utterance of the sentence, for clearly, if the event had not taken place, there would be no stress information. The point is simply that the perception of stress is not stimulus bound, which, in turn, means that a function going from some physical description to the perception of stress cannot, in the sense intended here, be carried out by a primitive

---

6. There may be other explanations for the empirical phenomenon, since the signal was distorted. (For example, Lieberman may have been examining the speech signal under the wrong physical description and thus inadvertently destroyed the stress-bearing features.) A sufficient number of experiments has been made, however, leading to the same general conclusions, to suggest that the principle is secure; for example, the perception of pauses and clicks is sensitive to linguistically defined phrase boundaries, hence, to factors far upstream in terms of information processing.

transducer. Of course, if we allowed a transducer to be a function going from, say, a Fourier analysis of the waveform to a syntactic parse of the sentence, and from there to the perception of stress (for example, a fairly advanced version of a computer speech-recognition system such as HEARSAY), then, in that extended sense of a "transducer," it would be a function that recovers stress from the physical event; thus the information must have been "in the stimulus." Clearly, the notion of transduction needs to be constrained sufficiently to prevent such vacuous use of the term, since, as we have noted, in that sense of *transducer*, entire organisms are nothing but transducers.

I have suggested that neither psychophysics nor neurophysiology nor functional analysis can solve the problem of discovering cognitive transducers. In this field there are no sure and easy ways; it is, as always, a matter of "inference to the best hypothesis." In the process of searching for the right characterization of transducers, however, the criteria described in this section provide essential constraints, while the goal of constructing a working system provides a salubrious discipline. It is possible that, when properly conceived (that is, without sacrificing generality for high performance in restricted domains), the task of implementing a system that deals directly with a natural environment is the closest thing we have to a discovery methodology.

Summary
In the discussion thus far I have insisted on the need for a principled constraint on what can count as a transducer. I have characterized a transducer as a function instantiated in the functional architecture, whose purpose it is to map physical events into cognitive, or computational, events. Roughly speaking, a transducer produces a code, C, of bounded size—say, an n-tuple of symbols—whenever it is stimulated by an event that is a member of a class of events that can be given a finite physical description, D, cast in terms of the primitive vocabulary of physics (or chemistry or some other basic, natural science). It is an approximation only to the extent that the relation between D and C can be modulated—primarily along a dimension of intensity—by the state of the organism. It cannot be freely altered to, for example, produce a code, C', which normally is produced by a different transducer or in response to a different description D'. Specifically, it cannot be modified by the cognitive system so as to change the semantic content it imparts to symbols in the cognitive system, though it can be affected by certain adjustments to sense organs, for instance, by adjustments in sensitivity or even by a general movement, as in the case of changing the direction of gaze. As I have already remarked, such a characterization does not exclude physically complex transducers. In particular, it does not exclude

transducers whose inputs are spatially and temporally extended. Thus, in many ways, the characterization is sympathetic to some of Gibson's claims, though it differs sharply from the "direct perception view."

The preceding discussion can be seen as an examination of some implications of the architecture-process distinction as it applies to the interface between systems whose regularities are captured in terms of intrinsic (that is, physical or biological) properties of the system and systems whose regularities are at least partly captured in terms of the properties of representations. Before we extend the discussion of these implications to more central, or cognitive, concerns, it should be instructive to observe how the ideas I have developed can be applied directly to an analysis of a class of theories of vision due to James Gibson, which claim that we see by "direct perception," without the benefit of inferences or representations.

Some Consequences of This Approach: Is Perception "Direct"?

One of the more influential schools of perception, outside of the information-processing tradition, is that of J. J. Gibson (summarized in Gibson, 1979). This approach, referred to as "direct realism," dates from the mid-1950s, but it has experienced a recent upsurge in popularity (Turvey, 1977; Neisser, 1976; Shaw and Bransford, 1977; see also the commentaries on Ullman, 1980). Like many groups that champion radical departure from a more or less conventional doctrine, Gibsonians have developed their own distinctive rhetoric, one that makes much of their theoretical writings bewildering to outsiders. If we take the claims made by this school at face value, we would conclude that direct realism is the exact antithesis of the computational approach. In particular, the computational view takes the position that perception and cognition involve a great deal of computation, which, in turn, necessitates speaking of primitive operations, of inference, memory, and, in particular, representation. These are all terms disparaged by direct realists, whose view is that, under ecologically normal circumstances, perception is direct in the sense that it involves no *construction* of enriched representation through the "epistemic mediation" of knowledge, expectations, memories, or inferences. Rather, it merely involves detection of information about the world, all of which is there in the optical invariances, needing only to be picked up—not, in any way, inferred or reconstructed.

Stated thus, the view is indeed radical. Clearly, it is opposed to the computational approach. Its program of eliminating the appeal to representations and other mental constructs essentially is the behaviorist program; indeed, it fails for some of the same reasons that behaviorism fails. Direct realism presupposes that organisms detect directly those categories of things in the world needed to account for the organisms' subsequent behavior. The same strategy is adopted by behaviorism. In a behavioral analysis, recognition of a stimulus, response, and reinforcer is presupposed in ways that are outside the theory; that is, a behavioral analysis cannot give an account (based on conditioning) of what constitutes a stimulus, response, or reinforcer. Thus these are objects the organism must individuate (or pick out or encode) prior to subsequent conditioning. Thus, in behavioral terms, the organism's environment consists of precisely those entities. This amounts to the assumption that organisms have transducers which respond to an environment under such a description (that is, not a physical description but a description based on perceptual categories and behavioral acts); it is precisely the assumption Gibson makes, though his categories are somewhat more subtle and include such things as "affordances."

The reason we find ourselves postulating a role for representations and inference in perception is: We require that what is "directly picked up" be only those properties for which the organism has transducers. Because transducers are primitive mechanisms of the functional architecture, they must be constrained in the ways I have been discussing. With tranducers constrained this way, we discover that what is transduced is not the same as what is perceived. For example, we perceive meaningful objects and relations categorized according to our knowledge of such things as their function; thus perception is, in general, highly penetrable by cognition. On the other hand, transduction is driven by the world in a way that is systematic when the world is described in physical terms (that is, terms in the projectable vocabulary of physics), as well as being stimulus bound and cognitively impenetrable. Thus perception is seen as the product of both transduction and cognition; it is perception that determines regularities in action.

Gibson's system is complex and manifold in detail, and by his own admission incomplete in many important respects. Without attempting to cover the approach comprehensively, I discuss some examples of its claims, to see how they connect with the analysis of transduction already given. A comprehensive critique of the direct realist position is provided in Fodor and Pylyshyn (1981), to which the reader is referred for clarification.

"Ecological Optics" and the Perception of Spatial Layout

According to Gibson, normal perception (that is, perception in an "ecologically valid" environment, as opposed to a perception laboratory) involves active exploration by an organism. This exploration can be viewed as the dynamic sampling of a space of potential, proximal stimulations. The totality of such potential stimulation is systematically and, in most cases, unequivocally related to the distal environment. It is the task of "ecological optics" to give an account of the way in which the space of proximal stimulations provides unambiguous information about objects and layouts (that is, three-dimensional arrangements of objects) in the environment.

There is nothing outrageous in this claim. Its point seems primarily to be one of emphasis, and it does lead to a unique experimental research style. Direct realism asserts that an interesting question about perception is, How does the organism explore the available stimulation by moving through the "ambient optical array" containing the information? This question contrasts with the question of how an organism infers the structure of the environment from the pattern of stimulation arriving at a set of anatomically distributed receptors. Turvey (1977) refers to the view implied by the first question as the *ordinal* conception of the perceptual input or image, and to the second as the *anatomical* conception.

In many ways, this is an interesting idea, since it emphasizes the active, exploratory nature of most visual perception. Clearly, much additional information would be available (hence, in principle, would not have to be inferred from knowledge of the world) if the organism could move about while actively sampling this information. The Gibsonian claim, however, goes well beyond this observation. The distinction between these two views of the image (the ordinal and the anatomical) is considered a question of how the proximal stimulus should be described; thus it is an issue relevant to our discussion. Turvey (1977, p. 69) puts it this way: "The question . . . is whether the light at the eye is to be described in the coordinates of the retina or in the coordinates of the environment." Since both are physical descriptions, the issue remains unresolved on that basis. How, then, does an organism gain access to the environmental coordinates? Through what energy transfers is such information conveyed? Following are two possible interpretations of the "ordinal view."

The first interpretation can be dealt with using conventional retinal images. Indeed, it is the approach taken by most contemporary computational models of vision. In this approach certain patterns of proximal stimulation—mostly, though not entirely, those located on the retinas— are converted into an internal representation which encodes certain proximal characteristics explicitly. It encodes certain stimulus-bound characteristics of the incident stimulation that the visual system must use later. Many of the characteristics that are explicitly encoded are ones which, under normal conditions, correlate reliably with distal properties of the scene (these are what Barrow and Tenenbaum, 1978, call "intrinsic scene characteristics"). Thus, in a certain sense, one might think of the transduction of such characteristics as tantamount to picking up distal properties of the scene. Of course, this is just a manner of speaking, since, without the proximal characteristics, the distal characteristics are not perceived; furthermore, the perception of distal scene properties can occur *without the presence of the distal scene*, providing the right proximal characteristics are present (that is, we get perceptual illusions). Nonetheless, in a limited sense, the process might be said to deal with "environmental coordinates."

The second possible interpretation of the view that the transduced stimulus must be described in environmental coordinates is more troublesome. According to this view, the actual spatial coordinates of objects in the environment can be detected directly *with no interpretation or inference*, providing some movement of the observer occurs. What an organism actually detects is the "ordinal image"—an "arrangement of differences in intensity in different directions from the eye" and a sample of the total "ambient optical array." In the Gibsonian view, this ambient, optical array unambiguously *provides information* about the three-dimensional layout of the environment without the organism having to make inferences or consult its memory or knowledge of the world. This is so because there is a mathematical relationship between the layout of objects in the scene and the optical array available to an active organism; presumably, such a relationship is derivable from some sort of projective geometry and from the laws of reflection, diffusion, and so on. To perceive the environment, the organism moves its various sensory systems through this optic array, and in so doing, simply *picks up the information that specifies the location of objects*.

What primarily makes this explanation of spatial perception vacuous is the lack of principled constraint on the notion of "information pickup." Unless we constrain what counts as "directly picking up" information, this way of describing perception skirts the entire problem of explaining perception by attributing it to the unconstrained "information pickup" function. Since whatever an organism can see is, in some sense, "specified by the light" (that is, if it were not for the light, it would not be seen), and since there are no restrictions on what qualifies as being directly "picked up," we might as well assume that the organism simply picks up directly whatever it can, in fact, perceive under some circumstance or other—for example, people, furniture, animals, the property of being far away, being honest, "affording" warmth or nourishment. (These, incidentally, are not fanciful examples. In being consistent in his attempt to avoid cognitive mediation, Gibson claims that these and other, similar properties are, in fact, directly picked up. See, for example, Gibson, 1979.) If that is what is directly picked up, there is, trivially, no problem involved in explaining perception. Indeed, there is no problem involved in *psychology* in general, since we directly pick up the causes of our behavior. In direct realism, it seems, the cognitivist's displaced homunculus has at last found a home in the information-pickup function. This—what Fodor and Pylyshyn (1981) call the "trivialization problem"—is the single most serious problem a direct realist confronts.

Fodor and Pylyshyn (1981) consider several possible ways Gibson might be viewed as intending to constrain what counts as the pickup of information or as constraining the properties that can be detected directly. We conclude that the various attempts made are inconsistent with one another. We further conclude that unless representations and inferences are admitted, it will continue to be impossible to prevent the trivialization of accounts of perception. To specify what may count as being directly picked up is to specify what can be transduced. I have already presented arguments for specific constraints on transduction; they are precisely the constraints necessary to prevent trivialization. As we have seen, however, they are also constraints that force us to postulate "epistemic mediation" in order to bridge the gap between what is transduced and what is perceived. Let us now look at why the Gibsonian view concerning the detection of spatial layout is excluded by my conditions on transduction.

The reason the coordinates of the distal scene are unlikely to be among those properties of a scene that are primitively transduced is partly that these coordinates do not univocally determine the perceived locations; perceived location is not stimulus-bound to a property such as "location in the scene." The reason is so simple as to be banal. It is this: For certain objects to be *perceived* as located at particular places in space, it is neither necessary nor sufficient that they actually *be* located at those particular places. It is easily demonstrated that *where* objects and visual features are seen to be located in space depends on, for instance, the relative positions of their projections on the two retinas, on their motion relative to each other as well as in relation to their positions on the retina, even in some cases on *what* they are seen to be, what size they are perceived to be, and so on. Because of this dependency, there are depth illusions; indeed, that's why it is possible to produce three-dimensional perception from two-dimensional displays, using a binocular stereoscopic viewer. Binocular stereograms work precisely because what the visual system transduces is not *literally* location in 3-D but rather some much more primitive properties, such as retinal disparity. To dismiss these results on the grounds that they were not produced in an "ecologically valid environment" is to misunderstand the nature of causal explanation. The way we demonstrate that A is not the cause of B in any science (at least since J. S. Mill) is to apply the method of differences in whatever environment is necessary for performing the experiment. What is done to demonstrate that B is not caused by A (but by X) is to show that B can be produced without the occurrence of A (not, however, without the occurrence of X).

Since three-dimension location is demonstrably not what actually serves as the input to the perceptual system, the perception of location in a 3-D frame of reference must be derived from something other than the primitive transducers, something that takes the output of the primitive transducers and constructs or derives the 3-D percept. A reasonable—though by no means established—hypothesis is that what produces the 3-D percept is the cognitive system itself.[7] Similarly, when illusions occur, a reasonable hypothesis is that one or another assumption involved in an inferential cognitive process fails to hold.

Many, of course, have ignored Gibson's more ambitious (and theoretically important) claims, taking him simply as providing sound arguments against sense-data theories and certain views of perception that take as their starting point instantaneous point-intensities on the retina as the proper description of the stimulus or as the transducer function. Gibson's research can be read as providing important methodological and empirical insights that are very much in keeping with the goals and program of cognitive science. In the remainder of this chapter I shall examine one or two of Gibson's claims from that perspective, suggesting (a) why some of the claims made by Gibson and his followers cannot be true, and (b) why other claims and criticism of earlier work, as well as some of their empirical results, are important and relevant to the cognitivist approach. Once again, this is not a general evaluation of the direct realism program; Fodor and I have provided that elsewhere. Rather, it is an examination of a few selected Gibsonian claims that may help illustrate the application of the functional-architecture-process distinction to certain problems in perception.

---

7. I say it is not established that this construction is carried out by the cognitive system, not because there is any doubt that it *is* a construction of some sort, but rather, that the question may still be open whether the constructions carried out by the low-level visual system merit the ascription "cognitive" in the fullest sense in which I am using the term, say, when I speak of "cognitive penetrability" as a prime indicator. The possibility I want to leave open is the one raised in chapter 5, that there may be combinatorial computational processes that are subpersonal or that are not carried out over cognitive or intentional representations. In fact, even if they are carried out over such representations, it might be that the representations involved are *internal* to the vision system and thus can neither enter into inferences outside that system nor be influenced by other beliefs (for a discussion of such modular systems, see Fodor, 1983). This point, however, is a minor one when compared with the issue of direct realism or constraining what is considered transduction.

Viewed one way, the Gibsonian program falls in the same camp as the research already cited, which is concerned with specifying transducer functions by functional analysis. As I remarked in that discussion, no matter how valuable such work is, if researchers aspire to achieve a perceptual theory (that is, a theory of how percepts are caused by events in the world), they cannot avoid worrying about whether the properties studied are transducible. Recall that the categories inferred from functional analysis typically are ones which, like most perceptual categories, are constructed from transducer outputs by inferential processes. The situation is exactly the same as that encountered in phonology, except that, compared with the entire domain of visual perception, phonology appears to involve a more tightly knit system and consequently has produced some rather clear, specific theories. In addition, contemporary phonologists have had the sense not to claim to be developing a theory of the entire sound-to-speech perceptual process.

To continue the parallel with phonology: It is possible that a successfully completed theory of ecological optics would provide a description of some constraints that hold among post-transducer perceptual properties, as phonology has done with some success. This kind of theory would be of considerable importance to a study of visual perception even if it provided no way to bypass the need for representations. As was discovered in artificial intelligence research in vision (especially the work of Waltz, 1975, and, more recently, in the work of Marr, 1982), capitalizing on such inherent constraints is important in allowing the visual system to avoid certain combinatorial processes in analyzing a scene. At the same time, it suggests possible transducers to look for by proposing properties of an idealized visual domain (the so-called natural constraints) which, if assumed by our visual system, would explain how the system apparently manages to be so efficient and veridical under normal circumstances. Although this is not at all the way direct realists view their enterprise, such a view might explain the affinity with the Gibson approach that some computationalists seem to feel.

If Gibson is read as searching for new kinds of transducer functions inferred from a functional analysis, as some people feel is the case, it might be interesting to see details of the proposals suggested by research done within the ecological optics framework, other than the "ordinal coordinates" and "affordances" readily excludable on the basis of the criteria I have introduced. In a publication of notes for his latest book, Gibson (1973) speculates on some features of an optic array that lead to perception of form.

The information-bearing features are things like . . . alignment or straightness (being "in line" but not necessarily a line as such) as against bentness or curvature; perpendicularity or rectangularity; parallelity as against convergence; intersections; closures and symmetries. These features are present in an unchanging array, but they are best revealed in a changing array, one kind of change being transformation. We have scarcely begun to understand them, and neither mathematics nor the Gestalt hypothesis has been adequate for the task. But it is along those lines that we would proceed. (p. 45)

Such proposals are not new to computational approaches to vision; similar features (but with a much richer set of differentiations) have formed the basis of such analyses of symbolic scenes as that of Waltz (1975). Much earlier, Gibson proposed more unusual and more carefully studied features as being relevant to perceptions of space and motion. Some of the best known are related to "optical texture." It can be shown that texture density, texture gradient, texture discontinuity, and the like are cues to depth and orientation of surfaces, while such optical-texture flows as expansion, contraction, acceleration, and relative motion (parallax) are cues to various perceptual phenomena, from approach-recede movements to shape and relative location. From these properties of the proximal stimulation, it is even possible to separate the observer's motion from that of objects in the environment.

Thus it becomes interesting, and relevant, to ask: Are such properties correlated with certain perceptual phenomena? and Are these properties ones for which a suitable transducer exists? Although the first question has received considerable attention in perception laboratories, little attention has been paid to the second question. Unless the properties in question are transduced in the constrained sense—unless they can be described in physical terms, are stimulus-bound, and are generally functions that can be viewed as instantiated in the functional architecture—they cannot be taken as the basis of perceptual phenomena. They, like sensations, the building blocks proposed by the British empiricists, are much more likely to be cognitive constructs than basic input properties. So far, there is only fragmentary evidence concerning such questions; but all the available evidence indicates that such cues underdetermine the percept. On the other hand, there is evidence of both the cognitive impenetrability of some perceptual features and the utility of some of the cues as bases for reliable perceptual inferences, providing the inferences are constrained in certain ways—for example, according to the assumption that there are certain natural constraints in the scene. Ironically, most of this work has been carried out by computer modelers (see, for example, Marr, 1982).

Detecting Invariance

Closely related—and subject to the same general remarks—is Gibson's focal interest in the notion of *invariance*. Because the notion of invariance raises problems that are somewhat different from those we have been discussing, it is considered separately. In discussing the differentiation theory of perceptual learning, Gibson (1966b, p. 271) characterizes the process as, "one of learning what to attend to, both overtly and covertly. For the perception of objects, it is the detection of distinctive features and the abstraction of general properties. This almost always involves the detection of invariants under changing stimulation. . . . The exploratory perceptual systems typically produce transformations so that invariants can be isolated. . . . And the action of the nervous system is conceived as resonating to the stimulus information. . . ."

The theme that perception involves the detection of invariance is ubiquitous in Gibsonian theory. Use of the word *detect*, in particular, suggests that, whereas exploration of the environment may be an active process, actual identification of the object or form is both passive and primitive, involving no cognitive intervention. And that, of course, is the direct realist philosophy: all the information is available in the physical event; one has only to reach out and resonate to it. Were it not for such claims about the primitiveness and noncognitiveness of detection, there would be little to object to in this way of speaking, for clearly there is a sense in which the recognition of, say, a cube could be viewed as the detection of properties invariant over the transformations of the proximal stimulation that maintain "cubeness."

In fact, it is a goal of computer vision research to discover a mapping from the proximal stimulation into systems of representation that distinguish between those aspects of an object invariant over transformations that maintain the object's identity from those that indicate its particular state (location, orientation, illumination, motion, and so on). It might even be said that it is the goal of linguistic theory to discover mappings from sentences into systems of representation (sometimes called "logical forms") invariant over certain transformations which might be called paraphrase.

Capturing invariance is the concern of every scientist. Gibson and his colleagues have made contributions by stressing that what are invariants depends on the transformations available and, at least in vision and haptic perception, that the transformations typically are under voluntary control. They have made additional contributions by pointing out that if the abstraction of invariants is viewed as the primary task, one is often led to investigate new ways of describing the proximal stimulus—which suggests useful transducers to look for. It is quite another matter to claim that the process of abstracting these invariants amounts to *focusing of attention* or making a selection.

Part of the problem is the same as that with the notion of information pickup: There are no constraints on the use of such terms as selection (or focusing attention). Saying that, in recognizing an object, a person simply focuses attention on, or selectively attends to, the object's invariance appears to remove the need for "epistemically mediated" computational processes. The need to draw on other knowledge appears not to arise, because one ignores those aspects of the stimulus that do not signal its invariance. Neisser (1976, p. 85) uses the analogy: "To pick one apple from a tree you need not filter out all the others; you just don't pick them. A theory of apple picking would have much to explain . . . but it would not have to specify a mechanism to keep unwanted apples out of your mouth."

And so it would not—for a reason that is significant. The rule for individuating (*not* "identifying") apples can be stated simply in the language of physics, in terms of physical coordinates. When this is true in perception—for example, when the principle for individuating an aspect of a stimulus can be stated in terms of time, space, and so on—and when the cognitive system has access to the terms specified through a transducer, it may indeed be possible to focus attention merely by ignoring irrelevant transducers. Unless "cubeness" can be defined in physical terms, however, so that a cubeness transducer becomes possible, talk of detecting the property of being a cube by attending to invariants remains a loose metaphor at best.

Temporal Order and Memory
The last claim of direct realism that we examine concerns the notions of temporal order and the role of memory. In a classic paper, Gibson (1966a) proposes a new way of viewing temporal order. He argues that it is incorrect to attribute apprehension of adjacent order to perception and apprehension of temporal order to memory. Although, in cognition, the case for the interchangeability of time and space seems convincing to me, there is little evidence that Gibson's arguments have had much impact in psychology. The dimensions of time and space are treated very differently, not only in cognitive psychology (where a minor exception is the acceptance of local-feature detectors for motion and intensity change), but in artificial intelligence as well. In computer modeling, whenever time is not ignored, invariably it is quantized or it appears as a tag associated with a state description (for example, in Winograd, 1972; Norman and Rumelhart, 1976). It has long been a puzzle to me why hierarchical, qualitative, descriptive structures are routinely used to represent spatial and semantic domains but never,

as far as I know, for temporal domains. Time, a curious dimension in psychology, remains a special problem in cognitive science. As noted in chapter 3, because computational processes are seen as running in real *time* (externally observable and cognitively significant) but not in real *space* (spatial location is not cognitively significant), the time dimension has been given special status.

Gibson was concerned that the conventional way of looking at temporal order differs from that of looking at spatial order, in that, at least in certain cases, spatial order is considered susceptible to direct, non-inferential pattern recognition (for example, by matching templates), whereas temporal order is always thought to require memory and a comparison stage. In contrast with this view (still prevalent today), Gibson proposed the following principles of temporal order apprehension, which he called "theorems." I quote the first four directly from Gibson (1966a).

> A succession can be perceived without having to convert all its elements into a simultaneous complex.

> Stimulation normally consists of successivities as well as adjacencies, and either will excite a receptive system.

> The detection of *different-from-before* is simply an alternative to the detection of *same-as-before*, and both are primitive.

> With increasing elaboration of the successive order of stimulation and the adjacent order of stimulation, limits are finally reached to the apprehension of both successive units and adjacent units.

In effect, "theorems" 1 through 3 assert that there are transducers for both spatially extended patterns and temporally extended (sequential) patterns. Therefore, they explicitly deny the need to appeal to memory in the detection of change. Although this may seem counterintuitive, it is nevertheless true that, from the perspective of our criteria for transduction, it makes no difference whether we use temporal or spatial coordinates so long as the stimulus event is described in physical terms. Thus Gibson's principles are quite compatible with the requirements I propose. Whether such transducers actually exist is an empirical question.

Still, the notion that *same-as-before* and *different-from-before* can be transduced without using memory seems troublesome. Surely, recognition that the person coming through a door is a different person from the one who earlier went in through that door involves consulting one's memory, no matter how brief the interval. Of course, for us, this example is excluded, because, by our previous criteria, *person* clearly is not a transducible category. Let us therefore consider a case in which the two events *are* transducible. Now, what can we say about the need for memory?

Suppose the first event has physical description D_1 and the second, physical description D_2. Then there is clearly a physical description, D_{12}, of the change event itself (assuming, for the sake of convenience in exposition, that time can be treated as quantized), namely, something like "D_1-followed-by-D_2" (or whatever physical predicate one uses to indicate succession). The question is: Is the temporally extended property D_{12} transduced? There is nothing in the "physical description" require-ment to preclude it, so the question becomes an empirical one. In fact, it reduces to the question whether there is a cognitive event or code C_{12} that is stimulus-bound to property D_{12} (that is, C_{12} occurs whenever the event D_1-followed-by-D_2 occurs). If there is such an event or code, we conclude that there is a transducer for D_{12}, hence, that detecting D_{12} requires no *cognitive* memory. (Latency of physical processes does not count as "memory" for our purposes unless the physical properties involved happen to be identical with computational or cognitive states.)

On the other hand, it is possible for an organism to indirectly "detect" D_{12} by methods other than transduction. For instance, the organism might transduce D_1 as C_1 and D_2 as C_2, then compare C_1 and C_2 by invoking a rule. On the basis of the rule it might "conclude" C_{12}. What is different in this case is that there *can* be circumstances in which an organism does not conclude C_{12} but something else, say, C', in which the relation between the difference in the two circumstances and the difference in the codes is explained only by reference to the content of certain representations, the organism's interpretation of the circum-stances, and the existence of the rule. That is partly what it means for C_{12} to be *inferred* or to be generated by a rule: It implies that the counterfactuals work out in certain ways, ways systematic only under a cognitive interpretation.

Thus the answer to the question, Is memory required in order to recognize *same-as-before* and *different-from-before*?, is, it depends whether the recognition is done by inference from the prior transduction of individual events D_1 and D_2, or by the direct transduction of D_{12}. To determine the answer to this question, we use the methods already discussed in this chapter, as well as those in chapter 5, where the equivalent problem arises in a context not involving transduction. After all, this is actually a special case of the general problem of deciding whether a particular observed regularity or function should be explained in terms of rules and representations (or, in the case of the examples discussed in chapters 7 and 8, tacit knowledge), or whether it should be explained in terms of intrinsic properties of the functional architecture. Thus, there is nothing special here: temporally extended patterns, like any other kind of pattern, *can* be primitively detected only if there is a transducer for the pattern.

A final concern is the question of spatial or temporal limits on transducer inputs. Empirically, it is clearly the case that we do not directly detect changes over long time periods or detect patterns over large spatial extents—the paradoxical perception of impossible figures being attributable to the latter. The range over which we can *perceive* (rather than transduce) patterns is limited, but the limits cannot be specified strictly in spatial or temporal terms; those depend on the pattern's conceptual complexity. For example, the ability to perceive a figure when it is presented in segments (either continuously by moving it behind a slot or through discrete "glances") depends on its figural integrity (its Gestalt) as well as the rate at which it is presented and on the distances involved (for example, Hochberg, 1968; Howard, personal communication).

The range over which transducers operate is also limited, but in this case the limits must be specified in physical terms (because their input must be specified in physical terms). This limitation of extension or range applies not only to space and time but also to frequency, intensity, and other physical dimensions. Thus, while transducers can be described as memory-free, perception and cognition, in general, cannot. Perceptual and cognitive processes that extend beyond the temporal limits of component transducers do involve memory in the true symbolic sense. Memory need not be implicated, however, merely because spatial-extent limits of certain transducers are exceeded, as in rapid eye movements, since there may be other transducers with spatially disparate receptive fields, or temporally extended "windows." Whether there are is an empirical matter; but, again, experiments with figures moving behind a slot (Parks, 1965; Howard, personal communication) suggest that it is possible spatially extended patterns considerably larger than the fovea are primitively transduced, that is, their detection involves no symbolic memory.

Chapter 7
Functional Architecture and Analogue Processes

I was at the mathematical school, where the master taught his pupils after a method scarce imaginable to us in *Europe*. The proposition and demonstration were fairly written on a thin wafer, with ink composed of cephalick tincture. This the student was to swallow upon a fasting stomach, and for three days following eat nothing but bread and water. As the wafer digested, the tincture mounted to his brain, bearing the proposition along with it.

Jonathan Swift, "Voyage to Laputa," *Gulliver's Travels*

Reasoning and the Language of Thought

The discussion of cognition thus far portrays mental activity as involving considerable ratiocination, or "reasoning through." According to this view, a major part of what goes on between input and output transducers involves goal-directed processes operating over semantically interpreted symbolic representations. Of course, in the strict sense, not everything that happens in these processes can be called inference. Much of it concerns "control processes," processes that determine which rule or operation is to be applied, as well as such information-handling operations as storage and retrieval, search, and recoding. Nonetheless, I argue that rationality and the application of truth-preserving operations remains the unmarked case. Even when strict truth preservation does not hold (as in guessing or using plausible though strictly invalid heuristic principles), the operations are rarely, if ever, semantically incoherent. Thus the mind is depicted as continually engaged in rapid, largely unconscious searching, remembering and reasoning and generally in manipulating knowledge—that is, "cognizing."

Because so much of this activity is at least semantically coherent, if not actually logical, representations typically are viewed as truth-bearing expressions. For that reason, I referred to them some years ago as *propositional* (Pylyshyn, 1973b). Since, however, propositions are abstractions, whereas representations are concrete entities, such representations should, strictly speaking, be referred to as "sentence analogues" or some similar term. They are, of course, not sentences in any natural or external (utterable) language. According to the view espoused here, they are symbolic expressions in an internal, physically instantiated symbol system sometimes called "mentalese" or the "language of thought."

The assumptions regarding cognition—(a) that it is dominated by a great deal of (largely unconscious) reasoning, and (b) that the primary form in which the representations are expressed consists of discrete sentencelike symbolic expressions—have come under considerable suspicion and criticism from some quarters. It is therefore important that we understand the status of these assumptions. It is particularly important that we see which aspects of these assumptions the cognitive science approach is committed to and which are contingent, empirical hypotheses (and, in the latter case, what reasons exist for holding the hypotheses).

We consider first the view that representations have the form of a "language of thought." The reasons for adopting this view have been discussed extensively (for example, Fodor, 1975), and they have been raised briefly in various contexts in this book. I do not elaborate them here except to point out what is at issue with respect to the ideas about representation I have been developing.

There are two general reasons for viewing representations as encoded in a language of thought. The first (discussed at length by Fodor, 1975, 1980c) concerns the opacity of propositional attitude attributions. If a person believes (wants, fears) *P*, then that person's behavior depends on the *form* the expression of *P* takes rather than the state of affairs *P* refers to; indeed, *P* may fail to refer to any actual or possible state of affairs (see end note 2 in chapter 2). If I believe that Mark Twain was a witty author, I do not have the same belief I would if I believed that Samuel Clemens was a witty author. Indeed, I might well deny the latter statement if I do not know that the two names belonged to the same person. Further, I would tend to do different things, depending on which belief I held; for example, I would tend to go to different sections of the public library, or would answer questions differently. Because the two beliefs refer to the same states of affairs (that is, they assert the same thing about the same person, hence, express the *same proposition*), the fact that they are distinct as beliefs suggests that beliefs depend on precisely how the two states of affairs are mentally represented or expressed. Thus, in some respects, distinguishing different beliefs resembles distinguishing two ways of saying something. In other words, beliefs have a grain more closely resembling that of quoted sentences than abstract propositions.

I do not wish to imply that holding a belief consists of storing a token of a belief sentence in English or some other natural language, since that would exclude nonverbal organisms and infants, not to mention that speakers of different languages can, or so we would like to believe, hold the same beliefs. If, however, we take the position that there is an internal, conceptual language (which we might call "mentalese"), then a natural explanation of what it is to hold a belief is that holding the belief consists in storing (in a special "active belief box") a token inscription of a sentence of mentalese. This account would explain why the two beliefs about Twain differ: They constitute different strings of internal symbols or different mentalese sentences—one using the mentalese term for "Mark Twain" and the other the mentalese term for "Samuel Clemens." These mentalese sentences—contributing, as they do, to distinct internal states—can enter into different patterns of reasoning and action. (The same is true, of course, even when no simple words—perhaps not even any two or three-word phrases—correspond to the concepts. For example, my idea of the strange thing I saw hovering over my backyard last night differs from my idea of the latest laser-created illusion my practical-joker-physicist neighbor likes to play with, even though the two events may be identical.)

It is common to discover that even logically equivalent beliefs and representations (for example, conjunctive versus disjunctive, positive versus negative ways of encoding exactly the same set of stimuli) can lead to very different behaviors (compare Johnson-Laird and Steedman, 1978; Hayes and Simon, 1976). The varying difficulty which subjects experience in reasoning about or remembering facts, depending on which of several logically equivalent forms they use to encode them, is prima facie evidence that some form of stored code is involved. Also, the fact that complexity of operations and recall can often be traced to the independently established complexity of the code suggests that the code has an intrinsic structure. Indeed, postulation of such a structure appears to be the most natural way to explain both the productivity of beliefs (the fact that the number of distinct beliefs does not seem to be bounded) and the fact that beliefs share similar component substructures. The beliefs that oranges are tasty and that they grow on trees, though different, are both about oranges. Together, they sanction the conclusion that some tasty things grow on trees—an inference that requires application of a rule sensitive to the component structure of the two beliefs in question. These and other phenomena (see chapter 3) are easily explained if we take the view that the representation of particular beliefs consists in the storage of token symbolic *expressions* in a specific manner.

Another, closely related consideration that recommends sentencelike symbolic expressions as the mode of cognitive representation derives from the importance placed on the rationality (or, at least, the semantic coherence) of much of cognition. Sentential predicate-argument structures are the only known means of encoding truth-valuable assertions for which there exist a (partial) calculus and at least certain combinatorial aspects of a semantic theory (that is, Tarskian model-theoretic semantics). This calculus, or proof theory, expresses truth-preserving operations. While both the formalism and the proof theory for the predicate calculus have many known limitations (see, for example, McCarthy and Hayes, 1969), it is important to note that no alternatives with equal expressive power have been developed. Of course, many data structures are widely used in artificial intelligence (for example, various "semantic nets"), many of which have clear advantages over the notation used in first-order logic. These data structures, however, are not substitutes for sentential structures. At best, they merely implement a subset of first order-logic which exploits special features of current computers to improve processing efficiency (for more on how exploiting certain features of the functional architecture can allow one to bypass certain inferential steps see chapter 4). The relation between semantic nets and the predicate calculus is discussed by David Israel (1984).

The recent successes in building "expert systems" in artificial intelligence began when the knowledge possessed by experts was systematically encoded in the form of "productions." These condition-action pairs encode the knowledge in simple rules, which correspond approximately to simple, conditional sentences. Very likely, the reason rules of this type (which are almost universal in the "expert system" field) have proved successful in spite of the existence of many complex forms of data structures in computer science is that the experts who serve as informants for the systems represent their knowledge in such small units. Another reason may be that such production systems depend heavily on a *recognition* capability, which many feel is also characteristic of human cognition (see, for example, Simon and Chase, 1973). Surely such reasons are highly inconclusive; at this stage, however, we cannot afford to ignore speculating what makes certain artifacts more successful than others at performing intelligently.

A growing number of people, while not disputing the general view I have been outlining, feel it is only a very small part of the overall account of cognition. They feel that there are large and important areas of cognition that do not involve ratiocination and the manipulation of sentential formulas. Some plausible candidates for areas that do not involve reasoning-type processes are learning, conceptual change, ontogenetic development, emotions, and, most significantly from my point of view, the large area of nonlinguistic or apparently nonlogical reasoning, such as intuitive or imagistic reasoning. In succeeding sections I examine several of these areas, reaching the conclusion that many of the claims are well founded: Cognition, as understood and conceived as a natural scientific domain, may well not include many of the areas that pretheoretical expectations had included. On the other hand, there are many areas where investigators, for the wrong reasons, have been misled into abandoning the cognitivist approach. The area of imagistic reasoning serves as the chief exemplar for this purpose, though discussion of the case is confined to chapter 8.

I begin by examining some reasons why cognitivist assumptions seem to be problematic in cases of apparent "nonlinguistic" reasoning. The larger issue—the location of the boundaries of representation-governed processes—is examined in chapter 9.

The Concept of an Analogue Process

The Attraction of Analogues

In many (perhaps most) clear cases of cognizing—specifically, activity through which we arrive at a decision, a solution to a problem, or an understanding of something—we are not aware that anything in particular is occurring, except, perhaps, occasional episodes of "inner speech" or some fleeting images. Frequently all we experience is the solution, together with the apprehension that it is the solution. Those who take such introspection seriously wish to preserve the distinction between what we are consciously aware of and what we are not consciously aware of. After all, that is the distinction which, pretheoretically, marks the difference between thinking and mere biological processes. Thus, Arnheim (1969) disparages a certain computational model of visual-analogy problem solving because the model must engage in a great deal of symbol manipulation involving pattern-matching, comparison, and inference. When people solve this kind of problem, Arnheim claims, they go through a quite different sequence of mental states, states involving a "rich and dazzling experience" of "instability," "fleeting, elusive resemblances," and being "suddenly struck by" certain perceptual relationships. Similarly, Hubert Dreyfus (1979) accuses computational modelers of not taking seriously such distinctions as that between *focal* and *fringe* consciousness, as well as ignoring our sense of oddness about the information-processing hypotheses.

Even among practitioners of cognitive science there is a reluctance to postulate much active cogitation where introspection reveals only the apparently automatic appearance of certain end products. Thus, Kosslyn, Pinker, Smith, and Shwartz (1979), who present a partially computational model of imagistic reasoning, are concerned that "none of the models of imagery based on artificial intelligence research treats the quasi-pictorial properties of images that people report when introspecting as functional properties of the representation." What the models in question postulate, instead, are various data structures and inferential procedures that occur over them. In other words, they treat the products of such problem solving processes as arising because subjects are *reasoning about* the envisioned geometrical properties, rather than as being *due to* the geometrical properties of some noncomputational (for example, physical or phenomenal) object, which the subject merely has to notice. I shall return to the imagery case; for the present, I merely point out that it appears universally repugnant to postulate reasoning processes in instances where introspection reveals answers are being "read off" or "noticed" or where they simply appear in some fashion in consciousness.

There is strong opposition as well to the notion that all cognition takes place over sentencelike objects. After all, our *experience* of numerous mental episodes reveals pictorial objects rather than sentential ones. Those who believe that other forms of representation are involved may turn out to be right. It is important, however, that the arguments for such forms of representation be made explicit. Often the reasons for positing something different (that is, analogues) are simply misconceived. For example, many believe that the discrete, languagelike nature of the postulated carriers of thought arises by false analogy with the discrete symbol structures of computers, and thus object to them on this ground alone. They point out that to adopt metaphors from current technology is to ensure the rapid obsolescence of one's ideas. The wax-tablet metaphor of the ancients gave way to the lever-and-gear metaphor of the eighteenth century, which gave way to the telephone-switchboard metaphor of the early twentieth century. Now we have the computer-software metaphor with its discrete languagelike, symbolic expressions.

The sentential-representation format has little to do with actual computing devices, however; rather, as has been mentioned, it is more closely related to formalist ideas in mathematics and logic. These ideas, which form the basis of symbolic logic, are the only scheme we have for capturing normative patterns of reasoning. All such formal systems require as a notation what Goodman (1968) calls a "symbol scheme." According to Goodman, the primary requirements for being a notational symbol-scheme are (a) *syntactic disjointness*, by which is meant each symbol token can be a member of only one symbol type, and (b) *syntactic finite differentiation*, by which is meant each pair of symbol tokens of distinct types can be finitely distinguished; that is, they cannot be arbitrarily similar. In providing this analysis of symbol systems, Goodman also provides a brief analysis of what it would be like to have a symbol system that is not a notational scheme, that is, a symbol system which violated one or both syntactic requirements. Goodman's taxonomy has been the basis of speculations about possible symbol systems that are nondiscrete, hence, intuitively appealing as an alternative account of mental representations for such domains as mental imagery (for example, Kolers and Smythe, 1979; Schwartz, 1981).

While nothing in the cognitivist account I have been sketching prohibits such a symbol scheme as a model of imagistic reasoning, it is far from clear what advantages it would have, except that of salving one's intuitions about the continuity and nondiscursiveness of images. The problem is not that such a proposal is likely to be false; rather, it is that we have no idea what explanatory advantage the proposal is supposed to gain us, because (a) there is nothing equivalent to a calculus, or even principles of composition, for what are called "dense symbol systems"; so we do not know what can be done with them, how elementary symbols can be combined to form complex representations, or the kinds of regularities that such symbols can enter into; and (b) there is no idea of a physical mechanism that could instantiate and process such symbols. The "analogue computing" view (to be examined) does not do this; it is not a symbolic system at all, inasmuch as none of its regularities require explanation at a separate symbol level, as is true of digital computing.

Thus we find widespread abhorrence of both the ratiocination and the discrete, articulated nature of the form of representation typical of cognitivist theories. A form of complex process that avoids both the logical, step-by-step character of reasoning and the discrete languagelike character of the representation is the analogue process. This process delivers its output in one bold step and has the desired property of continuity or holism. At the same time it can be achieved within material causal systems, just as the syntactic alternative can. It is no surprise, then, that so many have been attracted to this alternative in accounting for modes of reasoning that seem intuitively different from the deliberate, rational, linguistic kind we sometimes experience (for example, solving cryptarithmetic puzzles).

What Makes Something an Analogue Process?
A prototypical analogue computer differs from a prototypical digital computer in a great many ways, not all of which are relevant to arguments about the nature of mental processes and mental representation[1]. For example, analogue computers typically are special-purpose

1. In writing this section I have benefited by having access to an unpublished paper by

devices for solving systems of differential equations, which they usually do by representing time-varying values of variables by time-varying values of electrical properties. These computers typically are set up to solve a given set of equations by connecting components that correspond to some nth derivative of a variable and setting values of such physical parameters as resistances and capacitances to correspond to values of coefficients of the equations. There are, of course, other types of devices intuitively classed as analogue. For instance, we usually distinguish between analogue and digital watches and thermometers. Part of the reason for using the word *digital* in those cases is that digital versions do, in fact, use *digits* to display their value, though that is probably not a necessary property; a meter that indicates values by lighting up one of n arbitrarily arranged lights might also count as digital.

Thus, because typical analogue computers have numerous distinguishing properties, it is not obvious what people have in mind when they say certain mental functions can be performed analogically rather than digitally. In fact, often it is not even clear from the literature whether the term *analogue* is meant to apply to a process or to a form of representation. The etymology of the term (which is related to *analogy*) only makes matters worse. Some theorists consider any use of a physical model or analogy an instance of using an analogue—for example, Haugeland (1981a) counts the use of animals as research models for the human organism as a case of using an analogue. Obviously, some distinctions need to be made before the attraction of hypothesizing analogue processes in theories of cognition can be understood.

The most common interpretation of the analogue process is that it involves continuous, rather than discrete, forms of representation. Thus most computer science writers (for example, Minsky, 1967); psychologists (Banks, 1977); philosophers (Dreyfus, 1979; and, even more explicitly, Haugeland, 1981a) assume that it is the continuity (or density, as opposed to discreteness) of the form of representation that is the relevant distinction. That cannot be the right distinction, however, even between engineered analogue and digital devices, let alone different cognitive processes. An analogue watch does not cease to be analogue if its hands move in discrete steps, even if they do not pass through intermediate angles, as in the case of liquid-crystal-diode analogue watches. Similarly, an analogue computer does not become digital merely by being quantized. Conversely, a digital computer with arbitrarily extendable precision as in a Turing Machine, does not become

---

Block and Fodor (1972), in which many of these ideas are laid out. The approach I take differs in many ways from that of Block and Fodor; obviously they are not to blame for the use to which I put their insights.

an analogue computer when it uses the duodecimal number system or the Dewey system, despite the fact that these systems define dense sets of codes (there is a code between every pair of codes, no matter how close together members of the pair). In any case, the continuity, or density, criterion is not relevant for cognitive representations, since, presumably, at some level the nervous system is actually discrete—and, by this criterion, no discrete approximation to a continuous system qualifies as a true analogue.

David Lewis (1971) provides a better characterization. He defines an analogue process as one in which numbers (hence, presumably, any numerical magnitudes) are represented by primitive or nearly primitive physical magnitudes, or perhaps any magnitudes that can appear in reasonably general laws. By this means, Lewis gets around the discrete, yet analogue, counterexamples by locating the distinction in the nature of the underlying, representing dimension rather than in the values such a dimension actually takes. Thus a quantized encoding of some scale that uses discrete values of, say, length is still an analogue representation, since the underlying dimension (length) is a primitive physical magnitude. By this definition, the representation of time in a watch with discretely moving hands is still analogue, whereas the representation of time by the pattern of magnetizations of a computer memory is not, since, presumably, the arbitrarily complex disjunction of physical properties that make up the pattern of magnetizations does not itself figure in any law. This complex disjunction of physical properties is not, according to the usual use of the term, a projectable property.

The significance of the nonprojectability of the class of physical properties corresponding to distinct computational states of a digital computer is that the operation of the system, *as* a computer rather than a physical system, cannot be explained the way natural events typically are explained in science, by citing the value of the property in question and showing that the state transition is subsumed under some general, natural law. As we saw in chapter 3, the transition among what is treated as the *computational states* of a digital computer (that is, the states given a semantic interpretation in the computation) is nomologically arbitrary, inasmuch as any convenient equivalence class of physical states can be defined as a computational state. States that are convenient to engineer rarely have a simple physical description. Recall that characterizing digital computation involves specifying what I call an "instantiation function," which assigns sets of physical states to distinct computational states, as well as a "semantic interpretation function," which provides a regular scheme for pairing computational states and interpretations in the domain of the computation. Thus state-to-state transitions can involve arbitrarily many causal laws, and there can be different sets of laws that apply in each distinct instance of a state transition, which is why such sequences cannot be explained in terms of physical laws, even though each individual transition occurs because of some collection of physical causes.

The situation in analogue computing is different. Because the properties in terms of which we represent values of extrinsic variables are projectable properties involved in causal laws, the operation of an analogue process *can* be explained by appeal to the physical properties of the representation, together with the relevant natural laws. Hence, they can be explained without invoking what I have called the *symbol level*, with its syntactic properties. As it turns out, natural laws (at least, those outside quantum mechanics) invariably involve continuously varying magnitudes, so this criterion for analogicity does pick out systems with continuous, underlying representational dimensions.

Lewis's definition seems a reasonable way to characterize the intuitive notion of "analogue representation." One problem with the definition as it stands, however, is it ignores the relevance of the projectability criterion to the functioning of the system. Consequently, according to Lewis's criterion, it is possible for magnitudes to be represented in an analogue manner without the process itself qualifying as an analogue process. Consider a digital computer that (perhaps by using a digital-to-analogue converter to convert each newly computed number to a voltage) represents all its intermediate results in the form of voltages and displays them on a voltmeter. Although this computer *represents* values, or numbers, analogically, clearly it operates digitally.[2]

For the process, as opposed to the representation alone, to qualify as analogue, the value of the property doing the representing must play the right causal role in the functioning of the system. The process must unfold as it does *because* of the form taken by the analogue representation; that is, certain aspects of its behavior must be caused by the property used to represent magnitudes. There is little point in calling something an analogue process unless certain specifiable aspects of the system's operation are found to depend on its being analogue, that is, on particular analogue properties of the medium used for the encoding.

2. In this example both analogue and digital forms of representation occur. The point would remain even, however, if only the analogue form occurred. Block and Fodor (1972) give the example of a machine that represents numbers by electrical charge, adding numbers as follows. The machine has an ordered array of elements, each with a charge one unit larger than the previous element in the array. It adds n and m by first positioning its read head over the nth element, then moving the head by m elements, taking the value of the charge found there as the sum. Because it involves counting, this seems a clear case of a digital process.

Thus far, I have been concerned primarily with capturing the differences between intuitively clear cases of analogue, as opposed to digital, computing. Subsequently, I examine what appear to be deeper motivations for the appeal to analogue processing in cognitive theories and show that these motivations are closely related to the concerns that led me to distinguish *functional architecture* from *process*. There, I claim that, for purposes of cognitive theory, what is important about analogues is that the analogue properties used to represent certain things *constrain* the process in certain, specifiable ways, ways in which it would not be constrained if it were a digital system. I shall argue that it is the idea of constraints on a system's operation that, for cognitive science, constitutes the fundamental distinction on which the importance of the analogue-digital, or analogue-propositional, difference rests. Because this is precisely the point of the functional architecture-versus-process distinction as it is formulated in the preceding chapters, the criteria for distinguishing the latter two types of process are also important considerations in the case of analogues. The next section is devoted to developing this theme and to introducing the important concept of *cognitive capacity*.

Forms of Constraint on Processes: The Notion of Capacity

We get a hint of an important motivation behind positing analogue processes in cognition from the way Roger Shepard defines an analogue process. Shepard considered several different notions of analogicity, including "second-order isomorphism." Shepard (1975), however, asserts that in cognition an analogue process is one that goes through the same sequence of intermediate stages as the process represented would have gone through. This is an important idea, but, like Lewis's criterion, it fails to consider the reason *why* the process goes through that sequence rather than another. As we see in the example used in discussing Lewis's proposal, it is possible for a process to go through the sequence for clearly nonanalogue reasons. For example, in thinking about what happens when a batter hits a baseball, someone can think about the sequence of events in the minutest detail, faithfully following the sequence of events believed to have occurred. Regardless of whether the intermediate stages are represented by what would qualify as an analogue representation, this sequence clearly can be caused to occur by a process of reasoning that uses a sentencelike symbol system and carries out inferences between stages.

The difference between what happens in the example just given and what Shepard presumably has in mind is that, in the analogue case, because we have chosen to represent the baseball situation in a certain nonlinguistic way, it is *mandatory* that the system unfold according to the sequence specified. In our example, the system presumably could have gone through a quite different sequence while using exactly the same medium of representation and the same initial representation (this might be the case, for example, if the person did not know the rules of baseball). If the theory specifies that the sequence is fixed in a certain way, the theory must also state whether that way is determined by the medium of representation, by the representations (or beliefs) the system has, or merely by stipulation. In the last case, the theorist merely has observed that this is the sequence people go through, and specifies that the model should do the same, thereby mimicking the person being modeled.

An especially interesting example of an allegedly analogue representation that is equivocal as to the precise reason it leads to certain forms of behavior is the matrix representation of two-dimensional shape and layout discussed in chapter 4. A modeler (for example, Kosslyn and Shwartz, 1977; Funt, 1980) who claims that a two-dimensional spatial analogue is being used as the medium of representation in such a model is making a strong claim. The claim is much stronger than that the representation is similar to a computer's matrix data structure. Such a data structure simply provides a way to retrieve a piece of information in terms of pairs of index symbols which happen to be numerical values that can be treated like coordinates. There is nothing in a matrix, as a data structure, that *requires* it to behave in any way like a two-dimensional space. For example, nothing constrains a process to search for patterns in the matrix by examining "adjacent" cells, as opposed to examining them in any other order. (Even the notion of "adjacency" must be relativized to a certain extrinsic ordering defined on the pairs of index symbols; it is not an intrinsic property of symbols.) There is no requirement that only one "point" at a time be examined. Here, too, the notion of "point" is merely a way of viewing the matrix; nothing about the data structure per se requires preservation of any important properties of points. For example, there need not be a cell for each pair of index symbols within the range of symbols used to index the matrix; and there is certainly nothing about the data structure which requires that transformations over it be constrained in a way analogous to those that occur in real space (for example, there is nothing special about the operation corresponding to "rotating" or "translating" a form displayed in the matrix, as opposed to an operation which, say, transfers the contents of every cell to some arbitrary cell in the matrix).

When the matrix actually is used to model spatial reasoning, the way it is used is restricted so as to ensure that it behaves like a model of space. In other words, the way in which the representation is used has the property Shepard (1975) refers to as "second-order isomorphism," by which he means that the representation functions in ways similar to the thing represented or is functionally isomorphic to the object represented; that is, the system uses a representation in such a way that the relationship among tokens of representations is similar to that among tokens of the objects represented. Notice, however, that so far this is merely a stipulated constraint similar to the baseball example. Because in a computer model the constraint does not arise from properties of the data structure, we have to ask what enforces the constraint. There are two possibilities: the constraint may arise because the matrix is viewed as merely simulating a true analogue medium (for practical reasons), or it is simply a constraint imposed willy-nilly to make the process behave as though it were using real space. The latter answer represents a far different sort of constraint.

It is not enough merely to establish second-order isomorphism. As Steve Palmer (1978) has pointed out, to do so merely shows that the system can reason accurately about the objects it is thinking about. Establishing second-order isomorphism is insufficient because it makes a great difference whether the constraint on the system's behavior is attributed to (1) nomological requirements (as in Block's and Fodor's view of analogues), (2) relatively fixed structural properties of the representational system, or (3) the presence of other symbolic representations (goals and beliefs) in the system, and particularly to what these other symbols represent. Constraint (1) attributes the regularity to natural law; constraint (2) to the way people are constructed (perhaps to human nature); and constraint (3) to the representations' semantic content.

Note that second-order isomorphism is compatible with the condition that there be *no* relevant constraints due to physical or biological properties of the representation's instantiation. To get second-order isomorphism, all we need assume is that the organism has: (1) generally true beliefs, (2) the competence for valid reasoning, and (3) the goal of reasoning about the sequence of states an object would go through or the relationships that would be perceived when looking at a set of stimuli. Nothing more need be assumed about the material form the representation takes.

I shall have more to say about alternative types of explanation. Before discussing the general issue of constraints, however, it may be helpful to provide a simple (perhaps, in some ways, too simple), concrete example of what is at issue.

Intrinsic versus Semantic Constraints
Suppose I exhibited a black box into which I had inserted an electrode

or some other response recorder. We need not be concerned with what is in the box—though one possibility is that it contains a brain, as in figure 1. As we observe the box in its usual functioning, we discover that the ensuing record exhibits certain regularities. For example, we observe that frequently individual short pulses or pairs of short pulses occur in the record, that when there are both pairs and single pulses (as sometimes happens), the pair regularly appears to precede the single pulse. After observing this pattern for some time we discover occasional exceptions to its order—but only when the entire pattern is preceded by a pair of long and short pulses. Being scientists, we are most interested in explaning this regularity. What explanation is most appropriate?

The answer depends on the nature of the black box, particularly on what its *capacity* is beyond being able to produce the particular behavior we have observed (that is, not on what it is doing or what it typically does, but on what it *could* be doing in certain counterfactual situations). In this example, deliberately chosen to make a pedagogical point, I can confidently state that we would not find the explanation of the box's behavior in its internal structure, nor would we find it in any properties intrinsic to the box or its contents.

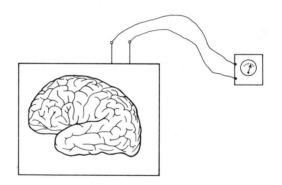

Figure 1. Systematic patterns of behavior recorded from an unknown black box. The problem is to explain the observed regularity.

Now, this might strike some people as an odd claim. How can the behavior of a system not be due to its internal construction or inherent properties? What else could explain the regularities exhibited? Ultimately, of course, it is the existence of certain properties in the box that govern its total behavioral repertoire or its capacity. But as long as we have sampled only some limited scope of this repertoire—say, what it "typically" or "normally" does—we may be in no position to infer its intrinsically constrained capacity; hence, the regularity observed may tell us nothing about the internal structure or the device's inherent properties.

I shall make this point more concrete by considering the question of why the black box in our example exhibits the regularity shown in the figure. As it happens, the real reason is simply that the black box is a box for transmitting (or, if you prefer, "thinking in") English words encoded in International Morse code. Thus the regularity we have discovered is entirely attributable to a spelling rule of English (*i* before *e* except after *c*), together with the Morse code convention. The reason providing a detailed description of the component structure and the operation of the box does not explain this regularity is, the structure is capable of exhibiting a much greater range of behaviors; *the observed constraint on its behavior is due not to its intrinsic capability but to what its states represent*. Constraints can exist at a number of levels (see chapter 3), each of which may require explanation in the vocabulary of different sciences.

Let us take another pair of examples, one much closer to the empirical cases discussed in chapter 8. First, we consider the regularities of perceptual color-mixing (for example, perceived yellow light and perceived red light mix to produce perceived orange light). What sort of account can we expect as an explanation of these regularities—one that appeals to intrinsic properties of the system, to certain internal biological mechanisms, or (as in the Morse-code example) one that appeals to properties of *what is represented* rather than properties of the system itself? The question is an empirical one, and I wish merely to point out what is at issue and the kinds of empirical considerations the answer depends on. Here, all the evidence points to the existence of a biological or biochemical mechanism which is responsible for the regularity. One reason for expecting such an account (apart from the fact that we have quite a large fragment of the account already in hand) is that the regularities appear largely insensitive to what subjects think they are looking at (within limits—see Delk and Fillenbaum, 1965), to what they believe about the actual color of the objects or the principles of color mixing, and to what the subjects believe is the purpose of the experiment.

Contrast this example with one in which an investigator seeks to discover the principles of what might be called "imaginal color mixing" or the "internal psychophysics of color." Similar experiments exist in psychology literature. The experimenter asks subjects to imagine certain colors and to superimpose them in the subjects' mental images. The instructions might be something like this: "Imagine a transparent yellow filter beside a transparent red filter. Now imagine that the two filters are slowly moved together until they overlap. What color do you see through the overlapped portion?" Suppose the investigator discovers a set of reliable principles governing the mixing of imagined colors. What explanatory account is likely to be correct in this case—one based on an appeal to biological or biochemical principles, or an account based on what is represented in the minds of the subjects, including what the subjects tacitly know about the principles of color mixing and what they understand their task to be? Again, it is an empirical question, though this time it seems much likelier that the correct explanation must advert to what the subject *believes* about the regularities of color mixing. The reason I say this is, it seems likely that the way colors mix in one's image will depend on what one knows about the regularities of perceptual color-mixing; after all, we can make our image whatever color we want it to be![3] The test for this explanation is to determine whether changing what a subject believes *by providing information* (possibly false information) changes the regularity in a logically explicable way. If it does, we say the regularity is "cognitively penetrable" (see chapter 5) and conclude that no account based solely on appeal to the intrinsic properties of a mechanism, or to what I called the "functional architecture," is, by itself, adequate to explain the regularity or the way in which it can be altered. I draw this conclusion (just as I did in the Morse-code example), not because of adherence to a dualist doctrine but because I know the evidence does not reveal a cognitively fixed *capacity*, inasmuch as the underlying mechanism is compatible with a wider range of behaviors than those embodied in the empirically observed regularity. What the biological mechanism does provide is a way to *represent*, or *encode*, the relevant knowledge, inference rules,

3. Note that we need not always use what we know in performing a particular task. Thus, if the experiment described above is carried out, people frequently do such things as free associate to the color names, guess, or do just about anything, depending on how the task is presented to them. Nothing much follows from this concerning the nature of their imagery mechanism. This suggestion can easily be verified by observing that the same thing happens when the experiment involves imaging a sequence consisting of a number, a plus sign, another number, and an equals sign, accompanied by instructions to imagine the next number that would appear. Here, too, subjects can refrain from using their knowledge of arithmetic, and can simply imagine any number. That, of course, would tell us nothing about the mechanisms of imagery; making valid inferences is not the only thing we can do with our knowledge.

decision procedures, and so on—not the observed regularity itself. (As I have already indicated in my discussion of functional architecture, the mechanism imposes certain resource-limited constraints, as well as providing the "control structure" for accessing rules and representations. It is these we must appeal to in explaining such performance features as deviations from logical omniscience.)

Even if one prefers to view the imaginal color-mixing case as involving some sort of analogue medium (a possibility many find attractive), it is apparent that, at least in this example, properties of the medium do not contribute to the explanation of *any* aspect of the observed phenomenon. In this case, the medium plays the same role as does the analogue representation of numbers in the example described in my discussion of Lewis's proposed definition of analogue computing, that is, where voltage is used as the form of representation of intermediate magnitudes (though these magnitudes were, in fact, computed digitally). In both cases, nothing about the medium constrains the sequence of representations that unfold, hence, postulation of such a medium is theoretically empty.

Those who speak of representations as involving an "analogue medium" (for example, Kosslyn et al., 1979; Attneave, 1974) usually assume that such a medium imposes constraints on processing (by, for instance, constraining the sequence through which a process must go or by determining which primitive operations may be applied—or, equivalently, which aspects of the information are "explicit" and can be read off the representation rather than having to be inferred). Here, I believe it is appropriate to refer to a hypothetical "medium of representation" such as this as being analogue, whether it has such further properties as continuity—and indeed, whether values of the domain represented are encoded in terms of projectable properties in the brain, as required by Block's and Fodor's (1972) or Lewis's (1971) definitions.

Putting aside the issue of continuity, it seems to me that the essential idea behind the use of the term *analogue* by most psychologists is captured precisely by what I have been calling *functional architecture*, inasmuch as both the notion of analogue and that of a function instantiated in the functional architecture are intended to emphasize that certain regularities must be explained by appealing to natural, intrinsic constraints, as opposed to semantic or extrinsic ones. Nonetheless, rather than cause further confusion by using the term *analogue*, which is reasonably well established outside cognitive science, I shall continue to refer to processes "instantiated by the functional architecture." In what follows I review some ideas behind the distinction between explanation by appeal to functional architecture and explanation by appeal to symbolic processes. (The reader is urged to review the discussion in chapters 4 and 5, where this distinction is introduced.)

Explanation and Functional Architecture
The example of the Morse-code box illustrates a point central to a great deal of my analysis thus far (especially the analysis in chapters 2 and 5), that two fundamentally different types of explanation are available for explaining a system's behavior. The first type of explanation appeals to the intrinsic properties of a system and provides a systematic account of "how the system operates." Such an account may require appeal to the natural laws governing these intrinsic properties, or it may require a longer, engineering-style account of different parts carring out certain functions and interacting in certain ways to produce the observed behavior (for a discussion of this type of explanation, see Haugeland, 1978). The second type of explanation appeals, roughly, to extrinsic properties or to properties and behaviors of real or imagined worlds to which the system bears a certain relation (called *representing*, or, more generally, *semantics*). The example illustrates the point that the appropriate type of explanation depends on more than just the nature of the observed regularities; it depends on the regularities that are *possible* in certain situations not observed (and which may never be observed, for one reason or another).

It is a general property of explanatory principles (as opposed to empirical generalizations) that they are "counterfactual supporting", that they make predictions in nonactual circumstances. In the case of the "special sciences" (sciences whose domain is confined to some limited range of natural phenomena), explanatory principles apply only within the domain of the science in question. For instance, one expects biological principles to say what happens under certain circumstances that have never arisen, provided thè circumstances are characterized in biological terms. Biology is not expected to, say, predict the motion of organisms dropped from a certain height or predict the future of organisms caught with their hand in the till. Similarly, biology is not expected to predict what would happen if an organism were pulverized and mixed with cement, since that range of alteration of circumstances takes the object outside the domain of biological explanation. In other words, in the special sciences, counterfactual conditions are relativized to those that define the domain of that science.

I am assuming that there are three separate levels, or sets of explanatory principles involved in cognition: the intentional (or semantic, or knowledge level) principles, the symbolic (or syntactic, or functional) level principles, and the physical (or biological) level principles. The first level concerns phenomena explainable by appeal to the semantic content of representations. They are the knowledge-dependent phenomena whose regularities are captured by principles that mention the system's goals and beliefs. Giving a full account, of course, requires discussing not only goals and beliefs but the functional (or symbol-processing) mechanisms that encode these goals and beliefs and make the system work, as well as the way in which such mechanisms are realized in brain tissue. In short, the other two levels of the account must also be given.

Here, the counterfactual-support criterion works by having knowledge-level principles predict events in certain counterfactual situations— that is, in any situation falling within the domain of knowledge-level principles. These principles enable us to answer such questions as: What would the organism do if. . . ? where the ellipsis is filled in by such phrases as *it came to believe that* P or *it adopted goal* G. Thus, in the color-mixing examples, the answer to what happens in the first example (perceptual color-mixing case) is not to be found at the knowledge level. That is so because it is an empirical fact that there are no such principles; the phenomenon is insensitive to goals and beliefs. Therefore, as long as only knowledge-level conditions are changed, there is no principle that says the behavior will change. On the other hand, if nonsemantic factors are varied, there are relevant principles that can, at least in principle, make predictions. These principles are to be found either at the symbol level (which, for example, might explain why some colors take longer to name or discriminate) or at the physical level, where actual color-mixing regularities can be dealt with in terms of the retinal color-encoding mechanism.

By contrast, the answer in the second case (imaginal color-mixing) *must* be dealt with at the knowledge level, because no other set of principles is equipped to express regularities that can be altered systematically and in a rationally explicable way by the semantic content of incoming messages (for example, instructions or facts)—which, by hypothesis, is the case in this example. To give a knowledge-level explanation we need an independent assessment of the subject's beliefs about the principles of color mixing (as might be inferred, for example, by some relatively unobtrusive measure, such as having subjects detect anomalous, perceptual color-mixing setups, as in Howard's experiment; see chapter 8). This, plus an independent assessment of the subject's goals (for example, to obtain the correct answer, outguess the experimenter, receive subject-participation credit, or get out as fast as possible), and an assumption of rationality as the unmarked case, gives us a basis for predicting the response under varying instruction and information conditions.

Put a different way, if we observe a certain, reliable, empirical regularity in the behavior of a system, we can ask for an explanation of why the system behaves as it does. Three classes of explanation are possible, depending on the ultimate form of the counterfactuals (the as-yet-unobserved cases). In the first class, the system behaves a certain way because of its beliefs and goals. This—the *intentional, or representational,* explanation—implies that in situations which differ only in information content (so that different beliefs or goals might be established), behavior may be different in predictable ways. In the second class, the system behaves as it does because of the kind of system it is, because of the way its nervous system or circuits are structured to encode information and to process these codes. This is the *functional architecture* explanation; it implies that in situations which differ along biological dimensions, behavior may be systematically and predictably different. Indeed, it might well be different in different organisms, in children, or in any other biologically different subject. (Presumably, biologists will eventually tell us what differences are relevant and whether certain properties are fixed or whether they can be changed by maturation, disease, diet, brain damage, ingesting drugs, or some other biologically explainable cause.) In the third class, the system behaves in such and such a way because it instantiates a natural law. This—the *analogue explanation* (at least, the version proposed by Fodor and Block)—implies that the system's behavior—under precisely the same description as that under which we want to explain it (that is, the description under which it is psychologically interpreted)—*must* unfold as it does in all possible circumstances, because the regularity in question is a necessary consequence of the particular physical properties that define the states of the system that are semantically interpreted.

What is special about the third class is not merely that the regularity itself is governed by natural laws (this is true of all alternatives, barring the truth of dualism or vitalism). What is special is that the regularity (under the relevant description of the behavior) is *explainable* by reference to such a law. Thus there is no need to appeal to anything else—for example, computations or representations. It is simply a straightforward unfolding of a physical process, much like the earth's orbit around the sun—something as well that we would not think of explaining by positing a representation of the Hamiltonian equation by the earth.

The nomological explanation, when it applies, wins by Occam's razor. We hypothesize no special principles when the basic laws cover the behavior under the description we have in mind. When the explanation does not apply, however, when the relevant (interpreted) behavioral regularity cannot be explained in terms of the lawful behavior of a projectable property of the system, then other factors come into play. For example, Fodor (1984) and Fodor and Pylyshyn (1971) argue that, in such cases, representations and inferences must be hypothesized. That position now seems too strong to me. Surely there are cases in which we do not need to posit representations in order to explain behavior, but in which behavioral regularities nonetheless cannot be subsumed under nomological laws—say, because the relevant properties are not projectable but, rather are some complex function of projectable properties, as is the case in typical artifacts such as engines. Such cases might, for example, require what Haugeland (1978) calls a "morphological explanation," an explanation that emphasizes structural constraints. In any case, the distinction between explanation by subsumption under a law and explanation by subsumption under many laws, together with a complex initial state (with topographical constraints) does not seem the correct way to draw the boundary between regularities that can be explained by reference to intrinsic properties (such as in the perceptual color-mixing example) and regularities that must be explained by reference to semantic or representational properties (such as in the imaginal color-mixing example or the Morse-code-box example).

It seems to me that the criteria for determining whether some hypothesized function is part of the functional architecture that were discussed in chapter 5 provide better criteria for deciding whether representations and inferences must be appealed to in order to capture a particular regularity. Chief among them is the criterion of cognitive penetrability. A regularity that is cognitively penetrable, we know, is not explainable solely by reference to intrinsic properties, either nomological or structural. If the regularity is not cognitively penetrable, however, we look for other evidence, for example, evidence of intermediate representational state, or of computational stages. For instance, I argue in chapter 5 that, to be instantiated directly by functional architecture, a function must not be inherently combinatorial. That is, certain inherently combinatorial functions (perhaps, parsing) with an infinite domain or range do not qualify as being instantiated by the functional architecture.[4]

4. Although the study of computational complexity (for example, the study of "NP complete problems") is concerned with "inherently combinatorial" problems, little is known about the complexity of functions that are independent of particular architectures, apart from some highly abstract speedup theorems of Blum (1967), theorems whose relevance to the problems at hand is not clear. Intuitively, it seems that functions such as parsing a sentence of a context-free language or deciding whether a number expressed in conventional notation is a prime are inherently combinatorial, in that there may exist no one-step algorithm for such functions realizable on a real machine. The same cannot be said of the function that determines whether any integer expressed in binary or decimal form is odd or even; this *can* be decided in one step by an algorithm that examines the

Such functions must be realized by computations in which intermediate expressions or representations are computed in the course of arriving at the output. On the other hand, if both the domain and the range are finite, the function can be realized by primitive table lookup, which, by the criteria discussed in chapter 5, qualifies as an instantiated function. As I have stated, it is not the overall complexity of the instantiation (that is, the amount of "wiring") that matters, but whether the system must go through intermediate *representational* states.

If the subfunction (as it is characterized in the model[5]) is rigid (for example, if it is "input bound" the way transducers were defined to be stimulus bound), then, barring special arguments that the input-output function must be combinatorial or arguments that representations or component subprocesses must be posited as part of a larger theory,[6] we have prima facie reason to take that function as instantiated rather than computed by a process operating over representations—whether or not the input or the output is encoded as a projectable property.

Based on such considerations, it is far from clear to me that the complex computations involved in deriving representations in "low-

---

numeral's least significant digit. What is needed is a result that is independent of the functional architecture of any computer. One way to obtain such a result is to find that physics imposes constraints on physically realizable processes. A small step in this direction was taken by Gandi (1980), who showed that certain minimal constraints can be derived from assumptions about the finite speed of information transmission. More realistic constraints are under investigation as well, in connection with understanding limits associated with space requirements in integrated circuit (VLSI) design; see Vuillemin, 1980; Chazelle and Monier, 1983. The study of perceptron devices by Minsky and Papert (1969)—who relate classes of geometrical predicates to classes of devices, particularly the "perceptron" class—is also a contribution to this sort of question in computational geometry. So far as I know, there is nothing comparable for the more general problem.

5. Of course, much depends on just how the subfunction is characterized, especially on what counts as its input. For example, the universal Turing machine is input bound under one way of characterizing it, and maximally plastic in another. It is impossible to determine whether some component is input bound outside the theory that specifies the component's function.

6. Such arguments are sometimes available. In the case of parsing natural language, there is evidence suggesting the availability of intermediate states of the parse tree. There are arguments as well (for example, Fodor, Bever, and Garrett, 1974) that the particular form of rules posited in some current syntactic theories must be represented and accessed in "interpreted mode," that is, consulted by the parser and used in the parse. This argument rests on the fact that linguistic universals, as they stand, are expressed over rules of a particular form. If there were no other way to express the universals (which there is not at the present), that would be an argument that the rules are represented and used. I must confess that I do not find this argument entirely persuasive, since it rests on the assumption that there is no alternative way to express universals. (There are other problems with the view that the grammatical rules are represented and accessed; see Stabler, 1983.)

level" vision systems (such as those discussed by Marr, 1982) are to be viewed as cognitive, representation-governed processes. That they can be realized on a digital computer is irrelevant, since the computer may simply be simulating brain processes that are not cognitive, any more than are simulations of the endocrine system or the dynamics of the musculature. The reason I feel they are probably not cognitive is that capturing the regularities of these processes seems not to require appeal to semantic properties. Even such general constraints on the process as the rigidity constraint or the continuity constraint (see Marr, 1982; Ullman, 1979), which are stated in terms of properties of the visible world, are not semantic properties that are encoded in any representations. Rather, they are descriptions of characteristics of the mapping from proximal stimulation to representation, worded so as to make clear why the process is veridical—indeed, to make clear the range of stimuli over which the process is veridical. Now, it may turn out that there is reason to view what goes on in these low-level vision systems as representational processes, as performing genuine inferences; but my inclination is to take their extreme inflexibility over cognitive variations (that is, their cognitive impenetrability) as evidence that their behavior may be explainable without reference to semantics. In other words, they may be merely complex neural processes that instantiate pieces of functional architecture—in this case, transducers.

The same could be said of all the mechanisms being developed by the "new connectionist" theorists (for example, Hinton and Anderson, 1981). These connection-type machines, you will recall, are ones which, it is claimed, can carry out certain cognitive functions or exhibit cognitive skills *without* symbolic representations. So far, however, *all* the functions that have been modeled by such mechanisms are cognitively impenetrable; they are chiefly functions like memory retrieval. The rigidity of these functions make it doubtful that they are anything but properties of the functional architecture. In other words, they are abstract models of the nervous system's instantiation of some operations of the functional architecture.

The preceding remarks also suggest that the proper place to look for neurophysiological constraints on cognitive models is precisely in functions hypothesized as part of the functional architecture—transducers, parsing, lexical access processes, aspects of phone recognition in speech, and so on. These functions are the basis of cognitive capacities as I define the term; it is their behavior that is most directly constrained by the inherent (especially structural) properties of the brain. In the case of representation-governed regularities, such as those involved in understanding natural languages, solving crossword puzzles, doing science, or appreciating a novel, any part of the achievement can depend crucially on *anything* one believes or knows. This massive holism makes it unlikely that topographical or structural constraints will show through in any direct way in the observed regularities. In such situations, anything, it seems, has at least the potential of being functionally, and hence structurally, connected to anything else.

The Search for Fixed Architectural Functions

If we take a broad view of the notion of functional architecture, we can recognize that proposals for components of the architecture discussed in the preceding section have frequently been made in psychological theorizing. In fact, they often characterize the differences that distinguish schools of psychology. For example, the dominant assumption, from the time of the British empiricists until about the early 1960s (and, in some quarters, even until today), was that the principal, built-in, functional capacity of organisms is their capacity to form associative links. For this assumption to be predictive, it was necessary as well to specify the type of entities over which associations could be formed (for behaviorists, these had to be defined behaviorally), as well as conditions on the formation and evocation of the links (such conditions as contiguity, reinforcement, and generalization gradients). This hypothetical capacity, like some contemporary nonbehaviorist proposals, was intuitively appealing because it agreed with informal observation of certain aggregate (that is, statistical) regularities of behavior, as well as behavior in certain highly controlled situations.

It is no accident that the controlled situations investigated from the conditioning perspective invariably involved suppression of what I call cognitive factors. The experimental paradigm was always contrived in such a way that beliefs, goals, inferences, or interpretations were, as much as possible, rendered irrelevant. Furthermore, critical observations generally were expressed as frequencies or probabilities, thus averaging over any remaining cognitive effects or strategies. Inevitably, however, cognitive factors still had an effect in the case of research involving human subjects. There, as Brewer (1974) persuasively and eloquently argues, the most plausible explanation of human-conditioning phenomena is one given in terms of change in belief. It is the most straightforward explanation of what reinforcers do: they inform the subjects of the contingencies so subjects can select a course of action based on their beliefs and utilities. Thus, the same effects typically can be produced by other ways of persuasively providing the same information, for example, explaining to subjects the conditions under which they will or will not be shocked, and backing up the story by showing them the wires.

I do not doubt the availability of ways of incorporating such results in the conditioning account, especially since individuation criteria for *stimulus, response,* or *reinforcer* are unspecified within the theory, thus allowing informal folk psychology to come to our aid in describing the situation appropriately and in smuggling knowledge of cognitive factors into the predictions. Whatever approach one takes to explaining such phenomena, however, Brewer's review and analysis of numerous studies makes it clear that even the simplest, most paradigmatic cases of conditioning in humans (for instance, classical conditioning of finger withdrawal to shock or conditioning of the eye-blink reflex) exhibit cognitive penetration, that is, they are radically yet systematically influenced by what the subjects believe or by what they are told or shown. Thus, even the simplest cases do not demonstrate that conditioning is a primitive function of the fixed architecture.

An intrinsic part of the conditioning account—and the only part that could conceivably explain novel behavior—is the notion of generalization. A more sophisticated, contemporary version of the generalization gradient is the similarity space. Just as conditioning requires dimensions along which it can generalize to new stimuli, so some contemporary theories which appeal to prototypes require dimensions of similarity in accounting for the relationships among prototypes and between prototypes and various exemplars or instances. Among the theoretical proposals for avoiding the complexities of inferential and problem-solving processes in accounting for such phenomena as recognition and classification (for example, Rosch, 1973), the most common proposal is the functional similarity space. Although Quine (1977), in speaking of a biologically endowed "quality space," gives no account of how such a space might be realized (presumably, neurophysiologically) or how the location of novel stimuli in the space are determined, a quality space still can be viewed as a possible component of the functional architecture. Thus, once again, it is appropriate to inquire whether this view can be sustained empirically.

The first thing to notice is that such a view cannot be applied to such stimuli as sentences, since it is clear that sentences can differ in an unbounded variety of relevant ways; that is, no finite set of dimensions or categories of comparison can exhaustively locate the meaning of a sentence in a similarity space.[7] While it seems likely that the same is true of visual patterns, the existence of *some* quantitative

7. The arguments given in Fodor and Pylyshyn (1981) for the nontransducibility of "sentencehood," based on arguments against the existence of projectable properties coextensive with membership of stimuli in the class "sentence," are also arguments against there being analogue representations of sentences, hence, of quality-space representations of sentences, since the latter is a clear case of analogue representation.

dimensions of similarity (size, orientation, brightness, hue) makes it less clear than it is in the language case. On the other hand, the strong interactions among such putative dimensions—demonstrated repeatedly by Gestalt psychologists—can also be cited in opposition to the view that such stimuli can be treated as varying along orthogonal dimensions in a similarity space.

A clear, simple demonstration of the inadequacy of the similarity-space view is found in the work of Roger Shepard, a pioneer of the multidimensional scaling technique. Shepard (1964) showed that when stimuli vary along several dimensions, subjects' judgments of their similarity can yield ratings that conform to a Euclidean metric along any dimension of variation, depending on what the subjects are instructed to attend to. When the subjects were not given specific attention instructions, however, and were left to attend to whatever they wished, the resulting data failed to conform to any metric (Euclidean or non-Euclidean) in the number of dimensions along which the stimuli varied. Shepard concluded that the noticing strategy of subjects determined the similarity structure of their judgments, and thus that the subjects could move at will from one possible similarity space to another. This is merely another way of saying the function described by the similarity space is cognitively penetrable. Thus it is determined at least in part by goals and beliefs rather than by properties of the functional architecture.

Many of the same arguments apply against the idea that memory storage is a form of "hologram," an idea that has received some currency (for example, Pribram, 1977), largely because holograms have the enticing property of being completely distributed memories that exhibit radical equipotentiality. If a pattern is stored in a hologram, and part of the hologram is destroyed, part of the pattern is not lost—the entire hologram simply loses some resolution. Holograms are also attractive because they exhibit a certain part-to-whole recall property wherein presentation of part of a scene leads to a degree of recall of the entire scene stored in the hologram. The holographic view has gained credence from evidence that a certain amount of spatial frequency analysis occurs in perception, since the theory of holograms is based on frequency-domain analysis. What holograms cannot account for—just as similarity spaces cannot—is the cognitive penetrability of the similarities and the generalizations observed in human memory. When people misrecognize a pattern similar to the one originally perceived, the dimension of similarity that accounts for the confusion is almost never one that is natural for holograms. We do not misrecognize a scene as one we have seen before when the scene is *geometrically* similar to the original (that is, similar with respect to locations and arrangement of features); rather, we misrecognize the scene if it is conceptually similar, if it contains similar thematic material, if we *interpret* it as involving the same participants, engaged in conceptually similar activities, and so on. We misrecognize conceptually similar scenes even though their geometry may differ radically. This is not the kind of failure of recall exhibited by a hologram. Holograms induce similarity or generalization gradients along quite different lines, lines thoroughly unnatural for human memory. (For a discussion of how perceptual memories are stored, see Pylyshyn, 1973b, 1978b.)

Once again, we probably could get around these counterarguments by allowing a cognitive component to preanalyze the stimulus prior to storage or recall. In these cases, however, where such added cognitive processes must be posited, it is no longer clear what function the space is serving other than as an ad hoc parameter to increase the precision of prediction. If we need a cognitive process to analyze and oversee the recognition, we already have a mechanism which, at least in principle, is capable of accounting for the similarity structure of the set of stimuli. Again, the burden falls on those who posit such a fixed function to demonstrate exactly what principled role the function plays, not merely to provide similarity judgments but as part of a general representational system.

In recent decades the psychophysical investigations that got psychology started as an experimental discipline (for example, Fechner's research) came under heavy criticism. Although usually not viewed in these terms, one problem with such studies is that many of the psychophysical laws being posited turned out to be cognitively penetrable (see, for example, Gregory, 1970; Howard, 1974; Rock, 1983). Almost any psychophysical *judgment* that requires the subject to selectively attend to certain specific aspects of the stimulus while ignoring other aspects will likely be cognitively penetrable. Among the best-known examples of a simple function found to be cognitively penetrable is the sensory threshold. The threshold was shown to be penetrable by subjects' beliefs concerning the utility of alternative responses, a finding that generated considerable interest in the theory of signal detectability (a decision theoretic and therefore cognitive analysis) as an alternative to the threshold function.

This is not to say that all aspects of perception are penetrable, even in the psychophysics examples. Signal detection theory assumes that only the decision stage (sometimes referred to as the "response-selection stage") is penetrable. Even in central processes, where the degree of plasticity is extremely high, it cannot be true that everything is cognitively penetrable. If it were, we would have no hope of developing a computational view of mind based on strong equivalence. If every function were cognitively penetrable it would mean, in turn, that we were mistaken either in our assumption that cognition is a natural, autonomous scientific domain or that we were mistaken in the view of computation we were using to explain cognition. Nonetheless, it is difficult to find examples of central processes that are clear instances of impenetrable architectural functions. Many attempts have been made to hypothesize content-independent principles that can account for properties of, say, memory retrieval (for example, the holographic model). These principles, possible candidates for architectural functions, include, for instance, the idea that information can be stored in the form of "sensory manifolds" or "images." I have argued (Pylyshyn, 1973b,1978b) that the empirical facts about the nature of memory confusion and failures of recall furnish strong evidence against such views. Indeed, the most plausible account of how long-term-memory retrieval occurs remains the reconstructive view of Bartlett (1932), which places general reasoning at the heart of at least some part of memory-retrieval processes, though it leaves open the possibility that other stages are basic operations of the architecture—as, indeed, they must be. The point is that we as yet have no empirically adequate proposal for such a stage.

The same is true of closely related proposals for memory access structures intended to function in the understanding and perception of language. Here, the problem to be resolved is how we bring the right knowledge to bear in the course of understanding sentences in discourse or in viewing a scene as a familiar one. The problem is, there is no way to specify the part of the overall data base of knowledge that is relevant to the task at hand.[8] Consequently, there is both a combinatorial explosion of possible items to take into account and an equally serious problem in deciding when to stop such inferences on the grounds that a "reasonable" interpretation has been found (since *reasonableness*, like *understanding*, is potentially a function of everything one knows).

Among the proposals for dealing with this combinatorial problem

8. One of my favorite examples of the use of arbitrary knowledge in even the simplest cases of understanding is drawn from Winograd (1972), who gives the following two sentences involving different pronominal assignments: (1) The city councillors refused the workers a permit for the demonstration because *they* were communists. (2) The city councillors refused the workers a permit for the demonstration because *they* feared violence. In these sentences it is clear that the reason we assign different referents to the italicized pronoun has to do with our practical knowledge of the world. I received a particularly cogent reminder that this is the case when I used this example in a talk I gave in Florence, Italy. The example lost much of its intended force because I had neglected to take into account that the city council of Florence consisted primarily of members of the Communist party, hence, many in the audience gave the pronoun *they* the *same* referent in the two sentences.

are such large-scale data structures as "frames" (Minsky, 1975) and "scripts" (Schank and Abelson, 1977). Even if there is something like these structures, however, they are relatively easy for people to override, given the motivation (that is, they are cognitively penetrable). In other words, people can still use arbitrary knowledge of the world to understand sentences and scenes; you cannot exclude any part of the knowledge base in advance, using some general prestructuring of that knowledge. Therefore, the content of such structures as frames and scripts must themselves be both analyzable and subject to reasoning by their users, which puts us back *almost* where we started. What we may have gained (and this is an empirical question that can be answered only if the frames-scripts proposal is specified well enough) is a summary of the aggregate regularities frequently, or typically, exhibited. The structures themselves tell us nothing about people's cognitive capacities, only about what are probably quite ephemeral habits of thought which people can change if sufficiently motivated. As in the case of free association, such structures summarize some of the patterns that emerge when people don't bother to think.

Perhaps the reason most central processes appear cognitively penetrable is that central cognitive processes more closely resemble deductions—where, under the appropriate circumstances, virtually any two concepts can be connected by some inference path. My own suspicions are that the functions that are part of the functional architecture of such higher level processes as thinking and common-sense reasoning are of two distinct kinds. On the one hand, there may be extremely primitive, elementary, symbol-processing operations (though they are unlikely to be the kind of operation found in contemporary serial digital computers); on the other, there may be properties of the functional architecture which impose extremely general constraints on data structures and on the control system. Furthermore, the primitive functions needed may even differ considerably in different parts of the cognitive system, though there may well be common resource allocation mechanisms, for example, a common control structure. We should not be surprised, however, by an apparent lack of highly constrained, functional properties of the type our folk psychology (which speaks freely of the limits of rationality, of recall, reasoning, or even belief change) might lead us to expect. This is an area in which we seek deeper explanatory principles, hence, an area where folk psychology is least likely to be of service. A comparable case—where some success has been achieved in seeking highly constrained, universal properties—is in the case of linguistic universals, or universal grammar. There, it has become obvious that properties of this sort can be found only at extremely high levels of abstraction, and at a considerable deductive distance from our intuitions and observations. I can see no reason to expect the situation to differ in other areas of cognition.

To expect such observations as those associated with the study of mental imagery to provide a direct route to a functional architecture of mind is to vastly underestimate the flexibility of mental processes. Even in those cases where, out of habit or for some other reason, people frequently do things in certain ways when they image, this need be of no special theoretical significance, since it may be due not to any general properties of mind but perhaps to certain longstanding habits (or so I argue in chapter 8). As I have repeatedly emphasized, mere statistical regularities need not tell us anything about mental capacity. More significant theoretical questions arise when we inquire which regularities are inviolable because they arise from fixed properties of mind, that is, from the functional architecture.

Rather than place the emphasis on explaining regularities which may well reflect little more than aggregate averages over various habits of thought, we should to be far more impressed with the extreme flexibility thought can take. For example, we should take seriously that, within the limits of our conceptual apparatus, there seems to be no specifiable limit to what the human mind can imagine or think.[9] As George Miller once put it, the salient property of mental life is surely the fact that we can will it to do practically anything we wish; given the appropriate goals and beliefs, by a mere act of will, we can alter our behavior and thoughts to a remarkable extent.

Although psychology typically has focused on the things we cannot do well or on the habitual patterns of behavior we display, we should not lose sight of the fact that a psychological theory of any interest must also account for the fact that a great many of these patterns and limitations can be overcome, thus telling us little about the underlying

9. Of course, the *unboundedness* of this flexibility is very likely an illusion. Surely we can think only thoughts expressible in terms of the concepts we possess. As Fodor (1980b, p. 333) colorfully puts it: *"From in here* it looks as though we're fit to think whatever thoughts there are to think. . . . It *would*, of course, precisely because we *are* in here. But there is surely good reason to suppose that this is hubris bred of an epistemological illusion. No doubt spiders think that webs exhaust the options." Nonetheless, within the bounds of our conceptual apparatus, it remains true that the reasoning capacity with which we are endowed appears to have the power of a Turing machine, though almost certainly our functional architecture is very different from that of Turing's original machine, and hence Turing machine algorithms are at most weakly equivalent to ours. Even though we *can* do many things with out minds, we cannot do them with equal ease. A very different story seems to be true of aspects of cognition that are not part of what we count as "central processes"; for example, it does not seem to be true of learning. Both concept learning (Keil, 1979) and language learning (Wexler and Cullicover, 1980) seem strictly constrained by properties of the functional architecture.

cognitive system. However uncomfortable may be the possibility that many of the functions studied by psychologists are not cognitively fixed mechanisms (in the sense that they are cognitively penetrable), we must be prepared to recognize that what is universal and biologically determined about the human mind may differ substantially from the sort of gross function we readily infer from patterns observed in behavior. It could well be—indeed, it seems extremely likely—that the major problem in understanding how cognition proceeds will be to explain how the vast store of tacit knowledge at our disposal is organized and how it is brought to bear in determining our thoughts, imaginings, and actions. To do this, we will need to pay special attention to formalisms adequate to the task of representing the relevant knowledge, rather than concentrating on the generation of *typical* behavior. This, in turn, presupposes that we take seriously such distinctions as those between competence and performance (see Chomsky, 1964; Pylyshyn, 1973a) or, to use McCarthy and Hayes's (1969) term, the distinction between the epistemological and heuristic problems of intelligence. A considerable advantage the computational view of cognition gives us is the potential to explore the more abstract issues formally and to work with longer deductive chains between observations and explanatory principles.

Chapter 8
Mental Imagery and Functional Architecture[1]

> To discover the nature of our *ideas* the better, and to discourse of them intelligibly, it will be convenient to distinguish them *as they are ideas or perceptions in our minds;* and *as they are modifications of matter in the bodies that cause such perceptions in us:* that so we may not think (as perhaps usually is done) that they are exactly the images and resemblances of something inherent in the subject; most of those of sensation being in the mind no more the likeness of something existing without us, than the names that stand for them are the likeness of our ideas, which yet upon hearing they are apt to excite in us.
>
> John Locke, From *An Essay Concerning Human Understanding*, XXIII, first published in 1690

Introduction: The Autonomy of the Imagery Process

It seems to me that the single most intriguing property of imagery—and the property that appears, at least at first glance, to distinguish it from other forms of deliberate rational thought—is that it has a certain intrinsic autonomy, in terms of both requiring that certain properties of stimuli (for example, shape and size) always be represented in an image, and with respect to the way in which dynamic imagery unfolds over time

Let us consider the second property. The experimental literature contains numerous anecdotes suggesting that to imagine a certain property we must first imagine something else. For example: To imagine the color of someone's hair we must first imagine their head or face; to imagine a certain room we must first imagine entering it from a certain

---

1. Parts of this chapter were adapted from my paper "The Imagery Debate: Analogue Media versus Tacit Knowledge," which appeared in *Psychological Review*, 1981, 88: 16–45. Copyright 1981 by the American Psychological Association. Reprinted with permission of the publisher.

door; to imagine a figure in a certain orientation we must first imagine it in a standard orientation and then imagine it rotating; to obtain a clear image of a tiny object one must first imagine "zooming in" on it. Sometimes, imagery even seems to resist our voluntary control. For example, in conducting a study of the mental rotation of images, I instructed subjects to imagine moving around a figure pictured as painted on the floor of a room. Several subjects reported considerable difficulty with one condition because the path of the imaginal movement was impeded by a wall visible in the photograph. They said they could not make themselves imagine moving around the figure because they kept bumping into the wall! Such responsiveness of the imagination to involuntary processes and unconscious control is a major reason why imagery is associated with the creative process: It appears to have access to tacit knowledge and beliefs through routes other than deliberate intellectual ones.

Other examples involving imaginal movement may be more compelling in this respect. Imagine dropping an object and watching it fall to the ground, or throwing a ball and watching it bounce off a wall. Does it not naturally obey physical laws? Imagine rotating the letter C counterclockwise through 90 degrees. Does it not suddenly appear to have the shape of a U without your having to deduce this? Imagine a square with a dot inside. Now imagine the width of the square elongating spontaneously until it becomes a wide rectangle. Is the dot not still inside the figure? Imagine the letters A through E written on a piece of paper in front of you. Can you not see by inspection that the letter D is to the right of the letter B? In none of these examples is there an awareness of what Haugeland (1978) calls "reasoning the problem through." The answer appears so directly and immediately available to inspection that it seems absurd to suggest, for example, that knowledge of topological properties of figures is relevant to the elongating-square example or that tacit knowledge of the formal properties of the relation *to the right of* (for example, that it is irreflexive, antisymmetric, transitive, connected, acyclic, and so on) are involved in the array-of-letters example. These and other, similar considerations have suggested to theorists that various intrinsic properties of imaginal representations are fixed by the underlying medium, and that we exploit these fixed, functional capacities when we reason imagistically. I believe this intuition is the primary motivation for the movement toward "analogue" processes.

Now, in general, these views are not implausible. We should be cautious, however, in what we assume is an intrinsic function instantiated by the underlying biological structure, as opposed to, say, a structure computed from tacit knowledge by the application of rules to symbolically represented beliefs or goals. In chapter 7, as well as Pylyshyn (1980a,1980b), I attempt to provide some necessary, though not sufficient, conditions for a function being instantiated in this sense. The condition I find particularly useful in clarifying this distinction, especially in the case of deciding how to interpret the observations already sketched, is the one I call the *cognitive impenetrability criterion*. Recall that I said a function is cognitively impenetrable if it cannot be altered in a way that exhibits a coherent relation to induced changes in subjects' goals and beliefs. For example, although a function might still count as cognitively impenetrable if it varied with such things as practice, arousal level, or ingestion of drugs, it would not be viewed as cognitively impenetrable if it changed in rationally explainable ways as a function of such things as whether a subject believes the visually presented stimulus depicts a heavy object (and hence, visualizes it as moving very slowly), whether the subject views it as consisting of one or two figures or as depicting an old woman or a young lady (in the well-known illusion) and, as a consequence, behaves in a way appropriate to that reading of the stimulus. I argued that cognitively penetrable phenomena such as the latter must be explained in terms of a cognitive rule-governed process involving such activity as logical inferences, problem solving, guessing, or associative recall, rather than in terms of the natural laws that explain the behavior of analogue process.

Many functions which appear at first to be biologically instantiated, and therefore alterable only in certain highly constrained law-governed respects, could, on closer inspection, turn out to be arbitrarily alterable in logically coherent ways by changes in subjects' beliefs and goals. That is, they could turn out to be cognitively penetrable and therefore require a cognitive-process account based on appeal to tacit knowledge and rules. The tremendous flexibility of human cognition, especially with respect to the more "central" processes involved in thinking and in common-sense reasoning, may well not admit of many highly constrained, nonprogrammable functions.

It might illuminate the nature of appeals to tacit knowledge if we considered some additional, everyday examples. Imagine holding in your two hands, and simultaneously dropping, a large object and a small object or two identically shaped objects of different weights. In your image, which object hits the ground first? Next, imagine turning a large, heavy flywheel by hand. Now imagine applying the same torque to a small aluminum pulley. Which—the flywheel or the pulley—completes one revolution in your image first? Now imagine a transparent yellow filter and a transparent blue filter side by side. Now imagine slowly superimposing the two filters. What color do you see in your image through the superimposed filters? Form a clear, stable image of a favorite familiar scene. Can you now imagine it as a photographic negative, out of focus, in mirror-image inversion, upside down? Next, imagine a transparent plastic bag containing a colored fluid that is held open with four parallel rods at right angles to the mouth of the bag in such a way that the cross section of the bag forms a square. Then imagine the rods being moved apart so that, with the plastic bag still tight around them, the rods now give the bag a rectangular, cross-sectional shape. As you imagine this happening, does the fluid in the bag rise, fall, or stay at the same level? (In other words, how does volume vary with changes of cross-sectional shape, the perimeter remaining constant?) Now imagine a glass half filled with sugar, and another nearly filled with water. Imagine the sugar being poured into the glass holding the water. Examine your image to determine the extent to which the resulting height of the water rises, if it rises at all.

These examples, it seems to me, are, in principle, no different from those in the list just presented. To many people, these imaginings unfold naturally, effortlessly, with no any need to reason through what happened; yet it seems clearer in these cases that whatever happens as the sequence unfolds in one's "mind's eye" is a function of the principles which one believes govern the events in question. Most people, in fact, tend to get several of these examples wrong. Clearly, the laws of dynamics or optics, and the principles of geometry that determine the relation between, say, the perimeter and the area of a figure are not intrinsic, or built in, to the representational media or to the mind's functional mechanisms. Not only must one have tacit knowledge of these laws and principles, but the way in which the imaginal events unfold naturally usually can be influenced with considerable freedom simply by informing the subject of the appropriate principle. Thus, what seems a natural, autonomous, unfolding process is cognitively penetrable; that is, it is under the control of an intellectual process, with all that this implies concerning the intervention of inferences and "reasoning through." As Harman (1973) argues, our intuitions concerning when inferences do or do not take place must give way before the logical necessity to posit such processes. The mind, it seems, is faster even than the mind's eye.

Another intriguing example, due to Ian Howard, demonstrates that even in the case of a simple task involving recognition of physically possible events, knowledge of physical principles is crucial—thus suggesting that, in the case of imaging, such knowledge is even more indispensable in explaining why images undergo transformations in certain, systematic ways. Howard (1978) showed that over half the population of undergraduate subjects he tested could not correctly recognize trick photographs of tilted pitchers containing colored fluids whose surface orientations were artificially set at various anomalous angles relative to the horizontal. Using the method of random presentation, and repeating the study with both stereoscopic photographs and motion pictures, Howard found that the subjects who failed the recognition task for levels as much as 30 degrees off the horizontal nevertheless, correctly reported that the fluid surface was not parallel to shelves visible in the background, thus showing that the failure was not one of perceptual discrimination. What was noteworthy was that postexperimental interviews, scored blindly by two independent judges, revealed that every subject who achieved a perfect score on the recognition test (that is, no stimulus with orientation more than five degrees off the horizontal failing to be correctly classified as anomalous) could clearly articulate the principle of fluid-level invariance, whereas no subject who made errors gave a hint of understanding the relevant principle. Here, unlike the typical case in such other areas as phonology, evidence of the relevant knowledge was obtainable through direct interviews. Even when direct evidence is not available, however, indirect behavioral evidence that tacit knowledge is involved frequently can be obtained, for example, by demonstrating "cognitive penetrability" of the phenomenon to new knowledge.

Once this kind of example is presented, no one finds at all surprising the claim that tacit knowledge is required for some forms of imagining. In fact, Kosslyn, Pinker, Smith, and Shwartz (1979) admit that both "image formation" and "image transformation" can be cognitively penetrable, hence, not explainable by appeal to properties of the imaginal medium. Given, however, that these examples are not distinguishable from earlier ones in terms of the apparent autonomy of their progression, why do we continue to find it so compelling to view such phenomena as those associated with mental scanning as providing evidence for an intrinsic property of the imaginal medium, or, as Kosslyn et al. (1979) put it, for the "spatial structure of the surface display"? Is it because such processes as mental scanning are more resistant to voluntary control? Is it inconceivable that we could search for objects in a mental image without passing through intermediate points, that we could compare two shapes in different orientations without necessarily first imagining one of them being at each of a large number of intermediate orientations?

I believe that what makes certain spatial operations resistant to a natural interpretation, in terms of knowledge-governed reasoning through, is primarily the "objective pull" I discuss in Pylyshyn (1978b). The objective pull results in a tendency to view the cognitive process in terms of properties of the represented objects—that is, in terms of the semantics of the representation—rather than the structure, or syntax, of the representation. This tendency, however, leads to a way of stating the principles by which mental processes operate that deprives the principles of any explanatory value, because it involves principles expressed in terms of properties of the represented object rather than in terms of the representation's structure or form. Yet expressing a principle in terms of properties of the domain represented begs the question why processing occurs in this fashion. The mechanism has no access to properties of the represented domain except insofar as they are encoded in the representation itself. Thus a principle of mental processing must be stated in terms of the formal structural properties of its representations, not what they are taken to represent in the theory.

Consider the following example. In describing their model, Kosslyn et al. (1979) are careful to abstract the general principles of the model's operation—an essential step if the model is to be explanatory. Included among such principles are, for example, "Mental images are transformed in small steps, so the images pass through intermediate stages of transformation"; and "The degree of distortion is proportional to the size of the transformational step." Shepard (1975) also cites such principles in discussing his image-transformation results.

In each case, these principles make sense only if such terms as *size* and *small steps* refer to the domain represented. The intended interpretation of the first principles ("Mental images are transformed," etc.) would have to be something like, "Representations are transformed in such a way that successive representations correspond to small differences in the scene being depicted." What we need, however, is a statement that refers only to the structure of the representation and its accessing process. We should be able to say something like, "Representations are transformed in small structural steps or degrees." Where, *small* is relative to a metric defined over the formal structure of the representation and the process. For example, relative to a binary representation of numbers and a machine with a bit-shifting operation, the formal, or syntactic, transformation from a representation of the number 137 to a representation of the number 274 is smaller than that from a representation of 137 to a representation of 140 (the former requires only one shift operation), even though the transformation clearly corresponds to a larger transformation in the intended semantic domain of abstract numbers. Thus in speaking (typically, ambiguously) about transformations of representations, it is important to distinguish between the intrinsic, syntactic domain and the extrinsic, semantic domain. Not only are the two logically different, but, as the example shows, quite different metrics, and thus quite different principles, can apply in the two cases.

Cognitive principles such as those invoked by Kosslyn et al. (1979),

Shepard (1975), and Anderson (1978) are theoretically substantive (that is, explanatory) only if they specify: (a) how it was possible to have formal operations with the desired semantic generalization as their consequence—for example, how one can arrange a formal representation and operations on it so small steps in the formal representations correspond to small steps in the represented domain; and (b) why these operations rather than some others which could also accomplish the task should be used. (This is the issue of making the underlying theory principled or of restricting its degrees of freedom by reducing the number of free parameters in it.) It is not enough simply to assert that representations do, in fact, have this property (because, for example, they are said to *depict* rather than merely *represent*). One reason it is not enough is that such a property is merely stipulated so as to conform to the data at hand; in other words, it is a free empirical parameter. Another reason is that, as with the cases already discussed, two distinct options are available to account for how this can happen: appeal either to tacit knowledge or to intrinsic properties of a representational medium, that is, to properties of the functional architecture. In other words, we can make the account principled by relating the process either to the rationality of the method adopted, given the organism's goals and tacit knowledge, or to the causal relations that hold among physical properties of the representational medium.

Tacit Knowledge and "Mental Scanning"

The Empirical Phenomena: Mental Scanning
In the following I examine some specific claims made about the phenomenon of reasoning with the aid of images. Since the study of mental imagery came back into fashion in the 1960s, hundreds of studies have been published, purporting to show that theories of imagery must make allowances for some fairly special properties, properties not shared by other modes of reasoning. Beginning in the 1970s, these studies have concentrated on the role of imagery in reasoning and problem solving rather than on imagery as a form of memory or imagery as an intervening variable in experiments on learning.

Among the best-known research on imaginal reasoning is that of Roger Shepard and his students (Shepard, 1978; Shepard and Cooper, 1982) and Steve Kosslyn and his associates. Kosslyn's work has been extensively reported—in numerous papers, in a summary in a review paper by Kosslyn et at. (1979), and in a book (Kosslyn, 1980). Because Kosslyn, having developed a detailed computer model of imagery, takes a more theoretical approach than most writers, and because his work is among the most influential of the "pictorialists"—to use Block's (1981) term—most of what follows is directed specifically at claims made by Kosslyn. My intention, however, is not to single out this one piece of research; everything I say applies equally to those "pictorialists" who feel that a special form of representation (often called an analogue medium) is needed to account for various experimental results in imaginal reasoning. It is just that Kosslyn's productivity and the explicitness of his claims make him an excellent spokesman for that approach.

The finding that became the basis for much of Kosslyn's theorizing is the "mental scanning result," used not only to argue that "images preserve distances"[2] and that they "depict information in a spatial medium" but also as a way to calibrate "imaginal distance" for such purposes as measuring the visual angle of the "mind's eye" (Kosslyn, 1978). Kosslyn's work has also been cited by Attneave (1974) as one of two results that most clearly demonstrate the analogue nature of the representational medium (the other is the "mental rotation" result that will be mentioned here only in passing). Hence, it seems a good place to start.

The scanning experiment (for example, Kosslyn, Ball, and Reiser, 1978) has been done many times, so there are quite a few variants. Here is a typical one. Subjects are asked to memorize a simple map of a fictitious island containing about seven visually distinct places (a beach, church, lighthouse, bridge, and so on), until they can reproduce the map to within a specified tolerance. The subjects are then asked to image the map "in their mind's eye" and focus their attention on one of the places, for example, the church. Then they are told the name of a second place, which might or might not be on the map. They are asked to imagine a spot moving from the first to the second place named (or, in some variants, to "move their attention" to the second place). When the subjects can clearly see the second place on their image, they are to press a "yes" button, or, if the named place is not

2. This claim is worded differently at different times, and depending on how careful Kosslyn is. Thus, in Kosslyn et al. (1979), it is put two different ways in two consecutive sentences. In the first, the authors claim that "these results seem to indicate that images do represent metrical distance"; in the second, they take the more radical approach, claiming that "images have spatial extent." (Kosslyn et al., p. 537) I contend that this vacillation between *representing* and *having* is no accident. Indeed, the attraction of the theory—what appears to give it a principled explanation—is the strong version (that images "have spatial extent"); but the only one that can be defended is the weaker version, a version, in fact, indistinguishable from the tacit knowledge view I have been advocating. Computerization of the theory does not remove the equivocation: There are still two options on how to interpret the simulation—as a simulation of an analogue or a surface with "spatial extent," or as a simulation of the knowledge the subject possesses about space.

on the map, the "no" button. The latter condition is usually there only as a foil. The result, which is quite robust when the experiment is conducted over hundreds of trials, shows that the time it takes to make the decision is a linear function of the distance traversed on the map. Because, to go from one point on an imagined map to a second point the mind's eye apparently scans through intermediate points, theorists conclude that all the intermediate points are on the mental map; hence, the representation is said to be a form of analogue.

This description, though accurate, does justice neither to the range of experiments carried out nor to the extremely intricate, detailed, highly interconnected model used to explain these and other results. I do not take the reader through the details of the model (they are summarized in the review papers and the book already cited), principally because I do not believe the details matter, neither for the main point of my criticism nor for what makes the model attractive to "pictorialists." The important point is that the explanation of the "scanning result" is to be found in the *intrinsic properties of the representational medium* rather than the tacit knowledge subjects have of the situation they are imagining. Therefore, it is an instance of explicitly positing a property of the functional architecture to account for a generalization. This makes our discussion of the issue, as it is developed in chapter 7, directly relevant to understanding these and many closely related findings.

Some Preliminary Considerations
In examining what occurs in studies such as the scanning experiment and those discussed in Kosslyn (1980), it is crucial that we note the difference between the following two tasks:

1a. Solve a problem by using a certain prescribed form of representation or a certain medium or mechanism; and

1b. Attempt to re-create as accurately as possible the sequence of perceptual events that would occur if you were actually observed a certain real event happening.

The reason this difference is crucial is that substantially different criteria of success apply in the two cases. For example, solving a problem by using a certain representational format does not necessarily entail that various incidental properties of a known situation be considered, let alone simulated. On the other hand, this is precisely what is required of someone solving task 1b. Here, failure to duplicate such conditions as the speed at which an event occurs constitutes failure to perform the task correctly. Take the case of imagining. The task of imagining something is the case, or considering an imagined situation in order to answer questions about it, does not entail (as part of the specification of the task itself) that it take a particular length of time. On the other hand, the task of imagining that an event actually happens before your eyes does entail, for a successful realization of this task, consideration of as many characteristics of the event as possible, even if they are irrelevant to the discrimination task itself, as well as entailing that you attempt to place them in the correct time relationships.

In discussing how he imaged his music, Mozart claimed: "Nor do I hear in my imagination, the parts successively, but I hear them, as it were, all at once. . . ." (See Mozart's letter, reproduced in Ghiselin, 1952, p. 45.) Mozart felt that he could "hear a whole symphony" in his imagination "all at once" and apprehend its structure and beauty. He must have had in mind a task best described in terms of task 1a. Even the word *hear*, taken in the sense of having an auditorylike imaginal experience, need entail nothing about the duration of the experience. We can be reasonably certain Mozart did not intend the sense of imagining implied in task 1b, simply because, if what he claimed to be doing was that he imagined witnessing the real event of, say, sitting in the Odeon Conservatoire in Munich and hearing his Symphony Number 40 in G Minor being played with impeccable precision by the resident orchestra under the veteran Kapellmeister, and if he imagined that it was actually happening before him in real time and in complete detail—including the most minute flourishes of the horns and the trills of the flute and oboe, all in the correct temporal relations and durations—he would have taken nearly 22 minutes for the task. If he had taken less time, it would signify only that Mozart had not been doing exactly what he said he was doing; that is, he would not have been imagining that he witnessed the actual event in which every note was being played at its proper duration—or we might conclude that what he had, in fact, been imagining was not a good performance of his symphony. In other words, if it takes n seconds to witness a certain event, then an accurate mental simulation of the act of witnessing the same event should also take n seconds, simply because, how well the latter task is performed, by definition, depends on the accuracy with which it mimics various properties of the former task. On the other hand, the same need not apply merely to the act of imagining that the event has a certain set of properties, that is, imagining a situation to be the case but without the additional requirements specified in the 1b version of the task. These are not empirical assertions about how people imagine and think; they are merely claims about the existence of two distinct, natural interpretations of the specification of a certain task.

In applying this to the case of mental scanning, we must be careful to distinguish between the following two tasks, which subjects might set themselves:

2a. Using a mental image, and focusing your attention on a certain object in the image, decide as quickly as possible whether a second named object is present elsewhere in that image; or

2b. Imagine yourself in a certain real situation in which you are viewing a certain scene and are focusing directly on a particular object in that scene. Now imagine that you are looking for (scanning toward, glancing up at, seeing a speck moving across the scene toward) a second named object in the scene. When you succeed in imagining yourself finding (and seeing) the object (or when you see the speck arrive at the object), press the button.

The relevant differences between 2a and 2b should be obvious. As in the preceding examples, the criteria of successful completion of the task are different in the two cases. In particular, task 2b includes, as part of its specification, such requirements as, subjects should attempt to imagine various intermediate states (corresponding to those they believe would be passed through in actually carrying out the corresponding real task), and that they spend more time visualizing those episodes they believe (or infer) would take more time in the corresponding, real task (perhaps because they recall how long it once took, or because they have some basis for predicting how long it would take). Clearly, the latter conditions are not part of the specification of task 2a, as there is nothing about task 2a which requires that such incidental features of the visual task be considered in answering the question. In the words of Newell and Simon (1972), the two tasks have quite different "task demands."

To demonstrate that subjects actually carry out task 2b in the various studies reported by Kosslyn (and, therefore, that the proper explanation of the findings should appeal to subjects' tacit knowledge of the depicted situation rather than to properties of their imaginal medium), I shall attempt to establish several independent points. First, it is independently plausible that the methods used in experiments reported in the literature should be inviting subjects to carry out task 2b rather than task 2a, and that, in fact, this explanation has considerable generality and can account for a variety of imaginal phenomena. Second, independent experimental evidence exists showing that subjects can, indeed, be led to carry out task 2a rather than 2b, and that when they do, the increase in reaction time with increase in imagined distance disappears. Finally, I consider several objections raised to the "tacit-knowledge" explanation, principally, cases in which subjects appear to have no knowledge of how the results would have turned out in the visual case. I then consider a number of interesting, important cases, possibly not explained by the tacit-knowledge view, in which subjects combine visual and imaginal information by, for example, superimposing images on the scene they are examining visually. I argue that these do not bear on the question under debate—namely, the necessity of postulating a special, non-inferential (and noncomputational) mechanism in order to deal with the imagistic mode of reasoning.

Task Demands of Imagery Experiments
With respect to the first point, all published studies of which I am aware, in which larger image distances led to longer reaction times, used instructions that explicitly required subjects to imagine witnessing the occurrence of a real physical event. In most scanning experiments subjects are asked to imagine a spot moving from one point to another, although, in a few experiments (for example, Kosslyn, 1973; Kosslyn, Ball, and Reiser, 1978, experiment 4), they are asked to imagine "shifting their attention" or their "glance" from one imagined object to another in the same imagined scene. In each case, what subjects were required to imagine was a real, physical event (because such terms as *move* and *shift* refer to physical processes) about whose duration they would clearly have some reasonable, though sometimes only tacit, knowledge. For example, the subjects would know implicitly that, for instance, it takes a moving object longer to move through a greater distance, that it takes longer to shift one's attention through greater distances (both transversely and in depth).

It is important to see that what is at issue is not a contamination of results by the sort of experimental artifact psychologists refer to as "experimenter demand characteristics" (see, for example, Rosenthal and Rosnow, 1969) but simply a case of subjects solving a task as they interpret it (or as they choose to interpret it, for one reason or another) by bringing to bear everything they know about a class of physical events, events they take to be those they are to imagine witnessing. If the subjects take the task to be that characterized as 2b, they will naturally attempt to reproduce a temporal sequence of representations corresponding to the sequence they believe will arise from actually viewing the event of scanning across a scene or seeing a spot move across it. Thus, beginning with the representation corresponding to "imagining seeing the initial point of focus," the process continues until a representation is reached that corresponds to "imagining seeing the named point." According to this view there is no need to assume that what is happening is that the imaging process continues until the occurrence of a certain imagined state is independently detected (by the mind's eye), say, because a certain "visual" property is noticed. The process could just as plausibly proceed according to a rhythm established by some independent psychophysical mechanism that paces the time between each viewpoint imagined, according to the speed the subject sets for the mental scanning. (We know such mechanisms exist, since subjects can generate time intervals corresponding to known magnitudes with even greater reliability than they can estimate them; see Fraisse, 1963.) Neither is it required that the process consist of a discrete sequence—all that is required is that there be psychophysical mechanisms for estimating and creating both speeds and time intervals. My point here is simply that the skill involved does not necessarily have anything to do with properties specific to a medium of visual imagery.

For the purpose of this account of the scanning results, we need assume little or nothing about intrinsic constraints on the process or about the form of the sequence of representations generated. It could be that the situation here is like that in the example discussed in chapter 7, where a sequence of numbers is computed in conventional digital manner and displayed in analogue form. In that example, I claim that positing an analogue representation is theoretically irrelevant. A similar point applies here. We might, for instance, simply have a sequence consisting of a series of representations of the scene, each with a different location singled out in some manner. In that case, the representation's form is immaterial as far as the data at hand are concerned. For example, we could view the representations as a sequence of beliefs whose contents are something like that the spot is now *here*, and now it is *there*—where the locative demonstratives are pointers to parts of the symbolic representations being constructed and updated.

Although the sequence almost certainly is more complex than I have described it, we need not assume that it is constrained by a special property of the representational medium—as opposed simply to being governed by what subjects believe or infer about likely intermediate stages of the event being imagined and about the relative times at which they will occur. Now, such beliefs and inferences obviously can depend on anything the subject might tacitly know or believe concerning what usually happens in corresponding perceptual situations. Thus the sequence could, in one case, depend on tacit knowledge of the dynamics of physical objects, and, in another, on tacit knowledge of some aspects of eye movements or what happens when one must "glance up" or refocus on an object more distant, or even on tacit knowledge of the time required to notice or recognize certain kinds of visual patterns. For example, I would not be surprised, for this reason, to find that it took subjects longer to imagine trying to see something in dim light or against a camouflage background.

The Generality of the "Tacit Knowledge" View

The sort of "tacit knowledge" view I have been discussing has considerable generality in explaining various imagery research findings, especially when we take into account the plausibility that subjects are actually attempting to solve a problem of type 1b. For instance, the list of illustrative examples presented at the beginning of this chapter clearly show that, to imagine the episode of "seeing" certain physical events, one must have access to tacit knowledge of physical regularities. In some cases, it even seems reasonable that one needs an implicit theory, since a variety of related generalizations must be brought to bear to correctly predict what some imagined process will do (for example, the sugar solution or the color filter case). In other cases, the mere knowledge or recollection that certain things typically happen in certain ways, and that they take certain relative lengths of time suffices.

Several other findings, allegedly revealing properties of the mind's eye, might also be explainable on this basis, including the finding (Kosslyn, 1975) that it takes longer to report properties of objects when the objects are imagined as being small. Consider that the usual way to inspect an object is to take up a viewing position at some convenient distance from the object that depends on the object's size and, in certain cases, other things as well (for example, consider imagining a deadly snake or a raging fire). So long as we have a reasonably good idea of the object's true size, we can imagine viewing it at the appropriate distance. Now, if someone told me to imagine an object as especially small, I might perhaps think of myself as being farther away or as seeing it through, say, the wrong end of a telescope. If I were then asked to do something, such as report some properties of the object, and if the instructions were to imagine that I could *see* the property I was reporting (which was the case in the experiments reported), or even if, for some obscure reason, I simply chose to make that my task, I would naturally try to imagine the occurrence of some real sequence of events in which I went from seeing the object as small to seeing it as large enough for me to easily discern details (that is, I probably would take the instructions as indicating I should carry out task 1b). In that case, I probably would imagine something that, in fact, is a plausible visual event, such as a zooming-in sequence (indeed, that is what many of Kosslyn's subjects reported). If such were the case, we would expect the time relations to be as they are actually observed.

Although this account may sound similar to the one given by some analogue theorists (for example, Kosslyn, 1975), from a theoretical standpoint, there is one critical difference. In my account, no appeals need be made to knowledge-independent properties of the functional architecture, especially not to geometrical properties. No doubt, the architecture—what I have been calling the representational medium—has some relevant, intrinsic properties that restrict how things can be represented. These properties, however, appear to play no role in accounting for any phenomena we are considering. These phenomena can be viewed as arising from (a) subjects' tacit knowledge of how, in reality, things typically happen, and (b) subjects' ability to carry out such psychophysical tasks as generating time intervals that correspond to inferred durations of certain possible, physical events. This is not to deny the importance of different forms of representation, of certain inferential capacities, or of the nature of the underlying mechanisms; I am merely suggesting that these findings do not necessarily tell us anything about such matters.

Everyone intuitively feels that the visual image modality (format, or medium) severely constrains both the form and the content of potential representations; at the same time, it is no easy matter to state exactly what these constraints are (the informal examples already given should at least cast suspicion on the validity of such intuitions in general). For instance, it seems clear that we cannot image every object whose properties we can describe; this lends credence to the view that images are more constrained than descriptions. While it is doubtless true that imagery, in some sense, is not as flexible as such discursive symbol systems as language, it is crucial that we know the nature of this constraint if we are to determine whether it is a constraint imposed by the medium or is merely a habitual way of doing things or is related to our understanding of what it *means* to image something. It might even be a limitation attributable to the absence of certain knowledge or a failure to draw certain inferences. Once again, I would argue that we cannot tell a priori whether certain patterns which arise when we use imagery ought to be attributed to the character of the biological medium of representation (the analogue view), or whether they should be attributed to the subject's possession and use, either voluntary or habitual, of certain tacit knowledge.

Consider the following proposals made by Kosslyn et al. (1979) concerning the nature of the constraints on imagery. The authors take such constraints to be given by the intrinsic nature of the representational medium, suggesting that what they call the "surface display" (a reference to their cathode ray tube proto-model) gives imagery certain fixed characteristics. For example, they state,

> We predict that this component will not allow cognitive penetration: that a person's knowledge, beliefs, intentions, and so on will not alter the spatial structure that we believe the display has. Thus we predict that a person cannot at will make his surface display four-dimensional, or non-Euclidean. . . . (Kosslyn et al., p. 549)

It does seem true that one cannot image a four-dimensional or non-Euclidean space; yet the very oddness of the supposition that we could do so should make us suspicious as to the reason. To understand why little can be concluded from this, let us suppose a subject insists that he or she could image a non-Euclidean space. Suppose further that mental scanning experiments are consistent with the subject's claim (for example, the scan time conforms to, say, a city block metric). Do we believe this subject, or do we conclude that what the subject really does is "simulate such properties in imagery by filling in the surface display with patterns of a certain sort, in the same way that projections of non-Euclidean surfaces can be depicted on two-dimensional Euclidean paper" (Kosslyn et al., 1979, p. 547)?

We, of course, conclude the latter. The reason we do so is exactly the same as that given for discounting a possible interpretation of what Mozart meant in claiming to be able to imagine a whole symphony "at once." That reason has to do solely with the implications of a particular sense of the phrase "imagine a symphony"—namely, that the task-1b sense demands that certain conditions be fulfilled. If we transpose this to the case of the spatial property of visual imagery, we can see that it is also the reason why the notion of imagining four-dimensional space in the sense of task 1b is incoherent. The point is sufficiently central that it merits a brief elaboration.

Let us first distinguish, as I have been insisting we should, between two senses of "imaging." The first sense of imagining (call it "imagine$_{think}$ X") means to think of X or to consider the hypothetical situation that X is the case or to mentally construct a symbolic model or a "description" of a "possible world" in which X is the case. The second sense of imagining (call this "imagine$_{see}$ X") means to imagine that you are seeing X or that you observe the actual event X as it occurs. Then the reason for the inadmissibility of four-dimensional or non-Euclidean imaginal space becomes clear, as does its irrelevance to the question of what properties an imaginal medium has. The reason we cannot imagine$_{see}$ such spaces is, they are not the sort of thing that can be seen. Our inability to imagine$_{see}$ such things has nothing to do with intrinsic properties of a "surface display" but, instead, with lack of a certain kind of knowledge: We do not know what it is like to see such a thing. For example, we have no idea what configuration of light and dark contours would be necessary, what visual features would need to appear, and so on. Presumably for similar reasons, congenitally color-blind people cannot imagine$_{see}$ a colored scene, in which case, it would hardly seem appropriate to attribute this failure to a defect in their "surface display." On the other hand, we do know, in nonvisual (that is, non-optical) terms, what a non-Euclidean space is like, hence we might still be able to *imagine*$_{think}$ there being such a space in reality (certainly, Einstein did) and thus solve problems about it. Perhaps, given sufficient familiarity with the facts of such spaces, we could even produce mental scanning results in conformity with non-Euclidean geometries. There have been frequent reports of people who claim to have an intuitive grasp of four-dimensional space in the sense that they can, for instance, mentally rotate a four-dimensional tesseract and *imagine*$_{see}$ its three-dimensional projection from a new four-dimensional orientation (Hinton, 1906, provides an interesting discussion of what is involved). If this were true, these people might be able to do a four-dimensional version of the Shepard mental rotation task.

If one drops all talk about the *geometry* (that is, the "spatial character") of the display and considers the general point regarding the common conceptual constraints imposed on vision and imagery, there can be no argument: *Something* is responsible for the way in which we cognize the world. Whatever that something is probably also explains both the way we see the world and how we image it. But that's as far as we can go. From this, we can no more draw conclusions about the geometry, topology, or other structural property of a representational medium than we can about the structure of a language by considering the structure of things that can be described in that language. There is no reason for believing that the relation is anything but conventional—which is precisely what the doctrine of functionalism claims (and what most of us implicitly believe).

The distinction between the two senses of *imagine* we discussed also serves to clarify why various empirical findings involving imagery tend to occur together. For example, Kosslyn et al. (1979), in their response section, provide a brief report on a study by Kosslyn, Jolicoeur, and Fliegel which shows that when stimuli are sorted according to whether subjects tend to visualize them in reporting certain of their properties, that is, whether subjects typically *imagine*$_{see}$ them in such tasks; then it is only those stimulus-property pairs that are classified as mental image evokers that yield the characteristic reaction time functions in mental scanning experiments. This is hardly surprising, since anything that leads certain stimuli habitually to be processed in the *imagine*$_{see}$ mode will naturally tend to exhibit numerous other characteristics associated with *imagine*$_{see}$ processing, including scanning time results and such phenomena as the "visual angle of the mind's eye" or the relation between latency and imagined size of objects (see the summary in Kosslyn et al., 1979). Of course, nobody knows why certain features of a stimulus or a task tend to elicit the *imagine*$_{see}$ habit, nor why some stimuli should do so more than others; but that is not a problem that distinguishes the analogue from the tacit knowledge view.

Some Empirical Evidence

Finally, it may be useful to consider some provisional evidence suggesting that subjects can be induced to use their visual image to perform a task such as 2a in a way that does not entail imagining oneself observing an actual sequence of events. Recall that the question is whether mental scanning effects (that is, the linear relation between time and distance) should be viewed as evidence for an intrinsic property of a representational medium or as evidence for, say, people's tacit knowledge of geometry and dynamics, as well as their understanding of the task. If the former interpretation is the correct one, then it must not merely be the case that people usually take longer to retrieve information about more distant objects in an imagined scene. That could arise, as already noted, merely from some habitual or preferred way of imagining or from a preferred interpretation of task demands. If the phenomenon is due to an intrinsic property of the imaginal medium, it must be a *necessary* consequence of using this medium; that is, the linear (or, at least, the monotonic) relation between time and distance represented must hold whenever information is accessed through the medium of imagery.

As it happens, there exists a strong preference for interpreting tasks involving doing something imaginally as tasks of type 1b—that is, as requiring one to *imagine*$_{see}$ an actual, physically realizable event happening over time. In most mental scanning cases it is the event of moving one's attention from place to place, or of witnessing something moving between two points. It could also involve imagining such episodes as drawing or extrapolating a line, and watching its progression. The question remains, however: *Must* a subject imagine such a physically realizable event in order to access information from an image or, more precisely, to produce an answer which the subject claims is based on an examination of the image?

A number of studies have been carried out in my laboratory suggesting that conditions can be set up which enable a subject to use an image to access information, yet which is done without the subject having to imagine the occurrence of a particular, real life, temporal event. That is, the subject can be induced to *imagine*$_{think}$ rather than *imagine*$_{see}$. For purposes of illustration, I mention two of these studies. The design of the experiments follows closely that of experiments reported in Kosslyn, Ball, and Reiser (1978). (See Pylyshyn, 1981, for additional details, and Bannon, 1981, for all the details of the design and analysis.) The subjects were required to memorize a map containing approximately seven visually distinct places (a church, castle, beach, and so on). Then they were asked to image the map in front of them and focus their attention on a particular named place, while keeping the rest of the map in view in their mind's eye. We then investigated various conditions under which the subjects were given different instructions concerning what to do next, all of which (a) emphasized that the task was to be carried out exclusively by consulting their image, and (b) required them to notice, on cue, a second named place on the map and to make some discriminatory response with respect to that place as quickly and as accurately as possible.

So far this description of the method is identical to that of the experiments by Kosslyn, Ball, and Reiser (1978). Indeed, when we instructed subjects to imagine a speck moving from the place of initial focus to another, named place, we obtained the same strongly linear relation between distance and reaction time as did Kosslyn, Ball, and Reiser. When, however, the instructions specified merely that subjects give the compass bearing of the second place—that is, to state whether the second place was north, northeast, east, southeast, and so on of the first, there was no relation between distance and reaction time. Similar results have also been obtained since by Finke and Pinker (1982).

These results suggest that it is possible to arrange a situation in which subjects use their image to retrieve information, yet where they do not feel compelled to imagine the event of scanning their attention between the two points—that is, to imagine$_{see}$. While this result is suggestive, it is by no means compelling, since it lacks controls for a number of alternative explanations. In particular, because a subject must, in any case, know the bearing of the second place on the map before scanning to it (even in Kosslyn's experiments), we might, for independent reasons, wish to claim that in this experiment the relative bearing of pairs of points on the map was retrieved from a symbolic, as opposed to an imaginal, representation, despite subjects' insistence that they did use their images in making judgments. Whereas this tends to weaken the imagery story somewhat (because it allows a crucial spatial property to be represented off the display and thus raises the question, Why not represent other spatial properties this way?, and because it discounts subjects' reports of how they were carrying out the task in this case while accepting such reports in other comparable situations), nonetheless, it is a possible avenue of retreat.

Consequently, another instructional condition was investigated, one aimed at making it more plausible to believe that subjects had to consult their image in order to make the response, while at the same time making it more compelling that they be focused on the second place and mentally "see" both the original and the second place at the time of the response. The only change in instructions made for this purpose was explicitly to require subjects to focus on the second place after they heard its name (for example, *church*) and, using *it* as the new origin, give the orientation of the first place (the place initially focused on) relative to the second. Thus the instructions strongly emphasized the necessity of focusing on the second place and the need actually to see both places before making an orientation judgment. Subjects were not told how to get to the second place from the first, only to keep the image before their mind's eye and use the image to read off the correct answer. In addition, for reasons to be mentioned, the same experiment was run (using a different group of subjects) entirely in the visual modality; thus, instead of having to image the map, subjects could actually examine the map in front of them.

What we found was that in the visual condition there is a significant correlation between response time (measured from the presentation of the name of the second place) and the distance between places, whereas in the imaginal condition no such relation holds. These results indicate clearly that even though the linear relation between distance and time (the "scanning phenomenon") is a frequent concomitant of imaging a transition between "seeing" two places on an image, it is not a necessary consequence of using the visual imagery modality, as it is in the case of actual visual perception; consequently, the linear-reaction time function is not due to an intrinsic (hence, knowledge- and goal-independent) property of the representational medium for visual images.

Such experiments demonstrate that image examination is unencumbered by at least one putative constraint of the "surface display" postulated by Kosslyn and others. Further, it is reasonable to expect other systematic relations between reaction time and image properties to disappear when appropriate instructions are given that are designed to encourage subjects to interpret the task as in 1a instead of 1b. For example, if subjects could be induced to generate what they consider small but highly detailed, clear images, the effect of image size on time to report the presence of features (Kosslyn, 1975) might disappear as well. There is evidence from one of Kosslyn's own studies that this might be the case. In a study reported in Kosslyn, Reiser, Farah, and Fliegel (1983), the time to retrieve information from images was found to be independent of image size. From the description of this experiment, it seems that a critical difference between it and earlier experiments (Kosslyn, 1975), in which an effect of image size was found, is that, here, subjects had time to study the actual objects, with instructions to practice generating equally clear images of each object. The subjects were also tested with the same instructions—which, I assume, encouraged them to entertain equally detailed images at all sizes.

Thus it seems possible, when subjects are encouraged to make available detailed information, they can put as fine a grain of detail as desired into their imaginal constructions, though, presumably, the total amount of information in the image remains limited along some dimension, if not the dimension of resolution. Unlike the case of real vision, such imaginal vision need not be limited by problems of grain or resolution or any other difficulty associated with making visual discriminations. As I have remarked, subjects can exhibit some of the behavioral characteristics associated with such limitations (for example taking longer to recall fine details); but that may be because the subjects know what real vision is like and are simulating it as best they can, rather than because of the intrinsic nature of the imaginal medium.

Other Arguments against the Tacit-Knowledge View

Access to Tacit Knowledge

Two major types of argument are used in opposition to the view that observed experimental effects in imagery studies are due to tacit knowledge. The first type involves showing that some effects of using the imagery mode appear in situations where subjects cannot report what would have happened in the perceptual case or, if they do have opinions, these opinions differ from the results observed in the imagery experiments. The second type of argument involves experimental demonstrations of reliable, apparently cognitively impenetrable effects in situations where images are combined with perception. I shall address the two types in turn.

There is nothing profound to say about the first type of argument. A well-known phenomenon in psychology is that access to knowledge is highly context dependent. It is common to find, for example, that subjects have good access to problem-solving tactics when the problem is worded one way, but not when the problem is worded another way (Hayes and Simon, 1976). It is equally common for people to exhibit an inability to express beliefs we know, for independent reasons, they hold. The science of linguistics would be much easier if this were not so. To take another example, few things are more obviously dependent on tacit knowledge than are various social customs, including rules of discourse; yet people can rarely articulate them when asked to do so. Surely it does not follow that such social skills are to be viewed as somehow part of the functional architecture, or that they result from properties of a medium of representation. Fluency of access to such knowledge, it seems, depends on the nature of the access key.

The concept of tacit knowledge—as a generalization and an extension of the everyday notion of knowledge (much as physicists' concept of energy is an extension of the everyday notion)—is one of the most powerful ideas to emerge from contemporary cognitive science (see Fodor, 1968a), though much remains to be worked out regarding the details of its form and function. It is already clear, however, that tacit knowledge cannot be freely accessed or updated by every cognitive process within the organism, nor can it enter freely into any logically valid inference; contradictions are much too common for that to be true. To claim that a regularity is determined by tacit knowledge is to claim that we can gain an explanatory advantage for a class of related regularities by appealing to the contents of such knowledge, that is, that we can capture certain generalizations that would otherwise be lost. The empirical argument that this is the correct view may be direct (for example, we can alter the regularity by suggesting to the subject that what is imagined works according to certain principles), or it may be indirect (if we posit that the subject believes P and draws inferences from this belief, an entire set of regularities can systematically be accounted for, even certain systematic errors, as in the case of the arithmetic skills studied by Brown and Van Lehn, 1980).

There are a number of experimental results showing that when people use imagery they exhibit certain regularities which resemble those of vision but which they are unlikely to know about, and which they cannot tell the experimenter about if asked what would happen in the comparable perceptual condition. For example, subjects provide evidence of systematic variations in resolution across the imaginal "field of view," even providing evidence for an imaginal analogue of the "oblique effect" wherein the resolution of lines is greater at horizontal and vertical orientations than at oblique orientations (reported in Kosslyn, 1981). The question is, Are we entitled to conclude that these properties must be inherent in the representational medium simply because the effects appear only when subjects are answering the question by visualizing, not when they are merely thinking about it in some other way?

The conclusion seems entirely unwarranted that in such experiments one is discovering properties of the functional architecture. All that may be occurring is that subjects are making inferences about what perception would be like from various bits of recollections, such as how they typically look at things in order to overcome the resolution limitations of the retina. My point is that a recall-and-inference story not only is compatible with the data, it is independently plausible in view of the nature of recall in general. It is true of recall in every domain that relevant facts frequently cannot be accessed without going through some particular sequence of access cues.

This sort of principle of successively cued access is ubiquitous. I cannot even recall the last two digits of my friend's telephone number without first recalling my friend's name and then recalling the initial five digits of the number. Similarly, as Roger Shepard points out, it is almost impossible to recall exactly where the doorknob is on one's front door without first recalling some other things about the door (which, by the way, need not include specifically visual features such as color, shape, and size). Other cases, involving problem-solving tasks, provide an even clearer illustration of this point. Shepard and Feng (1972) have shown that, to solve the problem of whether two marks on a paper template line up when the template is folded to make a certain shape, people must imagine going through a sequence of individual folds. I argue (Pylyshyn, 1978b) that this is because our knowledge of paper folding takes the form of knowing what happens when single folds are made (though it might not be true for a Japanese origami expert); hence, it has nothing special to do with imagery. In fact, what all the preceding examples show is that our tacit knowledge is indexed in various ways. Retrieval of the relevant bits can depend strongly on the contextual cues provided, as well as on the cue-setting strategies implicit in the sequence of accessing operations one uses.

We know on independent grounds that access to long-term memory is notoriously dependent on setting up the correct retrieval cues (see for example, Williams and Hollan, 1981). What cues and what sequence of cues works best depends on how the knowledge is structured, which, in turn, depends on how it was acquired in the first place (for some dramatic examples of the importance of learning-environment cues, see Smith, 1982). Thus it is clear that in cases such as those cited by Kosslyn (1981) there is no need to appeal to inherent properties of a representational medium in explaining why subjects provide one answer when they are imagining something and a different one—or none at all—when asked to think about the problem without invoking visual memories. That is precisely what is to be expected, given the exigencies of our access to our tacit knowledge.

Combining Imagery and Vision
Experiments involving the superimposition of images on actual visual stimuli are sometimes cited against the tacit-knowledge view (for example, Kosslyn et al., 1979). These experiments, however, differ from studies of purely imaginal thinking in several important respects that makes them largely irrelevant to this discussion. When a subject is instructed to view a display, then imagine a stationary or a moving pattern superimposed on it (as in the studies by Hayes, 1973; Finke, 1979; Finke and Pinker, 1983; Pinker and Finke, 1982; Shulman, Remington, and McLean, 1979; Shepard, 1978), there is no need to posit an internal medium of representation to explain the *geometrical rela-*

tionships that hold among features of the resulting construction; properties of the perceived background itself give us all the geometrical properties we need. For example, when a subject thinks of an imaginary spot as being *here* and then *there*, the locative terms can be bound to places in a percept whose position—as well as, perhaps, shape and other geometrical properties—are under direct stimulus control; hence, the relative spatial locations of these points continue to be generally veridical. Such locations can be examined in ways similar to our examination of other points in a scene.

Essentially this is equivalent to binding internal symbols to actual places in the stimulus, which, because they are in the actual stimulus, maintain their locations relative to each other, regardless of subjects' beliefs about space or what they are viewing (assuming only that perception is free of major time-varying distortions). Of course we cannot actually connect an internal symbol to a place in the distal scene, but we can do something that functionally is similar. Pylyshyn, Elcock, Marmor, and Sander (1978) have developed a model of the way in which internal symbols can be indexically bound to primitive perceptual features within a limited-resource computational system, as well as how such bindings enable the motor system to, say, point to bound features. More recently, we have shown experimentally that people can attentionally pick out as many as six elementary visual features in a scene consisting of twice that many identical features and keep track of them despite random movements of the features.

The binding of mental symbols to visual places is an important capacity. Without it, we could not, for example, count visually identical points on a display, since we would have no way of distinguishing the points already counted from those remaining. Given this capacity, however, we can see that certain geometrical properties of a visual display can be used in conjunction with "projected" images to provide some properties which otherwise would be natural to attribute to an internal, "surface display" or representational medium. Thus, if a subject imagines a spot moving from perceived location *A* to perceived location *B*, all that is required to ensure that the spot crosses some location *C* is: (a) the successive locations where the point is imagined to be must actually correspond to a certain path on the perceived stimulus (that is, the successive mental "locatives" in fact point to a certain sequence of adjacent places on the stimulus); and (b) place *C* must actually lie on that path, somewhere between *A* and *B*. In the pure imagery case, by contrast, subjects must not only imagine the spot as moving with respect to an imagined background, they must have tacit knowledge of such things as, if *C* lies between *A* and *B*, then going from *A* to *B* entails that one pass through *C*. A veridical imagination of the movement must also depend on knowing such things as, in this case, the point will move progressively farther from A and progressively closer to B (at the same rate), that the point adjacent to the current point and on the B side of the line from A to B is the next point passed through, that the location and shape of both A and B remain unaffected by the movement of the spot; and so on. Such properties are free for the asking in the superimposition case, on the assumption that we can keep attentional track of the several *actual* places in question.

Another way to put this is to say that certain geometrical properties of the layout being viewed (for example, the relative locations of its features) remain fixed because of the way the world is (in this case, rigid) and that different characteristics of it can simply be "noticed" or "perceived" by the viewer, including the relative position of a place being attended to, that is, a place "bound" to an internal, locative, indexical symbol. On the other hand, what remains fixed and what can be "noticed" in a purely mental image depends either on intrinsic properties of some medium of representation or subjects' tacit knowledge of the behavior of what they are imagining, as well as their ability to draw inferences from such knowledge—precisely the dichotomy I have been discussing throughout this book, and especially in chapter 7.

The notion that we can combine images and percepts by using "place tokens" (or, as Pylyshyn et al., 1978, call them, *Finsts*, for "instantiation fingers" since they behave somewhat like attentional "fingers") has far-reaching implications. It means not only that we can exploit geometrical properties of a scene being viewed but, apparently, that we can exploit some properties of the visual system itself. This finding is somewhat surprising. I shall tentatively examine some implications of the finding. The discussion is necessarily tentative, since it is based on ideas just beginning to be explored.

The proposal is sometimes made that imagery involves a way of feeding information "top down" from the cognitive system into some level of the visual system, where it is reprocessed. I have argued that, in general, this view is implausible, for numerous reasons (Pylyshyn, 1973b,1978b), one of which is that images are not uninterpreted objects available for "seeing." Another is that much of the visual system appears to be stimulus-bound (it can be activated only by incoming light). The attentional mechanism already sketched, however, provides for the possibility of certain highly specific kinds of interaction between the cognitive process and vision, hence, in principle, between imagery and vision.

Although the process called "low-level vision" (which I tentatively identified with transduction in chapter 7) is cognitively impenetrable, it has been shown that certain attentional processes can be applied to fairly low levels of the visual process. I call these *attentional processes* to emphasize that they have only the power to focus and select; they provide neither interpretations nor, even, hypotheses, as was maintained by the "new look" movement in perception (for example, Bruner, 1957). These processes have an influence closely resembling that exerted by eye movements, which clearly affect the very lowest levels of vision, though the effect is merely one of selecting and focusing.

It appears that something similar to eye fixation—but involving no physical movement, only mental processes—applies as well to very low-level visual processing. This is the attention allocation mechanism, already mentioned, associated with locating "places" (or "place tokens" or "Finsts") on the percept. These processes (referred to collectively by Ullman, 1983, as "visual routines") are necessary to explain, for example, the reaction-time function associated with "subitizing" (where reaction time varies linearly with the number of points even for numbers less than 5; Klahr, 1973) for the time it takes to decide whether a point is inside or outside a closed figure (Ullman, 1983), for the time it takes to decide whether two distinct points are on the same curve or on different ones (reaction time varies linearly with the contour distance between points; Jolicoeur, Ullman, and MacKay, 1983), and for the numerous studies showing that a point of maximal attention can be moved both voluntarily and involuntarily across the visual field without eye movement (for example, Posner, 1980; Tsal, 1983; Shulman, Remington, and McLean, 1979).

The discovery of primitive attentional processes is interesting because it helps explain how it is apparently possible to obtain a Muller-Lyer illusion by imaginally superimposing arrowheads on a pair of lines (Berbaum and Chung, 1981), as well as, perhaps, such other effects as aspects of "cognitive contours" and certain putative top-down effects on apparent movement (see the discussion in Ullman, 1979). Many of the effects discussed by Finke (1980) can be explained on the basis of these mechanisms. For example, the "movement adaptation effect" demonstrated by Finke (1979)—which exactly parallels the well-known visual prism adaptation phenomenon but which uses "imaginary" rather than visual feedback as to arm position[3]—can also be explained in

3. In the original experiment, subjects wear prism lenses which displace the perceived location of a target. They practice reaching the target while observing their hand initially miss its mark. Then, after a few minutes, they begin to adapt, and reach accurately. At this point the glasses are removed and the subjects are tested by having them reach for the target without seeing their hand. The test phase invariably shows an error in the direction opposite that of the prism displacement. What Finke did was replace the visual feedback in the training phase with directions to imagine that the hand misses the target to the same extent as occurred for the subjects in the visual adaptation experiment.

these terms. It appears that an attentional token located at a particular place in the visual field can serve many of the functions served by actual visual features located at that point.

These fascinating research topics have just begun to be investigated. They may help clarify some of the mystery surrounding the claims and counterclaims about the empirical properties of mental imagery. In particular, they might help explain why images appear to have spatial properties. Perhaps it is because *places* in an image can play an important role, in that they can be "bound," like pronouns, to places in a visual field or even to places in some motor command "space." After all, one of the most "spatial" properties of an image is that you can *point* to places and objects in your image. All of these speculations are open to further research, however. For now, it suffices to point out that the phenomena this discussion has addressed have nothing to do with the need to posit an internal analogue medium, especially not one which endows imagery with free geometrical properties the imager knows nothing about, apart from passively seeing such properties manifested on the imager's "internal display."

What Theoretical Claim about Imagery Is Being Made?

It has often been said that "imagery" models (for example, those of Kosslyn and Shwartz, 1977; Shepard, 1975) contribute to scientific progress because they make correct predictions and motivate further research. Although I do not wish to deny this claim, it is important to ask what it is about such imagery models that carries the predictive force. It is my view that there is only one empirical hypothesis responsible for the predictive success of the entire range of imagery models, that nearly everything else about these models consists of free, empirical parameters added ad hoc to accommodate particular experimental results. The one empirical hypothesis is this: *When people imagine a scene or an event, what occurs in their minds is, in many ways, similar to what happens when they observe the corresponding event actually happening.*

It is to the credit of both Shepard (1978) and Paivio (1977) that they recognize the central contribution of the perceptual metaphor. For example Shepard (1978, p. 135) states,

> Most basically, what I am arguing for here is the notion that the internal process that represents the transformation of an external object, just as much as the internal process that represents the object itself, is in large part the same whether the transformation, or the object, is merely imagined or actually perceived.

Paivio (1977, p. 71) has been even more direct in recognizing—and approving of—the metaphorical nature of this class of models:

> The criteria for a psychological model should be what the mind can do, so why not begin with a psychological metaphor in which we try to extend our present knowledge about perception and behavior to the inner world of memory and thought. . . ? The perceptual metaphor . . . holds the mirror up to nature and makes human competence itself the model of mind.

One general difficulty with metaphorical explanation is that, by leaving open the question of what the similarities are between the primary and the secondary objects of the metaphor, it remains flexible enough to encompass most eventualities. Such open-endedness, of course, is what gives metaphors their heuristic and motivational value. It is also what provides the feeling of having captured a system of regularities. In the case of the perceptual metaphor for imagery, however, the capturing of regularities is, largely, illusory, because it is parasitic upon our informal common-sense knowledge of psychology and our tacit knowledge of the natural world. I have argued that the reason I imagine things happening more or less as they happen in the world is not because my brain or my cognitive endowments are structured to somehow correspond to nature, but simply because I *know* how things generally happen—because I have been told, or have induced, some general principles. In other words, I possess a tacit physical theory good enough to predict correctly most ordinary, everyday, natural events most of the time. Now, the claim that our imagery unfolds just as our perceptual process unfolds trades on this tacit knowledge more insidiously because it does so in the name of scientific explanation.

The story goes like this. The claim that imagery is in some ways like perception has predictive value because it enables us to predict that, say, it will take longer to mentally scan longer distances, report the visual characteristics of smaller imagined objects, rotate images through larger angles, mentally compare more similar images, and so on. The account makes these predictions simply because we know that these generalizations are true of corresponding visual cases. Notice, however, that the reason we can make such predictions is not that we have a corresponding theory of the visual cases; it is simply that our tacit common-sense knowledge is sufficiently accurate to provide us with the correct expectations in such cases.

An accurate analogy to what is happening in these explanations would be to give, as a theory of Mary's behavior, the statement that Mary is much like Susan, whom we know well. That would enable us perhaps to make accurate predictions of Mary's behavior; but it scarcely qualifies as an adequate *explanation* of her behavior. Another parallel, one even closer in spirit to the metaphorical explanation of imagery, would be if we gave, as the explanation of why it takes longer to rotate a real object through a greater angle, that that is the way we typically perceive it happen, or if we explained why it takes more time to visually compare two objects of similar size than two objects of radically different sizes, by saying that is what happens in the mental comparison case. In both cases we can make the correct predictions as long as we are informally well enough acquainted with the second of each pair of situations. Further, in both cases, some nontrivial empirical claim would be involved. For instance, it would be the claim that perception is generally veridical, or that what we see generally corresponds to what we know to be the case. Although these are real empirical claims, no one takes them to have the theoretical significance attributed to corresponding theories of imagery, even though both may, in fact, have the same underlying basis.

Some models of imagery appear to go beyond mere metaphors. For example, Kosslyn and Shwartz (1977) have a computer model of imagery that accounts for a wide range of experimental findings. This is not a model of a large intellectual task, such as is the case in some artificial intelligence systems; it is a model of a small domain of phenomena. Hence, unlike artificial intelligence systems, no trick is involved in getting such a model to mimic the behavior in its domain if no principled constraints are imposed. The model can do this because it is, in fact, merely a simulation of some largely common-sense ideas about what happens when we image. That is why the principles it appeals to invariably are stated in terms of properties of the *represented domain*. For example, a principle such as "images must be transformed through small angles" clearly refers to what is being represented (since images themselves do not actually have orientations, as opposed to representing them). Yet that is often how we explain things in informal, everyday terms. We say we imagine things in a certain way because that's the way they really are. As I have remarked, a theory of the underlying process should account for *how* (that is, by what independently established mechanism) imagery comes to have this character; it should not use this very property as an explanatory principle.

Another consequence of the model being a simulation of common-sense views is that anything statable informally as a description of what happens in the mind's eye can easily and naturally be accommodated by the model. For example, Kosslyn et al. (1979) cite a subject who said she thought objects close together would take longer to image because it would be harder to see them or tell them apart. This is exactly the process that can easily be accommodated by the model. All that has to be done is to make the grain of the surface display whatever size is required to produce the effect. There is nothing to prevent such tuning of the model to fit individual situations. Therefore, these properties have the status of free parameters. Unfortunately, there is no limit on the number of these parameters that may be implicit in the model.[4] Similarly, in our experiment (in which subjects judged the compass bearing of one place relative to another), for some subjects we found a negative correlation between reaction time and distance from one focal point to another on the imagined map. The computer model would have little difficulty accommodating this result if the result turned out to be a general finding. In fact, it is hard to think of a result that could not be accommodated naturally—including, as we have seen, the possibility of representing non-Euclidean space. What is crucial here is not merely that such results can be accommodated but that the accommodation can be achieved without violating any fundamental design criteria of the model and without threatening any basic principle of its operation, without, for example, violating any constraints imposed by the hypothesized "surface display." What such a statement implies is that the truly crucial aspects of the model have the status of free parameters rather than structural constants.

To some extent, Kosslyn appears to recognize this flexibility in his model. In the last section of Kosslyn et al. (1979), he and his associates insist that the model be evaluated on the basis of its heuristic value. I agree. The ad hocness that goes with early stages of scientific modeling may well be unavoidable. We should make every effort, however, to be realistic and rid ourselves of all attendant illusions. One illusion that goes with this way of thinking about imagery is the idea that the model has an essential core that is not merely heuristic but which is highly principled and constrained. This core, which is immutable, is contained in the postulated properties of the "surface display" (or in the cathode ray tube proto-model). It involves the assumption that

---

4. True, it becomes embarrassing to have to change the model too often. It is also true that Kosslyn's model has been widely described; thus it is not subject to change for any minor reason. By now, however, the model has been patched to accommodate such a large variety of findings that it probably covers the complete range of experiments anyone would likely test it on. (After all, each new experiment is not testing an independent aspect of the model.) An examination of the model shows it has so many built-in assumptions that it is more like an encyclopedia than a theory. None of this, incidentally, is meant to detract from the numerous excellent ideas in the model, ideas about, for example, how structures are accessed or the distinction among classes of transformations. It is not the mechanics of the model that are problematic but rather the theoretical claims made about it—just as it is not the large number of clever experiments that went into the research program, or the fascinating data produced, that I find less than laudable; but the interpretations of them that are made.

there is an internal display medium with intrinsic geometrical (or geometry-analogue) properties. For example, Pinker (1980) claims that the "array structure" captures a set of generalizations about images. Without knowing which properties of the "array structure" are doing the work, however, and whether these properties can be altered by changes in the subject's beliefs, such "capturing" of generalizations may be no better than merely listing them. We need to know what it is about the intrinsic character of arrays that requires them to have the properties Pinker suggests (for example, that they represent shape, size, and locations implicitly in an integral fashion, that they are bounded in size and grain, that they preserve interpoint distances). If nothing apart from stipulation requires that arrays have these properties, then each property is precisely a free parameter.

For example, if the facts supported the conclusion that size, shape, and orientation are naturally factored apart in one's mental representation (as I believe they are), or that grain size is not homogeneous and varies as a function of what the subject believes the referent situation to be like (for example, how brightly lit, how detailed in its design, how important different features are to the task at hand), does anybody believe for a moment that this would undermine the claim that an "array structure" was being used? Clearly, all that would be required is minor adjustment in the system (for example, making resolution depend on additional features of the image, or allowing the cognitive process to access the "orientation" property in long-term memory). If that is the case, then it is apparent that claiming an "array structure" places no constraints on the phenomena that can be accommodated; that is, properties of this structure are free, empirical parameters. Thus, although one may have the impression there is a highly constraining core assumption crucial to the predictive success of the model, the way this impression is maintained is simply to give the rest of the system sufficient freedom to overcome any effort to empirically reject the core assumption. Therefore, whereas the intuitive appeal of the system continues to hang on the unsupported view that properties of imagery are determined by the intrinsic properties of an internal display medium, the system's predictive power may, in fact, come entirely from a single empirical hypothesis of imagery theory—namely, the perception metaphor.

The phenomenon of having the true appeal of a theoretical system derive from a simplified—and strictly false—view of the system while its predictions come from more complex, and more ad hoc, aspects is commonplace in science. Even the initial success of the Copernican world view might be attributable to such a characteristic. Copernicus published his epoch-making proposal, *de Revolutionibus*, in two volumes. The first volume showed how the solar-centered system could, in principle, elegantly handle certain aspects of stellar and planetary motions (involving reverse movements) without requiring such ad hoc devices as epicycles. In the second volume Copernicus worked out the details of his system for the more comprehensive case, which required reintroducing the ad hoc mechanisms of epicycles. In fact, Copernicus's system merely did away with the five major Ptolemaic epicycles, while retaining all the complexity associated with the greater number of minor ones needed to make the theory fit the observations. Of course, in time, Copernicus's system was vindicated, with the general principle of gravitation removing the remaining ad hocness.

The lesson for imagery is clear enough. For a theory of imagery to be principled, it is necessary correctly to locate the knowledge-independent functional properties. We must be critical in laying a foundation of cognitively impenetrable functions to serve as the basic architecture of a formal model—not simply because in this way we can get to the most primitive level of explanation, but, rather, because we can get a principled and constrained (and, therefore, not ad hoc) model only if we first fix those properties which are the basic functional *capacities* of the system. This does not mean we must look to biology to provide us with a solution (though we can use help from all quarters); the fixed functional capacities can be inferred behaviorally and specified functionally, as they are when computer architectures are specified. What it does mean is that, unless we set ourselves the goal of establishing the correct functional architecture or medium to properly constrain our models, we could well find ourselves in the position of having as many free parameters as we have independent observations.

Chapter 9

Epilogue: What Is Cognitive Science the Science of?

Aristotle, so far as I know, was the first man to proclaim explicitly that man is a rational animal. His reason for this view was one which does not now seem very impressive; it was that some people can do sums. . . . Nowadays, however, calculating machines do sums better than even the cleverest people, yet no one contends that these useful instruments are immortal or work by divine inspiration. As arithmetic has grown easier, it has come to be less respected. The consequence is that though many philosophers continue to tell us what fine fellows we are, it is no longer on account of our arithmetical skill that they praise us.

B. Russell, *Unpopular Essays*

Summary of Assumptions

In this book I have tried to address a number of issues in cognition. Before raising the question of what the term *cognition* applies to exactly, hence, what the domain of cognitive science includes, I shall summarize the ideas discussed and the claims made. That way, we can keep the general picture in mind.

1. Explaining human behavior differs from giving a true description of some (or even all) of its causes. Explanation requires that we "capture predictive generalizations," that we summarize what is systematic about the behavior in the most intellectually economical way. We need to describe the system in such a way as to exhibit maximal systematicity with the fewest assumptions. In doing that, we must find the correct categories over which to state the regularities. Different categories, or descriptive vocabularies, generally express different generalizations, though some categories may not reveal any regularities that survive application of the method of differences; that is, regularities that are "counterfactual supporting." That is why I say explanations apply to behavior "under a description."

2. We have at least excellent informal reasons for believing that there

are important generalizations that can be expressed under what I call a *cognitive* description that cannot be expressed under a neurophysiological, behavioral, or phenomenological description. A cognitive description would refer to stimulus conditions in terms of how people interpret (or *take*) them. For example, the causes of behavior would contain thoughts about and perceptions of such things as tables and chairs, friends, paychecks, hope for a raise, desire for tenure or a larger sailboat, fear of failure, lonely days and quiet nights—in short, the usual things, thoughts of which move people to act. A cognitive account would also describe behavior in terms of such actions as walking to a store, reaching for the salt, or looking for the person who borrowed your pencil. If that sounds like grandmother psychology, that's because much of grandmother's psychology is sound, not in its explanation of underlying mechanisms but in the *kinds* of regularities it addresses. We begin with these categories because that's where we at least have a clue that there is something systematic about human behavior. We do not end there, however; an explanation requires much more. Yet a theory that *ignores* truisms has started off on the wrong foot.

3. All indications are that certain central aspects of human behavior depend on what we believe and what we desire—on our knowledge, goals, and utilities and on our capacity to make inferences from our beliefs and desires and turn them into intentions to act. Although a philosophical defense of this thesis may not be straightforward, *everyone* except the professional skeptic, including practicing behaviorists, assumes this to be true. There are even impressive demonstrations (in the success of "expert systems" in artificial intelligence) that these constructs are *sufficient* to produce fragments of intelligent behavior. The only significant question remaining is, How is this fact compatible with some of our other dogmas, for example, the belief that behavior is caused by activity in the brain, that only physical things have causes (that is, dualism should be resisted), that explanations should be mechanistic, that they should, in principle, be falsifiable?

4. Thus far, only one solution has been proposed to the problem posed by the conundrums just stated, namely, that of reconciling a belief in materialism with the view that certain psychological generalizations (let us call them *cognitive generalizations*) must be stated in terms of the contents of, for instance, beliefs and goals. The solution is that the semantic contents of such mental states are *encoded* by properties of the brain in the same general way the semantic contents of the computer's representations are encoded—by physically instantiated symbol structures. In the case of computers, this idea has had a profound impact on our understanding of how it is possible for a mechanistic system to exhibit such semantic regularities as the preservation

by proofs of the semantical property of truth and the way in which the symbolic character of a mechanistic system overcomes the rigidity of behavior assumed to be inherent in physical systems (by exhibiting the property of "universality" or being able to imitate any other such symbol system).

5. Number 4 leads to the main thesis (or the basic working hypothesis) of this book. This hypothesis states that there is a natural theoretical domain within psychology which corresponds roughly to what we pretheoretically call *cognition*, in which the principal generalizations covering behavior occur at three autonomous levels of description, each conforming to different principles. These levels are referred to as the biological (or physical) level, the symbolic (or syntactic or sometimes the functional) level, and the semantic (or intentional) level, or as Allen Newell (1982) calls it, the "knowledge level." Although the vocabularies of these three levels are distinct, the levels interact in well-defined, principled ways; regularities at one level occasionally show through and modulate the regularities of other levels. Thus biological factors interact with symbol level generalizations by causing modifications in the basic computational resources, which I call the *functional architecture*. Such modulations may be due to biochemical influences, maturation, the triggering effect of environmental releasers, dendritic arborization, atrophy of neural function from disuse, and so on. These modulations also interact via transduction; but that is a somewhat different issue (see chapter 6). Note that symbol level generalizations (due to properties of the functional architecture) interact with such semantic level principles as rationality—principles concerned with drawing inferences or with the attainment of goals or the preservation of truth value over certain operations. As we saw in chapter 2, for instance, such interactions are expected because the symbol level principles that govern the functional architecture impose constraints on the way in which beliefs and goals can be accessed, on which inferences are drawn, and when. This explains why, for example, certain processes tend to be more error-prone, more difficult, or slower to complete than others. In general, it is the intrusion of symbol level principles that explains deviations from omniscience. Because these intrusions are a principled part of the theory, most arguments against the use of folk-psychology notions in cognitive science do not apply to the computational version of the representational view of mind. Such arguments (for example, Stich, 1984; P. M. Churchland, 1981) typically are concerned to show that semantic level generalizations encounter various difficulties, for example: the set of effective beliefs do not appear to be closed under deduction; there are systematic failures of logical reasoning or of rationality in general; there are individual differences in cognitive style; modes of reasoning are affected by emo-

tions. These phenomena, however, are an integral part of computational models. As I point out in chapter 2, semantic level principles alone do not determine particular instances of behavior. Constraints of functional architecture (or symbol level principles) must be taken into account as well, including, especially, principles governing the control structure (which might, for example, specify the accessibility of various representations as a function of such things as recency of use, the process currently active, and the general emotional state).

6. Although these ideas set the stage for viewing cognition as a species of computation, the goal of using computing to model and explain cognitive processes in detail raises an entirely new set of problems. In explaining cognition, one is not interested merely in arguing for the plausibility of cognition taking the form of computation; nor is one even interested in mimicking observed performance. Rather, one is concerned with showing how specific instances of behavior are generated by the mind, as well as relating this performance to certain cognitive capacities. This imposes the requirement that computational processes be "strongly equivalent" to processes that actually occur in the mind. Achieving strong equivalence requires that the computational model meet stringent conditions, to ensure a principled parallel between the model and the cognitive process. In particular, there must be a principled level of aggregation at which the parallel between the two holds. This level is defined as the boundary between those phenomena that must be explained in terms of semantic principles and those that do not. The latter are considered instantiated in what I call the *functional architecture* of the system, which provides the computational resources for realizing cognitive processes, just as a computer's "virtual machine" or programming language provides the resources for realizing running computer programs.

7. The distinction between functional architecture and cognitive process arises because different types of principles are required to explain the regularities in the two cases. My further assumption—that the way representational (or semantically expressed) processes are realized is by symbol systems (that is, computation)—provides us with several methodological criteria for deciding whether some observed regularity is indicative of a property of the functional architecture. One way we develop these criteria is to exploit certain ideas developed for the analysis of computer programs, suggesting indexes for the equivalence of two processes. We start by asking how it might be possible, by external observation, to determine whether two computers are performing the same algorithm. This leads to a criterion which I call *complexity-equivalence*, which relies on monitoring the computational-resource needs of the algorithm as a function of different inputs. A special case

of this criterion—one that is extremely important and which is widely used by psychologists, though its validity in particular cases has to be demonstrated independently—is "mental chronometry," which involves measuring the time it takes subjects to perform tasks.

8. In view of the definition of the boundary between functional architecture and representation-governed cognitive processes, a more direct test of whether some particular hypothesized function is instantiated in the functional architecture, or whether it is carried out by means of rules and representations, is to determine whether the hypothesized function itself is alterable according to semantic-level principles. We might investigate this empirically by determining whether the function can be altered in a semantically regular way by changing the subject's goals or beliefs (for example, by varying instructions). A function that can be altered in this way is said to be "cognitively penetrable," thus constituting evidence that the function is not instantiated in the functional architecture but is realized by a representational process, or that it is a computationally complex process.

9. The idea that certain functions can be explained without recourse to representations (hence, inferences and other semantic principles), whereas others cannot, is applied in several domains. Two domains that have received particular attention—because alternative theories exist that take a strikingly different point of view from that advocated here—are those of perception and mental imagery. I argue that contact between an organism and its environment, including its "internal environment," must be constrained in exactly the same way the functional architecture must be constrained, and for similar reasons. In fact, contact is made through a special function (not an organ) called a transducer, which is part of the organism's functional architecture, hence is subject to the same constraints (for example, it must be computationally primitive and cognitively impenetrable, or stimulus-bound). Because perception as a whole does not share these properties, perception is viewed as the product of both transduction and cognition, or inference.

10. The interest I have taken, in this book and elsewhere, in theories of mental imagery arises because the study of imaginal thinking constitutes one of several areas of cognition in which investigators feel that a computational view of the sort discussed here might have to give way to something different, perhaps an analogue process that does not go through a sequence of quasi-inferential steps and which uses nonarticulated representations. In this case, the process behaves in certain ways because of the intrinsic properties imparted to them by the medium of representation. From the point of view of the theory of cognition (or the theory framework) sketched here, this simply amounts to assigning to the functional architecture certain regularities

of the imaginal process. These *imagistic* theories, then, claim that when people use mental imagery, certain things happen in certain ways because of the inherent nature of the functional architecture (because of inherent properties of mind) and not because of the content of people's beliefs and goals and their capacity to reason. The same is true of other proposals for analogue explanations—for example, the process of recall, where holographic models are sometimes entertained. There are no logical or a priori reasons why such theories might not be true. In fact, I claim something like that must be true of *some* characteristics of reasoning, since every computational process exploits the properties of the functional architecture of the system on which it runs. At the same time, I argue that the evidence does not support some widely accepted proposals which attribute certain phenomena of recall or imaginal thinking directly to corresponding properties of the functional architecture. Rather, it appears that the observations in question are most plausibly interpreted as instances of semantic level generalizations, that is, as arising from inferential processes operating over subjects' beliefs and goals. The apparent cognitive penetrability of most such phenomena suggests that many of the salient characteristics of imagery are not built into the functional architecture. Included are such characteristics as the way images appear to mirror certain physical or geometrical properties of what is being imaged, such as the rigidity of objects under rotation or the impoverished visibility of small visual features or the necessity of scanning the image through intermediate points in order to access information from them (see chapter 8).

The distinction between functional architecture and representation-governed processes may be the most fundamental distinction proposed here, since it marks the boundary in the theory between two highly different kinds of principles—the kind stated in terms of semantics, in terms of properties of the *intentional objects* or *contents* of thoughts or other representations—and those that can be explained in more traditional, functional terms. For example, I could give a complex description of *how something operates* in terms of some combination of what it is made of, how the parts are connected, what each subpart does, and so on—all by appealing to natural laws or to a certain kind of black-box abstraction over them called a *function description*. Although the notion of functional description is imprecise, clearly, it does not include principles that mention the contents of representations, which, after all, typically include such nonexistent things as certain desired states of affairs.[1]

---

1. Some attempt has been made, however, to specify functionalism more precisely in terms of the "Ramsey-functional correlates" of a system; see, for example, Lewis, 1970.

The computational approach allows us to make sense of this talk—partly by providing an account of how such apparently nonphysical properties as semantical ones can explain the behavior of a physical system and partly by allaying our anxiety that this type of account might be either circular or dualistic—by demonstrating straightforward cases in which that sort of description holds without requiring any magic or deus ex machina (for example, by showing that processes of this type can be realized in certain programmed computers).

Carving Nature at the Joints

It has been fairly commonplace to say, ever since Plato first said it, that we must endeavor to "carve nature at her natural joints." Natural joints are not easy to find, however, and they cannot be specified in advance. There is no way to determine the phenomena that will cluster together to form the object of a special science except by observing the success, or lack of it, of attempts to build theories in certain domains. Despite general concurrence on this point, people are nonetheless extremely reluctant to accept a partition of phenomena that leaves out something they consider important—as though the development of a scientific field must be guided by a priori considerations of what matters to *us*. It should be clear to most observers of the history of science that there is precious little correspondence between the things about which we have adequate causal explanations and those that are most important to us *as people*. We may object, as does Alexis Zorba in Kazantzakis' novel when he cries out, "Why do people die? . . . all those damned books you read—what good are they? Why do you read them? If they don't tell you that, what do they tell you?" Yet it remains pretty generally true that answers to the truly important questions are not to be found in books of theory.

The converse is also true. There are many clear cases where important, practical regularities can be found in domains apparently lacking, or which perhaps are even incapable of supporting, true causal theories. For example, there are descriptive or taxonomic disciplines that catalogue a variety of useful regularities and perhaps even tie them together with elaborate systems which serve more as mnemonic aids than as explanations—as I believe is the case with Freudian theory. The Ptolemaic theory of astronomy, though it turned out to be false, provided a remarkably accurate means of astronomical reckoning, a means still in use today for navigational calculation. There are also numerous, useful,

---

This approach allows one to speak of the class of what might be thought of as, roughly, the "notational variants" of a theory, though it is not without difficulties in its application to psychology (for example, Block, 1978).

engineering disciplines based largely on systematic catalogues. I have long been impressed with how it is possible to do truly useful things in this world while being guided by an obviously false theory of why it works (behavior modification is a case in point, along with several other theoretical bases for therapy).

All of this should alert us both to the possibility that we are on the wrong track—there might be no natural explanatory domain of cognition—and that, even if there is such a domain, we may be wrong in several of our pretheoretical intuitions about it. One of the things we are most likely wrong about, judging from what has happened in other disciplines, are the boundaries of the domain. Despite the frequency with which we have been wrong in the past about the boundaries of the phenomena that constitute a scientific discipline, there is a strong reluctance to relinquish such pretheoretical intuitions.

A list of examples of the reluctance to part with a priori views of how phenomena must cluster can be found in studies of language—where the autonomy of phonology and syntax is still vigorously resisted, largely on such grounds as that the cluster we call "language" includes much more than grammar and phonology. And, of course, language, indeed, involves much more; but that does not mean we can develop a uniform, explanatory theory of language phenomena when the language phenomena are understood to include everything in the intuitively defined cluster. Inasmuch as language is used for communicating among people for countless different purposes, clearly the cluster referred to as *language* involves aspects of common-sense reasoning, social conventions, pragmatic goals (that is, "doing things" with words), and so on. We have every reason to believe that quite different principles are involved in those aspects of language that involve reasoning than in the aspects that involve recognizing a sentence's grammatical or thematic structure. Similar statements can be made about vision. What we see clearly depends on common-sense reasoning, expectations, cultural conditions, and so on. Recent successes in the study of visual perception, (see Marr, 1982) depend on separating certain processes (called "early vision") from the mass of knowledge-dependent processes ultimately involved in perception, that is, from the entire perceptual process whereby optical stimulation eventuates in beliefs about the world.

But there are more relevant examples. In viewing psychology as the science of mental life, many investigators have implicitly been committed to the view that principles should be sought that apply over the domain of conscious experiences, for example, J. S. Mill's principles of "mental chemistry," which govern our conscious thoughts, images, impressions, perceptions, feelings, and moods. This enterprise has met with little success, however. The reason most frequently given is a methodological one—it is very difficult to observe our experiences in an unobtrusive way. But there is another, perhaps even deeper, reason for the failure. If even the modest success in building small-scale theories in contemporary "information-processing psychology" is any indication, we have no right to the a priori assumption that the set of conscious contents is a natural domain. Among the things we are conscious of are some that follow quasi-logical principles (for example, common-sense reasoning), others that might follow associative principles (idle musings, mind wandering), and still others that may be governed primarily by biochemical principles (occurrences of pains, moods, or certain emotional states). Furthermore, it appears that, to account for some regularities, we must posit processes and mental states that behave exactly like some states of consciousness but which we are not in the least aware of. I consider it an empirical discovery of no small importance that if we draw the boundary around phenomena in such a way as to cut across the conscious-unconscious distinction, we find that we can at least formulate moderately successful minitheories in the resulting cluster. The literature on information processing is replete with persuasive examples of such models.

It is by no means obvious that, to develop explanatory theories, we must group deliberate reasoning and problem-solving processes with processes that seem to occur in a flash and with no apparent awareness that any mental activity is occurring, while at the same time leaving out such vivid mental contents as the experiences of pain, seeing a certain color, being dizzy, or feeling the pieces of a puzzle fall into place. Not only is this not obvious, it is vigorously opposed by many who view such regrouping as an indictment of information-processing psychology (as we see in chapter 7).

The conscious-unconscious distinction is not the only distinction we may have to cut through in seeking a natural domain within the set of phenomena now covered by the term *psychology*. It may turn out that large parts of such psychologically important domains as learning, development, emotion, mood, psychopathology, and motor skills will not be explained in the same way as other kinds of psychological regularities. Phenomena in such domains may have to be partitioned in ways different from the way in which pretheoretical intuitions and everyday common sense draw the boundaries. We simply have no right to require that the categories of phenomena in our evolving science follow particular a priori boundaries. The phenomena found to cluster in categories explainable by some uniform set of principles is something we will discover as we attempt to build theories beginning with clear cases. Thus, when John Haugeland (1978) disparages current information-processing theorizing on the grounds that it cannot deal with the development and control of motor skills or with the pervasive effects of moods on cognitive activity, or when Paul Churchland (1980) cites its inability to deal with what he calls "large-scale learning" or conceptual change, they are making presumptions about what should be included in a certain, natural, scientific domain. In particular, they are laying down the requirement that the role of moods, skills, and conceptual change be explainable within the same class of theory that would explain how people understand a sentence. We are no more entitled to set such a priori conditions on an evolving science than Galileo was in requiring, a priori, that planets follow the same laws of motion as cannonballs or that the generative semanticists were in requiring, a priori, that all acceptable-unacceptable distinctions among sentences be expressible within a common body of theory. It was an *empirical* discovery that planets do fall under the evolving laws of dynamics, and that some distinctions among sentences are not part of a developing linguistic theory (in fact, among those that are not part of such a theory are some familiar distinctions of prescriptive grammar, such as when to use *between* and when to use *among*). I shall consider a few of these possibly noncognitive effects in slightly greater detail.

Some Possible Noncognitive Effects: Learning, Development, and Moods

Let us consider a few salient examples of phenomena we have some reason to believe fall outside the semantic principles I claim characterize cognition. The view I describe in this book suggests, for example, that it is a mistake to take a monolithic view of cognitive change, as has been routine in most empiricist psychology and much of the early work in cybernetics aimed at developing "self-adaptive systems." The reason is, such change can be of two very different types. One type arises as a rational consequence of certain information-bearing events an organism experiences. The organism forms a cognitive *representation* as a result of these events, which allows it to apply rules to the representations and hence, infer certain beliefs about the world—in other words, draw inferences and induce plausible hypotheses. This type of change is what has long been known in the vernacular as "learning."

It is important that we distinguish this type of effect from other means of producing changes in an organism, including those due to variations in nourishment, growth and maturation of glands and organs (including the brain), injury and/or trauma, perhaps even changes due to noninformative aspects of reinforcement and practice—that is, effects beyond those that arise because the reinforcers serve as signals which inform subjects of the contingencies and hence, allow them to adjust their utilities accordingly (assuming there is such a thing as a non-informative aspect of reinforcers; see Brewer, 1974).

The reason for distinguishing two different types of relation between organisms and environments is the same as that for distinguishing different levels of description of processes in the preceding discussion: they follow quite different principles. For example, rational fixation of belief arising from environmental information, unlike just any arbitrary changes in biological state caused by the environment, can proceed in radically different ways, depending on how the organism *interprets* the stimulation, which, in turn, depends on its prior beliefs and utilities.

It is the knowledge-acquisition effect that concerns educators and which corresponds to the everyday notion of learning as "finding out about" something or other, of discovering something to be the case, of finding out how to do something. At the same time, the appropriateness of this type of process as an account of how certain states of an organism are arrived at, of how certain capacities are achieved, increasingly has come under question in recent years. More and more frequently, it is argued that the information in an organism's environment is too impoverished to allow it to logically infer certain representations that form part of its mature state. In the case of language, this argument has been made with particular force by Chomsky and others interested in the issue of language learnability, for example, Wexler and Cullicover, 1980. These critiques of the learning view frequently have been misunderstood as implying that the final cognitive competence (say, for language or conceptualization) is already present at birth or that no influence of the environment is necessary for its development. That is not the case. Environmental stimulation, sometimes of a highly specific sort, undeniably is necessary for the achievement of most cognitive competences. This is not the issue involved in arguments about learning, however. The stimulation required to produce in me the belief that the building I am in is on fire is extremely specific to that belief. Stimulations in that category stand virtually no chance of causing me to acquire the belief that the sky is falling or to acquire any other logically unrelated belief; yet the set of events with my belief that the building is on fire as their consequence are specific only in an informational or semantic sense—they need have nothing in common from the point of view of their physical form. I might hear a shout, be handed a note, see flames, smell smoke, hear a bell which I *interpret* to be a fire alarm, or even hear a tapping whose pattern corresponds to some prearranged, arbitrary code. Not only is this set of events open-ended, it can be changed systematically by the provision of other ancillary information, as in the case of prearranging the code convention or someone telling me that the fire alarm bell is being tested.

My point here is that mere specificity of environmental cause is no more reason to believe that the cognitive state attained is learned than is the effect of sunlight on skin color reason to believe that suntans are learned; something more is required to show that learning is involved. What is needed is a demonstration that the cognitive state is reached because environmental conditions have provided the organism with certain information about things in the world, information from which the organism can infer certain beliefs whose content is related to those conditions.

If that is what is needed, it should, at least in principle, be straightforward to inquire whether specific environmental conditions that do lead to the cognitive state in question provide sufficient information (or adequate premises), *in principle*, for the logical construction or induction of that state. If the answer is Yes, then learning is certainly a plausible hypothesis. If the answer is merely something like, "Yes, but only if the organism makes the following additional assumptions, or if for some reason it is prohibited from considering the following alternative hypotheses", then we at least know that the state is not attained solely by learning (at least not from the conditions in question). In such cases, something—for example, the "assumptions" or the constraints that prohibit certain hypotheses—must already have been present. We can then inquire in the same way whether *they*, in turn, could have been learned.

Sometimes the most plausible answer is No. For example, people who work on the problem of language learnability have shown, with only weak assumptions on the boundary conditions for language acquisition, that grammars cannot be learned without strong constraints on the grammars the organism can entertain as candidates. This is the burden of the research by, for example, Wexler and Cullicover (1980). Further, these abstract constraints, or "assumptions," could themselves not have been learned. If the arguments are sound, then this is a case in which the competence for learning grammars of a certain sort must be part of what I referred to as functional architecture. Consequently, they must either be part of the initial state or they must have developed from the initial state (with or without environmental influence) by noncognitive means (where, by *noncognitive*, I mean processes that do not operate on the basis of rules and representations, that are not inferential or otherwise knowledge-dependent). This is what cognitive theorists mean—or should mean—when they claim that some cognitive state or capacity is *innate*: not that it is independent of environmental influence but that it is independent of rule-governed construction from representations of relevant properties of the environment. In other words, the state or capacity is not systematically related to its environmental cause solely in terms of its semantic, or informational, content.

A closely related distinction arises in connection with research on vision by those working within the artificial intelligence tradition (or, as some vision people prefer to call it, "natural computation"). There, it has been demonstrated repeatedly that there is not enough information in patterns of light to warrant the perceptual beliefs that such light patterns give rise to; neither is there sufficient information to unequivocally determine the knowledge-independent, low-level, visual representations we form even of unfamiliar scenes. It has been shown by such investigators as Shimon Ullman (1979), however, that if certain assumptions about the nature of the distal environment are made, a unique mapping from proximal stimulus to such representations is possible. These assumptions include, for example, that visually interpretable scenes consist only of rigid, three-dimensional objects, that the surfaces in the scene are almost everywhere continuous, or that the reflectance of surfaces is nearly Lambertian. Such assumptions cannot be *inferred* from the light emanating from the scene; they must come from elsewhere. In particular, they must be internal to the visual system, since we know that the relevant part of the visual system is cognitively impenetrable. Further, if such assumptions are not inferred from other sources of information (and there is persuasive evidence that at least some of them are not; for example, two-week-old children appear able to distinguish surfaces differing only in their distance from the child), then they must be part of the initial state, or they must develop from the initial state by noncognitive means. That is, they are part of the functional architecture, and hence, change only according to the principles governing alterations of the architecture.

Similarly, the ubiquitous interaction between moods and general emotional states such as anger and depression is almost certain to involve a noncognitive component. I have already spoken of such interactions in connection with the cognitive penetrability condition (chapter 5). Moods and emotional states can be caused by cognitive states, just as the movements of my fingers as I type this sentence are caused by my thoughts and intentions. This causation, according to the view expressed in chapters 5 and 6, is mediated by a highly constrained process called transduction. Of course, moods and emotions may have noncognitive causes as well, such as hormonal and other biochemical fluctuations, disease, lesions of the central nervous system. Regardless of their origin, such changes may lead to further generalized effects on subsequent cognitive processes by affecting the functional architecture or the symbol level principles of the system.

The precise way in which alterations in the internal environment produce systematic changes in cognition remains a mystery. It seems reasonable to assume, though, that changing levels of biochemicals cannot, by itself, create arbitrary individual beliefs, for the reason that, as I argue in chapters 3 and 7, representational states must be articulated in certain ways that preserve the beliefs' semantic structure. Values of a physical parameter (such as chemical concentration or any other "projectable" property) cannot, in general, serve to encode beliefs. This is also why, as Fodor and I argue (Fodor and Pylyshyn, 1981), having a percept is not the sort of state a system conceivably can achieve by "resonating" to some property of the environment. On the other hand, as the discussion in chapters 5 and 6 suggests, *some* restricted subset of cognitive states must be of this kind; that is, they must be type identical with biological states, in order for an organism to have contact with a physical environment. This is what transduction is all about.

Although details of the way internal environments affect the cognitive system may remain a mystery, there is no problem with incorporating the right sort of functional interaction between noncognitive factors and cognition in a computational model (for example, Faught, Colby, and Parkinson, 1977; Colby, 1973; Tomkins and Messick, 1963). If we assume, for instance, that representations of beliefs are indexed according to some finite set of categories (say, certain affect valences), then the availability of these beliefs can be altered by changing the priority assigned different index categories as a function of the organism's affective states. This amounts to a sort of "activation" view of accessibility of representations. I do not know how realistic this device is, but it meets the criteria of allowing only a limited influence of affect state on cognition while allowing for extremely generalized effects on behavior. For example, a state of depression giving priority to beliefs categorized as having negative affect valence could account for the generally negative outlook depressed people have—without having to postulate any actual changes in stored beliefs associated with depression (other than those which might be derivable from the negatively marked subset of the depressed person's stored beliefs).

Such a hypothesis could explain why inferences and other cognitive processes characterized by a particular affective quality occur more frequently in certain situations (as happens in the case of happy or sad moods): the weighting mechanism in the control structure of the functional architecture simply results in the beliefs with negative affect being more readily available (that is, being the unmarked case or being the first beliefs encountered by a selection process). This is, in part, the device used by Colby (1973) in his model of paranoia, though Colby's model also incorporates mechanisms for altering the affect (or psychopathological) weightings as a function of both new inputs and new inferences.

This sketch is intended merely to highlight the premise that we cannot tell in advance of theory-development just what types of phenomena will find a natural home in the cognitive paradigm. The science must progress as it does in all disciplines: Start with what intuitively are clear cases, and attempt to develop a theoretical system. As the theory develops, we find that new phenomena, not originally anticipated to be part of the domain, fall naturally within the theory scheme, whereas others, originally expected to fall within the paradigm, are outside the theory scheme. In cognitive science it turns out, for example, that phenomena such as those associated with motor skills have a much larger cognitive (that is, knowledge-dependent) component (see, for example, Austin, 1974; Rumelhart and Norman, 1982), whereas others have major components that fall outside the cognitive paradigm. Therefore, criticisms of cognitive science that take the form of pointing out that it might be difficult to account for some phenomenon or other in terms of computational processes have little force. In the first place, no one knows exactly what phenomena can be encompassed by the computational story. In the second place, even if the examples are correct, they constitute a contribution to defining the boundaries of the field rather than an indictment of the approach. Of course, if, as time goes on, we find that *nothing* falls within the domain according to the way we went about partitioning it (that is, according to whether the process was knowledge-dependent), or if there is no principled distinction (given the appropriate idealizations) between phenomena that appear to be knowledge-dependent and those that do not, then the approach will be in difficulty. In my view, the evidence thus far is compatible with the existence of a significant, autonomous domain—as I have argued in this book.

A certain amount of stubbornness is associated with holding on to pretheoretical intuitions, and so there should be. Science progresses via a delicate balance between open-mindedness and prejudice. The former is, of course, the hallmark of science, as distinguished from revelation and other more autocratic systems of thought. Nonetheless, although everything is open to eventual overthrow, not everything can be overthrown immediately in the face of apparent counterexamples, as Kuhn (1972) clearly has shown. Such prejudice is essential; good ideas spring from what Kant called "the deepest recesses of the soul," and immediately face a barrage of objections, especially if they are reasonably novel ideas. It takes time to sort out relevant from irrelevant objections, to tune ideas and idealize the domain in the most perspicuous way. In the process, it is almost certain that one or another of our cherished beliefs will be scuttled for the higher goal of obtaining an intellectual grasp of what was once a set of unrelated, puzzling phenomena.

The eventual successes of cognitive science, if they come at all, will have to explain a variety of empirical phenomena. They will have to make their peace with various philosophical problems and face our pretheoretical intuitions of what makes sense. Of these various desiderata, it will be the latter that probably will have to give way most as deeper explanatory principles are discovered. We simply must be prepared to give up some of our pretheoretical ideas of how the mind works, as well as some of our ideas about what a scientific psychology can explain. William James (1892, p. 467) ends his treatise on psychology as a natural science with the following sobering conclusion, one that serves equally for the present attempt to build a natural science of cognition:

> When, then, we talk of "psychology as a natural science," we must not assume that that means a sort of psychology that stands at last on solid ground. It means just the reverse; it means a psychology particularly fragile, and into which the waters of metaphysical criticism leak at every joint, a psychology all of whose elementary assumptions and data must be reconsidered in wider connections and translated into other terms. It is, in short, a phrase of diffidence, and not of arrogance. . . . A string of raw facts; a little gossip and wrangle about opinions; a little classification and generalization on the mere descriptive level; a strong prejudice that we *have* states of mind, and that our brain conditions them. . . . This is no science, it is only the hope of a science . . . the best way in which we can facilitate [scientific achievements] is to understand how great is the darkness in which we grope, and never to forget that the natural science assumptions with which we started are provisional and revisable things.

References

Anderson, J. A., and G. E. Hinton. 1981. "Models of Information Processing in the Brain," in *Parallel Models of Associative Memory*, ed. G. E. Hinton and J. A. Anderson. Hillsdale, N.J.: Erlbaum, pp. 9–48.

Anderson, J. R. 1976. *Language, Memory and Thought*. Hillsdale, N.J.: Erlbaum.

Anderson, J. R. 1978. "Argument Concerning Representations for Mental Imagery," *Psychological Review* 85:249–277.

Appel, K., and W. Haken. 1977. "The Solution of the Four-Color Map Problem," *Scientific American*, October 1977.

Arbib, M. A. 1972. *The Metaphorical Brain*. New York: Wiley.

Arbib, M. A., and D. Caplan. 1979. "Neurolinguistics Must Be Computational," *Brain and Behavioral Sciences* 2:3: 449–483.

Arnheim, R. 1969. *Visual Thinking*. Berkeley: Univ. of California Press.

Ashby, W. R. 1956. *An Introduction to Cybernetics*. New York: Chapman and Hall.

Attneave, F. 1974. "How Do You Know?", *American Psychologist* 29:493–499.

Austin, H. 1974. "A Computational View of the Skill of Juggling," *AI Memo 330*, Massachusetts Institute of Technology: Artificial Intelligence Laboratory.

Backus, J. 1978. "Can Programming Be Liberated from the von Neumann Style? A Functional Style and Its Algebra of Programs," *Communications of the Association for Computing Machinery* 21:613–641.

Ballard, D. H., and C. M. Brown. 1982. *Computer Vision*. Englewood Cliffs, N.J.: Prentice-Hall.

Banks, W. P. 1977. "Encoding and Processing of Symbolic Information in Comparative Judgments," in *The Psychology of Learning and Motivation*, vol. 11, ed. G. H. Bower. New York: Academic Press.

Bannon, L. J. 1981. "An Investigation of Image Scanning: Theoretical Claims and Empirical Evidence," Ph.D diss., University of Western Ontario. Ann Arbor, Mich.: University Microfilms, no. 81-50,599.

Barlow, H. 1972. "Single Units and Sensation: A Neuron Doctrine for Perceptual Psychology," *Perception* 1:371–394.

Barrow, H. G., and J. M. Tenenbaum. 1978. "Recovering Intrinsic Scene Characteristics from Images," in *Computer Vision Systems*, ed. A. Hanson and E. Riseman. New York: Academic Press.

Bartlett, F. C. 1932. *Remembering: A Study in Experimental and Social Psychology*. Cambridge, England: The University Press; revised 1961.

Baylor, G. W. 1972. "A Treatise on the Mind's Eye: An Empirical Investigation of Visual Mental Imagery," Ph.D. diss., Carnegie-Mellon University. Ann Arbor, Mich.: University Microfilms, no. 72–12,699.

Berbaum, K., and C. S. Chung. 1981. "Muller-Lyer Illusion Induced by Imagination," *Journal of Mental Imagery* 5:1: 125–128.

Bever, T. G., J. A. Fodor, and M. Garrett. 1968. "A Formal Limitation of Associationism," in *Verbal Behavior and General Behavior Theory*, ed. T. R. Dixon and D. L. Horton. Englewood Cliffs, N.J.: Prentice-Hall.

Block, N. J. 1978. "Troubles with Functionalism," in *Perception and Cognition: Issues in the Foundations of Psychology*, ed. C. W. Savage, Minnesota Studies in the Philosophy of Science, vol. 9. Minneapolis: Univ. of Minnesota Press.

Block, N. J., ed. 1981. *Imagery*. Cambridge, Mass.: MIT Press, a Bradford Book.

Block, N. J., and J. A. Fodor. 1972. "Cognitivism and the Analog/Digital Distinction," unpub. paper.

Blum, M. 1967. "A Machine Independent Theory of the Complexity of Recursive Functions," *JACM* 14:2: 322–336.

Bobrow, D. G., and B. Raphael. 1974. "New Programming Languages for Artificial Intelligence Research," *Computer Surveys* 6:153–174.

Bransford, J. D., and M. K. Johnson. 1973. "Considerations of Some Problems of Comprehension," in *Visual Information Processing*, ed. W. Chase. New York: Academic Press.

Brewer, W. F. 1974. "There Is No Convincing Evidence for Operant or Classical Conditioning in Adult Humans," in *Cognition and the Symbolic Processes*, ed. W. B. Weiner and D. S. Palermo. Hillsdale, N.J.: Erlbaum.

Brindley, G. S. 1970. *Physiology of the Retina and Visual Pathways*, 2nd ed. Baltimore: Williams and Wilkins.

Bromberger, S. 1966. "Why-question," in *Mind and Cosmos: Essays in Contemporary Science and Philosophy*, ed. R. G. Colodyn. University of Pittsburgh Series in the Philosophy of Science, vol. 3. Pittsburgh: Univ. of Pittsburgh Press.

Brouwer, L. E. J. 1964. "Intuitionism and Formalism," in *Philosophy of Mathematics*, ed. P. Benacerraf and H. Putnam, Englewood Cliffs, N.J.: Prentice-Hall.

Brown, I. D. 1962. "Measuring the 'Spare Mental Capacity' of Car Drivers by a Subsidiary Auditory Task," *Ergonomics* 5:247–250.

Brown, J. S., and R. B. Burton. 1978. "Diagnostic Models for Procedural Bugs in Basic Mathematical Skills," *Cognitive Science* 2:155–192.

Brown, J. S., and K. Van Lehn. 1980. "Repair Theory: A Generative Theory of Bugs in Procedural Skills," *Cognitive Science* 4:379–426.

Bruner, J. 1957. "On Perceptual Readiness," *Psychology Review* 64:123–152.

Butterfield, H. 1957. *The Origins of Modern Science: 1300–1800*. Toronto: Clark Irwin.

Chazelle, B., and L. Monier. 1983. "Unbounded Hardware Is Equivalent to Deterministic Turing Machines," *Theoretical Computer Science* 24:123–130.

Chomsky, N. 1957. "Review of B. F. Skinner's Verbal Behavior," in *The Structure of Language*, ed. J. A. Fodor and J. J. Katz. Englewood Cliffs, N.J.: Prentice-Hall.

Chomsky, N. 1964. *Current Issues in Linguistic Theory*. The Hague: Mouton.

Chomsky, N. 1975. *The Logical Structure of Linguistic Theory*. New York: Plenum.

Chomsky, N. 1976. *Reflections on Language*. New York: Fontana.

Chomsky, N. 1980. "Rules and Representations," *Behavioral and Brain Sciences* 3:1: 1–15.

Churchland, P. M. 1980. "Plasticity: Conceptual and Neuronal," *Behavioral and Brain Sciences* 3:133–134.

Churchland, P. M. 1981. "Eliminative Materialism and the Propositional Attitude," *Journal of Philosophy* 78:2: 67–90.

Churchland, P. S. 1980. "Neuroscience and Psychology: Should the Labor Be Divided?", *Behavioral and Brain Sciences* 3:133.

Clowes, M. B. 1971. "On Seeing Things," *Artificial Intelligence* 2:79–116.

Cohen, J. 1966. *Human Robots in Myth and Science*. London:George Allen and Unwin.

Colby, K. M. 1973. "Simulations of Belief Systems," in *Computer Models of Thought and Language*, ed. R. C. Schank and K. M. Colby. San Francisco: W. H. Freeman.

Cummins, R. 1975. "Functional Analysis," *Journal of Philosophy* 72:741–765.

Davidson, D. 1970. "Mental Events," in *Experience and Theory*, ed. L. Foster and J. W. Swanson. Amherst: Univ. of Massachusetts Press.

Davies, D. J. M., and S. D. Isard. 1972. "Utterances as Programs," in *Machine Intelligence*, vol. 7, ed. B. Meltzer and D. Michie. Edinburgh: Edinburgh Univ. Press.

Davis, M., ed. 1965. *The Undecidable: Basic Papers on Undecidable Propositions, Unsolvable Problems and Computable Functions*. Hewlett, New York: Raven Press.

Delk, J. L., and S. Fillenbaum. 1965. "Differences in Perceived Color as a Function of Characteristic Color," *American Journal of Psychology* 78: 290–295.

Dennett, D. C. 1971. "Intention Systems," *Journal of Philosophy* 63: 87–106.

Dennett, D. C. 1978a. *Brainstorms*. Cambridge, Mass.: MIT Press, a Bradford Book.

Dennett, D. C. 1978b. "Toward a Cognitive Theory of Consciousness," in *Perception and Cognition: Issues in the Foundations of Psychology*, ed. C. W. Savage, Minnesota Studies in the Philosophy of Science, vol. 9. Minneapolis: Univ. of Minnesota Press; reprinted in *Brainstorms*, Cambridge, Mass.: MIT Press, a Bradford Book.

Dennett, D. C. 1982. "Beyond Belief," in *Thought and Object*, ed. A. Woodfield. Oxford: Oxford Univ. Press.

de Saussure, F. 1959. *Course in General Linguistics*. New York: Philosophical Library.

Donders, F. C. 1969. "On the Speed of Mental Processes (1868–1869)," *Acta Psychologica* 30:412–431.

Dretske, F. I. 1981. *Knowledge and the Flow of Information*. Cambridge, Mass.: MIT Press, a Bradford Book.

Dreyfus, H. L. 1979. *What Computers Can't Do: A Critique of Artificial Reason*. 2d ed. New York: Harper & Row.

Duncker, K. 1935. "On Problem Solving," *Psychological Monographs* 58:5 (no. 270).

Fahlman, S. E. 1979. *NETL: A System for Representing and Using Real-World Knowledge*. Cambridge, Mass.: MIT Press.

Fahlman, S. E. 1981. "Representing Implicit Knowledge," in *Parallel Models of Associative Memory*, ed. G. E. Hinton and J. A. Anderson. Hillsdale, N.J.: Erlbaum.

Farley, A. 1974. "A Visual Imagery and Perception System," Ph.D. diss., Carnegie-Mellon University, Pittsburgh.

Faught, W. S., K. M. Colby, and R. C. Parkinson. 1977. "Inferences, Affects, and Intentions in a Model of Paranoia," *Cognitive Psychology* 9:153–187.

Feldman, J. A., and D. H. Ballard. 1982. "Connectionist Models and Their Properties," *Cognitive Science* 6:205–254.

Finke, R. A. 1979. "The Functional Equivalence of Mental Images and Errors of Movement," *Cognitive Psychology* 11:235–264.

Finke, R. A. 1980. "Levels of Equivalence in Imagery and Perception," *Psychological Review* 87:113–132.

Finke, R. A., and S. Pinker. 1982. "Spontaneous Imagery Scanning in Mental Extrapolation," *Journal of Experimental Psychology: Learning, Memory, and Cognition* 8:2: 142–147.

Finke, R. A., and S. Pinker. 1983. "Directional Scanning of Remembered Visual Patterns," *Journal of Experimental Psychology: Learning, Memory, and Cognition* 9:3: 398–410.

Fodor, J. A. 1965. "Explanation in Psychology," in *Philosophy in America*, ed. M. Black. Ithaca: Cornell Univ. Press.

Fodor, J. A. 1968a. "The Appeal to Tacit Knowledge in Psychological Explanation," *Journal of Philosophy* 65:627–640.

Fodor, J. A. 1968b. *Psychological Explanation*. New York: Random House.

Fodor, J. A. 1975. *The Language of Thought*. New York: Crowell.

Fodor, J. A. 1978a. "Computation and Reduction," in *Perception and Cognition: Issues in the Foundations of Psychology,* ed. C. W. Savage, Minnesota Studies in the Philosophy of Science, vol. 9. Minneapolis: Univ. of Minnesota Press.

Fodor, J. A. 1978b. "Tom Swift and His Procedural Grandmother," *Cognition* 6:229–247.

Fodor, J. A. 1980a. "Methodological Solipsism Considered as a Research Strategy for Cognitive Psychology," *Behavioral and Brain Sciences* 3:1: 63–73.

Fodor, J. A. 1980b. Reply to Putnam, in *Language and Learning: The Debate between Jean Piaget and Noam Chomsky,* ed. M. Piattelli-Palmarini. Cambridge, Mass.: Harvard Univ. Press.

Fodor, J. A. 1980c. *Representations.* Cambridge, Mass.: MIT Press, a Bradford Book.

Fodor, J. A. 1983. *The Modularity of Mind: An Essay on Faculty Psychology.* Cambridge, Mass.: MIT Press, a Bradford Book.

Fodor J. A. 1984. "Why Paramecia Don't Have Mental Representations," unpublished paper.

Fodor, J. A., and Z. W. Pylyshyn. 1981. "How Direct Is Visual Perception? Some Reflections on Gibson's 'Ecological Approach,' " *Cognition* 9:139–196.

Fodor, J. A., T. Bever, and M. Garrett. 1974. *The Psychology of Language.* New York: McGraw-Hill.

Forgy, C. L. 1979. "On the Efficient Implementation of Production Systems" (Tech. Rep.). Department of Computer Science, Carnegie-Mellon University.

Forster, K. I. 1963. "Accessing the Mental Lexicon," in *New Approaches to Language Mechanisms,* ed. R. J. Wales and E. Walker. Amsterdam: North-Holland.

Forster, K. I. 1979. "Levels of Processing and the Structure of the Language Processor," in *Sentence Processing: Psycholinguistic Studies Presented to Merrill Garrett,* ed. W. E. Cooper and E. C. T. Walker. Hillsdale, N.J.: Erlbaum.

Fosdick, L. D., and L. J. Osterweil. 1976. "Data Flow Analysis of Software Reliability," *ACM Computing Surveys,* 8:305–330.

Fraisse, P. 1963. *The Psychology of Time.* New York: Harper & Row.

Frazier, L., and J. D. Fodor. 1978. "The Sausage Machine: A New Two-stage Parsing Model," *Cognition* 6:291–325.

Frege, G. B. 1980. "The Foundations of Arithmetic: A Logico-Mathematical Inquiry into the Concept of Number," Second edition, trans. by J. L. Austin. Evanston: Northwestern Univ. Press.

Funt, B. V. 1980. "Problem-Solving with Diagrammatic Representations," *Artificial Intelligence* 13:3: 201–230.

Gandi, R. 1980. "Church's Thesis and Principles for Mechanisms," in *The Kleene Symposium,* ed. J. Barweis, H. J. Keisler, and K. Kunen. Amsterdam: North Holland, pp. 123–148.

Geach, P. 1957. *Mental Acts.* London: Routledge & Kegan Paul.

Geach, P. 1980. "Some Remarks on Representations," *Behavioral and Brain Sciences* 3:1: 80–81.

Ghiselin, B. 1952. *The Creative Process.* New York: New American Library.

Gibson, J. J. 1966a. "The Problem of Temporal Order in Stimulation and Perception," *Journal of Psychology* 62:141–149.

Gibson, J. J. 1966b. *The Senses Considered as Perceptual Systems.* Boston: Houghton Mifflin.

Gibson, J. J. 1973. "On the Concept of 'Formless Invariants' in Visual Perception," *Leonardo* 6:43–45.

Gibson, J. J. 1979. *An Ecological Approach to Visual Perception.* Boston: Houghton Mifflin.

Goodman, N. 1954. *Fact, Fiction, and Forecast.* University of London: Athlone Press.

Goodman, N. 1968. *Languages of Art.* Indianapolis: Bobbs-Merrill.

Gregory, R. L. 1970. *The Intelligent Eye.* New York: McGraw-Hill.

Guzman, A. 1968. "Decomposition of a Visual Scene into Three-Dimensional Bodies," *AFIPS Proceedings, Fall Joint Computer Conference* 33:291–304.

Hanson, A., and E. Riseman, eds. 1978. *Computer Vision Systems*. New York: Academic Press.

Hanson, N. R. 1958. *Patterns of Discovery*. Cambridge: Univ. of Cambridge Press.

Harman, G. 1973. *Thought*. Princeton, N.J.: Princeton Univ. Press.

Haugeland, J. 1978. "The Nature and Plausibility of Cognitivism," *Behavioral and Brain Sciences* 2:215–260.

Haugeland, J. 1981a. "Semantic Engines: An Introduction to Mind Design," in *Mind Design*, ed. J. Haugeland. Cambridge, Mass.: MIT Press, a Bradford Book.

Haugeland, J. 1981b. *Mind Design*. Cambridge, Mass.: MIT Press, a Bradford Book.

Hayes, J. R. 1973. "On the Function of Visual Imagery in Elementary Mathematics," in *Visual Information Processing*, ed. W. G. Chase. New York: Academic Press.

Hayes, J. R., and H. A. Simon. 1976. "The Understanding Process: Problem Isomorphs," *Cognitive Psychology* 8:165–180.

Hebb, D. O. 1949. *Organization of Behavior*. New York: Wiley.

Hebb, D. O. 1968. "Concerning Imagery," *Psychological Review* 75:466–477.

Hess, E. 1975. "The Role of Pupil Size in Communication," reprinted in *Mind and Behavior, Readings from Scientific American*, ed. Atkinson and Atkinson. San Francisco: Freeman, 1980.

Hewitt, C. 1977. "Viewing Control Structures as Patterns of Passing Messages," *AI Journal* 8:3: 323–364.

Hinton, C. H. 1906. *The Fourth Dimension*. London: George Allen and Unwin.

Hinton, G. E., and J. A. Anderson. 1981. *Parallel Models of Associative Memory*. Hillsdale, N.J.: Erlbaum.

Hochberg, J. 1968. "In the Mind's Eye," in *Contemporary Theory and Research in Visual Perception*, ed. R. N. Haber. New York: Holt, Rinehart & Winston.

Howard, I. P. 1974. "Proposals for the Study of Anomalous Perceptual Schemata," *Perception* 3:497–513.

Howard, I. P. 1978. "Recognition and Knowledge of the Water-Level Principle," *Perception* 7:151–160.

Hubel, D. H., and T. N. Weisel. 1968. "Receptive Fields and Functional Architecture of Monkey Striate Cortex," *Journal of Physiology* (London), pp. 195, 215–243.

Huffman, D. A. 1971. "Generating Semantic Descriptions from Drawing of Scenes with Shadows," *Tech. Report AI TR-271*, Cambridge, Mass.: Massachusetts Institute of Technology Artificial Intelligence Laboratory.

Israel, D. J. 1984. "On Interpreting Semantic Network Formalisms," *International Journal of Computers and Mathematics* (in press).

James, W. 1892. *Text Book of Psychology*. London: MacMillan.

Johnson, N. F. 1972. "Organization and the Concept of a Memory Code," in *Coding Processes in Human Memory*, ed. A. W. Melton and E. Martin. New York: Winston.

Johnson-Laird, P. N., and M. J. Steedman. 1978. "The Psychology of Syllogisms," *Cognitive Psychology* 10:64–99.

Julicoeur, P., S. Ullman, and M. F. MacKay. 1983. "Boundary Tracing: An Elementary Visual Process," unpub. manuscript, Department of Psychology, University of Saskatchewan.

Julesz, B. 1971. *Foundations of Cyclopean Perception*. Chicago: Univ. of Chicago Press.

Julesz, B. 1975. "Experiments in the Visual Perception of Texture," *Scientific American* 232:34–43.

Just, M. A., and P. A. Carpenter. 1976. "Eye Fixations and Cognitive Processes," *Cognitive Psychology* 8:441–480.

Keil, F. 1979. *Semantic and Conceptual Development: An Ontological Perspective*, Cambridge, Mass.: Harvard Univ. Press.

Klahr, D. 1973. "Quantification Processes," in *Visual Information Processing*, ed. W. Chase. New York: Academic Press.

Knuth, D. E. 1968. *Fundamental Algorithms. The Art of Computer Programming*, vol. 1. Reading, Mass.: Addison-Wesley.

Koestler, A. 1959. *The Sleep Walkers*. New York: Macmillan.

Kohler, W. 1947. *Gestalt Psychology, An Introduction to New Concepts in Modern Psychology*. New York: Liveright.

Kolers, P. A., and W. E. Smythe. 1979. "Images, Symbols and Skills," *Canadian Journal of Psychology* 33:3: 158–184.

Kosslyn, S. M. 1973. "Scanning Visual Images: Some Structural Implications," *Perception and Psychophysics* 14:90–94.

Kosslyn, S. M. 1975. "The Information Represented in Visual Images," *Cognitive Psychology* 7:341–370.

Kosslyn, S. M. 1978. "Measuring the Visual Angle of the Mind's Eye," *Cognitive Psychology* 10:356–389.

Kosslyn, S. M. 1980. *Image and Mind*. Cambridge, Mass.: Harvard Univ. Press.

Kosslyn, S. M. 1981. "The Medium and the Message in Mental Imagery: A Theory," *Psychological Review* 88:46–66.

Kosslyn, S. M., and J. R. Pomerantz. 1977. "Imagery, Propositions, and the Form of Internal Representations," *Cognitive Psychology* 9:52–76.

Kosslyn, S. M., B. J. Reiser, M. J. Farah, and L. Fliegel. 1983. "Generating Visual Images:Units and Relations," *Journal of Experimental Psychology: General*, 112:2: 278–303.

Kosslyn, S. M., and S. P. Shwartz. 1977. "A Data-Driven Simulation of Visual Imagery," *Cognitive Science* 1:265–296.

Kosslyn, S. M., T. M. Ball, and B. J. Reiser. 1978. "Visual Images Preserve Metric Spatial Information: Evidence from Studies of Image Scanning," *Journal of Experimental Psychology: Human Perception and Performance* 4:46–60.

Kosslyn, S. M., S. Pinker, G. Smith, and S. P. Shwartz. 1979. "On The Demystification of Mental Imagery," *Behavioral and Brain Sciences* 2:4: 535–548.

Kowalski, R. 1979. "Algorithm = Logic + Control," *Communications of the ACM* 22:7: 425–438.

Kuhn, T., ed. 1972. *The Structure of Scientific Revolutions*. New edition. Chicago: Univ. of Chicago Press.

Kyburg, H. E., Jr. 1983. "Rational Belief," *Behavioral and Brain Sciences*, 6:2: 231–273.

Lewis, D. 1970. "How to Define Theoretical Terms," *Journal of Philosophy* 67:427–444.

Lewis, D. 1971. "Analog and Digital," *Nous*: 321–327.

Lieberman, P. 1965. "On the Acoustic Basis of the Perception of Intonation by Linguists," *Word* 21:40–54.

Lindsay, P. H., and D. A. Norman. 1977. *Human Information Processing: An Introduction to Psychology*. Second edition. New York: Academic Press.

Mackworth, A. K. 1973. "Interpreting Pictures of Polyhedral Scenes," *Artificial Intelligence* 4:121–137.

Marcus, M. 1979. *A Theory of Syntactic Recognition for Natural Language*. Cambridge, Mass.: MIT Press.

Marr, D. 1976. "Early Processing of Visual Information," *Philosophical Transactions of the Royal Society* 275:483–524.

Marr, D. 1977. "Artificial Intelligence—A Personal View," *Artificial Intelligence* 9:37–48; also published as MIT AI Memo 355.

Marr, D. 1982. *Vision*. San Francisco: W. H. Freeman.

Marr, D., and H. K. Nishihara. 1977. "Representation and Recognition of Spatial Organization of Three-Dimensional Shapes," *Proceedings of the Royal Society of London, Series B* 200:269–294.

Marslen-Wilson, W., and L. K. Tyler. 1980. "The Temporal Structure of Spoken Language Understanding," *Cognition* 8:1: 1–71.

Massaro, D. W. 1975. *Experimental Psychology and Information Processing*. Chicago: Rand McNally.

McAlister, L. L. 1976. *The Philosophy of Brentano*. London: Duckworth.

McCarthy, J., and P. Hayes. 1969. "Some Philosophical Problems from the Standpoint of Artificial Intelligence," in *Machine Intelligence 4*, ed. B. Meltzer and D. Michie. Edinburgh: Edinburgh Univ. Press.

Miller, G. A. 1984. "Informavores," in *The Study of Information: Interdisciplinary Messages*, ed. F. Machlup and U. Mansfield. New York: Wiley.

Miller, G. A., E. Galanter, and K. H. Pribram. 1960. *Plans and the Structure of Behavior*. New York: Holt, Rinehart & Winston.

Minsky, M. L. 1967. *Computation: Finite and Infinite Machines*. Englewood Cliffs, N.J.: Prentice-Hall.

Minsky, M. L. 1975. "A Framework for Representing Knowledge," in *The Psychology of Computer Vision*, ed. P. H. Winston. New York: McGraw-Hill.

Minsky, M. L., and S. Papert. 1969. *Perceptrons*. Cambridge, Mass.: MIT Press.

Minsky, M. L., and S. Papert. 1972. Artificial Intelligence Progress Report. Artificial Intelligence Memo No. 252, Massachusetts Institute of Technology.

Mitchell, D. B., and C. L. Richman. 1980. "Confirmed Reservations: Mental Travel," *Journal of Experimental Psychology: Human Perception and Performance* 6:58–66.

Moran, T. 1973. "The Symbolic Imagery Hypothesis: A Production System Model," Ph.D. diss., Carnegie-Mellon University.

Neisser, U. 1976. *Cognition and Reality*. San Francisco: W. H. Freeman.

Newell, A. 1962. "Some Problems of Basic Organization in Problem-Solving Programs," in *Self-Organizing Systems*, ed. A. Yovitts, G. T. Jacobi, and G. D. Goldstein. New York: Spartan.

Newell, A. 1970. "Remarks on the Relationship between Artificial Intelligence and Cognitive Psychology," in *Theoretical Approaches to Non-Numerical Problem Solving*, ed. R. Banerji and M. D. Mesarovic. New York: Springer-Verlag.

Newell, A. 1972. "A Theoretical Exploration of Mechanisms for Coding the Stimulus," in *Coding Processes in Human Memory*, ed. A. W. Melton and E. Martin. Edinburgh: Edinburgh Univ. Press.

Newell, A. 1973a. "Artificial Intelligence and the Concept of Mind," in *Computer Models of Thought and Language*, ed. R. C. Schank and K. Colby. San Francisco: W. H. Freeman.

Newell, A. 1973b. "Production Systems: Models of Control Structures," in *Visual Information Processing*, ed. W. Chase. New York: Academic Press.

Newell, A. 1980. "Physical Symbol Systems," *Cognitive Science* 4:2: 135–183.

Newell, A. 1982. "The Knowledge Level," *Artificial Intelligence* 18:1: 87–127.

Newell, A., and H. A. Simon. 1972. *Human Problem Solving*. Englewood Cliffs, N.J.: Prentice-Hall.

Newell, A., and H. A. Simon. 1976. "Computer Science as Empirical Inquiry," *Communications of the Association for Computing Machinery* 19:113–126.

Nicod, J. 1970. *Geometry and Induction*. Berkeley: Univ. of California Press.

Nisbett, R. E., and L. Ross. 1980. *Human Inference: Strategies and Shortcomings of Social Judgment*. Englewood Cliffs, N.J.: Prentice-Hall.

Norman, D. A., and D. E. Rumelhart. 1975. *Explorations in Cognition*. San Francisco: W. H. Freeman.

Nudel, B. 1983. "Consistent-Labeling Problems and Their Algorithms: Expected-Complexities and Theory-Based Heuristics," *Artificial Intelligence* 21:1: 135–178.

Osgood, C. E. 1963. "Psycholinguists," in *Psychology: A Study of a Science*, ed. S. Koch. New York: McGraw-Hill.

Paivio, A. U. 1977. "Images, Propositions and Knowledge," in *Images, Perception, and Knowledge*, ed. J. M. Nicholas. Dordrech: Reidel.

Palmer, S. F. 1978. "Fundamental Aspects of Cognitive Representation," in *Cognition and Categorization*, ed. E. H. Rosch and B. B. Lloyd. Hillsdale, N.J.: Erlbaum.

Parks, T. 1965. "Post-Retinal Visual Storage," *American Journal of Psychology* 78:145–147.

Pascual-Leone, J. 1976. "Metasubjective Problems of Constructive Cognition: Forms of Knowing and Their Psychological Mechanism," *Canadian Psychological Review* 17:2: 110–125.

Pike, K. L. 1967. *Language in Relation to a Unified Theory of the Structure of Human Behavior*. The Hague: Mouton.

Pinker, S. 1980. "Explanations in Theories of Language and of Imagery," *Behavioral and Brain Sciences* 3:1: 147–148.

Pippenger, N., and M. J. Fischer. 1979. "Relations among Complexity Measures," *Journal of the Association for Computing Machinery* 26:2: 361–381.

Posner, M. I. 1978. *Chronometric Explorations of Mind*. Hillsdale, N.J.: Erlbaum.

Posner, M. I. 1980. "Orienting of Attention," *Quarterly Journal of Experimental Psychology* 32:3–25.

Pribram, K. H. 1977. *Languages of the Brain*. Englewood Cliffs, N.J.: Prentice-Hall.

Putnam, H. 1960. "Minds and Machines", in *Minds and Machines*, ed. A. Anderson. Englewood Cliffs, N.J.: Prentice-Hall.

Putnam, H. 1967. "The Mental Life of Some Machines," in *Intentionality, Minds and Perception*, ed. H. N. Castaneda. Detroit: Wayne State Univ. Press; reprinted in "Mind, Language and Reality," *Philosophical Papers*, vol. 2. Cambridge, England: Cambridge Univ. Press.

Putnam, H. 1973. "Reductionism and the Nature of Psychology," *Cognition* 2:131–146.

Putnam, H. 1975. "The Meaning of 'Meaning'," in *Minnesota Studies in the Philosophy of Science*, ed. K. Gunderson. Minneapolis: Univ. of Minnesota Press 7:131–193.

Putnam, H. 1981. "Computational Psychology and Interpretation Theory," Conference on Foundations of Cognitive Science, University of Western Ontario, London, Canada.

Pylyshyn, Z. W. 1972. "The Problem of Cognitive Representation," Research Bulletin No. 227, Department of Psychology, University of Western Ontario.

Pylyshyn, Z. W. 1973a. "The Role of Competence Theories in Cognitive Psychology," *Journal of Psycholinguistics Research* 2:21–50.

Pylyshyn, Z. W. 1973b. "What the Mind's Eye Tells the Mind's Brain: A Critique of Mental Imagery," *Psychological Bulletin* 80:1–24.

Pylyshyn, Z. W. 1974. "Minds, Machines and Phenomenology," *Cognition* 3:57–77.

Pylyshyn, Z. W. 1978a. "Computational Models and Empirical Constraints," *Behavioral and Brain Sciences* 1:93–99.

Pylyshyn, Z. W. 1978b. "Imagery and Artificial Intelligence," in *Perception and Cognition: Issues in the Foundations of Psychology*, ed. C. W. Savage, Minnesota Studies in the Philosophy of Science, vol. 9. Minneapolis: Univ. of Minnesota Press.

Pylyshyn, Z. W. 1979a. "Do Mental Events Have Durations?", *Behavioral and Brain Sciences* 2:2: 277–278.

Pylyshyn, Z. W. 1979b. "The Rate of 'Mental Rotation' of Images: A Test of a Holistic Analogue Hypothesis," *Memory and Cognition* 7:19–28.

Pylyshyn, Z. W. 1979c. "Validating Computational Models: A Critique of Anderson's Indeterminacy of Representation Claim," *Psychological Review* 86:4: 383–394.

Pylyshyn, Z. W. 1980a. "Cognition and Computation: Issues in the Foundations of Cognitive Science," *Behavioral and Brain Sciences* 3:1: 111–132.

Pylyshyn, Z. W. 1980b. "Cognitive Representation and the Process-Architecture Distinction," *Behavioral and Brain Sciences* 3:1: 154–169.

Pylyshyn, Z. W. 1980c. "Complexity and the Study of Human and Machine Intelligence," in *Mind Design*, ed. J. Haugeland. Cambridge, Mass.: MIT Press, a Bradford Book.

Pylyshyn, Z. W. 1981. "The Imagery Debate: Analogue Media versus Tacit Knowledge," *Psychological Review* 88:16–45.

Pylyshyn, Z. W. 1984. "Plasticity and Invariance in Cognitive Development," in *Neonate Cognition: Beyond the Blooming, Buzzing Confusion*, ed. J. Mehler and R. Fox. Hillsdale, N.J.: Erlbaum.

Pylyshyn, Z. W., E. W. Elcock, M. Marmor, and P. Sander. 1978. "Explorations in Visual-Motor Spaces," *Proceedings of the Second International Conference of the Canadian Society for Computational Studies of Intelligence*, University of Toronto.

Quine, W. V. O. 1977. "Natural Kinds," in *Naming, Necessity, and Natural Kinds*, ed. S. P. Schwarts. Ithaca: Cornell Univ. Press.

Regan, D., and K. I. Beverley. 1980. "Visual Responses to Changing Size and to Sideways Motion for Different Directions of Motion in Depth: Linearization of Visual Responses," *Journal of the Optical Society of America* 70:11: 1289–1296.

Restle, F. 1959. "A Metric and an Ordering on Sets," *Psychometrika* 24:3: 207–219.

Rey, G. 1980. "Penetrating the Impenetrable," *Behavioral and Brain Sciences* 3:149–150.

Richman, C. L., D. B. Mitchell, and J. S. Reznick. 1979. "Mental Travel: Some Reservations," *Journal of Experimental Psychology: Human Perception and Performance* 5:13–18.

Rock, I. 1983. *The Logic of Perception*. Cambridge, Mass.: MIT Press, a Bradford Book.

Rosch, E. 1973. "On the Internal Structure of Perceptual and Semantic Categories," in *Cognitive Development and the Acquisition of Language*, ed. T. E. Moore. New York: Academic Press.

Rosenthal, R., and R. L. Rosnow, eds. 1969. *Artifact in Behavioral Research*. New York: Academic Press.

Rumelhart, D. E., and D. A. Norman. 1982. "Simulating a Skilled Typist: A Study of Skilled Cognitive-Motor Performance," *Cognitive Science* 6:1–36.

Ryle, G. 1949. *The Concept of Mind*. London: Hutcheson.

Schank, R. C., and R. P. Abelson. 1977. *Scripts, Plans, Goals and Understanding*. Hillsdale, N.J.: Erlbaum.

Schwartz, R. 1981. "Imagery—There's More to It than Meets the Eye," in *Imagery*, ed. N. Block. Cambridge, Mass.: MIT Press, a Bradford Book.

Scott, D. S., and C. Strachey. 1971. "Toward a Mathematical Semantics for Computer Languages," in *Proceedings of the Symposium on Computers and Automata*, ed. J. Fox. Brooklyn, N.Y.: Polytechnic Press.

Searle, J. 1980. "Minds, Brains, and Programs," *The Behavioral and Brain Sciences* 3:3: 417–457.

Shannon, C. E. 1950. "Programming a Computer for Playing Chess", *Philosophical Magazine* 41:256–275.

Shaw, R. 1971. "Cognition, Simulation and the Problem of Complexity," *Journal of Structural Learning* 2:4: 31–44.

Shaw, R. E., and J. Bransford, eds. 1977. *Perceiving, Acting, and Knowing: Toward an Ecological Psychology*. Hillsdale, N.J.: Erlbaum.

Shepard, R. N. 1964. "Attention and the Metrical Structure of the Similarity Space," *Journal of Mathematical Psychology* 1:54–87.

Shepard, R. N. 1975. "Form, Formation, and Transformation of Internal Representations," in *Information Processing in Cognition: The Loyola Symposium*, ed. R. L. Solso. Hillsdale, N.J.: Erlbaum.

Shepard, R. N. 1978. "The Mental Image," *American Psychologist* 33:125–137.

Shepard, R. N., and S. Chipman. 1970. "Second-Order Isomorphism of Internal Representations: Shapes of States," *Cognitive Psychology* 1:1–17.

Shepard, R. N., and L. A. Cooper. 1982. *Mental Images and Their Transformations.* Cambridge, Mass.: MIT Press, a Bradford Book.

Shepard, R. N., and C. Feng. 1972. "A Chronometric Study of Mental Paper Folding," *Cognitive Psychology* 3:228–243.

Shulman, G. L., R. W. Remington, and J. P. McLean. 1979. "Moving Attention through Visual Space," *Journal of Experimental Psychology: Human Perception and Performance* 15:522–526.

Simon, H. A. 1969. *The Sciences of the Artificial,* Compton Lectures. Cambridge, Mass.: MIT Press.

Simon, H. A., and W. G. Chase. 1973. "Skill in Chess," *American Scientist* 61:394–403.

Smith, S. M. 1982. "Enhancement of Recall Using Multiple Environmental Contexts during Learning," *Memory and Cognition* 10:405–12.

Stabler, E. P. 1983. "How Are Grammars Represented?", *Behavioral and Brain Sciences* 6:3: 391–420.

Sternberg, S. 1966. "High-Speed Scanning in Human Memory," *Science* 153:652–654.

Sternberg, S. 1969. "The Discovery of Processing Stages: Extensions of Donders' Method," *Acta Psychologica* 30:276–315.

Stich, S. 1984. *Folk Psychology and Cognitive Science: The Case against Belief.* Cambridge, Mass.: MIT Press, a Bradford Book.

Tomkins, S., and S. Messick, eds. 1963. *Computer Simulation of Personality.* New York: Wiley.

Townsend, J. T. 1974. "Issues and Models Concerning the Processing of a Finite Number of Inputs," in *Human Information Processing: Tutorials in Performance and Cognition,* ed. B. H. Kantowitz. Hillsdale, N.J.: Erlbaum.

Treisman, A., and H. Schmidt. 1982. "Illusory Conjunctions in the Perception of Objects," *Cognitive Psychology* 14:1: 107–141.

Tsal, Y. 1983. "Movements of Attention across the Visual Field," *Journal of Experimental Psychology: Human Perception and Performance* 9:523–530.

Turing, A. M. 1937. "On Computable Numbers, with an Application to the Entscheidungsproblem," *Proceedings of the London Mathematical Society* 42:230–265.

Turing, A. M. 1950. "Computing Machinery and Intelligence," in *Mind*; reprinted 1964 in *Minds and Machines,* ed. A. R. Anderson. Englewood Cliffs, N.J.: Prentice-Hall.

Turvey, M. T. 1977. "Contrasting Orientation to the Theory of Visual Information Processing," *Psychology Review* 84:67–88.

Tversky, A., and D. Kahneman. 1974. "Judgment under Uncertainty: Heuristics and Biases," *Science* 185:1124–1131.

Ullman, S. 1976. "On Visual Detection of Light Sources," *Biological Cybernetics* 21:205–212.

Ullman, S. 1979. *The Interpretation of Visual Motion.* Cambridge, Mass.: MIT Press.

Ullman, S. 1980. "Against Direct Perception," *Behavioral and Brain Sciences* 3:3: 373–415.

Ullman, S. 1983. "Visual Routines," *AI Memo 723,* Massachusetts Institute of Technology, Artificial Intelligence Laboratory.

Uttal, W. 1967. "Evoked Brain Potentials: Signs or Codes?", *Perspectives in Biology and Medicine* 10:627–639.

von Neumann, J. 1966. "Rigorous Theories of Control and Information," in *Theory of Self-Reproducing Automata.* Urbana: Univ. of Illinois Press, pp. 42–56.

Vuillemin, J. 1980. "A Combinational Limit to the Computing Power of V.L.S.I. Circuits," *Proceedings of the 21st Annual Symposium on the Foundations of Computer Science,* I.E.E.E., pp. 294–300.

Waltz, D. 1975. "Understanding Line Drawings of Scenes with Shadows," in *The Psychology of Computer Vision,* ed. P. H. Winston. New York: McGraw-Hill.

Wasserman, G. S., and K. L. Kong. 1979. "Absolute Timing of Mental Activities," *Behavioral and Brain Sciences* 2:2: 243–304.

Waterman, D. A., and A. Newell. 1971. "Protocol Analysis as a Task for Artificial Intelligence," *Artificial Intelligence* 2:285–318.

West, R. F., and K. E. Stanovich. 1982. "Source of Inhibition in Experiments on the Effect of Sentence Context on Word Recognition," *Journal of Experimental Psychology: Human Memory and Cognition* 8:385–399.

Wexler, K., and P. Cullicover. 1980. *Formal Principles of Language Acquisition.* Cambridge, Mass.: MIT Press.

Williams, D. M., and J. D. Hollan. 1981. "The Process of Retrieval from Very Long-Term Memory," *Cognitive Science* 5:87–119.

Winograd, T. 1972. "Understanding Natural Languages," *Cognitive Psychology* 3:1–191; also published by Academic Press.

Young, R. M. 1973. "Children's Seriation Behavior: A Production System Analysis," Ph.D. diss., Department of Psychology, Carnegie-Mellon University.

Young, R. M., and O'Shea, T. 1981. "Errors in Children's Subtraction," *Cognitive Science* 5:153–177.

Index

Marslen-Wilson, W., 112
Massaro, D., xix, 135
Meaning, problem of, xx, 23, 40, 43–44
Mechanism (computational), 49, 52, 71, 76
Mental
  chemistry, 264
  chronometry, 261. *See also* Reaction time
  imagery. *See* Imagery
  rotation, 232
  scanning, 231–245, 252
Mentalese. *See* Language of thought
Messick, S., 270
Mill, J. S., 184, 264
Miller, G., xi, 45, 80, 97, 222
Mimicry of behavior, xv, 43, 53, 76, 98, 115, 260. *See also* Weak equivalence
Minsky, M., 54, 158, 200, 214n4, 221
Monier, L., 71, 72n, 214n4
Moods, 265–266, 269–270
Moran, T., 112
Mozart, W. A., 234, 240
Müller, J., 163
Müller-Lyer illusion, 250

Natural kinds, xii, 35, 113
Neisser, U., 179, 188
Newell, A., xiii–xivn1, 24, 30, 32–33, 36, 51, 54, 72, 80, 82–84, 88n1, 107–108, 109n1, 112, 123, 127, 131, 235
"New Look" in perception, 135, 174, 250
Newton, I., xv
Nicod, J., 18, 104
Nisbett, R. E., 20
Nishihara, H. K., 84
Nomological laws, 3, 53, 56–57, 140, 152n1, 201, 212–213, 215
Norman, D. A., 100, 157, 188, 271
Nudel, B., 84
Null detection task, 175

Objective pull, 229
Oblique effect, 246
Occam's Razor, 212
Opaque context, 4, 194
Osgood, C. E., 41
O'Shea, T., 113
Osterwell, L. J., 119

Paivio, A. U., 251–252

Palmer, S. F., 205
Pandemonium model, 157
Papert, S., 158, 214n4
Parallel processing, 73. *See also* Connectionist models
Parkinson, R. C., 270
Parks, T., 14, 191
Pascual-Leone, J., xiiin1, xix
Peano axioms, 58, 61, 100
Perceptron, 214n4
Physical level, 24, 62, 132, 136, 140–141, 145, 148–149, 151, 210–211, 259
Physiology. *See* Biological level
Piaget, J., 104
Pike, K. L., 13
Pinker, S., 197, 229, 243, 247, 255
Pippenger, N., 71
Place token, 164, 249–250
PLANNER, 81, 97
Plato, 263
Posner, M., xix, 126, 135, 250
Post, E., 49–50
Pribram, K. H., 80, 97, 218
Primal sketch, 164
Prism adaptation, 250
Production systems, 81–83, 196
Program, 88–95. *See also* Algorithm
Projectable properties, 15, 140, 152n1, 165–166, 169, 201–212, 209, 213–214, 217n7, 270
PROLOG, 70, 82, 97
Propositional attitudes, 29n4, 34, 65n4, 194
Protocol analysis, 112
Psychological reality, 40, 87–88. *See also* Strong equivalence
Psychopathology, 265
Ptolemaic astronomy, 256, 263
Putnam, H., 7, 24, 30
Pylyshyn, Z. W., xviii–xix, 69, 85, 109–110n1, 122–123, 135–137, 141, 148, 164, 180, 183, 193, 213, 217n7, 219–220, 223, 227, 229, 242, 247–249, 270

Qualia, 45
Quine, W. V. O., 217

Ramsey-functional correlates, 262–263n1
Raphael, B., 81
Rationality, Principle of, 20, 34, 38–39, 136, 193, 196, 211, 259